The

Modern Encyclopedia

of

Russian *and* Soviet

Literature

CONTRIBUTORS

Gilman H. Alkire
Occidental College

Susan Amert
*Dept. of Slavic Languages
  and Literatures
Yale University*

Patricia Arant
Brown University

Howard I. Aronson
The University of Chicago

Milica Banjanin
Washington University, St. Louis

Vahan D. Barooshian
Wells College

J. Neville Birdsall
The University of Birmingham

John E. Bowlt
University of Texas

Eugene K. Bristow
Indiana University

Julia Brun-Zejmis
University of New York at Buffalo

John Colarusso
McMaster University

Garland E. Crouch, Jr.
University of New Orleans

George A. Genereux
Davis, California

Peter Hodgson
University of Southern California

George L. Kline
Bryn Mawr College

Serge Kryzytski
Oberlin College

Lauren G. Leighton
University of Illinois, Chicago Circle

Kathleen Lewis
Austin, Texas

A.B. McMillin
The University of Liverpool

Philip G. Maloney
University of Montana

Robert Mathiesen
Brown University

Priscilla Meyer
Wesleyan University

Ellendea Proffer
Ann Arbor, Michigan

John Sadouski
Queen's University, Canada

Karl Horst Schmidt
Institut für Germanistik, Bonn

Richard D. Sylvester
Colgate University

Michael Ulman
The University of New South Wales

Audrone B. Willeke
Miami University

Arvids Ziedonis, Jr.
Muhlenberg College

SOVIET CONTRIBUTORS

N.V. Baranskaia
A.A. Belkin

M.P. Shtokmar
O. Zosenko

The
Modern Encyclopedia
of
Russian and Soviet
Literature

Edited by
Harry B. Weber

Vol. 3

BIBLE, GEORGIAN - CHAINIKOV, KUZ'MA PAVLOVICH

Academic International Press

1979

THE MODERN ENCYCLOPEDIA OF RUSSIAN AND SOVIET LITERATURE
Volume 3

Copyright © 1979 by Academic International Press

Library of Congress Catalog Card Number: 75-11091
ISBN: 0-87569-064-5

Title page by King & Queen Press
Typography by Marsha Garza and Bess Roggenbuck

Printed in the United States of America

By direct subscription with the publisher.

*A list of Academic International Press publications
is found at the end of this volume.*

ACADEMIC INTERNATIONAL PRESS
Box 555 Gulf Breeze FL 32561 USA

Preparation of this volume

was greatly facilitated by the

support of

The University of Iowa

Iowa City

Comments, criticisms, corrections and suggestions are welcomed by the Editor and by the publisher.

Persons wishing to contribute to MERSL are invited to contact the Editor:

Harry B. Weber, Department of Russian, University of Iowa, Iowa City, Iowa 52242

B

BIBLE, GEORGIAN. Although the precise details still constitute an historical problem, it is clear that the foundations of Christianity in Georgia reach back into the mid-fourth century. Even though the faith reached the Georgians from a number of different sources, the early links were very closely tied with Armenia. In common with the Armenian church, the Georgians at first followed the Monophysite opposition to the decisions of the Council of Chalcedon (A.D. 451) and later (about A.D. 505/6) rejected the Henoticon of the emperor Zeno: yet in about A.D. 600 the Georgian church accepted the Chalcedonian definition, and thereafter remained in communion and close theological and cultural contact with the Byzantine church and empire. The history of both church and people is one of rising and sinking fortunes as the country constituted a frontier region between Byzantium and the various Eastern peoples who were in the ascendancy at different times. This produced a martyr history throughout the centuries, and the first original Georgian literature arose to commemorate the earliest martyrs. The greatest period of Georgian unity and independence was in the eleventh to the thirteenth centuries, brought to an end by the Mongol invasions. After several centuries of domination by Turks and Persians, Georgia became part of the Russian empire at the end of the eighteenth century. Nationalist movements found their eventual expression in the independent republic from 1918 until 1921, when the country was made part of the USSR, at first as part of the Transcaucasian Republic and since 1937 as the Georgian SSR.

This political and ecclesiastical history is the background to the history of Bible translation into the Georgian language. The first influences are clearly from Armenia, but at an early stage there began a series of revisions to a Greek standard. In the eighteenth century, as the Russian influence grew, revisions were made from the Slavonic, while as a result of native scholarship, the twentieth century has seen an upsurge of Georgian philology, producing a series of learned editions, and a revised ecclesiastical text. No modern Georgian translation has appeared, however. The most convenient method of presentation at this stage of scholarship is to treat of the several parts of scripture, and to describe their history through the eyes of recent research.

It is the Gospels which have attracted most scholarly attention both in Georgia and elsewhere. This centered on the Adish manuscript, discovered in the early years of the century, and published in facsimile in 1916: it contains the Four Gospels and is dated A.D. 897. Its text may be found in two publications: firstly that edited by R.P. Blake in *Patrologia Orientalis* (vol. 20, pt. 3; vol. 24, pt. 1; vol. 26, pt. 4; with M. Brière) and brought to a conclusion after Blake's death by Brière (*PO* vol. 27, p. 3), between 1928 and 1955; secondly, that of Akaki Shanidze, in 1945. In both cases the text was presented in comparison with that in other ancient manuscripts, Blake and Brière giving the variant readings of the Opiza and Tbet manuscripts, Shanidze (in parallel) the text of two manuscripts deriving from the same monastery of Shatberd as the Adish codex. Study of these materials by Blake and others shows that the Adish manuscript presents a text derived from an Armenian base, and the other manuscripts a related text, revised from a Greek base. There are a number of other manuscripts of this latter type unedited, but the Adish manuscript remains a unique witness to its form of the text. In the early twenties, other early texts began to come to light; these were both palaeographically much older than Adish and the others previously edited, and also contained texts in early forms of Georgian (technically known as khanmeti and haemeti) known to have become extinct in the standard literary language by the first half of the seventh century. More have recently been discovered. Their content (where this is a gospel text) does not, however, agree, as was at first assumed, with the older Adish text, but is more closely affiliated to the revised texts of the other edited manuscripts: readings in common with Adish do sporadically occur. This variety (analogous to that of the pre-Hieronymian or "Old" Latin) is borne out by the gospel allusions and quotations in the oldest hagiographical texts: no adequate historical explanation has yet been found. Both the Adish text and that of the other manuscripts prove on analysis to bear clear marks of the original Armenian and of the Syriac lying behind that. Since the Syriac tradition was influenced by Tatian's gospel harmony, harmonistic readings have survived even into the Georgian version; but the hypothesis that that gospel harmony was known early in Georgian Christian history and may be seen in the Martyrdom of St. Eustace of Mtskheta, has been shown to be erroneous. The text reflected in the Martyrdom shows features analogous to that of the khanmeti fragments. All the texts hitherto described, while differing among themselves in various particulars, are known as the "Old Georgian," in contradistinction to the revised text due to the work of two Georgian Athonite monks, St. Euthymius and St. George the Hagiorite in the eleventh century. This is the text found in most manuscripts. In the printed Georgian Bible it was corrupted by Slavonic influences, but a revised text was published in 1963.

The rest of the New Testament has only more recently been edited in its oldest Georgian forms. Critical editions of the Acts of the Apostles appeared within a few years of each other, by Abuladze in 1949 based on eight manuscripts (one from Athos, the rest from Georgia), analyzed into four redactions, and by Garitte in 1955 from two Sinai manuscripts. Garitte's text corresponds to the earliest of the four recensions identified by Abuladze, of which the second is a revision to a Greek standard. The two later recensions identified by Abuladze are the work of St. George the Hagiorite, and a revision of this about A.D. 1100 by one of the most renowned Georgian translators, Ephrem Mtsire (the Small), who worked in the Black Mountain near Antioch and in Jerusalem (both important centers of Georgian monasticism). Similar patterns of redactional analysis have revealed themselves in the Catholic Epistles, edited in 1956, and in the Paulines, which appeared only in 1974. Two khanmeti fragments of Romans and Galatians were already known in scholarly edition, which correspond textually to the oldest Pauline stratum. The Apocalypse was accepted as canonical only late amongst many Eastern churches, and its translation into Georgian did not take place until the eleventh century as the work of St. Euthymius. This was accompanied by the commentary of Andreas of Caesarea (erroneously called "of Crete" in the Georgian tradition, following a frequent confusion of the Greek). This work was edited in 1961 by Imnaishvili.

Apart from the Gospels, little work has been done on the textual affiliations within the New Testament tradition of these various Georgian recensions. The Georgian philologists have concentrated upon linguistic and literary matters. In the Gospels, the close links of the earliest forms with the Syriac and Armenian tradition are clear. The Greek standard of the first revision (that is, the second form of "Old Georgian" text) is related to forms known in Egypt and Palestine in the third century, and in a number of Greek minuscules. It has thus played a part in the research and debate concerning the so-called "Caesarean text." In Acts, work by Garitte indicates an Armenian base for the earliest translation, and the recently published text of the Paulines appears to confirm the hypothesis of a similar base in that case, erected by Conybeare. This may be true, too, of the Catholic epistles, as Molitor has proposed, but his opinion that similar Syriac and Armenian influences may be found in the Georgian version of the Apocalypse is not only completely unlikely on historical grounds, but will not stand close examination of the alleged evidence. A detailed analysis of the text, collated against the whole tradition both of the Greek and of the versional evidence, however, still awaits execution.

In the case of the Old Testament we are not so far advanced. In Western Europe and America, R.P. Blake has been a standard source of reference. In articles published in 1926 and 1929 he described two manuscripts recently come to light, one from the monastery of Gelati, one a dated manuscript (A.D. 978) written in Oshki but preserved in the Iveron monastery of Mt. Athos. The Gelati manuscript, which is defective, contains part of the Octateuch and the Prophets; the Oshki manuscript, too, has lost a number of leaves, and the whole of Numbers, Deuteronomy, and Joshua are thus missing and large parts of Leviticus and Job. The Gelati manuscript, although it caused a stir when discovered, proved on examination to represent a late text, rather slavishly following Greek idiom; the Oshki text, however, is clearly earlier and shows traces of ultimate Armenian origin, although knowledge of the Greek is not absent. (Blake says the contrary of this in the 1926 article, but in the publication about to be mentioned had rectified his opinion.) Blake's edition of the Prophets, based on the Oshki manuscript with an apparatus criticus from a Jerusalem manuscript, was posthumously published between 1961 and 1963 in *Patrologia Orientalis* (vol. 29, pts. 2-5; vol. 30, pt. 3). In the meanwhile, the Georgian scholar Shanidze had published from the Oshki manuscript the surviving parts of Genesis, Exodus, Leviticus, Judges, Ruth, Job and Isaiah, and Blake himself (in 1926 and 1929) the (apocryphal) IV Esdras from the Oshki and Jerusalem manuscripts. Some fragments in the khanmeti form of the language had also come to light from Genesis, Jeremiah and Proverbs; and still unpublished are khanmeti fragments of Judges and Deuteronomy. We also possess an important edition of the rubrics of the ancient lectionary of the church of Jerusalem (preserved in Georgian and Armenian); the text of the lections has not been published *in extenso*.

From Georgian sources, apart from the material mentioned, and editions of Ecclesiastes and the Song of Songs (in 1920 and 1924) and of the Psalter (in

1960), we have recently a number of detailed studies in preparation for an eventual edition. Thus we have access to analyses of the textual transmission and attestation of Genesis, Exodus, Leviticus, Ruth, the first, second, and fourth books of Kingdoms, the first book of Paralipomena (Chronicles), Nehemiah, Proverbs, Esther and Lamentations. There are naturally differences of detail between these different parts, but in outline it may be said that the Oshki manuscript and its related manuscripts (such as the Jerusalem manuscript which retains considerable importance) present the earliest text known to us, which generally evinces its ultimate derivation from an Armenian version, but shows signs too, that the redactors were aware of Greek texts, frequently of "Lucianic" type. The Gelati manuscript represents a twelfth-century text, child of a Grecophile period in Georgian literary activity. The printed Georgian Bible (1743) is often based upon it, sometimes with corrections from the Slavonic. In the case of Proverbs (and the same is true of a fragment of I Esdras known to us), the khanmeti fragment presents a distinct form of text from either of these. While it is the "Lucianic" text-type that is found in many Georgian recensions, the Hexaplaric text resulting from the work of Origen has also left traces, for instance, according to Blake's analysis, in the text of Jeremiah in the Gelati manuscript, and other manuscripts have marginalia in which traces of the Jewish Greek versions of Aquila and Symmachus have been found.

The so-called apocryphal or deuterocanonical books did not form part of the Georgian canon of scripture, although (in parallel to the marginal uncertainties shown in the history of the canon everywhere) the Wisdom of Solomon, the Wisdom of Jesus ben-Sira, and IV Esdras were included in copies of the Bible at various times.

It is clear that work on the Georgian Bible is far from finished. When the philologists have concluded their work, the textual critics, particularly in the field of Septuagint studies, will have at their disposal new data which will not prove insignificant; while within the purely Georgian field, the history of Biblical scholarship and of exegesis, native and translated, still awaits our study.

The original object of the translation of scripture into the Eastern languages of Christendom was (to use a phrase of Western religious history) that they might be "understanded of the people." The processes of revision which mark the evolution of the Georgian version are clearly related to this, as well as the theologically motivated desire to ensure close equivalence of the Georgian and the Greek original. But by the time of the work of Ephrem Mtsire, the emergent literary language elsewhere than in the religious sphere is already a form of modern Georgian, as the great national epic of Rustaveli, *The Man in the Tiger's Skin*, shows. Had the development of Christianity in the East followed the pattern of the sixteenth-century upheaval in the West, we might have seen a vernacular translation; however, events did not move in that direction, nor was there later Protestant infiltration leading to modern translation, in contrast with the Armenian area. This means that scripture and theological literature in general is accessible to learned folk, and has had a great moulding effect upon the language; but the influence upon the uneducated has been indirect. There is some religious literature in modern Georgian—for instance, the maxims of Ahikar, and an apocryphal gospel are known—but it may be significant that these are both translations from Armenian, and probably do not reflect a spontaneous movement within Georgian Christianity. This remains, in its use of scripture, clearly within the pattern of Eastern Orthodoxy, with the strengths and splendors of that tradition, and with its shortcomings also.

References: [The Library of Congress system of transliteration for Georgian titles is used in this bibliography.] R.P. Blake, "Ancient Georgian Versions of the Old Testament," *Harvard Theological Review,* vol. 19 (1926), 271-297; – – –, "The Georgian version of Fourth Esdras from the Jerusalem Manuscript," (1926), 299-375; K. Lake, R.P. Blake, S. New, "The Ceasarean Text of the Gospel of Mark," *Harvard Theological Review,* vol. 21 (1928), 208-404; – – –, "The Athos Codex of the Georgian Old Testament," *Harvard Theological Review,* vol. 22 (1929), 33-56; Akaki Shanidze, *Two old recensions of the Georgian gospels according to three Shatberd mss.* (Tbilisi, 1945); I. Abuladze, *Sak'me mocik'ult'a* [The Acts of the Apostles] (Tbilisi, 1949); G. Garitte, *L'ancienne version géorgienne des Actes des Apôtres* (Louvain, 1955); M. Tarchnišvili, *Geschichte der kirchlichen georgischen Literatur* (Rome, 1955); K. Lort'k'ip'anidze, *Kat'olike epistolet'a k'artuli versiebi* [Georgian versions of the Catholic epistles] (Tbilisi, 1956); J. Molitor, *Monumenta Iberica Antiquiora. Textus chąnmeti et haemeti ex inscriptionibus, s. Bibliis et patribus* (Louvain, 1956); M. Šanidze, *Psalmunis dzveli k'art'uli redak'ciebi* [Old Georgian redactions of the Psalter] (Tbilisi, 1960); I. Imnaišvili, *Iovanes Gamocxadeba da misi t'argmaneba* [The Revelation of John and its interpretation] (Tbilisi, 1961); D.M. Lang, *Catalogue of Georgian and other Caucasian printed books in the British Museum* (London, 1962); J.N. Birdsall, "Traces of the Jewish Greek Biblical Versions in Georgian Manuscript Sources," *Journal of Semitic Studies,* vol. 17 (1972), 83-92; D. Barrett, *Catalogue of the Wardrop Collection and other Georgian books and manuscripts in the Bodleian Library* (Oxford, 1973); *Mravaltavi* (annual of the K. Kekelidze Institute of MSS.), vols. 1-3 (Tbilisi, 1971-73); K. Žoceniże and K. Danelia, *Pavles epistolet'a k'art'uli versiebi* [Georgian versions of Paul's epistles] (Tbilisi, 1974); J.N. Birdsall, " 'The Martyrdom of St. Eustathius of Mzheta' and the Diatessaon: an investigation," *New Testament Studies,* vol. 22 (1976), 215-223; Entries: "Georgien," "Georgische Kirche," in *Kleines Woerterbuch des Christlichen Orients* (Wiesbaden, 1976); B.M. Metzger, *The Early Versions of the New Testament,* vol. IV: *The Georgian Version* (Oxford, 1977), 182-214.

J. Neville Birdsall

BIBLE, CHURCH SLAVONIC. The first Bible translations into Slavic were the work of two highly educated Byzantines from Thessalonica, the brothers Constantine (Cyril) and Methodius, who were fluent in Slavic as well as in their native Greek. According to several reliable historical sources, Constantine and Methodius were sent as Christian teachers to Great Moravia in 863, and soon extended their activity to nearby Pannonia also. Before his departure from Constantinople, Constantine invented an alphabet for Slavic (the glagolitic alphabet) and composed a homily on the Gospel text, "In the beginning was the Word, and the Word was with God, and the Word was God" (John 1:1). Upon their arrival, the brothers began training a number of Moravians, and soon also Pannonians, for the priesthood. Partly to expedite this, and partly for reasons of theological principle, they translated the requisite liturgical books from Greek and instituted Christian worship in a Slavic language. This language is now usually named Church Slavonic (or, less appropriately, Old Slavonic); several varieties of it are still used as liturgical languages by the Slavic Orthodox Churches, and under certain conditions also by the Roman Catholic Church.

Several of the liturgical books translated by Constantine and Methodius contained Biblical texts: the Gospel Lectionary (Evangeliarium), the Epistle Lectionary (Epistolarium), the Old Testament Lectionary (Prophetologium or Paroemiarium), and the Psalter with its appended Canticles from the Old and New Testaments (Psalterium). (A Lectionary is a book containing the lections, or liturgical readings, from a particular part of the Bible in the order of their liturgical use during the course of the Church year.) The ninth-century *Life of Methodius* and the early tenth-century Bulgarian writer John the Exarch state that at least three of these four books—they do not mention the Prophetologium—had already been translated by the time of Constantine's death in 869. Soon the Gospel Lectionary was expanded into a complete translation of the Four Gospels (Tetraevangelium) and the Epistle Lectionary into a complete translation of the Acts of the Apostles and their Epistles (Apostolus). All six of these books—Evangeliarium, Tetraevangelium, Epistolarium, Apostolus, Prophetologium, and Psalterium—have come down to us in many manuscripts, the oldest of which were written in the eleventh and twelfth centuries, and philological investigations of the extant texts have fully confirmed the testimony of the historical sources summarized above.

The *Life of Methodius* states further that Methodius, assisted by several shorthand writers (tachygraphers), translated the remainder of the Bible, except for the books of the Maccabees, in the course of eight months (March-October 26) shortly before his death in 885. Several other historical sources, some of which are independent of the *Life of Methodius,* make the same claim with less circumstantial detail; and one of these sources, the *Brief* (or *Prologue*) *Life of Constantine and Methodius,* says expressly that the translation was completed in the year 884. Although such a rapid translation of so much text may seem impossible at first, a simple and obvious calculation will show that it could have been accomplished by translating only a few pages (about as much as the book of Ruth) each day, and thus was well within the capability of a person such as Methodius. This translation is not now extant in its entirety, and most probably it was a casualty of the violent measures by which Christian worship in Church Slavonic was abolished in Great Moravia shortly after Methodius's death. However, some small parts of Methodius's translation may have survived, and may be extant among the numerous later translations of parts of the Bible into Church Slavonic. Several scholars have argued that this is true of the extant translations of the books of Ruth, Zephaniah, Haggai, Zechariah, Malachi and Revelation, and of a peculiar translation of the book of Daniel (with excerpts from Jeremiah and Baruch added) preserved in certain *Chronographs;* but the published philological studies of these texts fall short of proving this hypothesis.

Church Slavonic continued to be cultivated outside of Great Moravia, and especially in Bulgaria, where several of Constantine and Methodius's leading disciples had found refuge. Here during the reign of Emperor Symeon (893-927) Church Slavonic translations were made of many Greek texts, including the following parts of the Bible: the Octoteuch (that is, the eight books from Genesis through Ruth), the Tetrabasileium (that is, I-IV Kingdoms, which in Western Bibles are usually named I-II Samuel and I-II Kings), the Sixteen Prophets (that is, Isaiah, Jeremiah with Lamentations and Baruch, Ezekiel, Daniel, and the twelve Minor Prophets from Hosea through Malachi) with commentaries mostly by Theodoret of Cyrrhus, Job with a commentary by Olympiodore of Alexandria, Proverbs, Ecclesiastes with a commentary, the Song of Songs with a commentary by Philo of Carpasia, and the Wisdom of ben Sirach (that is, Ecclesiasticus). There is also an early translation of Esther from the Hebrew which may have been made in Bulgaria at this time, but which is usually considered to have been made in Kievan Russia during the eleventh or twelfth century, and a translation of Revelation with a commentary by Andrew of Caesarea which may have been made in Bohemia during the tenth or eleventh century (perhaps only the commentary is of this provenance, and the text itself is one of Methodius's translations, as already remarked). Most of these translations have hardly been subjected to any penetrating philological investigation which would settle the question of their origins; the views summarized above are merely the most reasonable yet advanced.

Until the end of the fifteenth century these translations circulated only as separate groups of related books. (The same is generally true of the Greek originals. No more than twelve of the several thousand extant Greek Biblical manuscripts up to the end of the fifteenth century contain the complete Bible, or even the complete Old Testament.) The Tetraevangelium, Apostolus and Psalterium were frequently copied (sometimes with commentaries by various authors), as were the three Lectionaries (Evangeliarium, Epistolarium and Prophetologium). The book of Revelation with its commentary usually circulated in a volume by itself. The Octoteuch and the Tetrabasileium, sometimes with Esther added, were copied together either as a single volume or as a two-volume set (divided either after Deuteronomy or after Ruth). The Sixteen Prophets with their commentaries made a volume by themselves. The remaining five Old Testament books circulated in a variety of combinations, usually by themselves but occasionally as appendices to the Octoteuch and Tetrabasileium or to the Sixteen Prophets.

Occasionally these Bible translations occur in the same manuscript as non-Biblical texts. The "wisdom" books (Job, Proverbs, Ecclesiastes, Sirach) may be found with various translated collections of proverbs and sayings, including a collection of sayings extracted from the pagan playwright Menander. The historical books (Octoteuch and Tetrabasileium) and historical excerpts from the Sixteen Prophets are sometimes found together with translations of certain Byzantine Chronicles and of Josephus Flavius's *Jewish War*; the resulting compendia of Jewish, Greek and Roman history are called *Chronographs*. The *Chronograph* in its original form was probably made in Bulgaria during Emperor Symeon's reign, although none of the extant manuscripts is older than the fifteenth century. The *Chronograph* is particularly important because only in it is preserved the above-mentioned peculiar translation of Daniel (with excerpts from Jeremiah and

Baruch) which may be part of Methodius's original translation of the Old Testament into Church Slavonic.

There is also a briefer work called the *Paleia* (from Greek *Palaia Diatheke,* "Old Testament") containing a summary of Biblical history in the form of paraphrases and excerpts of parts of the Old Testament. This seems to be a work of Slavic origin, made from the translations described above. The oldest extant manuscript of the *Paleia* was written in 1406.

At the end of the fifteenth century Archbishop Gennadius of Novgorod, in his efforts to combat a certain heretical movement, found it desirable to have a complete text of the Bible in Church Slavonic. He therefore brought together copies of all the earlier Church Slavonic translations of various books of the Bible (as listed above), and then commissioned a translation of the remaining parts. Curiously enough, his translators worked from a copy of the Roman Catholic Bible in Latin (the Vulgate), following its text and also its canon. Their translation, which was completed ca. 1493, contained the following books: I-II Chronicles, I-III Esdras, Nehemiah, Tobit, Judith, Esther (the parts not found in the Hebrew, nor in the earlier Church Slavonic translation made from the Hebrew), Wisdom of Solomon, I-II Maccabees; they also translated brief passages in certain other books (notably in Jeremiah and Ezekiel) to fill up gaps in the earlier translation from the Greek. The result of their labors was the first complete text of the Bible in Church Slavonic since the time of Methodius. At least four manuscripts of this text, which is usually called Gennadius's Bible, are extant (the oldest written in 1499), and there is evidence that several others once existed. Moreover, all printed editions of the Church Slavonic Bible are based on this text (with various revisions).

The first edition of the Church Slavonic Bible, printed by Ivan Fedorov at Ostroh (in Volynia) in 1580-1581, was published by Prince Constantine of Ostroh in order to provide the Orthodox populace of the Ukraine and Belorussia (at that time within the Grand Duchy of Lithuania and the Kingdom of Poland) with a means of defense against the attempts then being made by various missionaries to convert that populace to Protestantism or to Catholicism. By the standards of its time, the Ostroh Bible was a solid work of scholarship. The text of Gennadius's Bible was extensively revised and corrected against the Greek Orthodox Bible (the Septuagint), with occasional reference to the Vulgate and various Catholic and Protestant translations into Czech and Polish. The former translations of Esther, the Wisdom of Solomon and the Song of Songs were replaced by new translations from Greek, and a translation from Greek of III Maccabees (absent from Gennadius's Bible) was added.

The second edition of the Church Slavonic Bible, printed at Moscow in 1663, purports to be a close reprint of the Ostroh Bible, but in fact it has been rather heavily revised. The circumstances of this revision are unknown.

During the eighteenth century a series of Imperial Commissions sitting from 1712 through 1756 undertook a further, more thorough revision of the Church Slavonic text against the Greek. The result of their labors was published during the reign and under the patronage of the Empress Elizabeth of Russia, and therefore is known as Elizabeth's Bible. The first edition of Elizabeth's Bible was published at St. Petersburg in 1751, the second edition (embodying the Commission's final corrections) at Moscow in 1756. The text of these editions is in actual fact not very different from that in the edition of 1663; the great bulk of the corrections made by the Imperial Commissions were in matters of grammar and orthography (but the books of Tobit and Judith were newly translated from Greek.) It is the text of the edition of 1756 that is found in all subsequent editions of the Church Slavonic Bible (Catholic and Protestant as well as Orthodox ones, wherever published). The one exception is a reprint of the Ostroh Bible, published by Old Believers at Moscow in 1914.

Thus the presently received text of the Church Slavonic Bible contains five historical layers, as follows: (1) translations made by Constantine and Methodius in Great Moravia about 863-885; (2) translations made in Bulgaria for Emperor Symeon about 893-927; (3) translations made in Russia (Novgorod) for Archbishop Gennadius about 1493; (4) translations made in the Ukraine (Ostroh) for Prince Constantine about 1580; and (5) translations made in Russia for Empress Elizabeth about 1751. Most of these translations are from Greek, but those in layer 3 were originally from Latin (although they have by now been extensively revised against the Greek).

The presently received text of the Church Slavonic Bible also embodies at least two different views as to which books belong in the Bible (to use more technical language, two different canons of Scripture). Gennadius's Bible followed the Roman Catholic Vulgate of the fifteenth century, manuscripts of which contained not only all the books presently regarded as canonical by the Roman Catholic Church (as defined by the Council of Trent in 1546), but also three others: The Prayer of Manasseh and II-III Esdras (now usually termed II-IV Esdras by Western scholars, inasmuch as the book of Nehemiah is counted by the Roman Catholic Church as the canonical II Esdras). The Orthodox editors of the Ostroh Bible followed the Orthodox canon of Scripture (its six-fold definition is given by Apostolic Canon 85, Canon 60 of the Council at Laodicea, Canon 27 of the Council at Carthage, and pronouncements by St. Athanasius the Great, St. Gregory of Nazianzus, and St. Amphilochius of Iconium), and thus added II Maccabees, which the Roman Catholic Church has never regarded as canonical. They did not, however, exclude III Esdras (now usually termed IV Esdras by Western scholars), although it has never been regarded as canonical by any Orthodox Church and is not extant in Greek. (The private opinion of many Orthodox theologians, that only those books of the Old Testament now extant in Hebrew and now canonical for Judaism are truly canonical for the Orthodox Church, has no support in Orthodox canon law and may be left out of account here.)

The table on page 10 gives the contents of the Church Slavonic Bible, indicating to which of the five historical layers (as specified above) the translation of each book belongs and which books are regarded as not canonical by the Orthodox Churches, by the Roman Catholic Church, and by most Protestant Churches. The Church Slavonic names of the books are given in English translation, and those few books which bear different names in the Septuagint, the Vulgate or the Authorized (King James) Version are noted.

Despite the diverse origins of its parts, Elizabeth's Church Slavonic Bible strikes the reader as a unitary work. The language is archaic and majestic, but it

Empress Elizabeth's Church Slavonic Bible

Old Testament

Book	Layer
Genesis	2
Exodus	2
Leviticus	2
Numbers	2
Deuteronomy	2
Joshua	2
Judges	2
Ruth	2
I-II Kingdoms[1]	2
III-IV Kingdoms[2]	2
I-II Chronicles	2
†Prayer of Manasseh	3
I Esdras[3]	3
Nehemiah[4]	3
†II Esdras[5]	3
*Tobit	5
*Judith	5
Esther	4
*(Additions to Esther)[6]	4
Job	2
Psalter	1
Proverbs	2
Ecclesiastes	2
Song of Songs[7]	4
*Wisdom of Solomon	4
*Wisdom of ben Sirach[8]	2
Isaiah	2
Jeremiah	2
Lamentations	2
*Epistle of Jeremiah[9]	2
*Baruch	2
Ezekiel	2
Daniel	2
*(Additions to Daniel)[10]	2
Hosea	2
Joel	3
Amos	3
Obadiah	3
Jonah	3
Micah	3
Nahum	5
Habakkuk	5
Zephaniah	4
Haggai	4
Zechariah	2
Malachi	1
*I Maccabees	2
*II Maccabees	2
†III Maccabees[11]	4
‡III Esdras[12]	3

New Testament

Book	Layer
Matthew	1
Mark	1
Luke	1
John	1
Acts	1
James	1
I-II Peter	1
I-III John	1
Jude	1
Romans	1
I-II Corinthians	1
Galatians	1
Ephesians	1
Philippians	1
Colossians	1
I-II Thessalonians	1
I-II Timothy	1
Titus	1
Philemon	1
Hebrews	1
Revelation	2

[1] I-II Samuel in Vulgate and Authorized Version.

[2] I-II Kings in Vulgate and Authorized Version.

[3] Ezra in Authorized Version, II Esdras 1-10 in Septuagint.

[4] Nehemiah, i.e. II Esdras in Vulgate, II Esdras 11-23 in Septuagint.

[5] III Esdras in Vulgate, I Esdras in Authorized Version Apocrypha, I Esdras in Septuagint.

[6] The Rest of Esther in Authorized Version Apocrypha.

[7] Song of Solomon in Authorized Version.

[8] Ecclesiasticus in Vulgate and Authorized Version Apocrypha.

[9] Baruch 6 in Vulgate and Authorized Version Apocrypha.

[10] The Song of the Three Holy Children. The History of Susanna, and Bel and the Dragon in Authorized Version Apocrypha.

[11] followed by ‡ IV Maccabees in Septuagint; III-IV Maccabees not in Vulgate or Authorized Version Apocrypha.

[12] IV Esdras in Vulgate, II Esdras in Authorized Version Apocrypha, not in Septuagint.

1-5 = five historical layers of translations. *not canonical for most Protestants. †not canonical for most Protestants or for Catholics.
‡not canonical for most Protestants, for Catholics or for Orthodox.

is also very familiar to an Orthodox reader who has regularly attended church services (which are in the same language). An attentive reader will find a few unfamiliar words (for example, *tul*, "quiver," in Russian *kolchan*), or unfamiliar forms of familiar words (*vel'blud*, "camel," in Russian *verbliud*), or familiar words with unfamiliar meanings (*zhivot*, "life," but in Russian "stomach"; *trus*, "earthquake," but in Russian "coward"), but these are relatively rare. More frequent are grammatical forms and constructions which are no longer used in literary Russian (for example, *skazakh*, "I said," in Russian *skazal; prikosnutisia emu*, "to touch it," in Russian *prikosnut'sia k nemu*, with the preposition *k*). But the great majority of Church Slavonic words and grammatical forms and constructions are used also in Russian, and have the same meaning in both languages, so that many passages are perfectly clear to an attentive Russian reader, and he will understand at least the gist of even the most obscure passages. Literary depictions of Church Slavonic texts as completely incomprehensible to uneducated Russians, for example, in Chekhov's tale "Peasants," are exaggerations. The greatest obstacle to comprehension, which some Russians feel very keenly, is not the language, but the very great differences between modern ways of viewing and evaluating the world and the much more archaic ways in the Bible: these can range from what are hardly more than differences of idiom or style (for example, *nos tvoi iako stolp livanskii, smotriaiai litse damaska*, "thy nose is as the tower of Lebanon which looketh toward Damascus," Song of Songs 7:4) to differences of a much more fundamental character, such as Galatians 3:13 in any language. Exactly the same remarks could be made about an English reader of the King James version of the Bible; the difficulties in comprehension are about the same in each case.

Until the end of the nineteenth century the Church Slavonic Bible was virtually the only Bible available to Russians, and its role in the development of Russian literature is similar to that which the King James version of the Bible has played in the development of English or American literature. The first commonly available translation of the entire Bible into Russian was published only in 1876, and its utterly graceless language and style still hinder its acceptance by Russians. Therefore a close acquaintance with Empress Elizabeth's version of the Church Slavonic Bible is essential for any serious study of the classics of Russian literature.

References: Chistovich, "Ispravlenie teksta slavianskoi Biblii pered izdaniem 1751 g.," in *Pravoslavnoe obozrenie*, 1 (1860), 479-510, 2 (1860), 41-72; A. Bobrov, *Krest'ianin i kniga* (Vladimir, 1908); M. Jugie, *Histoire du Canon de l'Ancien Testament dans l'Église grecque et l'Église russe* (Paris, 1909); I.E. Evseev, "Gennadievskaia Bibliia 1499 goda," *Trudy XV-go Arkheologicheskogo s"ezda v Novgorode, 1911* (Moscow, 1916), II, 1-21; – – –, "Rukopisnoe predanie slavianskoi Biblii," in *Khristianskoe chtenie*, 91 (1911), 435-450, 644-660; – – –, "Ocherki po istorii slavianskogo perevoda Biblii," *Khristianskoe chtenie*, No. 92 (1912), 1261-1285, 1342-1374, No. 93 (1913), 192-213, 350-373, 469-493; M. Rešetar, "Zur Übersetzungstätigkeit Methods," *Archiv für slavische Philologie*, No. 34 (1913), 234-239; J. Schweigl, "La Bibbia slava del 1751 (1756)," *Biblica*, No. 18 (1937), 51-73; N.A. Meshcherskii, "K voprosu ob izuchenii perevodnoi pis'mennosti Kievskogo perioda," *Uchënye zapiski Karelofinskogo pedagogicheskogo instituta,* Seriia obshchestvennykh nauk, No. 2 (1955) :1, 198-219; W. Schneirla, "The Orthodox Old Testament Canon and the so-called Apocrypha," *St. Vladimir's Seminary Quarterly,* new series, 1 (1957), 40-46; F. Grivec, *Konstantin und Method: Lehrer der Slaven* (Wiesbaden, 1960); R. Večerka, *Slovanské počátky české knižni vzdělanosti* (Prague, 1963); I. Ševčenko, "Three Paradoxes of the Cyrillo-Methodian Mission," *Slavic Review,* 23 (1964), 220-236; A. Dostál, "The Origins of the Slavonic Liturgy," *Dumbarton Oaks Papers,* 19 (1965), 67-87; R. Mathiesen, "An Emendation to the Vita Methodii xv," *Zbornik za filologiju i lingvistiku* (Novi Sad), 10 (1967), 51-53; A.P. Vlasto, *The Entry of the Slavs into Christendom* (Cambridge, 1970); Ch. Hennick, "Das Neue Testament in altkirchenslavischer Sprache: Der gegenwärtige Stand seiner Erforschung und seine Bedeutung für die griechische Textgeschichte," *Die alten Übersetzungen des Neuen Testaments, die Kirchenväterzitate und Lektionare,* ed. K. Aland (Berlin & New York, 1972), 403-435; G. Freidhof, *Vergleichende sprachliche Studien zur Gennadius-Bibel (1499) und Ostroger Bibel (1580/81)* (Frankfurt, 1972); "Zur ersten Übersetzung des 3. Buches der Makkabäer im Ostslavischen," *Slavistische Studien zum VII. Internationalen Slavistenkongress* (München, 1973), 75-80; B.A. Uspensky, "The Influence of Language on Religious Consciousness," *Semiotica,* 10 (1974), 177-189.

Robert Mathiesen

BIBLIOTÉKA DLIA CHTÉNIIA (lit.: Library for Reading). A conservative monthly journal of "literature, science, the arts, industry, news, and fashion," issued in Petersburg from 1834 to 1865. *Biblioteka* was published by A.F. Smirdin, and edited chiefly by O.I. Senkovskii, whose numerous articles and feuilletons appeared in the journal frequently under the pseudonym "Baron Brambeus." *Biblioteka* was the first Russian so-called "thick" journal (up to 30 printer's sheets) and started the "commercial trend" in Russian journalism. It is given credit for inculcating an interest in the public for reading journals. Oriented primarily to provincial readers—small landowners, officials, merchants—the journal enjoyed unheard-of popularity in the late 1830s with a circulation of some 7,000 copies. The publication in 1834-35 of works by Pushkin ("Queen of Spades," "Tale of the Dead Tsarevna and the Seven Bogatyrs") lent to the success of *Biblioteka.* The journal gave prominent space to such topical genres as the society tale and tales of adventure—Lermontov's "Khadzhi-Abrek" and Aleksandr Bestuzhev-Marlinskii's *Caucasian Sketches.* However, the journal relied primarily upon the works of second-rank writers, such as N.V. Kukol'nik and V.G. Benediktov, D.V. Davydov, V.I. Dal, and N.A. Polevoi. In the section devoted to foreign literature, *Biblioteka* published works by Balzac, George Sand, William Thackeray, Eugène Sue, and Alexandre Dumas.

Beginning in 1836 the journal battled with Pushkin's *Sovremennik* (The Contemporary) and, over the next decade, spoke out against Belinskii, Gogol, and the "Natural School." The liberal critics of the time sharply condemned its ideas as conservative, and the tone of its literary criticism as superficial. In 1848 A.V. Starchevskii became editor, followed by A.V. Druzhinin (1856), A.F. Pisemskii

(1859) and P.D. Boborykin (from 1864 until the journal closed in 1865). In the 1850s and 1860s such authors as Lev Tolstoi ("Three Deaths"), Aleksandr Ostrovskii (the play *The Pupil*), Ivan Goncharov, N.S. Leskov (with the antinihilist novel *No Way Out*), and A.A. Fet occasionally contributed to the journal. Articles by N.I. Pirogov, P.N. Tkachev, P.L. Lavrov, N.V. Shelgunov, and Alexander Humboldt appeared from time to time in columns covering "The Sciences and the Arts," or "News from the Scholarly World." See also SENKOVSKII, O.I. and JOURNALS, RUSSIAN.

References: "Biblioteka dlia chteniia" in Brokgauz-Èfron, *Novyi entsiklopedicheskii slovar'*, vol. 6 (Pb., 1911); V.G. Belinskii, "Nichto o nichem," *Polnoe sobranie sochinenii*, II (M., 1953); N.V. Gogol', "O dvizhenii zhurnal'noi literarury v 1834 i 1835 godu," *Polnoe sobranie sochinenii*, VIII (M., 1952); N.G. Chernyshevskii, "Ocherki gogolevskogo perioda russkoi literarury," *Polnoe sobranie sochinenii*, III (M., 1947); D.I. Bernshtein, *"Biblioteka dlia chteniia," Uchenye zapiski kafedry russkoi literatury Moskovskogo gos. ped. in-ta*, fascicle 2 (M., 1939); L.Ia. Ginzburg, *"Biblioteka dlia chteniia* v 1830-kh godakh: O.I. Senkovskii," in *Ocherki po istorii russkoi zhurnalistiki i kritiki*, vol. I (L., 1950); V. Kaverin, *Baron Brombeus* (M., 1966).

BICHÚRIN, NIKITA YAKOVLEVICH [monastic name: IAKINF] (1777-1853). Russian Orientalist, traveller and translator. Bichurin was born on 29 August (9 September) 1777 in the family of a village church-reader of Chuvash nationality. Upon completion of the seminary in Kazan, he was sent in 1807 to China as head of the Church mission in Peking and remained there until 1822. During his 14 years in Peking he studied the Chinese language and the history of China and its culture. His extensive research led to the publication of many books and articles, and translations into Russian of a great number of Chinese historical and geographical works, a descriptive study of China and other Asian countries, and two books about Tibet. Bichurin's works treat many aspects of ancient, medieval and modern Chinese history, the history of Chinese culture and philosophy and also China's international relations. Bichurin firmly believed the ancient Chinese chronicles are more complete and more reliable as a source for the history of the peoples of Central Asia than the Greek chronicles. Pushkin and Belinskii took a great interest in the writings of Bichurin, and he was highly respected by the exiled Decembrists with whom he had made friends on his travels in Siberia. Bichurin's rich and factual material makes it possible to study the everyday existence and the cultural and spiritual values of many peoples. The literature which Bichurin collected during his stay in China and during his journeys to Mongolia, China and Tibet, as well as the Museum collections, is housed in the Institutes of Oriental Studies and Ethnography of the Soviet Academy of Sciences. He was a corresponding member of the Academy of Sciences (from 1837) and of the Asian Society in Paris. Bichurin died on 11 (23) June 1853.

Works: Zapiski o Mongolii, 2 vols. (Pb., 1828); *Istoricheskoe obozrenie oiratov ili kalmykov s XV stoletiia do nastoiashchego vremeni* (Pb., 1834); [Chinese Grammar] *Khan'-vyn'-tsamyn'* (Pb., 1838); *Kitai, ego zhiteli, nravy, obychai, prosveshchenie* (Pb., 1840); *Statisticheskoe opisanie Kitaiskoi imperii* (Pb., 1842); *Kitai v grazhdanskom i nravstvennom sostoianii*, 4 pts. (Pb., 1848); *Sobranie svedenii o narodakh, obitavshikh v Srednei Azii v drevnie vremena,* 3 vols. (M.-L., 1950-1953); "Iakinf Bichurin (Avtobiograficheskaia zapiska)," *Uchĕnye zapiski Akademii Nauk po I i III otdeleniiam,* vol. 3 (1855).

Translations from Chinese: Opisanie Tibeta v nyneshnem ego sostoianii, 2 pts. (Pb., 1828); *Istoriia pervykh chetyrĕkh khanov iz doma Chingisova* (Pb., 1829); *Opisanie Chzhungarii i Vostochnogo Turkestana v drevnem i nyneshnem sostoianii,* 2 pts. (Pb., 1829).

References: N.S. Shchukin, "Iakinf Bichurin," *Zhurnal ministerstva narodnogo prosveshcheniia,* No. 9, ch. XCV (September 1857); M.P. Pogodin, "Biografiia Iakinfa Bichurina," *Besedy v Obshchestve liubitelei rossiiskoi slovesnosti pri Moskovskom universitete,* No. 3 (1871); N.S. Moller, "Iakinf Bichurin v dalĕkikh vospominaniiakh ego vnuchki," *Russkaia starina,* Nos. 8-9 (1888); *Istoriia izucheniia vostoka v Evrope i Rossii,* 2nd ed. (L., 1925); L.V. Simonivskaia, "Bichurin kak istorik Kitaia," *Doklady i soobshcheniia istoricheskogo fakul'teta MGU,* No. 7 (1948); D.M. Tikhonov, "Russkii kitaeved pervoi poloviny XIX v. Iakinf Bichurin," *Uchĕnye zapiski LGU* [seriia vostokovedcheskikh nauk], No. 179, vol. 4 (1954).

BIELIÁUSKAS, ALFONSAS (b. 1923). Lithuanian writer. Bieliauskas was born on 5 October 1923 of working-class parents in the village of Naujieji Neveronys in the district of Kaunas. Throughout his career he has combined political activity and Party functions with journalistic and literary efforts. Orphaned at a young age Bieliauskas worked at manual labor while attending secondary school in Kaunas. At this time he became active in the underground Communist youth organization. During the Nazi occupation of Lithuania he went to Russia (1941-44) and returned with the Soviet troops to become the first secretary of the Communist youth organization in post-war Kaunas (1944-46). He continued his education at the universities of Kaunas and Vilnius, completing his studies in Lithuanian literature in 1951. Active in journalism since his secondary school days, he joined the editorial staff of the newspaper *Tarybų Lietuva* (Soviet Lithuania) in 1946, then became assistant editor (1951-54) and finally chief editor of the journal *Švyturys* (The Beacon). He is a member of the Soviet Writers' Union and has held the influential post of chairman of the Soviet Lithuanian Writers' Union from 1970 to 1976. Member of the Communist Party since 1944, he has served on the Central Committee of the Lithuanian Communist Party (1971-76) and since 1971 as deputy to the Supreme Soviet of the Lithuanian Republic. Bieliauskas has been awarded numerous honors for his political and literary activities. In 1965 the Soviet Lithuanian Republic awarded him special recognition for his contributions to culture.

The development of Bieliauskas as a writer parallels major trends in Soviet Lithuanian literature during the post-war decades. His early publications were journalistic sketches in which he described with optimistic zeal the dedication of farmers and workers to the building of a new socialist order. These sketches were published in a number of volumes: "Happiness Is Born Thus" (Taip gimsta laimė, 1949, with co-author V. Radaitis) describes rural collectivization; "Firm Hands" (Tvirtos rankos, 1950) and "People and Machines" (Žmonės prie staklių, 1955) present positive models of workers. From these direct attempts to shape public opinion Bieliauskas turned to the art of the novel, the genre in which he has made his principal contribution as a writer. His first three novels—*Work Street* (Darbo gatvė, 1956), *Roses Bloom Red* (Rožės žydi raudonai, 1959), and *We Shall Meet Again, Wilma*! (Mes dar susitiksim, Vilma!, 1962)—are traditional narratives with branching plots, stereotyped characters and conflicts based primarily on class struggle. However, during the post-Stalin "Thaw" he was one of the first writers to experiment with new narrative techniques. His novel *Kaunas Romance* (Kauno romanas, 1966) ushered in a trend toward the psychological novel of introspection narrated from a limited, internal perspective and utilizing stream of consciousness techniques. The protagonist is no longer a "positive hero," a model to be imitated, but a weak, confused, struggling individual who must come to terms with his own guilt and with the injustice of the Stalin era. Bieliauskas' fifth novel, *When It Rained* (Tada kai lijo, 1977) continued to experiment with a stream of consciousness mode of narration, obliterating the boundaries between past time and the present through random associations and recurring symbolic figures. These five novels present a line of development from the political epic of class struggle to the psychological novel of introspection, a development typical of Lithuanian prose in the post-Stalin period.

The author has stated more than once that his books are his biography, and rightly so, for many autobiographical elements can be found in the novels, especially in the characterizations of the central characters. The main protagonists of his novels have many traits in common, for they are basically one and the same character seen with increasing depth and truthfulness. In the center of each novel stands an upright, hard-working, ambitious young man, dedicated to the new social order. Of poor, working-class origins he is unpolished and naive, but eager to better himself. He tends to fall in love with an "unsuitable" girl, a refined daughter of the bourgeoisie, so that the external class struggle is internalized through conflicting loyalties.

The first novel, *Work Street*, depicts the final days of Nazi occupation in a provincial Lithuanian town. Focus is on external action: the heroic resistance of workers and Communist partisans against the Nazis and the local capitalists. The sentimental and tragic love story of the youthful worker Paul Giniotis and a bourgeois girl dominates the intrigues of the other stereotyped characters. The novel was later revised under the new title *She Loved Paul* (Ji mylejo Paulį, 1976).

The action of the next novel, *Roses Bloom Red,* is set in the early post-war years. It depicts the intense ideological struggle that divided friends and families. The hero, Vytas Čeponis, returns from his wartime refuge in Russia to the city of Kaunas after its liberation from the Nazis. Idealistic, moral and hard-working, he assumes leadership of the Communist youth organization. His love for the daughter of a pre-war state official ends unhappily since she is unable to free herself from her mother's influence and her own materialistic tendencies. Čeponis abandons her with a clear conscience as he departs to pursue his education and career aspirations (he hopes to become a writer) in the capital city, Vilnius. The class conflict is personalized through the love story as well as through the antagonisms within the hero's own family. In a suspenseful midnight chase Čeponis kills his own cousin, a nationalist "bandit" and enemy of the new state. *Roses Bloom Red* was awarded the Lithuanian Republic's prize for literature in 1959. It has been dramatized on stage and has supplied the libretto for an opera.

A transition to first-person narration occurs in *We Shall Meet Again, Wilma!* Saulius Juozaitis, a somewhat younger version of Čeponis, relates his wartime experiences. The Nazi invasion of Lithuania catches the young Communist activist by surprise. He flees in panic, barely ahead of the invaders, into the depths of Russia. His picaresque wanderings and adventures, his meetings with friends against the backdrop of war are narrated as flashback episodes from a secure refuge in the forests of Siberia. Saulius comprehends the chaos he has witnessed within the framework of a cosmic struggle between the forces of inhumanity and greed bred by the capitalist system and the forces of a new and just social order. The major conflicts in the novel quickly fall into place along class lines. Plot intrigue is provided by the German girl Wilma, who moves in and out of the hero's life and whom he comes to love. Her mysterious reticence raises the demons of jealousy and suspicion, yet is finally explained *deus ex machina* by a document that reveals her secret mission against the Nazis. The first-person narration provides a more intimate understanding of the protagonist's states of mind, revealing moments of doubt and self-questioning through stream of consciousness. However, the novel's structure—mechanical shifts between the present and the past in alternating chapters—stands at variance with the personal mode of observation. The author's manipulative presence is clearly felt in the structuring of the parallel time levels and in the unexpected, external resolutions of personal conflicts.

The world of Bieliauskas' first three novels conveniently falls into clear-cut black and white, good and evil categories. Their plots contain the ingredients of a melodramatic "thriller": heroes and villains, innocent maidens, attempted seductions, fratricide, and unexpected coincidences. These novels belong to the category of light entertainment, like a "Western" or detective story, where interest is sustained by the unraveling of an involved plot, and the desire for justice is satisfied by a conclusion that punishes the evildoer, rewards the good and re-establishes a state of harmony.

The tendency away from external action toward psychological insight and an internal point of view, evident in *We Shall Meet Again, Wilma!*, found fuller expression in the next novel *Kaunas Romance*. From the perspective of a disintegrating Stalinist era, the protagonist and first-person narrator of the novel, Sigitas Sėlis, tormented by guilt and doubt, looks back some fifteen years to his youth. The events that occur during the present time level—a span of about twenty-four hours—are presented in a chaotic stream of consciousness. Dislocated images of the present, by association, serve for Sėlis as bridges to confront the past. In contrast to the present, these past episodes are interior monologues narrated in a chronological and coherent manner. They recount the first post-war years of a working-class youth, a functionary in the Communist youth organization. But now the smooth façade and moral certitude of the earlier heroes breaks down, revealing fear, guilt, outright careerism and personal betrayal. Under the repressive atmosphere of the Stalinist "Personality Cult," Sėlis had deserted his beloved Geda, the niece of a pre-war government minister. After her deportation he had quickly married the daughter of a security police chief, assuring his own career. In the confrontation with his guilty past Sėlis gradually determines to break away from the sterile path of conformity and cowardice. By refusing for the first time to obey unjust orders from his superior he risks his career. Declining further advancement he resolves to return to his childhood cottage, to the simple life of a factory worker. *Kaunas Romance* stimulated considerable literary discussion, especially with regard to the stream of consciousness form, still new to Lithuanian literature in the sixties. The interest of readers and critics in the non-heroic character of Sėlis helped modify the critical position which required that fictional protagonists serve a didactic-exemplary function.

A decade later the novel *When It Rained* continued the psychological, introspective approach. The primary events in the novel, as in two of the earlier works, take place immediately after the war. The protagonist, Aurimas Gluosnis, is again a poor working-class youth who returns to Kaunas from Russia and earns a respected place for himself as a Communist youth leader. Yet driven by the ambition to become a writer he resigns his political position against the wishes of the Party and returns to school. In spite of a national prize awarded for a short story, a political campaign against him terminates his literary career. The major issue in the novel is a literary controversy: What type of literature does the new socialist society need? Remnants of the bourgeois intelligentsia at the university insist on the primacy of aesthetic considerations and suggest avant-garde Western writers as models. Communist activists, on the other hand, call for a politically committed literature, aggressive in its dedication to and adulation of the new order. Gluosnis is unwilling to join either camp. For him writing is an intuitive, introspective activity, an attempt to convey personal truths, subjective insights. His refusal to compromise these truths leads to outward defeat. Bieliauskas in this novel touches upon an important problem: the dilemma of an individual who must reconcile subjective experience with the conflicting demands of "objective," ideologically-defined, truths. The protagonist suffers a spiritual collapse, verges on suicide, seeks oblivion in erotic experiences and security in idealized, romantic love. As in *Kaunas Romance* the conclusion is unsatisfactory—the individual seeks to escape from the complexities and contradictions of the emerging social order by returning to a simpler stage of his existence. Gluosnis departs for the provinces to fight the nationalist partisans. He chooses a path that promises to be clearer and simpler, but which offers no solution to the problem of truth posed by the novel.

A number of structural and stylistic flaws are common to both of the psychological novels: sub-plots and minor intrigues create a sprawling, formless structure; secondary characters, stereotyped by social class, are reminiscent of the earlier novels; repetitive leitmotifs and rhetorical metaphors evoke a melodramatic tone that characterizes Bieliauskas' style in general. As a novelist Bieliauskas has expanded the concept of Socialist Realism by introducing new stylistic forms and topical, even controversial themes. He has contributed to the emergence of the modern psychological novel in Lithuanian literature. Yet the scope of his works is limited by his ideologically schematic treatment of significant human issues.

Several of the novels have been translated: *Roses Bloom Red* into Russian, Polish, Slovakian, Latvian, Estonian; *We Shall Meet Again, Wilma!* into Russian, German, Latvian; *Kaunas Romance* into Russian, Ukrainian, Polish, Slovakian, German, Latvian, Estonian, and Hungarian.

In addition to his novels Bieliauskas has published numerous essays on literary criticism. These have been collected in two volumes, *Roads and Monuments* (Keliai ir paminklai, 1963) and *Emphatic Dreams* (Išdrožti sapnai, 1973). As a literary critic Bieliauskas assumes the primary function of literature to be a tool for social change. However, he has also argued eloquently for a broadened concept of socialist literature, for innovation and variety in style and structure, for a non-didactic approach to fictional protagonists, for high aesthetic standards and openness to modern world literature.

Works: Taip gimsta laimė (with V. Radaitis, Vilnius, 1949); *Tvirtos rankos* (Vilnius, 1950); *Žmonės prie staklių* (Vilnius, 1955); *Darbo gatvė* (Vilnius, 1956; revised edition entitled *Ji mylejo Paulį*, Vilnius, 1976); *Rožės žydi raudonai* (Vilnius, 1959); *Mes dar susitiksim, Vilma!* (Vilnius, 1962); *Keliai ir paminklai* (Vilnius, 1963); *Kauno romanas* (Vilnius, 1966); *Išdrožti sapnai* (Vilnius, 1973); *Tada kai lijo* (Vilnius, 1977).

References: E. Bukelienė, "Dar kartą apie psichologizmą," *Pergalė,* No. 5 (1967), 123-133; Vytautas Kubilius, "Vidinis Monologas," *Pergalė,* No. 5 (1968), 132-150; Algirdas Antanaitis, "New Trends in the Soviet Lithuanian Novel," *Litaunus,* vol. 16, No. 2 (1970), 13-19; Algimantas Bučys, *Romanas ir dabartis* (Vilnius, 1973), 192-205; Audrone B. Willeke, "Socialist Realism and the Psychological Novels of Alf. Bieliauskas," *Journal of Baltic Studies,* vol. 8, No. 4 (1977), 294-300.

Audrone B. Willeke

BIGÉEV, ZAGIR [pseudonym of: BIGEEV, MUKHAMMED-ZAGIR] (1870-1902). Tatar writer. Bigeev was born in Rostov-on-the-Don in 1870. He studied in a Russian school, then at a madrasah (Moslem school) at Kazan, and later became a mullah. In the novel *The Thousands, or The Beautiful Khadicha* (Meng-nar iaki gůzal kyz Khadicha, 1887) Bigeev spoke out against hypocrisy and greed which incite people to crime. In the novel *Great Sins* (Gònalie kabair, 1890) he gives a broad and depressing social picture of the self-seeking rich, grinding poverty and venal lawyers. Bigeev attributed the existence of social evil to the poor preparation given students at the madrasah, an idea which is stressed in all his works. He also wrote the book *A Journey through Mesopotamia* (Mavaraén-naherda saiakhat, published posthumously in 1908). Bigeev died in Rostov-on-the-Don in 1902.

Works: Povest'lar (Kazan, 1960).

References: F. Émirkhan, "Ädäbiiatka gaid," *Äl'islakh,* Nos. 44, 47 (1908); M. Gainullin, "Zahir Bigiev," *Sovet ädäbiiaty,* No. 9 (1944); M. Gainullin, *Tatar ädäbiiaty XIX iòz* (Kazan, 1957).

BIÍSHEVA, ZAINAP ABDULLOVNA (b. 1908). Bashkir writer, CP member since 1941. Biisheva was born on 2 (15) January 1908 in the village of Tuimbe-tovo (now the Kugarchin Raion). She completed the Orenburg Bashkir Pedagogical Technicum. Biisheva is the author of the book *The Boy Partisan* (Partizan malai, 1942), the novelette *Kiunkhylyu* (1949), the novelette in verse *Gul'iamal* (1953), and the plays for children *On the Christmas Tree* (Ělkala, 1948) and *Friendship* (Duthlyk, 1950). The novelette *Let's Be Friends* (Duth bulaiyq, 1954) is devoted to the friendship of children of different nationalities. In the novel *The Oppressed* (Kămhetelgăndăr, 1959) the difficult life of the Bashkir woman and her adjustment to the Revolution are depicted.

Works: *Hailanma ăthărihăr* (Ufa, 1964); *Mökhăbbăt hăm năfrăt* (Ufa,1965); *Kămhetelgăndăr. Uiaanyu* (Ufa, 1968); *Izbrannye proizvedeniia* (Ufa, 1969) [text in Bashkir] ; *Volshebnyi Kurai: p'esy* (Ufa, 1972) [text in Bashkir] ; In Russian translation: *Strannyi chelovek* (Ufa, 1963); *Unizhennye*, pt. 1 (M., 1965); *U Bol'shogo Ika. Emesh: romany* (M., 1974).

BIKBÁI, BAIAZIT GAIAZOVICH (1909-1968). Soviet Bashkir wirter. Meritorious Artist of the Bashkir ASSR (1957). Bikbai was born in the family of a teacher in the village of Kaltai (now Kuiurgazin Raion) on 9 January 1909. He is a teacher by training. His first collection of poems was published in 1932, *Current days* (Ütep barghan köndăr), followed by *Beyond the Forest* (Urman artynda, 1934), *Sunny Days* (Qoiashly kön, 1934), *Why is Sea-Water Salty* (Dinggath hyuy ningă tothlo, 1939). *Bright Land* (Yagty er, 1941). During World War II a collection of Bikbai's poems came out entitled *I Sing Praises of the Land* (1941), *The Kerchief* (1942), *Fiery Lines* (1943). Bikbai wrote the plays *Karlugas*(1938), *The Motherland Calls* (1941), *Children of One Family* (1942), *Salavat* (1940-54), *Kakhym Turia* (1957) and also librettos for the operas *Karlugas, Azat* and *Salavat Yulaev*. In the novel *When the Akselian Floods Its Banks* (Aqselăn tashqanda, 1956) Bikbai writes of the improvements in the Bashkir village which the Soviet regime has brought. Bikbai died on 2 September 1968 in Ufa.

Works: *Hailanma ăthărihăr* (Ufa, 1959); *Zhivye istochniki* (Ufa, 1968) [text in Bashkir] ; *Izbrannye proizvedeniia* (Ufa, 1969) [text in Bashkir]. In Russian translation: *Stikhotvoreniia* (Ufa, 1949); *Doroga* (Ufa, 1955); *Utrennii svet* (Ufa, 1967).

References: L.G. Barag and F.M. Khatirov, "Tvorchestvo Baiazita Bikbaia," in *Istoriia bashkirskoi sovetskoi literatury*, vol. 2 (Ufa, 1961).

BIKCHENTÁEV, ANVER GADEEVICH (b. 1913). Soviet Bashkir writer who also writes in Russian, member CP since 1941. Bikchentaev was born in Ufa in the family of a white-collar worker on 4 October 1913. He received training in the Advanced Literature Courses of the Union of Writers of the USSR in 1956, although he was first published in 1933. He wrote sketches and stories about the life of workers during the five-year plans before World War II. His stories about the heroic exploits of Soviet soldiers and the Soviet Army's liberation of German-occupied lands were anthologized in *Red Poppies* (Krasnye maki, 1944) and *Short Stories about the Russian Soldier* (Novelly o russkom soldate, 1946). Bikchentaev is the author of the novelette *The Right to Immortality* (Pravo na bessmertie, 1950)—depicting the heroic exploits of A. Matrosov—and of the novelette *Grand Orchestra* (Bol'shoi orkestr, 1957), about Soviet children. He also wrote *The Swans Remain in the Urals* (Lebedi ostaiutsia na Urale, 1956), a novel about the exploration for Bashkir oil.

Works: Ḣailanma ăthărt̂hăr, 2 vols. (Ufa, 1962-64). Bikchentaev's latest works in Russian translation are: *Bakenshchiki ne plachut* (Ufa, 1961); *Ad"iutanty ne umiraiut* (M., 1963); *Ia ne suliu tebe raia* (M., 1965); *Morskoi bog* (M., 1966); *Proshchaite, serebristye dozhdi: povesti* (M., 1973).

References: Istoriia bashkirskoi sovetskoi literatury, part 2 (Ufa, 1966).

BIKHBUDÍ, MUKHAMMED KHODZHA [or: BEHBUDI, MAHMUD HOJA] (1874-1919). Uzbek writer. Jadid leader, editor, founder of modern Uzbek literature. First publishing in 1901, Bikhbudi wrote textbooks in Uzbek and Persian for use in the Jadid (New School) movement in Uzbekistan (1908-1920). In the city of Samarkand he edited the newspaper *Samarqand* (1914) and later the journal *Aina* (Mirror), which served as a rallying point for educated people of the time. Not only did he produce newspaper articles, but encouraged the literary talent of many young Uzbeks. Bikhbudi's play *The Parricide* (Padarkush, 1911) is the first drama in Uzbek literature in the European sense and earned its author the appellation "Father of Uzbek theater." Bikhbudi was sympathetic to the revolution but was a Pan-Turkic nationalist interested in creating a Soviet Republic of Turkestan. Bikhbudi was considered the best educated and most effective political and social figure of all the Jadids of that era. His opposition to the Emir of Bukhara led to his imprisonment and murder on 25 March 1919. By the mid-thirties Jadidism had been declared counterrevolutionary, and Bikhbudi's activities have not been publicized in the Soviet Union. See also JADIDISM.

References: A. Saadi, "Bikhbudi i pisateli vokrug nego," *Turkestan,* Nos. 207-208 [in Uzbek] ; A. Samoilovich, "Literatura tiurkskikh narodov," in *Literatura Vostoka,* fascicle 1 (Pg., 1919); *Zeravshan,* No. 23 (Samarkand, 1923) [issue devoted to Bikhbudi] . Various references will be found in E. Allworth, *Uzbek Literary Politics* (The Hague, 1964).

BIKKÚLOV, SHARIF SAGADATOVICH (b. 1924). Soviet Bashkir writer, member CP from 1944. Bikkulov was born in a peasant family in the village of Karlaman on 28 May 1924. He completed university training as a teacher, graduating from the Pedagogical Institute in 1949. The principal themes of his verse and narrative poems are the creative work of Soviet people described in the collection "Aspiration" (Yntylyu, 1947), *To My Contemporary* (Zamandashyma, 1951), and the themes of the struggle for peace—in the narrative poem *Tian Ge Chan* (1954)—and friendship and love of young people in the narrative poem *Across Thresholds* (Ḣikăltălăr asha, 1957) and others.

Works: Iat̂hghy, uit̂har (Ufa, 1955); *Tòshòrăm it̂htăremă* (Ufa, 1959). In Russian: *Na rassvete* (Ufa, 1953).

BILÉTS'KYI, OLEKSANDR IVANOVYCH (1884-1961). Soviet Russian and Ukrainian literary scholar, editor, Academician (USSR) since 1958 and Ukrainian Academy of Sciences since 1939. The son of an agronomist, Bilets'kyi was born in Kazan on 21 October (2 November), 1884. He graduated in 1907 with a degree in history and philology from Kharkov University and returned there as professor in 1920. First published in 1909, Bilets'kyi's first significant study was "The Faust Legend in Connection with the History of Demonology" (Legenda Fausta v sviazi s istoriei demonologii, 1911-1912). In 1914 Bilets'kyi published a number of articles on the works of Simeon Polotskii. Bilets'kyi's range of interests was extraordinarily wide and varied, encompassing the literatures of various countries and peoples. His articles deal not only with the history of Russian literature (Pushkin, Gogol, Lermontov, Dostoevskii, Leonov and others), but also with west European and classical literatures, and with literary theory. Among his aritcles on Ukrainian writers are studies of the work of P. Tychyna, M. Ryl'skyi, V. Sosiura, T. Shevchenko, I. Nechui-Levyts'kyi, Panas Myrnyi, M. Kotsiubyns'kyi, Lesia Ukrainka, and I. Franko. Bilets'kyi wrote the book *Forty Years of Ukrainian Literary Studies (1917-1957)* (Ukrains'ke literaturoznavstvo za sorok rokiv (1917-1957), 1957). He was chief editor and the author of a number of sections of volumes 1 and 2 of the *History of Ukrainian Literature* (Istoriia ukrains'koi literatury, 1954-57). In several of his works he turned to the study of the ties between Russian, Ukrainian and other Slavic literatures. Bilets'kyi also carried on extensive administrative and professional work: he held the post of Vice-President of the Academy of Sciences of the Ukrainian SSR, was for many years the Director of the Shevchenko Institute of Literary Studies in Kiev, and was a member of the editorial board of the *Soviet Ukrainian Encyclopedia.* He died 2 August 1961 in Kiev.

Works: Starinnyi teatr v Rossii (M., 1923); "V masterskoi khudozhnika slova," in *Voprosy teorii i psikhologii tvorchestva,* vol. 8 (Kharkov, 1923); "Ocherednye voprosy izucheniia russkogo romantizma" in *Russkii romantizm* (L., 1927); *Karl Marks. Fridrikh Engel's i istoriia literatury* (M., 1934); *Khrestomatiia davn'oi ukrains'koi literatury (Doba feodalismu)* (Kiev, 1949); *Ivan Franko* (Kiev, 1956); *Ukrains'ka literatura seredinshykh slov'ian'skykh literatur* (Kiev, 1958); *T.G. Shevchenko* (M., 1959); *Vid davnyny do suchasnosti. Zbirnyk prats' z pytan' ukrains'koi literatury,* 2 vols. (Kiev, 1960); *Vybrani pratsi* (Kiev, 1960); *Ukrains'ka literatura* (Kiev, 1961); *Davnia ukrains'ka i davnia rosiis'ka literatura* (Kiev, 1965); *Zarubizhini literatura* (Kiev, 1966); *Antychna literatura* (Kiev, 1968).

References: M.K. Gudzii, *Oleksandr Ivanovych Bilets'kyi* (Kiev, 1959); N. Gudzii, B. Derkach, "Aleksandr Beletskii" in *Literaturnye portrety,* vol. 1 (Kiev, 1960), 248-73; N. Gudzii, "Bol'shoi sovetskii uchěnyi," *Voprosy literatury,* No. 12 (1961), 187-92.

BILÉTS'KYI-NOSENKO, PAVLO PAVLOVYCH (1774-1856). Ukrainian writer. Bilets'kyi-Nosenko was a native of Priluki Uezd (now Chernigov Oblast) where he was born to the aristocracy on 27 (15) August 1774. He was educated in St. Petersburg Aristocratic Pension, then entered military service, and after 1798 supervised schools until 1840. Bilets'kyi's works (more than 60 titles) are quite diverse in content and include treatises on aesthetics, economics, philosophy, medicine, agriculture, and many other subjects. Since they remained largely unpublished, however, Bilets'kyi was little known during his lifetime. Only a few of his literary works have since been published. His works written in Ukrainian deserve attention: *Gorpinida, or Captured Persephone, a Farcical Poem in Three Songs* (Horpynyda chy vkhoplenaia Prozerpyna, zhartlyvaia poema v tr'okh pisniakh, published in 1876) is an imitation of Kotliarevs'kyi's *Aeneid* and a free translation from the Russian of Kotel'nitskii's *The Abduction of Persephone,* interspersed with inserted genre pictures in a purely Ukrainian spirit. Under the influence of Karamzin's *History* and Walter Scott's novels, Bilets'kyi wrote *Zinovii Bohdan Khmel'nyts'kyi, A Historical Picture of the Events, Morals, and Customs of the 17th Century in the Ukraine* (Zinovii Bohdan Khmel'nytskyi, istoricheskaia kartina sobytii, nravov i obychaev XVII v. v Malorossii, 1829) and *Ivan Zolotarenko* (1839), a dramatic tale in one act. In addition Bilets'kyi translated and reworked several ballads and romances from German into Ukrainian. His *Linguistic Expressions of Superstitions among the Ukrainians, Their Wedding Rites with Folk Songs* (Lingvisticheskie pamiatniki poverii u malorossiian, ikh svadebnye obriady s narodnymi pesniami, 1839-40), contains information about many customs, rites, and beliefs which have since disappeared. Also useful was his *A Hermeneutic, Linguo-historical, and Geographic Dictionary with an Explanation of the True Meaning of Archaic Words Found in Russian Chronicles* (Slovar' germenevticheskii, lingvistiko-istoricheskii, geograficheskii, s iz'iasneniem istinnogo smysla slov zastarelykh, vyshedshikh iz upotrebleniia, nakhodiashchikhsia v letopisiakh rossiiskikh). He died in Priluki in 1856.

Works: Horpynyda, chi vkhoplenaia Prozerpina (Kiev, 1871); *Prykazky,* 4 parts (Kiev, 1871); *Hostinets' zemliakam, Kazky slipoho bandurista . . .* (Kiev, 1872).

References: N.I. Petrov, *Ocherki istorii ukrainskoi literatury XIX st.* (Kiev, 1884); [a list of Belets'kyi-Nosenko's works] *Moskvitianin,* No. 8 (1855); B.S. Butnik-Sivers'kii, " 'Malorossiiskii slovar' i 'Grammatika' P. Bilets'koho-Nosenka," *Naukovi zapiski IM AN USSR,* vols. 2-3 (1946), 207-13; V.I. Maslov, "Neizdannyi roman P.O. Beletskogo-Nosenko *Zinovii Bogdan Khmelnitskii* (1829)," *Naukovi zapiski (Kievskii universitet),* vol. 13, fasc. 2, No. 6 (1954), 121-40; G.A. Nud'ga, "Pavlo Bilets'kyi-Nosenko," in *Burlesk i travestiia v ukrains'koi poezii pershoi polovyny XIX st.* (Kiev, 1959), 572-75.

BILIÁRSKII, PĒTR SPIRIDONOVICH (1819-1867). Russian linguist, Slavist, professor of Russian literature, Academician of the St. Petersburg Academy of Sciences. Born in 1819, Biliarskii received his education at Kazan Seminary and the Moscow Spiritual Academy. Among his works, particular attention was attracted by *Fate of the Church Language* (Sud'by tserkovnogo iazyka), *On Middle Bulgarian Vocalism* (O sredne-bolgarskom vokalizme, 1847), and *On the Cyrillic Part of the Reims Gospel* (O Kirillovskoi chasti Reimskogo evangeliia, 1848). In this work Biliarskii subjected to a thorough grammatical and orthographic analysis the Middle Bulgarian dialect, which, as a transitional step between Old Slavonic and Modern Bulgarian, can serve as a key to the understanding of the language of old church texts. His *Materials for a Biography of Lomonosov* (Materialy dlia biografii Lomonosova, 1865) was very valuable as an attempt to prepare a critical edition of Lomonosov's works, and was intended by Biliarskii to mark the one-hundredth anniversary of the celebrated author's death. In addition Biliarskii published in *Zhurnal ministerstva narodnogo prosveshcheniia* a series of extensive book reviews, chiefly about Slavic philology and Russian literature. Finally, he translated Wilhelm von Humboldt's essay of 1836, *Linguistic Variability and Intellectual Development* (O razlichii organizma chelovecheskogo iazyka, 1859). Biliarskii died on 2 (14) January 1867 in Odessa.

BILIŪNAS, JONAS (1879-1907). Lithuanian writer. The son of a peasant, Biliūnas was born on 3 March 1879 in the village of Niūronys (now the Anykščiai Raion of the Lithuanian SSR). He studied in the city of Liepaja and at the University of Derpt (Tartu), where he was expelled for revolutionary activities. Biliūnas was a member of the Social Democratic Party of Lithuania. In 1903 he went abroad and studied in Leipzig and Zürich. Appearing in the press in 1898, Biliūnas was the first in Lithuanian literature to write on the theme of the growth of the class consciousness of workers: "Without Work" (Be darbo, 1903), "The First Strike" (Pirmutinis streikas, 1903). After 1905 he retired from active involvement in social issues and pessimistic notes appeared in his work. However, even in this period Biliūnas wrote in the tradition of critical realism about the difficult life of workers and their struggle against exploitation, as in the tales "The Light of Happiness" (Laimės žiburys, 1905), "Along the Neman," (Nemunu, 1905), "Joniukas" (1906), and the novelette A Sad Tale (Liūdna pasaka, 1907). Biliūnas' works are distinguished by their lyricism, compositional balance, and subtle psychological portraiture. He died on 8 December 1907 in Zakopane, Poland; his remains were returned to Lithuania in 1953.

Works: Lazda. Ubagas. Svečiai. Brisiaus galas (Vilnius, 1906); *Paveikslai, apysakos ir eiles* (Tilze, 1913); *Raštai* (Kaunas, 1937); *Rinktiniai raštai* (Gunzenhausen, 1946); *Raštai* (Kaunas, 1947); *Lazda* (Kaunas, 1959); *Rinktinė* (Kaunas, 1960); *Žvaigždė* (Vilnius, 1965); *Apsakymai* (Kaunas, 1967). In Russian translation: *Pervaia stachka. Rasskazy* (Vilnius, 1952); *Svetoch schast'ia: povesti i rasskazy* (Vilnius, 1964).

References: V. Kapsukas, *Jono Biliūno biografija* (Philadelphia, 1917); V. Mykolaitis, "Jonas Biliūnas," *Židinys,* Nos. 8-9 (1929); J. Ambrazevičius, *Lietuvių rašytojai* (1938); K. Korsakas, "Jonas Biliūnas," in *Literatūra ir kritika* (Vilnius, 1949); K. Umbrasas, *Jonas Biliūnas* (Vilnius, 1956); *Lietuvių literatūros istorija,* vol. II (Vilnius, 1958); B. Pranskus, "J. Biliūno kūrybos socialiniai bruožai," in *Lietuvių literatūros gretose* (Vilnius, 1959).

BILL'-BELOTSERKÓVSKII, VLADIMIR NAUMOVICH (1884-1970). Soviet Russian playwright. Born in Aleksandriia, Kherson Province, to a poor Jewish family on 28 December 1884 (9 January 1885), Bill'-Belotserkovskii ran away from home at 15 to become a sailor, and for the next decade travelled abroad. In 1911 he arrived in the United States and stayed until 1917, holding a series of unskilled jobs. He returned to Russia after the February Revolution and ended up in Moscow, where he joined the Communist Party in September and took part in the October Revolution. During the Civil War he was engaged in Party work and served as chairman of the Simbirsk (now Ul'ianovsk) Party Committee. Returning once more to Moscow in 1921, he worked in the Proletkult (the Proletarian Culture organization), and continued his active Party work in the organizational section of the Central Committee of the CP, and later served in the *Glavrepertkom* (the Central Committee for the Control of Repertory, established in 1929).

From the very beginning of his career as a playwright, Bill'-Belotserkovskii aligned himself with proletarian literary groups. Like other adherents of the theory of proletarian art, he believed in the subordination of art to political ends and in the creation of a new art by and for the proletariat. These views account for the blatant tendentiousness of his literary work, his wholesale rejection of the pre-Revolutionary literary heritage, and his distrust for the academic theaters. After his involvement in the Proletkult, he joined RAPP (the Russian Association of Proletarian Writers) in 1925. He was a leader of the extremist "Proletarian Theater" group, which broke with RAPP in 1927 and made virulent attacks on theaters and playwrights that diverged from the strict proletarian line. The Moscow Art Theater was a frequent target. Bill'-Belotserkovskii himself wrote to Stalin in 1929, denouncing the theater for its intention to stage Bulgakov's *The Flight,* and criticizing Bulgakov's plays for their anti-Soviet content. The play was soon withdrawn from the repertory. He was one of the first to call for Party control of literary groups. Co-authoring an article in *Pravda* entitled "For Bolshevik Leadership on the Theater Front" (November 17, 1931), Bill'-Belotserkovskii attacked RAPP for numerous mistakes of its leaders (Averbakh and Afinogenov were mentioned by name) and called for the consolidation of all Proletarian groups under Party leadership. This article anticipated by five months the Party resolution of 23 April 1932, which dissolved all Proletarian organizations and created the single Union of Soviet Writers.

Bill'-Belotserkovskii had no formal education nor any special training for the theater. He began his literary career in Moscow in 1917, writing several short stories and sketches based on his life abroad. Collected under the title *Laughter through Tears* (Smekh skovz' slezy, 1929), the book was issued in Simbirsk, where his first two plays were also written and staged. Both were propaganda plays; the first, *Beefsteak, Rare* (Bifshteks s krov'iu, 1920) was based on one of his short stories and received Second Prize in the 1920 All-Russian Drama Competition. Set in America, the play depicted the miserable plight of unemployed workers and their growing class consciousness. Its loose, episodic structure, the reduction of the *personae* to mouthpieces for political views, the inattention to plot, the spurning of nuance and subtlety in favor of black-and-white contrasts and sharp conflicts—all of these traits anticipate the main tendencies of Bill'-Belotserkovskii's mature style. *Stages* (Ėtapy, 1921), his second play, was written in the vein of the allegorical propaganda play, where the action takes place on some abstract level, and which, instead of individualized characters, has conventional, allegorical *personae* representing entire socio-economic phenomena. The play showed various stages in the development of the human race, and climaxed in a symbolic struggle between Labor and Capital reminiscent of Maiakovskii's *Misteriia Buff.* Bill'-Belotserkovskii never returned to the allegorical mode, and his other plays follow the line of *Beefsteak, Rare,* where political issues are treated in a more realistic manner.

His next two plays concern the reverberations of the Russian Revolution abroad and belong to that category of Soviet plays devoted to the theme of the approaching "World Revolution." *Echo* (Ėkho, 1922; first staged in 1924), like *Beefsteak, Rare,* is set in America, and shows the efforts of dockworkers to prevent the shipment of arms to the Whites during the Civil War. *Steer to the Left!* (Levo rulia!, 1923; first staged in 1926) depicts the growing sympathy for the

Bolsheviks among a group of foreign sailors, who eventually mutiny to stop the delivery of arms to the Whites in Arkhangelsk. Both works consist of a string of separate episodes, each of which illustrates some aspect of the characters' everyday life or some political idea, not necessarily tied to the main theme. In *Echo,* the order of the episodes is interchangeable. *Steer to the Left!* has more of a sense of development, but still there is no sustained buildup of tension. In both plays the action moves freely from place to place, and there are a multitude of *personae* who are characterized only with regard to their social class or political views. *Echo* and *Steer to the Left!* were praised by contemporary critics on ideological grounds, but were condemned for the glaring flaws in their composition.

Later in his career, Bill'-Belotserkovskii returned twice to the theme of the decay of the capitalistic West and the impending "World Revolution." Following a trip to Germany in 1928-29, he wrote *The West Is Restless* (Zapad nervnichaet, staged in 1931), which depicts the rising revolutionary consciousness of German workers. In *Around the Ring* (Vokrug ringa, 1948; originally titled *Skin Color,* produced in 1949), Bill'-Belotserkovskii treated the same theme in the setting of the American South, with a focus on the prevailing racial oppression. Neither play was successful.

It was Bill'-Belotserkovskii's treatment of Soviet events and issues that won him his place in the history of Soviet drama. His foremost play, *Storm* (Shtorm, 1924—performed December 1925) deals with the Civil War period. Set in 1919 in a small Ukrainian town, the drama grew out of the author's own Civil War experiences in Simbirsk. The main heroes are the wise and dedicated Chairman of the local CP Committee and his right-hand man, the colorful, enthusiastic, one-legged sailor Vilenchuk. The chief villains are introduced at the very beginning: the Whites, a typhoid epidemic, local bandits, hostile peasants, and undesirables in the local Party organization. The subsequent scenes show the Party Chairman in action, striving to maintain order and morale, resolving disputes, chairing meetings, rising to emergencies, and liquidating the enemies. *Storm* culminates in a surprise attack on the town by the Whites. A fierce battle ensues, and, in the final scene, just as the sailor is shouting news of the Red victory, the dead body of the Chairman is carried on stage. This ending anticipates that of V. Vishnevskii's *An Optimistic Tragedy* (1933), a play which helped to formulate the notion of Soviet tragedy.

Like Bill'-Belotserkovskii's earlier plays, *Storm* is composed of a series of episodes, but here the episodic format is well-suited to the subject matter. The continual presence of the Party Chairman on stage and the relatively quick tempo of the action lend the play a cohesiveness lacking in the other plays. It should be noted that the play was considerably reworked at the hands of Liubimov-Lanskoi and his theater collective at the Moscow Trade Union Theater. The original title, *Typhoid,* was changed, the play was streamlined, and the characters were individualized to a greater extent. Despite the reworking, *Storm* still suffers from superfluous scenes and incidents, intended to illustrate some aspect of the Civil War struggle but not successfully integrated into the play. The play was criticized for its crude language and its schematic character treatment; the

Bolsheviks and their sympathizers are portrayed in glowing colors, while the negative figures are reduced to caricatures.

It was precisely the one-sided portrayal of the positive figures that won the play its acclaim. *Storm* is still cited today as the first Soviet play to bring the positive hero to the stage: the Party Chairman is resolute and self-disciplined; he has no private life and lives only for the Party. *Storm* was the first Civil War play to glorify the guiding role of the Party leader. Earlier treatments of the period, such as A. Neverov's *The Civil War* (1920), had represented it on a massive scale as a struggle between whole groups of people, none of whom were singled out for individual treatment. *Storm* made a sharp break with this tradition, and it was highly influential, spawning a series of plays about the Party hero during the Civil War. The play was very popular with audiences of the time and was staged in theaters throughout the Soviet Union and in Eastern Europe. Bill'-Belotserkovskii revised it twice, in 1935 for an edition of his plays and for a 1952 revival of the play by the Mossoviet Theater. None of his other plays achieved the success of *Storm.*

Bill'-Belotserkovskii turned to the period of the New Economic Policy (NEP) in his next play *Calm* (Shtil', 1926; staged in 1927). It is a continuation of *Storm* and focuses on the sailor Vilenchuk, who tries to reconcile himself to life under NEP, but at heart cannot accept it and yearns for the simpler days of the Revolution and Civil War. The play has the obligatory positive and negative characters, but the satirically drawn negative figures were received by audiences much more enthusiastically than the positive ones, whose speeches were a mishmash of Party slogans and platitudes. The most popular scenes were the satiric pictures of the communal kitchen and the beer hall. *Calm* was condemned both for its lack of convincing positive heroes and for its compositional weaknesses. Critics saw in the figure of the sailor an autobiographical element, and accused Bill'-Belotserkovskii himself of not fully accepting NEP. The play did not last long on the stage, and it has not been published in the Soviet Union.

Moon on the Left (Luna sleva, 1927) was Bill'-Belotserkovskii's only attempt at comedy, and it was a failure. It belongs to that branch of Soviet literature dealing with the "women's question," and concerns the role of romantic love in the life of the new Soviet hero. The plot is highly contrived and the characters are flat and unconvincing. Performances of the play tended to deteriorate into farce.

His next play, *The Voice of the Depths* (Golos nedr, 1928), was a construction play written in response to the First Five-Year Plan. It deals with the reconstruction of a Donbass mine in 1920-21, but it was topical both in its celebration of labor and in its depiction of "wreckers" (saboteurs). The first wrecker trials (the so-called Shakhty affair) had made headlines earlier in 1928. Like other construction plays, such as N. Pogodin's *Tempo* (1929), its cast of characters breaks down into the builders, the wreckers, and the Party hero who saves the day. The episodes of this artless play are linked weakly, if at all, but *The Voice of the Depths* met with temporary success because of its topicality.

Life Is Calling (Zhizn' zovet, 1933; premiered in 1934) is generally regarded by Soviet critics as Bill'-Belotserkovskii's most important play after *Storm.* It marked a striking departure from his earlier works, for it was an attempt at a truly psychological drama. In contrast to the scores of *personae* in the earlier plays, it has just six characters, and its plot is much more distinct. The play centers on the role of the intelligentsia in the new Soviet society typified by the main character, Professor Chadov, an elderly Bolshevik scientist who concocts a grandiose scheme for the agricultural development of Siberia. He suffers a stroke and must either stop working or risk death. He chooses the latter, and lives to see his project accepted by other Soviet scientists. There is a secondary plot involving a love-triangle between his daughter, her husband, who is incapable of adjusting to the new society, and a Party man of the positive hero variety. *Life Is Calling* met with limited success. The plot of the play is far-fetched, the dialogue is stiff and unnatural, and character treatment is heavy-handed. A maximalist at heart, a lover of extreme contrasts, a specialist in overstatement, Bill'-Belotserkovskii was not able to meet the demands of the psychological drama for nuance and subtlety.

Life Is Calling in effect marked the end of Bill'-Belotserkovskii's career as a dramatist. Two of his last plays, *The Border Guards* (Pogranichniki, 1937) and *The Duel* (Poedinok, 1940), were never staged. The former shows heroic scenes at a Soviet border outpost, while the latter grew out of the autobiographical story "The Wild Voyage" (Dikii reis, 1937). After 1937 Bill'-Belotserkovskii devoted himself to prose and produced a series of sketches and short stories based on his travels through Europe and America. The stories are crudely done and lack literary merit. Collections of them appeared regularly in the forties and fifties, and they are still reissued periodically along with collections of the plays.

Today Bill'-Belotserkovskii is remembered only as the author of *Storm,* the first Soviet play to bring the positive hero to the stage. It initiated an influential trend in Soviet dramaturgy and produced numerous offspring, many of which were far superior to it. The most important of these was Vsevolod Ivanov's *Armored Train 14-69* (Bronepoezd 14-69, 1927). Bill'-Belotserkovskii's other dramatic works were of negligible significance.

Works: P'esy (M.-L., 1940); *Rasskazy* (M., 1940); *Rasskazy* (M., 1947); *Varvarskii bereg* (M., 1949); *Po tu storonu* (M., 1950); *Izbrannoe* (M., 1954); *P'esy* (M., 1955); *Put' zhizni. Rasskazy* (M., 1959); *Izbrannye proizvedeniia,* 2 vols. (M., 1962); *Izbrannye proizvedeniia,* 2 vols. (M., 1976). In English: *Life is Calling* (N.Y., 1938).

References: K. Rudnitskii, "Bill'-Belotserkovskii," *Portrety dramaturgov* (M., 1961), 7-65; G.A. Lapkina, "Bill'-Belotserkovskii," *Ocherki istorii russkoi sovetskoi dramaturgii 1917-34* (L.-M., 1963), 195-214; A. Boguslavskii, V. Diev, A. Karpov, *Kratkaia istoriia russkoi sovetskoi dramaturgii* (M., 1966), 89-95.

Susan Amert

BILOÚS, DMYTRO HRYHOROVYCH (b., 1920). Soviet Ukrainian poet and satirist, member CP since 1948. Bilous was born in the village of Kurmeny, Sumy Oblast, on 24 April, 1920, the son of peasants. During World War II he worked at radio stations in Moscow and wrote materials for the Ukrainian partisans. In 1945 he graduated from Kiev University and in 1948 finished his graduate work with a specialty in Ukrainian literature. He was first published in 1943, and his first collection of satirical poems *Oskolochym!* came out in 1948. In his lampoons and couplets Bilous attacks warmongers, bureaucrats, sycophants and people who always "play it safe." He also writes for children and translates, mainly from Bulgarian.

Works: Veseli oblychchia (Kiev, 1953); *Zygzag* (Kiev, 1956); In Russian translation: *Dobrogo zdorov'ia* (Kiev, 1951); *Antologiia ukrainskoi poezii,* vol. 2 (M., 1958); *Krytychnyi moment* (Kiev, 1963).

References: O. Vyshnia, "Pro Dmytra Bilousa," *Tvory,* vol. 2 (1956).

BILOZERS'KA-KULISH, OLEKSANDRA MIKHAILIVNA: *see* BARVINOK, HANNA

BÍLYK, IVAN [pseudonym of RUDCHENKO, IVAN YAKOVYCH] (1845-1905). Ukrainian folklorist, ethnographer, literary critic and writer. Bilyk was born in Mirgorod on 2 September 1845. He compiled and published the anthologies *Popular South-Russian Tales* (Narodnye iuzhnorusskie skazki, 1869-1870) and *Carters' Folk songs* (Chumats'ki narodni pisni, 1874) with an ethnographical introductory article. In Bilyk's cycle of critical articles "A Review of Literary News" (Peresmotr literaturnykh novostei) in the journal *Pravda* (1873), he deplored the absence of ideology and national narrowness in literature and supported principles of realism and a populist respect for "the people." Bilyk translated into Ukrainian Turgenev's stories "Khor' and Kalinych" and "Bezhin Meadow." Together with his brother Panas Mirnyi, Bilyk wrote a novel on social themes called *The Bullocks Don't Roar, Do They, When the Troughs Are Full?* (Khiba revut' voly, iak iasla povni? 1880) which gave an almost whole century's history of the Ukrainian village. In the eighties Bilyk became an important civil servant and espoused conservative views.

Works: Narodnye iuzhnorusskie skazki, 2 vols. (Kiev, 1869-70); *Chumatskie narodnye pesni* (Kiev, 1874); *Khiba revut' voly, iak iasla povni?* (Geneva, 1880); *Ukrains'ki narodni kazky,* 2nd ed. (Katerinoslav-Kam'ianets-Leipzig, 1920; rept., N.Y., 1957).

References: I. Franko, *Narys istorii ukrains'ko-rus'koi literatury do 1890 r.* (Lvov, 1910); M.P. Komyshanchenko, *Literaturna dyskusiia 1873-1878 rokiv na Ukraini* (Kiev, 1958); M.D. Bernshtein, *Ukrains'ka literaturna krytyka 50-70-kh rokiv XIX st.* (Kiev, 1959); M.E. Syvachenko, *Istoriia stvorennia romana "Khiba revut' voli, iak iasla povni?"* (Kiev, 1957).

BILYLÓVS'KYI, KESAR OLEKSANDROVYCH [pseudonyms: TSEZAR BILYLO, IV. KADYLO] (1859-1934). Ukrainian poet and publisher. Bilylovs'kyi was born on 20 February 1859 in the village of Stolypivtsi in Poltava Province. He studied medicine at Derpt University (Tartu), Leipzig, and Vienna; throughout his life he worked as a doctor. Bilylovs'kyi began writing poetry while still in the gymnasium. His first published work was a German translation of a poem by Shevchenko in 1876. In 1877 Bilylovs'kyi began to publish his poetry in *Nauka* and *Nyva.* At the same time he wrote songs, which were set to music by a Galician composer. Many of his poems appeared in the Galician newspaper *Svit,* and his poetry, articles, and letters were carried in *Zoria.* When he returned to Russia, Bilylovs'kyi joined a small group of Ukrainian writers, contributed poetry and two tales to an almanac called *Skladka* (1887, 1893), and after the publisher's death, himself undertook the publishing of the third and fourth volumes of the almanac (Kharkov, 1896; Petersburg, 1897). In addition to *Skladka,* Bilylovs'kyi contributed to the almanacs *Vik* and *Ukrains'ka Muza.* Bilylovs'kyi possessed an unquestionable lyric talent, and a sense of verse imparts elegance and charm to many of his poems. Works such as "In the Spell of Love" (V charakh kokhannia) and "Evening Song" (Vechirnia pisnia) have attained great popularity. In addition to his translations of Shevchenko, Bilylovs'kyi translated works by Goethe and Schiller into Ukrainian.

BÍNKIS, KAZYS (1893-1942). Lithuanian poet and playwright. Binkis was born in a peasant family on 4 November 1893 in the village of Gudeliai (now the Papilys Raion of the Lithuanian SSR). He studied at the University of Berlin and began to publish in 1909. In his first book *Poems* (Eilėrašciai, 1920), Binkis celebrated the Lithuanian countryside and village life. In the 1920s he organized the Lithuanian Futurists and issued an anthology of poems entitled *100 Springs* (100 pavasariŲ, 1926). Later he moved away from Futurism and wrote several long humorous poems on social themes, such as "Tamošius Bekepuris." As a playwright Binkis is best known for his play *Shoots* (Atžalynas, 1938), about student life, and his anti-military drama *Dress Rehearsal* (Generalinė repeticija, 1940; published posthumously in 1958). Both plays are among the best examples of pre-Soviet Lithuanian dramaturgy. Binkis is the author of children's verse *The Fisherman* (1928) and *The Rabbits' Rebellion* (1936), and has translated poems by Pushkin. He died on 27 April 1942 in Kaunas.

   Works: Antanas Smetona, 1874-1934 (Kaunas, 1934); *Lyrika* (Chicago, 1952); *Baltasis vilkas. Pasaka* (Brooklyn, 1953); *Rinktinė* (Vilnius, 1955); *Poezija* (Vilnius, 1963); *Generalinė repeticija: pjesės, straipsniai, pasisakymai* (Vilnius, 1965); *Atsiskyrelis Antanelis* (Vilnius, 1968); *Kiškių sukilimas* (Vilnius, 1971); *Lyrika* (Vilnius, 1972); *Raštai* (Vilnius, 1973-). In Russian translation: *Rybolov* (Vilnius, 1950); *Antanelis neliudimyi* (Vilnius, 1952).

   References: B. Pranskus, "Kazio Binkio satyrinės poemos," in K. Binkis, *Kriaučius Motiejus* (Kaunas, 1947); V. Galinis, "Kazys Binkis," *Pergale,* No. 4 (1960).

BIRCHBARK LETTERS *see* BERESTIANYE GRAMOTY

BIRIUKÓV, NIKOLAI ZOTOVICH (1912-1966). Soviet Russian writer. Biriukov was born in the family of a textile factory worker in Orekhovo-Zuevo on 1 (14) February 1912. He graduated from the Moscow Institute of Foreign Languages and the Gor'kii Institute of Literature. His first published work was a novelette *In the Villages* (Na khutorakh, 1938). Biriukov's novel *The Gull* (Chaika, 1945; Stalin Prize, 1951) tells of the life and heroic death of the partisan Liza Chaikina. In his novel *Waters of the Naryn* (Vody Naryna, 1949) he describes the construction of the Great Fergana Canal; the book is based on the writer's travels in Central Asia. His travels across the Soviet Union have led to a book of sketches *On the Peaceful Land* (Na mirnoi zemle, 1952), devoted to the builders of the Kuibyshev GES (Hydro-Electric Station), to the workers of the Gor'kii automobile factory, to the ship-builders of Sormovo. Biriukov also published his novel

The First Thunder (Pervyi grom, 1957) which deals with the history of the labor movement of the end of the nineteenth century. In 1959 Biriukov's historical novel about the Revolution came out entitled *Through Enemy Crosscurrents* (Skvoz' vikhri vrazhdebnye). Biriukov died on 31 January 1966.

Works: Tvĕrdaia zemlia (Simferopol, 1964); *Na krutykh perevalakh* (Simferopol, 1965).

References: G. Ershov, "Vsegda v stroiu," *Krym,* No. 21 (1959); Sh. Viadro, "Zhizn'–podvig," *Sovetskaia Ukraina,* No. 5 (1959); N. Matveeva, "O zhizni i tvorchestve N. Biriukova," *Istoriko-kraevedcheskii sbornik,* 2nd ed., [Orekhovo-Zuevskii kraevedcheskii muzei] (M., 1959); L. Zharikov, G. Ershov, M. Kotov, *Nash sovremennik–Nikolai Biriukov* (M., 1967).

BIRIUKÓV, PAVEL IVANOVICH (1860-1931). Eminent social figure, biographer of L.N. Tolstoi. In 1884 met Tolstoi and became a proponent of Tolstoi's teachings. He was a publisher both in Russia and abroad and took an active part in the publishing house Posrednik.

In 1893 Biriukov worked together with Tolstoi organizing assistance for the famine victims of the Samara district. He signed the petition written by Chertkov and approved by Tolstoi in defence of the Dukhobors under the title "Help!" (Pomogite!), for which he was exiled in February 1897 to Kurland Province. After 1898 he lived abroad, returning from time to time to Russia. In Geneva Lenin used to visit Biriukov. In 1906 Biriukov began to publish memoirs and other materials relating to Tolstoi. His four-volume work was the first attempt at a detailed biography of the great writer; it is of particular value in that Tolstoi himself made suggestions concerning the materials to be included.

Works: Dukhoborets Pĕtr Vasil'evich Verigin (Geneva, 1903); *Biografiia L'va Nikolaevicha Tolstogo,* 4 vols. (M.-Pg., 1922-23). In English translation: *Leo Tolstoy, His Life and Work* (N.Y., 1906); *The Life of Tolstoy* (London, 1911).

References: L.N. Tolstoi, *Polnoe sobranie sochinenii,* vol. 63 (M.-L., 1934), 227-30.

BÍRKERTS, ANTONS (1876-1971). Soviet Latvian literary scholar and writer. Birkerts first got acquainted with Marxist literature in the nineties, took part in the revolution of 1905, and published some of his poetry in the underground party press. His main works are devoted to the study of the life and works of Jānis Rainiś, whom Birkerts had known very well and whose friend he was. His monographs *J. Rainis* (1919), *The Life of J. Rainis* (1925), *Rainis in Life and Work* (Rainis dzîve un darbā, 1930) and others contain valuable factual material which to this day are widely used by historians of Latvian literature.

Works: Daildarbi un atmiņas (Riga, 1958); *Latviešu intelligence savas ciņās un gaitās* (Riga, 1927); *Kopoti raksti* (Riga, 1928); *Rudolfs Blaumanis* (Riga, 1932); *J. Rainis Slobodskas trimdā* (Riga, 1961); *J. Rainis Pleskavas trimdā* (Riga, 1964).

BÍRZE, MIERVALDIS [pseudonym of BĒRZIŅŠ] (b. 1921). Soviet Latvian writer. Birze was born on 21 March 1921 in the city of Rūjiena. In 1940 he joined the Komsomol, and during World War II was imprisoned in various prisons and concentration camps. After victory over Germany Birze returned to Riga, and in 1949 graduated from the University of Latvia with a degree in medicine. Birze's first stories about everyday life were published in the collection *First Flowers* (Pirmie ziedi, 1956). Birze's best works, the novella "One Apple" (Viēns ābols, 1956) and the novelette *The River Flows Even under the Ice* (Ari zem ledus upe tek, 1957) deal with the German occupation. This novel, for which Birze was awarded the State Prize of the Latvian SSR in 1958, has been translated into the languages of the peoples of the USSR as well as Czech. Birze is the author of humorous stories collected in the book *Unlucky Dog* (Nelaimīgais suns, 1959).

Works: Visiem rozes dārza ziedi . . . (Riga, 1957); *Tā nebija pēdējā diena* (Riga, 1961); *Kā radās stāsts* (Riga, 1961); *Sajaukta diagnoze* (Riga, 1963); *Smilšu pulkstenis* (Riga, 1964); *Lielā žurija* (Riga, 1970); *Izlase* (Riga, 1971); *Ari tāds bija rīts* (Riga, 1972); *Sūkās ar melno* . . . (Riga, 1973). In Russian translation: *Stroptivyi utoplennik* (Riga, 1963); *Pesochnye chasy* (M., 1966); *Ne vse vernulis' domoi* (M., 1971). In English translation: *Yet Icebound Rivers Flow* (M., 196-).

BÍRZNIEKS-ÚPĪTIS [Real name: BIRZNIEKS], **ERNESTS** (1871-1960). Latvian writer, People's Writer of the Latvian SSR (1947). Birznieks-Upītis was born 6 April 1871 in Tukums Uezd, Dzirciem county, on Bisnieki estate (now Kandava Raion) in a peasant family. He was educated at the Tukums district school, then was employed as a private tutor in his own county. In 1893 he moved to the Caucasus, where he worked as a teacher and librarian. Birznieks-Upītis set up the "Dzirciemnieki" Publishing House (1908-21), which published Latvian books favorable to the democratic and liberal writers Jānis Rainis, Sudrabu Edžus and others. In 1921 he returned to Latvia to work in the libraries of Riga. Birznieks-Upītis began to write in the eighties under the influence of Latvian folklore. In 1891 he published his first story "The Mother." After that he wrote stories, sketches and fairy tales, mainly about the life of hired farm hands or village artisans—*The Stories of Upitis* (Upiša stāsti, 1900), *From the Morning* (No rīta, 1912), *Towards Evening* (Pret vakaru, 1913), *The Stories of the Grey Stone* (Pelēkā akmena stāsti, finished in 1907, published 1914). In the twenties Birznieks-Upītis wrote a cycle of Caucasian stories, entitled *In the Caucasian Mountains* (Kaukaza kalnos, 1924), *Caucasian Stories* (Kaukaza stāsti, 1927). At that same period Birznieks-Upītis began to write for children—*The Fairy Tales of Nina* (Ninas pasaciņas, 1922-24), *Bucis i Ulla* (1924), *Our Friends* (Mūsu draugi, 1925) *Skaidrite* (1926) and others. Later he published stories for children *Granddaughter Dace* (1949); *Lively Janitis* (1955). Among Birznieks-Upitis' significant works is the trilogy *The Diary of Pastarin* (Pastariņa diēnasgrāmata, 1922), *Pastarin in School* (Pastariņš skolā, 1923), *Pastarin in Life* (Pastariņš dzīvē, 1924), in which the author describes his childhood and school years. He died on December 30, 1960.

Works: Pasaku valsti (Riga, 1928); *Nīnas pasaciņas* (Riga, 1934); *Mūsu sēta* (Riga, 1946); *Kopoti raksti,* 6 vols. (Riga, 1946-50); *Bubulis* (Riga, 1948); *Izlase* (Riga, 1951); *Pastariņs dzīvē* (n.p., 1960); *Zem ābeles* (Riga, 1964); *No rita. Izlase* (Riga, 1971). In Russian translation: *Dnevnik Pastarinia* (Riga, 1951); *Pastarin' v shkole* (Riga, 1953); *Rasskazy serogo kamnia* (Riga, 1955); "Avtobiografiia," *Sovetskie pisateli,* vol. III (M., 1966), 69-84.

References: A. Vilsons, *Tautas rakstnieks E. Birznieks-Upītis* (Riga, 1956); E. Kazaine, *Ernesta Birznieka-Upītis* (Riga, 1966).

BÍTOV, ANDREI GEORGIEVICH (b. 1937). Russian prose writer. Bitov was born in Leningrad on 27 May 1937, into a long line of Leningraders. In 1942 during the siege his mother took him via the "road of life," the only escape route over Lake Ladoga, to the Urals and later to Tashkent. They returned to Leningrad in 1944, where they lived on Aptekarskii Island in a household headed by his grandmother, consisting of her three children and fifteen grandchildren. Bitov had no idea what to do upon graduating from high school, but partly because of a love of travel, decided to become a geologist and entered the Leningrad Mining Institute in 1956. There he went to a meeting of a society of student poets which included G. Gorbovskii and Aleksandr Kushner, and, because of the "official" nature of recent Soviet literature, was astounded to find people writing about their own thoughts and feelings. Seeing Fellini's *La Strada* around the same time, Bitov first realized the possibility of "the contemporary expression of contemporary reality." He wanted desperately to join the literary group, but not having written anything, submitted some poems by his older brother as his own and was accepted as a member. The poems he subsequently wrote, however, were better received than those of his brother, and he began writing poetry so intensely that he stopped studying and as a result was expelled from the Institute.

After working as a stevedore and a lathe operator, Bitov joined the army, serving in construction units until demobilization. In 1958 he married the writer Inga Petkevich with whom he has a daughter, Anna, born in 1962. He was reinstated at the Mining Institute, where he continued writing. Summer geological expeditions provided material for his first prose works, and when he finished the Institute in 1962, he signed an agreement for his first book and for a film scenario, whereupon he decided to become a professional writer.

His short stories appeared in a variety of journals and then in the collections *The Big Balloon* (Bol'shoi shar, 1963), *Such a Long Childhood* (Takoe dolgoe detstvo, 1965), *A Summer Place* (Dachnaia mestnost', 1967), *Apothecary Island* (Aptekarskii ostrov, 1968), *Way of Life* (Obraz zhizni, 1972), *Seven Journeys* (Sem' puteshestvii, 1976), and *Days of Man* (Dni cheloveka, 1976).

Bitov's work is divided between psychological stories about an urban hero and "travel notes." The latter genre is represented in *Seven Journeys* which includes "One Country" (Odna strana, 1968), "Trip to a Childhood Friend" (Puteshestvie k drugu detstva, 1968), "Armenian Lessons" (Uroki Armenii, 1969), "The Wheel" (Koleso, 1971), "Gambling" (Azart, 1972), and "Nature's Choice" (Vybor natury, 1971-1973). Using the travel note form, Bitov describes exotic parts of the USSR he has been commissioned to write about, but it is readily apparent that this level merely supplies the warp to his woof: he is most interested in the nature of space and time, and in integrating his thoughts about language, culture and communication into his experience of "the foreign." The travels are narrated by the traveler, whose isolation as detached observer, sometimes forcibly deprived by language barriers of the possibility of communication, distills to its essence the isolation of Bitov's urban hero.

The most important of Bitov's stories about this hero, given various names in successive stories, make up *Days of Man*. The book is a "novel with ellipses" written over a ten-year period, which chronicles the development of Aleksei Monakhov (from the Russian *monakh*, "monk," suggesting a special sort of isolation) and of Bitov himself. Monakhov is to a large degree an autobiographical hero, but there is a well-defined distance between author and persona, a distance created by the author's greater insight and self-irony, rather than by a difference of world views.

The subject of the book is the growth of Monakhov's self-awareness, a growth which gradually, though never totally, bridges the distance between Bitov and his hero. Monakhov suffers from a sort of automatism, living in a dreamlike state and refusing to make his thoughts fully conscious. He allows himself to steal from his aunt without acknowledging it to himself ("The Garden" [Sad]), to behave badly to a girl without admitting his own selfishness ("Penelope" [Penelopa]), and to live in cranky isolation in the midst of his family ("Life in Windy Weather" [Zhizn' v vetrennuiu pogodu]).

The first five stories establish Monakhov's character, and its origins; the second five describe a series of awakenings through which he begins to break out of his self-preoccupation. Two poignant moments in childhood begin the book: in "The Big Balloon" the purity and vividness of a child's vision, told with fairy-tale simplicity, is set against a harsh post-war background. "The Leg" (Noga) shows the early stages of hypersensitivity that contribute to Monakhov's isolation: he struggles home on his injured leg facing humiliation by his peers and reprimand from his family much the same way as in "The Door" (Dver'), almost ten years later, he waits for his girlfriend Asia all alone on the stairwell, trying to lessen the pain with another rationalizing monologue.

"The Garden" and "The Loafer" (Bezdel'nik) are stories of adolescence. Monakhov is on the verge of realizing that he is allowing himself the egotism of adolescence in the name of preserving the ideals of childhood; he begins to notice the escapist nature of his fantasies and the dangerous consequences of relating to the world the way children do. Bitov does not deny that children can be as cruel to each other as adults, but he sees childhood as a stage of life at which no discrepancy has yet developed between the inner self and the masks put on for the benefit of others. Children are capable of total, unselfconscious absorption in life, and so are still proof against the deadening artificialities of the adult world. In "The Loafer" Aleksei's superior's excitement over the American stapler is empty and perverted in contrast to the little boy's involvement in the snow city he builds in the park. But Aleksei belongs to neither world: the boy refuses to play with this "uncle," and the boss scolds him for sloppy work. The problem is to reconcile the demands of responsible adulthood with the values represented by childhood.

Monakhov's parents serve throughout the novel as a point of calibration of his emotional growth. In the first half of the book he weighs his actions against their potential disapproval, but in the second he is finally responsible only to himself, so that the revelations he experiences are capable of changing him. In "Penelope" Aleksei is able to realize that he has betrayed both the heroine and himself. He watches a movie of *The Odyssey* with a girl he meets in the theater—she is thereby associated with the model of fidelity, Penelope—but disposes of her unfeelingly because of her bizarre appearance, which suggests recent release from prison. His interaction with her makes him think about his own reactions and about his habitual unwillingness to make such thoughts fully conscious. Thought about thought is Bitov's main concern. In "The Image" Monakhov realizes the subjectivity of love, a realization begun at the end of "The Garden" and only fully believed some ten years later when he meets Asia by chance after long separation. Her reality as an individual is irrelevant, Monakhov realizes: well-defined but flat, lacking any concerns but the most immediate and self-serving, Asia is rendered almost as a caricature of the Other Woman, the side of the coin which has Mother/Wife as its obverse. Asia, like the nameless wife and mother, also has a real-life prototype, but Bitov is almost exclusively interested in his hero's inner world; as with Dostoevskii, the only "reality" the reader can establish is the hero's construction of his own perceptions.

In "Life in Windy Weather," Monakhov, now a husband, a father, and a writer, is placed in a space he has to define for himself; without reacting to an external event or others' demands, he tries to find meaning and inner stability, the absence of which has led to awkwardness with his father, annoyance with his wife and his work, and inattention to his son. It is through his one-year-old son that he finds a new peace, this time not by joining the child in his games as in "The Loafer," but by re-learning his perception of the world. Monakhov finally understands the mutual dependency of father and son, and attains an adult self-image which is independent of the roles other people construct for him. In "Life in Windy Weather" Aleksei creates an acceptable version of himself through fiction, and can decide that sufficient meaning resides in the natural world around him, the pleasures of daily family life, and in his work. As a writer, Monakhov can reconcile fantasy and subjective reality, which he has associated with childhood, with the "reality" of adulthood. Bitov suggests that fiction is a means of renovating one's perception analogous to seeing life through the eyes of a child— an idea similarly stated in stories of Yurii Olesha, but Bitov denies any influence.

The last pair of stories form an epilogue in flashback form with the older generation as the nominal heroes. Asia's father (Infantiev) suffers from an even more severe opaqueness than Monakhov which it takes the death of his wife to shatter. Only then does he perceive the whole level of existence of the unspoken, the emotional, even of the mystical, that he had totally rejected all his life. Aleksei's Uncle Dickens ("The Soldier") is another isolated old man; the epilogue presents two possible variations of Monakhov's future, were he to neglect the struggle for self-awareness. When Uncle Dickens dies, Aleksei comes into possession of some short stories the old man had written in his youth, and the circle is complete: Aleksei gains insight into Dickens as an independent person, no longer distorted by Aleksei's need of him, just as Bitov creates Aleksei for the reader in a process which attains self-awareness for all three—author, hero and reader.

The commentary on the nature of prose fiction in "The Soldier" sensitizes us to the implicit discussion of the function of literature throughout the book, because finally, Andrei Bitov's real hero is literature. His novel *Pushkin House* is dedicated to the Russian literary tradition, the preservation of which provides the essential meaning of Bitov's work and life.

Bitov speaks mostly about Pushkin and Gogol, yet in important ways he is responding particularly to Dostoevskii. Dostoevskii discovers a fantastic world in everyday existence; the diseased vision of his heroes reveals the diseased nature of reality. Bitov, too, concentrates on his hero's vision, but both the hero and his reality are commonplace, while it is the mode of perception that is rendered extraordinary.

But Bitov acknowledges no influences on his work. The scene in "The Loafer" in which the young hero projects his guilt onto a fallen horse would remind anyone who has read *Crime and Punishment* of Raskolnikov's dream of the peasant beating the mare, but Bitov explains the similarity by a kind of collective unconscious: the ideas, myths and symbols of a culture are in the air, and the fallen horse is part of a shared imagery.

The 1960s began a new period in Soviet literature with the emergence of many young writers who produced what came to be known as "Young Prose." They wrote short stories about the problems of their contemporaries who were growing up, unlike their fathers' generation, in conditions of peace and prosperity. The leaders of "Young Prose," Aksënov and Gladilin, were from Moscow; Bitov, who began to publish a few years later than they, is very much a Leningrad writer. While he, too, discusses the problems of adolescence, he does so in an abstract and psychological way characteristic of the Leningrad tradition. His focus on "thought about thought" (Lev Anninskii) caused conservatives to attack him for excessive subjectivity, preoccupation with personal trivia, and lack of moral purpose, all of which is antithetical to the Soviet view that literature must educate the reader to be a better member of society. But as Bitov's stories have appeared, the sincerity of his search for spiritual values and the high quality of his art have been increasingly recognized.

Works: Aptekarskii ostrov (L., 1963); *Bol'shoi shar* (L., 1963); *Takoe dolgoe detstvo* (L., 1965); *Dachnaia mestnost'* (M., 1967); *Obraz zhizni* (M., 1972); *Sem' puteshestvii* (L., 1976); *Dni cheloveka* (M., 1976); *Pushkinskii dom* (Ann Arbor, Mich., 1978).

References: L. Anninskii, "Tochka opory: éticheskie problemy sovremennoi prozy," *Don,* No. 6 (1968), 168-81; V. Solov'ëv, "Problema talanta," in *Puti k khudozhestvennoi pravde* (L., 1968), 262-95.

Priscilla Meyer

BLAGÍNINA, ELENA ALEKSANDROVNA (b. 1903). Soviet Russian poetess. Blaginina was born on 14 (27) 1903 in Yakovleva village, Orlov Province, in the family of a railroad worker. In 1925 she graduated from the Briusov Higher Literature and Art Institute in Moscow. First published in 1921, Blaginina writes mainly for pre-school children: the books of poems *Autumn* (Osen', 1936), the narrative poem *Sadko* (1936), *That's the Way Mama Is* (Vot kakaia mama, 1939), *Let Us Sit in Silence* (Posidim v tishine, 1940), *Rainbow* (Raduga, 1948), *Little Light* (Ogonëk, 1950) and others (see bibliography below). Blaginina's poems are lyrical and have a singing quality. Blaginina is also a translator of the Ukrainian writers T. Shevchenko, Lesia Ukrainka, L. Kvitko and others.

Works: Gori-gori iasno! (M., 1944); *Alёnushka* (M., 1959); *Trudnye stikhi* (M., 1960); *Lodochki* (M., 1966); *Okna v sad* (M., 1966); *Nauchus'-ka ia chitat'* (M., 1966); *Osen' sprosim* (M., 1969); *Travushka-muravushka* (M., 1971); *Ugadaite, gde my byli?* (M., 1972).

"BLAGONAMÉRENNYI" ("Well-Intended"). A journal published by A.E. Izmailov from 1818 to 1826. The journal appeared monthly from 1818-1821, weekly from 1822-1825, and for the remaining year two numbers appeared as a biweekly. The journal was intended to give the members of the Free Society of Lovers of Russian Literature, Science, and the Arts a special organ for the publication of their works. *Blagonamerennyi* was published in an extremely careless and slipshod manner: the numbers were delayed by several months, two or three were often combined into one, and they were much shorter than promised. Izmailov, the publisher, regarded his negligence with genial, but cynical humor, but the fact that he was also president of the Society perhaps explains the public's forgiveness. As for content, the most frequently encountered items were theatrical reviews. The journal had a "philanthropy" section, which contained information on paupers and donations, as well as reports on the latter's use. Izmailov presented himself to the public as a good-natured old friend, who, in an hour of leisure, had decided to chat a little about one thing or another. He often admitted that the articles appearing in the journal were bad and apologized for the tardy publication. *Blagonamerennyi* made no lasting contribution to the developing tradition of Russian journalism.

BLAGOSVÉTLOV, GRIGORII EVLAMPIEVICH (1824-1880). Russian journalist. The son of a priest, Blagosvetlov was born on 1 (13) August 1824 in Stavropol-Kavkazskii. In 1851 he graduated from Petersburg University with a degree in law. While a student he participated in the activities of a circle of intellectuals studying liberal contemporary political theory, organized by I.I. Vvedenskii. Blagosvetlov was a teacher in several military institutions but was dismissed and placed under police surveillance in 1856 for "pernicious thinking." From 1857 to 1860, he lived abroad, participating to some extent in the editorial activities of A.I. Gertsen and serving as tutor to Gertsen's children. Blagosvetlov was an active participant in the revolutionary underground of the sixties, and was a member of the Central Committee of the organization "Land and Freedom" in 1862. From 1860 he edited the journal *Russkoe slovo,* taking a position in the polemics which the journal conducted with the *Sovremennik* close to that of D.M. Pisarev's. From 1866 to 1880 Blagosvetlov served as the editor of the journal *Delo.* He managed to attract to these journals the liberal writers of the sixties and seventies. Blagosvetlov's first articles were of a literary-historical and critical nature. Thereafter he devoted his work to public education, the equality of women and other economic, political and historical problems. Blagosvetlov died on 7 (19) November 1880 in Petersburg.

References: "G.E. Blagosvetlov," *Delo,* No. 11 (1880) [nekrolog i bibliografiia]; S.A. Vengerov, *Kritiko-biograficheskii slovar',* vol. 3 (Pb., 1892); B. Kozmin, "G.E. Blagosvetlov i *Russkoe slovo,*" *Sovremennik,* kn. 1 (1922); N.V. Shelgunov, *Vospominaniia* (M.-Pg., 1923); P.V. Bykov, *Siluëty dalëkogo proshlogo* (M.-L., 1930); G. Prokhorov, "Sud'ba literaturnogo nasledstva G.E. Blagosvetlova," *Literaturnoe nasledstvo,* Nos. 7-8 (M.-L., 1933); P.N. Tkachëv, "Izdatel'skaia i literaturnaia deiatel'nost' G.E. Blagosvetlova," *Shestidesiatye gody* (M.-L., 1940); F. Kuznetsov, "Zhurnal'nyi ékspluatator ili revoliutsionnyi demokrat? (G.E. Blagosvetlov)," *Russkaia literatura,* No. 3 (1960).

BLÁGOV, ALEKSANDR NIKOLAEVICH (1883-1961). Soviet Russian poet, member CP since 1940. Blagov was born on 20 November (2 December) 1883 in the village of Sorokhta, Kostroma Province. From the age of 14 Blagov worked as a weaver and later participated in the revolutionary movement of the workers in Ivanovo. First published in 1909, Blagov's pre-Revolutionary poems describe the hard life of the textile workers and express the hatred for the factory: "The Moan of a Weaver-Woman" (Ston tkachikhi, 1910), "Thought" (Duma, 1941), the narrative poem "Ten Letters" (Desiat' pisem, 1915-16), and others. After the Revolution, labor continued to be the principal theme of Blagov's poems, and particularly the labor of textile workers in such poems as "Trilogy" (Trilogiia, 1943-48), "Our Factory" (Nasha fabrika, 1950), and "Word of the Weaver Woman" (Slovo tkachikhi, 1950). Some of Blagov's poems have been set to music—"Song of the Old Weaver" (Pesn' starogo tkacha), "The Woman-Spinner" (Priadil'shchitsa) "The March of the Textile-Workers" (Marsh tekstil'shchikov).

   Works: Pesni rabochego. Stikhotvoreniia (1909-1919) (M., 1919); *Izbrannoe* (Ivanovo, 1953); *Stikhi* (M., 1960).

   References: G. Maksimov, "A.N. Blagov," *Pisateli tekstil'nogo kraia* (Ivanovo, 1953).

BLAGOVESHCHÉNSKII, NIKOLAI ALEKSANDROVICH (1837-1889). Russian writer. A native of Moscow, Blagoveshchenskii was born on 19 April (1 May) 1837 in the family of a priest. He completed the Petersburg theological seminary and from 1858 to 1860 was assigned to the Archimandrite Porfirii as an artist and accompanied him to Mt. Athos and to Jerusalem. While there he wrote a number of sketches and made about 400 drawings of the places visited. Upon his return to Petersburg Blagoveshchenskii audited courses at the University and taught in the Sunday schools aimed at educating and indoctrinating workers with liberal ideas. He first appeared in print in 1862 when Dostoevskii published his sketch "From the Recollections of a Visitor in Jerusalem" (Iz vospominanii byvalogo ob Ierusalime) in his journal *Vremia* (No. 2). Blagoveshchenskii's writings were also published in the liberal journals *Sovremennik* and *Russkoe slovo.* His books *Afon* (1864) and *Among the Pious* (Sredi bogomol'tsev, 1871), which revealed uncomplimentary aspects of monastery life, were on the index of forbidden books. In 1863-66 Blagoveshchenskii was the editor-publisher of the journal *Russkoe slovo,* then the editor of *Zhenskii vestnik,* contributed to *Nedelia,* and *Otechestvennye zapiski.* The features characteristic of the liberal literature written by non-aristocratic intellectuals of the sixties are also shared by Blagoveshchenskii's writings. He wrote the first biography of the writer and fellow seminarian N.G. Pomialovskii (1864). His novel *Before Dawn* (Pered rassvetom, 1865-66) depicted the life of a liberal *raznochinets* (non-aristocratic intellectual). And in his sketches of 1870-73 Blagoveshchenskii detailed the working conditions in Russian factories. In the mid-seventies he moved to the Caucasus where he worked as the Secretary of the Tersk Statistical Board (from 1875) and edited the unofficial part of the *Terskie vedomosti,* beginning in 1880. Blagoveshchenskii died on 1 (13) June 1889 in Vladikavkaz.

Works: Povesti i rasskazy (Pb., 1873); *Semidesiatye gody na fabrikakh i zavodakh* (M.-L., 1929); "Nikolai Gerasimovich Pomialovskii (Biograficheskii ocherk)" in N.G. Pomialovskii, *Polnoe sobranie sochinenii,* vol. 1 (M.-L., 1935).

References: S.A. Vengerov, *Kritiko-biograficheskii slovar',* vol. 3 (Pb., 1892); A.M. Shanygin, "Roman N.A. Blagoveshchenskogo 'Pered rassvetom,' " *Uchënye zapiski LGU. Filologicheskaia seriia,* No. 19 (1954); S.B. Rassadin, "Roman demokrata-shestidesiatnika N.A. Blagoveshchenskogo," *Nauchnye doklady Vysshei shkoly. Filologicheskie nauki,* No. 2 (1959).

"BLÁGOVEST" (lit.: the ringing of the church bell before services). Russian journal existing from 1883 to 1897. From 1883 to 1889 *Blagovest* was published in Nezhin by G.I. Kul'zhinskii. In 1890 the journal moved to Petersburg under the editorship of N.N. Filippov; a year later A.V. Vasil'ev issued it as a supplement to his journal *Russkaia beseda.* The publication was clearly Slavophile in tendency. *Blagovest* ceased publication in 1897 along with *Russkaia beseda,* and its subscribers were transferred to Sharapov's *Russkoe slovo.*

BLANK, BORIS KARLOVICH (1769-1826). Russian writer. In his youth Blank served in several Guard regiments, retiring in 1797 with the rank of lieutenant-colonel, and became the Mozhaisk Marshal of Nobility in 1805. A close friend of Prince Shalikov, the publisher of *Moskovskii zritel'* (The Moscow Spectator), *Aglaia,* and *Damskii zhurnal* (The Lady's Journal), Blank contributed assiduously to these journals, producing from 1806 to 1826 a total of 329 poems and 14 articles. Blank also translated one of Ann Radcliffe's novels (from its French translation) with the Russian title *The Living Corpse* (Zhivoi mertvets, 1806 and 1816), and Justus Friedrich-Wilhelm Zacharia's poem "Die Tageszeiten" (Chetyre chasti dnia, from the French, 1806). All of Blank's many works are typical of the Sentimentalism that flooded Russian literature in the first quarter of the nineteenth century at the hands of the imitators of Karamzin. Blank died around 1826 on his estate near Lipetsk.

References: S.A. Vengerov, *Kritiko-biograficheskii slovar',* vol. 3 (Pb., 1892), 362-68.

BLÁUMANIS, RŪDOLFS (1863-1908). Leading Latvian modern realist of the turn of the century. Blaumanis began his literary activities in the 1880s with works of prose and continued in this genre throughout his lifetime, completing about 250 works in all: articles and feuilletons for newspapers and journals, long tales and masterful short stories. From the 1890s on Blaumanis also wrote seventeen plays—dramas and comedies—based largely on his earlier prose works, and he composed lyrical, philosophical, and humorous-satirical poetry.

Blaumanis was born on 1 January 1863 (20 December 1862) and grew up in the country. His parents originally worked on the Baltic German country estate of Ergli, in Vidzeme, as cook and chambermaid. But when Blaumanis was five years old, his parents rented the nearby Braki farm from the same estate. From early childhood Blaumanis observed the German and Latvian cultures: his elementary and high school education was conducted in German, but he learned Latvian traditions, folklore, and language from the farmhands of Braki, and folk songs and colorful Latvian expressions from his mother. After his graduation from the Second Riga District German Commercial School, Blaumanis worked briefly in the capital in the office of a brewery, which was also an agency for the Russian Lloyds and a fire insurance company of Moscow; thus his work required also some knowledge of the Russian language. Early signs of tuberculosis forced Blaumanis to return to farm life in Braki in 1885. He worked briefly as bookkeeper and steward-apprentice on the country estate of Koknese, but returned again to Braki in 1887 and devoted himself henceforth to writing.

His early stories and short stories were published—often simultaneously in German and in Latvian—in the Riga journals and newspapers *Zeitung für Stadt und Land* (Newspaper for Town and Country), *Balss* (Voice), and *Baltijas Vestnesis* (Baltic Messenger). Already with these early prose works Blaumanis surpassed Apsīšu Jēkabs, A. Apsitis and other contemporary prose writers of early Latvian Realism—especially those of the National Awakening period, who had stressed national consciousness, purity of language, folklore, and Latvian traditions. But he also surpassed many writers of the so-called New Current who had influenced Blaumanis to concentrate on the present rather than the past, and to deal with immediate issues concerning society in general and farm life in particular. Blaumanis had enthusiastically prepared himself for a literary career by reading and studying classical and modern authors such as Goethe, Schiller, Walter Scott, Thackeray, Dickens, Maupassant, Gogol, Tolstoi, Korolenko, Sologub (whose "Evil Spirit" he translated into Latvian, 1885), Peter Rosegger, and others. Blaumanis continued writing in both German and Latvian until 1893, and thereafter mainly in Latvian. Through the Baltic German poet Victor von Andrejanoff Blaumanis became involved in poetry and in Nietzsche's philosophy, which prompted him to reevaluate his own religious beliefs, rejecting church traditions but keeping the essence of Christianity.

When his health improved, Blaumanis worked in Riga in 1890-93 on the staff of *Zeitung für Stadt und Land* as reviewer of the Latvian press and theater and as part-time dispatcher. It was the beginning of his journalistic career, which he continued with brief periods of respite, until the last year of his life, 1908. This work was physically very demanding and time consuming, leaving little free time for his belles-lettres, but beyond providing his main, though meagre income, it opened new avenues to the world beyond the borders of the Russian Empire and thus enabled Blaumanis to escape from provincialism. He wrote articles and stories, and his plays, beginning with the comedy *Thieves* (Zagli, 1891), were immediately performed at the Riga Latvian Theater and elsewhere in Latvia. Blaumanis was a member, then secretary, of the Theater Commission of the Riga Latvian Association in 1890-93.

When his father died in 1894, Blaumanis, as the eldest son, was forced to take over the management of the Braki farm. He used this time as much as possible for creative writing and the further study of literary styles and genres of his own (mostly with the help of German publications on these subjects), despite poor health with its resulting nervousness and bouts of insomnia. Quite unexpectedly, in the summer of 1895 Blaumanis was told by his physician that he no longer had tuberculosis, and his renewed joy in life found expression in some of his best lyrical and philosophical poetry dealing with the themes of love, search for meaning in life, and thankfulness to the Creator for the dignity of man. He even wrote comedies for the theater, and while critic Jansons and poetess Aspazija and others of the liberal *Dienas Lapa* (Daily Paper) in Riga attacked the comedies, calling them frivolous and oblivious to the demands of the times, Blaumanis continued to write several of them before turning to dramas and serious short stories again in 1897.

Pēteris Zālīte, the new editor of *Mājas Viesis* (Houseguest), *Mājas Viesa Mene-šraksts* (Houseguest Monthly) and *Dienas Lapa,* invited Blaumanis to join the staff, and Blaumanis returned to Riga in 1898 as editor of literary contributions, especially beginners' works, for all three publications. He was exceptionally dedicated to this task, and several of the beginners became his proteges and close friends—many of them now well-known writers and poets such as J. Rainis, Aspazija, A. Brigadere, J. Akurāters, K. Skalbe, A. Niedra, A. Austriņš, L. Laicēns, J. Jaunsudrabiņš, and others. He was also close to many of the best Latvian actors in Riga and created roles specifically suited to them. When Zalite supported in his German-owned publications the German faction for majority in the Riga City Council, Blaumanis and several other prominent Latvian writers and critics on the staff demonstratively quit the *Dienas Lapa.* Blaumanis moved to St. Petersburg in the winter of 1901 to accept the position of editor of the feuilleton section and the humorous-satirical section "At the Edge of the Bog" (Purva malā) on the Latvian-language newspaper *Pēterburgas Avizes* (Petersburg News). This newspaper had been famous particularly during the initial period of publication, 1862-65, under Krišjanis Valdemārs and other well-known Young Letts (jaunlatvieši), but by the turn of the century was struggling with financial difficulties. Using the pseudonym "Ditchdigger" (Grāvracis), for the next two years Blaumanis attacked mostly social ills of the time with his humorous satirical poems until he returned once more to Braki, ill and practically destitute (he was not paid for months).

The punitive expeditions that were led in the Latvian countryside by German barons and Russian gendarmes against the sympathizers of the 1905 revolution and also against the Latvian intelligentsia forced Blaumanis to move to Riga, where he worked for the democratic newspaper *Latvija* from early 1906 as editor of the feuilleton section and the humorous-satirical section "The Woodpile" (Skaidiena). Using the pseudonym "Polisher" (Puliers) and others, Blaumanis published many satirical poems and short prose works attacking various social problems, deploring the hardships caused by the punitive expeditions, and dismissing decadence as art. For a brief period Blaumanis was also chief editor of *Latvija,* and he was named playwright for the Riga Latvian Theater for the 1907/ 08 season. However, when he became seriously ill on a visit to Braki in early spring and his condition worsened to acute tuberculosis, all his ambitions, especially the completion of two philosophical plays, were thwarted.

Lacking funds, Blaumanis tried to improve his health at home in Braki. There he wrote his last play, a one-acter, *A Saturday Evening* (Sestdienas vakars, performed posthumously in 1908, publ. 1909), which expressed his physical suffering and premonition of death, and his despair that his best works would remain unwritten. He longed for a final cleansing and freedom of his soul. Realizing Blaumanis' grave condition, and his dire financial situation, his friends hastily collected funds and took him by railroad for treatment to the Takaharju Sanatorium in Finland, where he died on 22 August 1908. Blaumanis was buried in his native Ergli.

The apathy expressed by an elderly artist on Christmas Eve at the beginning of Blaumanis' first story, "Found Again" (Wiedergefunden, 1882) strongly resembles Faust's monologue on Easter morning, but the artist's gradual finding of faith and love with the help of a little child echo Blaumanis' own search for these values. "Found Again" deals with life in the city. After his Koknese experience of friendship and unrequited love, and his encounter with the despotic estate manager, Blaumanis realized that the countryside was his real realm for characters in novelettes and short stories, and later dramas.

Blaumanis' early literary period in 1887-90 produced immediately several important stories, published both in German and in Latvian: "Weed" (Unkraut/Nezāle, 1887), "A Horse, Three Cows, and Hundred Rubles" (Ein Pferd, drei Kühe, und hundert Rubel: Eine Livlandische Bauerngeschichte/Zirgs, trīs govis un simts rublu, 1887), "Thunderstorm" (Das Gewitter/Negaiss, 1887), "Always in the Pink" (Immer lilla/Aizvien lillā, 1888), "Money in the Stockings" (Nauda zeķēs, 1889), and the tragic short story "Raudup's Widow" (Die Raudupwirtin/Raudupiete, 1889). These tales were realistic accounts of the harsh life of the 1880s and 1890s, when economic pressures and exploitation by the German landlords caused many farmers to go bankrupt and despair, become calculating, and squander their belongings on alcohol. Blaumanis also noted the haughtiness of some affluent Latvian farmers of that time and the uprightness or subserviency of poor farm workers. He exposed heavy drinking as a curse, as some previous German and Latvian writers had done, but Blaumanis for the first time emphasized that it was a physical illness which could be cured only through total abstention. Blaumanis showed how immorality and excessive wealth often led to disaster, as in "Always in the Pink" and "Raudup's Widow," and warned against unjust exploitation of orphans as child laborers in "The Weed," which deals with the mistreatment of a foundling. The latter story also deals with the question of fate and revenge, similar to Gogol's "Terrible Vengeance" (Blaumanis was fascinated with Gogol). He stressed the importance of following one's heart in marriage in "A Horse, Three Cows, and Hundred Rubles" and "Money in the Stockings." The latter story deals also with the problem of conscription, the burden of which fell unfairly on farmhands. As a conservative, Blaumanis supported the patriarchal ways of life in the changing times and struggle between the old and new generations in "Thunderstorm." He stressed the need to control one's passions and temptations in "Raudup's Widow," the main character of which deliberately lets her child drown, so that she can propose to a poor but handsome farmhand.

These motifs and prototypes of the 1880s and 1890s appear with variations also in Blaumanis' later short stories and plays. He remained loyal to his contemporary peasant society, even though at the turn of the century some socialist and liberal critics clamored for a more sophisticated content in Blaumanis' works, urging him to concern himself more with scientific subjects and socio-political problems. The themes of greed, love and passions, alcoholism, scheming, suffering inflicted on self and others, fate, religion, superstition, the demonic forces in life, the search for meaning, purity of heart, and other themes Blaumanis analyzed realistically and without direct moralizing. They are as contemporary today as they were in his own time, and thus Blaumanis' early themes and characters have gained a certain universality, just as Chekhov's characters have, even though they seem firmly anchored in their own time. Like Chekhov, Blaumanis approached his characters with pity, but also with humor and ridicule. He suffered with them and often cried over their fate. This was true especially of his character Krustins, the wayward adolescent in *Thunderstorm,* who through his father's neglect and his mother's overprotectiveness is too weak to withstand the temptations of drinking and gambling and who in the end is shot as a thief by his own father.

During the 1890s Blaumanis wrote his best short stories. "Frost in Spring" (Salna pavasarī, 1898) is based on the theme of closeness between man and his horse: when the young maiden in the story suddenly changes her mind and promises herself in marriage to an eighty-year-old wealthy widower, the disappointed young suitor tells his troubles to his horse. "Wader in the Bog" (Purva bridējs, 1898) also stresses the theme of marrying according to one's heart rather than for a financially more secure life; this time, however, the complication is that Kristine does give an affirmative answer to Edgars, the man she loves, although he is an alcoholic. "Andriksons" (1898) tries to show that both sides can be right and wrong: it is a struggle between a Latvian renter and his German landlord. "In the Shadow of Death" (Nāves ēnā, 1899), based on a newspaper report of fishermen lost at sea on an ice floe, concentrates the action in a truly Chekhovian way in a very limited period of time and space, where seemingly nothing happens as the days drag on, but where tension is created through the inward struggle of the men fighting for their lives.

Blaumanis is credited with having perfected the Latvian short story. His mastery is evidenced particularly in the fluid, euphonic language, in the development of dramatic effect through wave-like increases and decreases of tension leading to the climax, and in the realistic, objective, psychological analysis of people observed in real life (most of his characters were either his own relatives, friends, proteges, or neighbors of the Ergli district). He firmly believed that reality was more powerful than fiction.

Blaumanis is perhaps best remembered today for his plays, which continue to be performed each year in Latvia and abroad. In his first humorous story "Crazy Isaac" (Trakais Izaks, 1887), Blaumanis created the comic character of the Jewish panhandler Abrams, who became an integral part of most of his comedies. Blaumanis himself loved to portray him on stage with the Ergli theater group, to the immense delight of the audience. Very much alive with Blaumanis' good-natured humor are especially the comedies *Trine's Sins* (Trīnes grēki, 1897), concerning an old maid turned matchmaker, and *Tailordays at Silmači* (Skroderdienas Silmačos, 1902), which includes folk songs of the summer solstice called "*Jāņu dziesmas*" and other musical interludes, as well as the antics of the Jewish panhandler Abrams. Blaumanis' dramas *Indrāni* (The Indrani Farm, 1904) and *In the Fire* (Ugunī, 1906) as well as one-acter *A Saturday Evening* (Sestdienas vakars, 1909) are also still performed regularly. *Indrāni*, like Chekhov's *The Cherry Orchard*, deals with problems of modernization and its effects on patriarchal country life. *In the Fire*, a love story, elaborates the themes of the earlier short story "Wader in the Bog," based on Blaumanis' experiences on the Koknese estate. The events of the 1905 Revolution in Latvia and its aftermath are portrayed and interpreted in several poems, and in the one-act comedy *After the First Meeting* (Pēc pirmā mītina, 1909), which ridicules some of the radical changes proposed by the socialists. His unfinished drama in verse *Living Water* (Dzīvais ūdens, 1914) was also intended as an analysis of various political and religious problems of the revolution, and has certain parallels with the themes of miracle, mystery, and authority discussed in Dostoevskii's "Grand Inquisitor." Blaumanis also left unfinished his drama *Genoveva* (1908), an original play based on Hebbel's *Genoveva* of 1843 and, like the German work, is written in iambic pentameter. Blaumanis had hoped to gain international recognition with his *Genoveva*.

As a poet, Blaumanis was best in his several short lyrical poems and several lengthy philosophical poems in the 1895-98 period, when he believed he had been cured of tuberculosis and gratefully sought to embrace life anew and accept its challenges to seek inward perfection. "Unawareness" (Vēl tu nezini, 1895) and "Furtively" (Kā zagšus, 1896) were both set to music by composers A. Kalniņs and E. Dārziņš, and Jurjānu Andrejs, respectively, and are still popular. "Ode" (Oda, 1896), "My Prayer" (Mana lūgšana, 1897), and "Renatus" (1898) are among his best philosophical poems. His humorous-satirical poems on sociopolitical problems of that time have some historical value.

Although Blaumanis worked in all genres except the novel his greatest contributions to Latvian literature were made in the short story and the theater. His most popular plays have been performed continuously in Latvia and in Latvian centers in the West, while his short stories "Frost in Spring" and "In the Shadow of Death" have been made into motion pictures in Soviet Latvia. Blaumanis spent especially his last ten years in intense literary activity. He wrote a total of 61 tales, 15 plays, 100 lyrical and philosophical poems in Latvian, 13 poems in German, 133 humorous-satirical poems, 101 translations of poems in German or Latvian, 51 satirical feuilletons, and 130 articles and reviews in Latvian or German. He also maintained an extensive correspondence with writers, poets, artists, composers, critics, and friends. All major works have been translated into German, Estonian, Lithuanian, Czech, Swedish, Finnish, and Russian; some also into Danish, French, Ukrainian, Hungarian, English, Esperanto, Polish, Hebrew, and Chinese.

Works: Pie skala uguns (Jelgava, 1893); *Kopoti raksti,* 7 vols. (Jelgava, 1909-14); *Kopoti raksti,* 12 vols. (Riga, 1923-28); *Kopoti raksti,* 5 vols. (Riga, 1946-49); *Kopoti raksti,* 12 vols. (Waverly, Iowa, 1942-58); *Kopoti raksti,* 8 vols. (Riga, 1958-60); *Izlase* (Riga, 1968); *Speka ozols.* Dzejolu izlase (Riga, 1969). In Russian translation: *Izbrannoe* (Riga, 1952); *Rasskazy* (M., 1952); *P'esy* (M., 1959); *Vesennie zamorozki: rasskazy* (M., 1975). In English translation: *The*

Builders of New Rome and Other Lettish Tales (London-Toronto, 1924) [Contains "In the Jaws of Death," "Raudup's Widow," and "Andrikson"] ; "The Prodigal Son," in *The Tricolor Sun* (Cambridge, 1936); *In the Lap of Happiness* (M., 1957) [Contains "Raudup's Widow," "Story about the Pig That Could Talk," "Money in the Stocking," "Odd Man Out," "In the Lap of Happiness," "The Shadow of Death," "The Pug-Dog, or Accident in Terbata Street"] ; "In the Shadow of Death," in *Latvian Literature* (Toronto, 1964).

References: Rudolfs Blaumanis: Atmiņu kopojums (Riga, 1923); A. Birkerts, *Rūdolfs Blaumanis dzīvē un darbā* (Riga, 1930); A. Vilsons, *Latviešu literatūras klasiķis Rūdolfs Blaumanis* (Riga, 1956); K. Karkliņš, "Monografija: Rūdolfs Blaumanis," in R. Blaumanis, *Kopoti raksti,* vol. XII(Waverly, Iowa, 1957); *Rūdolfs Blaumanis laika biedru atmiņās* (Riga, 1962); Arvids Ziedonis, Jr., "The Dramatic Works of Rūdolfs Blaumanis," *Journal of Baltic Studies,* 3, Nos. 3/4 (1972), 198-212; Antons Stankevičs, *No Braku kalna* (Riga, 1973) [a biographical novel] ; Arvids Ziedonis, Jr., "The Prose of Rūdolfs Blaumanis," *Baltic Literature and Linguistics* (Columbus, Ohio, 1973); — — —, "Problems of Modernization in Blaumanis' *Indrāni* and Chekhov's *The Cherry Orchard,"* in *Probleme der Komparatistik und Interpretation: Festschrift für Andre von Gronicka zum 65. Geburtstag* (Bonn, 1978).

Arvids Ziedonis, Jr.

BLIÁKHIN, PAVEL ANDREEVICH (1887-1961). Soviet Russian writer, member CP since 1903. The son of a peasant, Bliakhin was born on 25 December 1886 (7 January 1887) in the village of Verkhodym (now Saratov Oblast). He took part in the revolution of 1905, suffered political exile, and after 1917 was given Party and government posts. He was first published in 1919 as an anti-religious propagandist. In 1923-26 Bliakhin's revolutionary adventure novel called *Little Red Demons* (Krasnye diavoliata) won great popularity. Bliakhin is the author of the film scenarios *Little Red Demons* (1923), *Bolshevik Mamed* (1925), *Judas* (Iuda, 1929), the plays *Through Victory to Peace* (Cherez pobedu k miru, 1920), and *Declaration of the Commune* (Provozglashenie kommuny, 1920). The novelettes which make up his autobiographical trilogy—*At Sunbreak* (Na rassvete, 1950), *Moscow Aflame* (Moskva v ogne, 1956), *Days of Rebellion* (Dni miatezhnye, 1959)—provide a panorama of the Revolution of 1905 and of the revolutionary struggle of the proletariat in Astrakhan, Baku, Tiflis, and Moscow. Bliakhin died on 19 June 1961 in Moscow.

Works: V chadu kadil'nom (M., 1928); *Na rassvete* (M., 1952); *Dni miatezhnye* (M., 1961); *Gody velikikh ispytanii* (M., 1966).

References: A. Kondratovich, "Sil'nye dukhom," *Novyi mir,* No. 12 (1955); O. Mikhailov, "Moskva v ogne," *Moskva,* No. 3 (1957); V. Khobin, "Takie ne umiraiut," *Oktiabr',* No. 5 (1967).

BLINÓV, PËTR ALEKSANDROVICH (1913-1942). Soviet Udmurt writer, member CP since 1939. Blinov was born on 17 December 1913 in Pekshur (now the Selty Raion of the Udmurt ASSR). In 1931 he finished the Novo-Multan Pedagogical Institute and was first published a year later. He worked in the editorial offices of the Udmurt newspapers *Udmurt kommuna* and *Egit bol'shevik.*

Blinov's novel *The Desire to Live* (Zhit' khochetsia, 1940), about the disorderly early life and the rehabilitation of a teen-age vagabond is popular among Udmurt readers. During World War II he was political adviser of his company and was killed in action near Smolensk on 7 January 1942.

Works: Ulem potė, 3rd ed. (Izhevsk, 1952). In Russian translation: *Zhit' khochetsia* (Izhevsk, 1960).

References: Ocherki istorii udmurtskoi sovetskoi literatury (Izhevsk, 1957); *Pisateli Udmurtii* (Izhevsk, 1963), 20-22.

BLIÚMMER, LEONID PETROVICH (1840-1888). Russian writer, journalist. The son of a military officer, Bliummer was born in Enikale in the Caucasus on 25 December 1840. He spent his childhood years in the Caucasus, and without having completed his secondary school education, began to teach in the village of Krutoiarovka, in Poltava Province. At age 16 Bliummer submitted articles from Krutoiarovka to *Odesskii vestnik.* In the following year he moved to Petersburg, embarked upon the study of Chinese at Petersburg University, and began to contribute to *Severnaia pchela* with his "Letters on Russian Journalism" (Pis'ma o russkoi zhurnalistike), and to other Petersburg publications, especially *Svetoch.* Bliummer also issued *Ukrainian Songs* (Khokhlatski spivki) in 1857, under the pseudonym "Krutoiarchenko." He abandoned the study of Chinese and in 1861 passed the entrance examination to read law at Moscow University. Later he emigrated abroad, became acquainted with members of the revolutionary movement, issued the journal *Svobodnoe slovo,* first in Berlin and then in Brussels, published the newspaper *Vest'* in Berlin and the newspaper *Evropeets* in Dresden. Recalled to Russia in 1865, Bliummer was tried and sentenced to exile in a Siberian settlement. Pardoned in 1871, he returned to Russia, found work as an attorney and resumed his literary activities. Bliummer's Siberian impressions found reflection in the novel *Around Gold* (Okolo zolota, 1871), published separately under the title *In The Altais* (Na Altae, 1886) and in the collection of tales *Without a Trace* (Bez sleda, 1887). Bliummer continued his journalistic activities in various cities until virtually the end of his life. A number of his articles on Tolstoi's book *Roman Catholicism in Russia* were issued separately under the title *The Papacy and Russia* (Papstvo i Rossiia).

References: S.A. Vengerov, *Kritiko-biograficheskii slovar',* vol. 3 (Pb., 1892), 441-44.

BLOK, ALEKSANDR ALEKSANDROVICH (1880-1921). Russian Symbolist poet. Blok was born in Petersburg on 16 November 1880 at the home of his maternal grandfather Andrei N. Beketov, a distinguished botanist who was at that time Rector of the University of St. Petersburg. Blok's grandmother, mother and aunts were translators and writers. His father was a professor at the University of Warsaw, where he taught public law and wrote on jurisprudence; he was also an accomplished musician.

Blok's parents were separated shortly after his birth, were divorced in 1889, and both subsequently remarried. The poet grew up in the predominantly feminine, sheltered and intellectual environment of his mother's family at Shakhmatovo, the Beketov family estate outside of Moscow. After his mother remarried in 1889, the family moved back to Petersburg, where Blok completed his gymnasium work and entered the university as a law student. In the third year of his legal studies he realized that he had chosen the wrong discipline; in 1901 he transferred to the Faculty of Philology, which he completed in 1906.

Blok's works reflect the major events of his private as well as public life. In 1903 he married Liubov Dmitrievna Mendeleeva, daughter of the famous chemist; she was the inspiration for his early poetry. At the same time Blok became interested in the philosophy of Vladimir Solov'ëv. The Russo-Japanese War of 1904-1905 and the Revolution of 1905 played a part in shaping Blok's outlook on life, as did his interest in the V. Kommisarzhevskaia Theater. It was there in 1906 that he met N.N. Volokhova, an actress who inspired several cycles of his poetry. Blok traveled abroad a number of times. His trip to Italy in 1909 was important because it inspired an excellent cycle of poems. Blok's father died in Warsaw in the same year, and Blok met his half-sister Angelina there for the first time. In 1914 Blok met the opera singer L.A. Delmas, who also inspired a number of poems. Like many intellectuals, Blok had foreseen the catastrophic events of World War I and the October Revolution. In 1916 Blok was drafted into the army as a "time-keeper" in an engineering division of the militia which was digging trenches behind the front line in the area of the Pinsk marshes. He enthusiastically welcomed the Revolution of 1917 as a new "musical" era. One of the few members of the intelligentsia who were willing to collaborate with the new regime, Blok was appointed in May of 1917 as editor of reports of the Special Investigation Committee of the Provisional Government that was investigating the Tsar's ministers and high officials. During 1918 he worked as a member of the editorial board of the "World Literature" series, a translation project organized by Gor'kii immediately after the October Revolution to provide employment for members of the intelligentsia. In the following year he was appointed an editor of the German Literature Section of "World Literature," and undertook a new edition of Heine's works.

Towards the end of his life, in the midst of the Civil War, Blok was busy preparing revised editions of his works and sorting out his diary and notebook materials as well as serving on several commissions and boards. It was clear that his health was failing; his specific illness has been variously reported as depression, neurasthenia, endocarditis, or venereal disease. In May of 1921 he took a turn for the worse, and died on 7 August 1921.

Although Blok had started writing at the end of the eighteen-nineties, his work was first published in 1903. He divided his poetry into three volumes, which he called a "novel in verse." Each volume, as he repeatedly pointed out, signified a specific stage in his life and creative work. Blok considered each poem essential to the structure of a chapter; several chapters constituted a volume, and each volume was part of what he called, using religious terminology, a "trilogy of incarnation." Blok continued to revise the structure of these volumes throughout his life.

The main theme of *Poems: First Book* (1898-1904) is expressed in the cycles "Before the Light" (Ante lucem, 1898-1900) and "Poems about the Beautiful Lady" (Stikhi o Prekrasnoi Dame, 1901-1902). This theme is the poet's love for a Woman, for the most part his beloved Liubov Mendeleeva, whom he later married. Blok's love for a real woman is merged with his interest in the mystical conception of the Eternal Feminine in German literature, and in the Divine Feminine, also referred to as "Sophia," developed by the poet-philosopher Vladimir Solov'ëv. Sophia was an inspirational force of divine love, as she was a companion to God. She was also an intermediary between the realms of God and man. This fusion between the divine and human in Sophia helps explain the role Liubov Blok played for the poet as the supposed earthly incarnation of the perfect being represented by Sophia. Blok's poetry also incorporates Solov'ëv's imagery of snow-storms, frosts, mists, dark clouds, dreams and premonitions.

In this early poetry Blok perceived himself as a knight who, humbly, in solitude and prayer, awaits a sign of grace from the Beautiful Lady. This mysterious woman is called "The Majestic Eternal Woman," "The Radiant Face," "Woman," "She," "The Peerless Lady," "The Unattainable," "Eternal Hope," or "The Purest." The tone of the poems resembles that of troubled religious prayers, and the Beautiful Lady has certain attributes of the Holy Virgin. Hidden meaning is attributed to her every word and gesture. The Lady appears indifferent, cold, haughty, stern, veiled in azure; she reveals herself in mysterious sounds. The poet wants to come to her temple to fall at her feet, as her servant or lover, but always as a slave. He is persistently a solitary observer, unnoticed by the woman he secretly follows, and she is an apparition, a "Russian Venus."

Although the "Poems about the Beautiful Lady" are filled with the expectation of an actual appearance of the mysterious feminine creature, Blok's faith in the reality of the vision contains a discordant note of fear and doubt as early as 1901: "I feel terrible; your face will change." The appearance of doubles in the poetry strengthens the feeling of possible deception. The derisive, older double of the poet, in some instances a harlequin, becomes a rival for Her love.

In the "Crossroads" (Rasput'ia, 1902-1904) section of the first volume, many poems are dedicated to the Beautiful Lady and show humble reverence, but the tone of doubt becomes more pronounced. The poet, who seems to be losing faith in his Lady, now assumes the mask of a buffoon who grimaces at the crossroads and tells silly tales to which the crowd responds with "Enough!" The image of the poet as buffoon foreshadows some of the themes that were introduced later in Blok's plays. In several of the poems new social themes connected with the city, one of the dominant themes of the second book, are introduced.

Blok's doubts about his mystical feminine principle and its earthly incarnation became particularly strong after his marriage in 1903, although to the end of his life his wife remained his main spiritual support and inspiration. Both pursued their separate interests and careers. Liubov was an actress and they were often apart. Her infatuation with the poet Andrei Belyi (Boris Bugaev), who together with Sergei Solov'ëv was an ardent supporter of the cult of the Beautiful Lady, left Blok with an increasing sense of despair.

The poetry of the second book (1904-1908), which had originally appeared as two separate collections entitled *Unexpected Joy* (Nechaiannaia radost', 1906) and *The Land in Snow* (Zemlia v snegu, 1908), is considered transitional. It deals with great spiritual turmoil, doubt, search and a surrender to passion. Part of it represents a move toward a new poetic landscape, the city. After the poet has passed through the swamps and marshes inhabited by "The Little Priest of the Bog" (Bolotnyi popik) and "The Night Violet" (Nochnaia Fialka) of a dream, he enters the world of the city. Although the initial inspiration of the early poetry is not lost, it can never be completely recaptured.

The central cycle of the second book is dedicated to the city, at that period the subject of Blok's interest, partially under the influence of the poetry of Valerii Briusov and French Symbolist poetry. It is in the city that Blok seeks "in the magical whirlwind and light, the terrible and beautiful visions of life." The duality stated here is characteristic of Blok's city poetry as a whole. On one level his city represents an attempt to grasp the external world as an escape from the confines of the self. On another level Blok populates his city with grotesque caricatures (invisible beings, dwarfs, skeletons). Yet, just as he had failed to retain the rapture inspired by the Beautiful Lady, Blok also fails to find asylum in the city because the self remains alienated, lonely and desperate, drowned in wine and debauchery. Blok's city exists equally in life and in the imagination.

The world of the city is like a "gigantic whore-house" where one finds prostitution, humiliation, stench, factory smoke and "repulsive cars." The city is perceived as a spider that devours nature and constricts the people who live in it. That world differs from the sense of soaring heights and spaces associated with the world of an ideal Beauty. Licentiousness and evil in the city are aptly expressed in the poem "The Invisible Being" (Nevidimka), in which the metropolis is portrayed as Babylon, presided over by the Mother of Harlots and Abominations.

A new type of woman can be encountered in Blok's city poetry, generally the prostitute, who is both a synthesis of the real woman of the city in "The Last Day" (Poslednii den'), and the mysterious woman of the poet's imagination in "The Unknown Woman" (Zeznakomka). In "The Unknown Woman" an encounter with a woman in a suburban restaurant full of drunks and discordant noises arouses in the poet an inner vision of beauty. The sound of the woman's silk dress and her perfume, mixed with the poet's drunken stupor, allow him to recapture for a moment the Beyond of the Beautiful Lady. But he is not sure whether the vision he sees is real or a drunken dream. The poem ends on the note that "truth is in wine." The wine prevents the poet from distinguishing between this world and some other world, between dream and reality. A similar duality is found in the poem "In the Restaurant" (V restorane), in the play *The Unknown Woman,* and in a number of poems that touch on the theme of the Unknown Woman.

The "Snow Mask" (Snezhnaia maska, 1907) and "Faina" (Faina, 1906-1908), cycles of the second book, were Blok's "snowy baptism" into the world of passion and poetry, inspired by his affair with the actress Natalia Volokhova. "Snow Mask" contains thirty poems written between 29 December 1906 and 13 January 1907, and initially dedicated "to the tall woman in black, with winged eyes, in love with the fires and the darkness of my snowy city." The poetry is so highly personal that Blok was afriad that it might not be understood. The poet is depicted as a captive of the mysterious woman, the temptress, the fallen star.

The predominant images are those of snow, storms, night, comets, fallen stars, and wind. The poet feels that "in life—there is only prose," that he has somehow failed Volokhova. In the poem "Voices" (Golosa) he is pierced by "needles of snow." In "And Snow Again" (I opiat' snega) he weaves a chain of "snowy strands" around the woman, but the design of this snow imagery is created and destroyed almost simultaneously: "The storm builds a white cross,/ And the snowy cross is scattered about."

The "masks" that whirl through the snow storms in the section "The Masks" were inspired by a masked ball arranged by the actresses of the V. Kommisar-zhevskaia Theater, with which Volokhova was associated. The poet's experience is a combination of masks and reality: "Return, o mask, my soul." In the poem "Heart Devoted to the Blizzard" (Serdtse predano meteli) the poet implies that he has forgotten everybody since his heart has been caught in the whirl of the snow storm. He himself is going to the cross asking: "Pierce me . . ./ With a needle of snowy fire!" In reality Volokhova, who in a sense represented for Blok the spirit of Russia, was cool to the poet. She did not want to be merely the in-spiration for the whirlwind of Blok's poetry of blizzards and snowstorms, of "dancing masks on the white snow under the stormy sky . . ."

The "Faina" cycle includes poems to Volokhova and poems about Russia. In "Autumn Love" (Osenniaia liubov') the poet is crucified on the cross of love, but the woman who looks at him is no longer the cruel snow maiden, but stern Mother Russia. In the poem "Incantation by Fire and Darkness" (Zakliatie ognem i mrakom), his passion for Volokhova and his love for the country are bound together. Yet the poet is unable to satisfy either his passion or his love for the movement of "free Russia." He asks the accordion and the dancing Volokhova to drive him mad and carry him away because "The impossible became possible,/ And the possible became a dream." Blok had resigned himself both to his life and his art. But the image of a "cold, lifeless flower" that arose out of the snow suggests that the experience is a product of his art rather than of his life.

Blok's *Third Book* (1907-1921) contains his mature poetry. Even here there is still a sense of irrationality, chaos, and cosmic forces. The poem "To the Muse" (K muze) opens the main section of the third volume, "The Terrible World" (Strashnyi mir, 1909-1916). "To the Muse" most aptly describes the temptation and the curse of beauty. The muse and the beloved are merged into one image. The terrible world is still primarily the world of the city, and Blok's poetic in-spiration fluctuates between the ideal Beauty of the early poetry and the new type of evil beauty found in the city. Blok's search for the infinite through sin, suffering and humiliation has been seen as representing a change from the "ideal of the Madonna" to the "ideal of Sodom." A note of despair becomes more prominent in the poetry ("Humiliation"), and his diary entries for the period re-flect Blok's heavy drinking and the drowning of his despair in debauchery.

The lifelessness of human existence in the city is most aptly expressed in a group of five poems entitled "Dances of Death" (Pliaski smerti). The living are portrayed as more dead than the dead, the dead only hiding the "rattling of bones." The second poem of the group, the famous "Night, a street, a lamp, a pharmacy" (Noch', ulitsa, fonar', apteka) expresses the absurdity of human ex-istence in the city:

Night, a street, a lamp, a pharmacy.
A senseless, dim light.
Even if you live another quarter of a century—
It will all be the same. There is no way out.
You will die—you will begin again at the beginning,
And everything will repeat itself as of old:
The night, the icy ripple on the canal,
The pharmacy, the street, the lamp.

No human being is present in this wintry, dark poem, and even the water is frozen in its attempted motion.

The "Retribution" (Vozmezdie, 1908-1913) cycle of poems reflects the idea that the betrayal and renunciation of pure, ideal love cause a guilt that demands retribution. Impotence and despair at the loss of ideal love permeate these poems, and the lyrical "I" tries to forget what happened the day before, tries "To love Her again in heaven,/ And to deceive her on earth."

A group of poems "Iambs" (Iamby, 1907-1914) was dedicated to Blok's half-sister Angelina, whom he met for the first time in Warsaw at the time of his father's funeral. They contain political overtones and indignation against the social-political order. Blok's poetry and correspondence throughout 1908 and the early part of 1909 are full of despondency, pessimism and anger. His relationship with his wife was strained, particularly after she joined Meierkhol'd's theatrical group in February of 1908 and was frequently away from home.

When Blok's wife returned in August of 1908 she was expecting another man's child. Blok accepted the child and seemed about to find a new meaning in life, but the child died a week after it was born. The loss deepened Blok's bitterness and despair and his sense of revolt against the world. In order to forget the unhappy experience he and his wife traveled to Italy in May of 1909. This trip resulted in a number of poems, diary entries, letters, and unfinished prose sketches, "Lightning Flashes of Art" (Molnii iskusstva). "The Italian Poems" (Ital'ianskie stikhi, 1909) show an aesthetic detachment and a new interest in the plastic arts. The point of departure in the poems is Italy as Blok saw it, its cities and its art. In these poems Blok achieved the clarity and economy of effect that he had been striving for, which for him was a form of defense against the chaos of external existence and his own internal turmoil.

In early March of 1914 Blok became infatuated with the opera singer L.A. Demas, whom he had first seen in the role of Bizet's Carmen. The result was a cycle of poems "Carmen." In 1920 Blok wrote that in March of 1914 he had given himself to the elements as completely as he had in 1907 when he wrote "The Snow Mask." Delmas inspired other poems as well. "The sleepy whirl-, wind" that the confused soul of the poet enters in this poetry is an apt description of his impression of the singer whose song inspires Blok's "creative dreams," memories of spring, gypsy melodies.

From the time of the 1905 Revolution on, the themes of Russia occupied a prominent place in Blok's poetry. It was to this theme that Blok had "consciously and irrevocably dedicated his life," as he said in a letter to Stanislavskii of 9 December 1908. The "Russia" cycle of poems (1907-1916) expressed Blok's very personal love for his country. Russia in his poetry is usually personified and appears according to Blok's mood either as "drunken Rus," or "destitute Finnish Rus," or a "bride," a "friend," a "beloved one." Blok's love co-exists with his anger, disgust and anguish because of his country's faults. He was aware of all the dirt, ignorance and brutality of Russia, yet he saw this very lack of civilization as her sign of vitality. "On the Field of Kulikovo" (Na pole Kulikovom), a lyrical treatment of the Battle of Kulikovo (1380) in which the Tatars were defeated, considers Russia's heroic past and implies the historical crisis and suffering Russia was to face again. Blok saw his fate as tied closely to that of his country: "We are the children of Russia's terrible years/ We do not have the strength to forget anything." But Blok is also able to foresee another future industrial Russia in the poem "New America" (Novaia Amerika).

Blok also worked on the theme of Russia in his longer autobiographical poem, "Retribution," from 1910 until 1921. The poem was originally inspired by the death of his father in 1909, but the concept was later enlarged to incorporate the theme of destiny in three generations of his family with the theme of Russia and its suffering. Blok worked on this unfinished poem with many interruptions. The first part was completed in 1916. In 1921, before he died, Blok was still trying to continue his work on the second and the third parts. In writing the poem Blok used the Beketov family legends, historical materials and memoirs of the period 1870-1890. The epigraph for the poem: "Youth—that is retribution" was taken from Ibsen's *The Master Builder.*

Involvement with his country's destiny continued in the longer poem "The Twelve" (Dvenadtsat', 1918). In his note about the poem Blok says that in January of 1918 for the last time he gave himself to the elements just as blindly as he had in January of 1907 (Volokhova), or in March of 1914 (Delmas). During and after the composition of "The Twelve," Blok wrote, he heard for several days a terrible rumble produced by the collapse of the old world. He started the poem on 8 January 1918 and finished it on the 28th; it was first published on the 18th of February 1918.

"The Twelve" is Blok's masterpiece and Blok considered it "the best I have written, because I lived then in the present." The poem has to be seen as the highest point of Blok's poetic career that brings together many of the familiar motifs and symbols of his earlier poetry—the snow scenes, the wind, love triangle, beloved turned prostitute—while at the same time the dynamic force of the spirit of the new imbues the whole poem. "The Twelve" is rich in details peculiar to their time and place: military uniforms, weapons, clothing, money, the language and contemporary music of the streets (*chastushka*). Blok also carefully incorporated the political jargon of the day and newspaper reports of the prohibition of looting and drunkenness.

The compositional principle of contrast and dissonance underlies the whole poem. Conversational language, slang expressions, obscenities, topical references, the deliberate interruption of the narrative by questions, exclamations and bits of dialogue, street songs and march rhythms are all incorporated into the poem. The poem is built with precision, its twelve parts corresponding to the title and the number of Red Guards it portrays. Different parts of the poem form a circular structure through the repetition of imagery. There is a combination of realism and symbolism, a rich polyphonic quality with many transitions and breaks, and a clever use of the language and rhythms of popular songs. The musical effect of dissonance is accompanied by a sense of movement, the change from one rhythmical form to another.

In the first part of the poem Blok introduces the actors of his drama: the old woman, the poet, the priest, the bourgeois, ladies, prostitutes, a beggar. These are all representatives of a society that stands at a crossroad in history. There are also topical references to the Constituent Assembly (dispersed on 6 January 1918), to the Bolshevik desire to end the war with Germany, which was thought by many to be treason, and to a meeting of prostitutes at which they attempted to establish trade union rules for themselves. Part one also asks the main question of the poem "What is ahead of us?" which is followed in part twelve by a series of questions to which the answer seems to be: Jesus Christ.

The twelve guardsmen, who resemble convicts, want freedom without the moral restrictions imposed by Christian ethics. Their march through the wind-swept, snowy city is intermingled with the story of Vanka, a bourgeois turncoat, and of Katka, a prostitute. Katka is senselessly killed by her former lover Petrukha, now a member of the guard. He is upset because of what he has done, yet his comrades urge him to continue his ceaseless revolutionary march because there are more important tasks ahead of them.

The bourgeois, introduced in part one of the poem, continues to stand on the street as a silent question mark and is followed by the mangy dog, which symbolizes the old world. The immobility of the old world is contrasted to the ceaseless movement and force of the revolution, symbolized by the wind whose strength increases. The snowstorm turns into a blizzard as the twelve march ready for anything, without pity, their rifles aimed at an invisible enemy. The twelfth section of the poem asks a number of questions: "Who else is there?" "Who's in the snow drift - come out!" "Speak up, who goes there?" "Who's waving the red flag?" "Who goes there with the step of a fugitive,/ Hiding behind every house?" All of these questions are accompanied by the raging blizzard and shooting. And we learn:

> ... So they march with sovereign tread,
> At their heels, the hungry dog,
> At their head - with a bloody flag,
> And unseen behind the storm,
> And unharmed by a bullet,
> With gentle step above the storm,
> Dusted with the pearly snow,
> With a garland of white roses,
> At their head is Jesus Christ.

The poem has aroused numerous controversies over the difficulty of explaining the appearance of Christ at the end of the poem, an ending which Blok himself questioned in his notebooks. Blok spells the name of his Christ in the way the Russian schismatics do, as *Isus,* rather than the modern *Iisus.* This spelling suggests that Blok had the schismatic Jesus of the Old Believers in mind, rather than the Orthodox Christ. But this is not an "explanation," since the Christ of the Old Believers is hardly the gentle feminine figure of Blok's poem. In his notebook Blok comments that he himself, at times, hated that feminine apparition, but could not replace the image with another. Soviet critics have commented on the lack of concreteness in Blok's political vision. In his perceptive essay on Blok in *Literature and Revolution* Trotskii said of Blok's poem: "To be sure, Blok is not one of ours, but he reached towards us. And in doing so, he broke down." Nevertheless, Trotskii considered the poem "the most significant work of our epoch." Other Soviet critics object to Blok's portrayal of the Guards as rabble.

The creative frenzy brought on by the composition of "The Twelve" soon abated. "The Scythians" (Skify), written in two days, was published in February of 1918. This poem could be considered the end of Blok's major poetic inspiration. Blok admonishes Europe in "The Scythians" to take heed and make attempts at friendship with Russia, the Asiatic sphinx that both loves and hates the old world. His plea is for brotherhood. The poem reflects Blok's thoughts on the problems of Russia, Europe and Asia since the time of the Revolution of 1905.

In an essay "On Lyric Poetry" (O lirike, 1907) Blok says: "Lyric poetry is 'I' the macrocosm. The whole world of the lyric poet lies in his mode of perception." This statement is a perceptive description of his poetry, in which the allusive and the emotional powers of the word enable him to recreate the mood of his intensely personal experiences and states of mind.

The repeated use of certain words—stars, dreams, sleep, magical, fog, shaddows, dawn, the road—strengthens the allusive quality of Blok's poetry. Very often things are defined by what they are not, and by qualities they do not possess. Blok deliberately uses negative constructions. Words of different categories are often juxtaposed to achieve new meanings.

Blok has been called "the poet of metaphor." But his images are symbols in that they retain both a concrete and an abstract meaning. Blok also gives an impression of the irrational to his poetic style by his frequent use of catachresis, an intentional misuse of words that often includes logical and semantic contradictions, as, for example, "The fires of a white-winged blizzard." He rather underlines the paradoxical quality of the words to create an impression of the irrational, the supra-real, and the fantastic. The most characteristic examples of this device can be found in poems that depict agitated passionate feelings and the ecstasy of love. Blok makes bold use of the logically contradictory, the dissonant, as an artistic device to express his general conception of the world as irrational.

Another striking quality of Blok's verse is the uncanny sense of rhythm it projects. In his opinion the poet was the bearer of rhythm, and music was the essence of being. Blok applied his musical concepts to philosophy, art and history. What he called the "Spirit of Music" seemed to be an elemental, vital, urgent, intense force, similar to what he experienced at moments of poetic inspiration. In his essay "The Collapse of Humanism" (Krushenie gumanizma, 1919) Blok distinguishes between a historical, calendar concept of space and time, and of musical space and time in which we live only when we are close to nature and surrender to its elemental force. Apparently Blok's perception of the Revolution within this latter category of musical space and time explains his enthusiastic response to its rumble. Yet Blok the poet ceased to hear any "sound" after he had written "The Twelve" and "The Scythians." The poet whose very silence was once full of sounds *(zvuchnaia tishina)* lived until his death in a soundless space. The impression of an unresolved, heavily stressed dissonance, in accordance with the music of that period, brings "The Twelve" close to what Northrop Frye calls the "technical" use of the word musical, while Blok's earlier poetry could be called "sentimental" (in Frye's terminology) implying recognized Symbolist (Verlaine) melifluousness.

Blok's standing as one of the greatest Russian poets is based on his lyric poetry, his lyric dramas (see entry below) and "The Twelve." He made a considerable number of innovations in Russian prosody. Blok helped break away from the traditional syllabo-accentual (or syllabo-tonic) verse, used from the time of Trediakovskii and Lomonosov, which is based on the regular alternation of stressed (strong) and unstressed (weak) syllables. Instead, Blok began making use of accentual verse called *dol'niki*, used until then only in popular poetry in Russia and in translations of Western poetry. With accentual verse the number of stressed syllables per line is constant, while the number of unstressed syllables between the stresses is variable—one, two or three syllables. From about 1890 various types of romantic *dol'niki* began to be widespread in the original works of the Russian Symbolist poets. Blok is considered the creator of the modern *dol'niki*; his experiments formed the basis for future developments. The overwhelming majority of *dol'niki* in Blok's verse can be found in his first book, and it is here that *dol'niki* became an integral part of the Russian poetic language.

Blok also made great use of the technique of repetition and syntactic parallelisms. The most characteristic repetitive device in Blok's poetry (and in Symbolist poetry in general) was the symmetry of the first and last lines of either the stanza or the whole poem, the so-called *kol'tso,* or "ring." There is great variation in the use of this device.

Assonances give Blok's poetry fluidity and an attempt at orchestration: "I veiut drevnimi pover'iami . . ." (The Unknown Woman). Blok used both assonance and alliteration and enriched the tonal effect with internal rhyme. He carefully arranged vowels and consonants to evoke a specific mood. In his early poetry, for example, he strongly favored the vowel *a* in describing the Beautiful Lady; her appearances are frequently depicted by assonances with *a* (Oná molodá i prekrásna bylá).

Imperfect rhymes *(netochnye rifmy)* were introduced into Russian poetry by Briusov, who was inspired by the French Symbolists. Yet the canonization of imperfect rhyme in twentieth-century Russian poetry belongs to Blok. Before 1902 imperfect rhymes were rare in Blok's poetry. From 1902 on, under Briusov's influence and Blok's acquaintance with the Symbolists, the use of imperfect rhyme became more varied in his poetry. The second book of Blok's poetry has a large number of imperfect rhymes, particularly when he departs from the laws of syllabo-accentual versification, or when he does not adhere to strophic composition, or uses catachresis to create an impression of irrationality. Blok incorporated into Russian verse not only assonance, but also consonance, for example: *solntsa: serdtsa; rozakh: rizakh.* In his third book Blok returned to more traditional forms of meter and rhyme.

Blok has been associated with the Symbolist movement that arose in Russia in the 1890s as a revolt against the literary tradition of realism in prose that dominated much of nineteenth-century Russian literature, and against the civic poetry of the second half of the nineteenth century. In its formative years this movement was under the influence of French Symbolist poetry that was actively translated in Russia. The movement was not homogeneous: the so-called aesthetic school, led by Briusov, was mainly influenced by French Symbolism; and the Ivanov-Belyi, nationally-oriented trend was partially inspired by German philosophy. The distinction between the two trends was not clear-cut; what united them was their refutation of the past and its language. For Briusov Russian Symbolism was mainly a poetic school. Briusov considered the mysticism of Blok's early poetry an alien element in Symbolism. Belyi, however, as early as 1905, thought that poetry and philosophy were inseparable. Symbolism for him was a conception of life. For Ivanov and Blok the poet was a theurgist, and poetry a religious act. In his essay "On the Present State of Russian Symbolism" (O sovremennom sostoianii russkogo simvolizma, 1910) Blok wrote that the poet is first and foremost a theurgist and a possessor of secret knowledge. Therefore, only the poet is capable of interpreting the unknown reality in whose existence he believed. But Blok's views had changed by 1905 and he came to the conclusion that art and religion were incompatible. He refused to be drawn into any schools and believed that the poet had a right to chose his own themes. The year 1910 saw the crisis of Symbolism in Russia. Blok's essay on Symbolism was one among many theoretical statements that were made by Russian Symbolist poets that year.

In a number of essays, letters and diary entries written between 1907 and 1919 Blok demonstrated his concern about the relationship between the intelligentsia and the people, a question that had occupied the mind of many Russian thinkers. Blok's approach was emotional, allusive and lyrical. He believed that the intelligentsia and its way of life was doomed and he condemned the isolation of the intelligentsia from the people. The people, in his opinion, were a vital force asking for answers which the liberal intelligentsia, searching for its own answers, failed to give them (" 'Religious Quests' and the People," 1907). In his essay "The People and the Intelligentsia" (Narod i intelligentsiia, 1908) Blok suggested that the intelligentsia should renounce its "aestheticism, individualism and despair" and a "will to die," because their views were opposed to those of the people who represented a life force and a "will to live." The starving, brutally abused people, he thought, had been brought to the limit of endurance and might revolt and destroy the intelligentsia. Blok hoped that a common meeting ground would be found. But his views were not accepted by the public or the various levels of the intelligentsia, particularly his hope that the Revolution would bring change. In "The Intelligentsia and the Revolution" (Intelligentsiia i revoliutsiia, 1918) Blok foresaw difficult tasks for his country, yet perceived its ultimate victory. The fierce and stormy aspect of the Revolution was accepted by Blok as a sign of the new, as a sign of something great, as "music of the future."

Although Blok was not a theoretician or philosopher, his essays show sincere interest in Russia's destiny. He offered no concrete program for action and was at times unclear in his approach. Blok, however, was primarily a poet, and it is in the realm of poetry where his greatness has been assured.

Works: Sobranie sochinenii, 12 vols. (L., 1932-36); *Polnoe sobranie sochinenii v dvukh tomakh* (L., 1946); *Sochineniia v dvukh tomakh* (M., 1955); *Sobranie sochinenii v vos'mi tomakh* (M.-L., 1960-63); *Zapisnye knizhki* (M., 1965); *Sobranie sochinenii v shesti tomakh* (M., 1971).

References: Kompozitsiia liricheskikh stikhotvorenii (Pb., 1921); *Rifma. Eë istoriia i teoriia* (Pb., 1923); V. Zhirmunskii, *Vvedenie v metriku. Teoriia stikha* (L., 1925); – – – , *Voprosy teorii literatury* (L., 1928); *Literaturnoe nasledstvo,* vols. 27-28 (M., 1937); B.O. Unbegaun, *Russian Versification* (London, 1956); G. Donchin, *The Influence of French Symbolism on Russian Poetry* (The Hague, 1958); *Blokovskii sbornik* (Tartu, 1964); R. Kemball, *Aleksandr Blok: A Study in Rhythm and Metre* (The Hague, 1965); M.L. Gasparov, "Russkii trekhudarnyi dol'nik," *Teoriia stikha* (L., 1968); *Selected Poems of Aleksandr Blok,* ed., J.B. Woodward (London, 1968); K. Taranovsky, "Certain Aspects of Blok's Symbolism," *Studies in Slavic Linguistics and Poetics in Honor of Boris Unbegaun* (N.Y., 1968); I.M. Mashbits-Verov, *Russkii simvolizm i put' Aleksandra Bloka* (Kuibishev, 1969); J. Bailey, "Blok and Heine: An Episode from the History of Russian *dol'niki,*" *Slavonic and East European Journal,* vol. XIII, No. 1 (1969); *Alexander Blok: Selected Poems,* ed., A. Pyman (Oxford, 1972); R.A. Maguire, "Macrocosm or Microcosm? The Symbolists on Russia," *Review of National Literatures,* vol. III, No. 1 (1972); S.D. Cioran, "Vladimir Solovyov and the Divine Feminine," *Russian Literature Triquarterly,* No. 4 (1972); *Blokovskii sbornik II* (Tartu, 1972); L. Vogel, *Aleksandr Blok: The Journey to Italy* (London, 1973); L. Ginzburg, *O lirike* (L., 1974); D. Maksimov, *Poeziia i proza Al. Bloka* (L., 1975); S. Hackel, *The Poet and the Revolution* (London, 1975); *Tezisy I Vsesoiuznoi (III) konferentsii "Tvorchestvo A.A. Bloka i russkaia kul'tura XX veka"* (Tartu, 1975); J. Forsyth, "Prophets and Supermen: 'German' Ideological Influences on Aleksandr Blok's Poetry," *Forum for Modern Language Studies,* vol. XIII, No. 1 (1977), 33-46.

Milica Banjanin

BLOK, ALEKSANDR: THE DRAMATIC WORKS. Aleksandr Blok gave a significant share of his personal life, as well as generous portions of his expository writings and poetic works, to the theater and drama. Interested in theater since childhood, Blok subsequently performed roles like Romeo, Hamlet, and Chatskii (the hero of Griboedov's *Woe from Wit*) in amateur productions, referred to himself as a "theater person," and even dreamed of taking up the profession as dramatic actor. His greatest role—in the striking image of Zinaida Gippius and Boris Eikhenbaum—was perhaps that of Symbolist Poet who was, in both his public and private life, as inseparably fused with his Role and his Poetry as is the Tragic Actor with his Mask and his Soliloquy. In 1906 Blok became seriously affiliated with the professional theater, "fell profoundly in love" with it, and "remained true to it his whole life" (D'iakonov). Blok completed four plays that year.

His first play, *The Little Show Booth* (Balaganchik), was originally written for the intended, but never realized, opening of theaters conceived by persons associated with the literary almanacs *Fakely* and *Zhupely* in St. Petersburg. Developed from his poem of the same title, the play was published in *Fakely* in April. That summer he began his second play, *The King in the Square* (Korol' na ploshchadi). That autumn the management of the Theater of V.F. Komissarzhevskaia decided to produce his first play, and their preparations drew Blok into the activities of that theater. Following the completion of *The King in the Square,* for example, V.E. Meierkhol'd, who had recently joined the staff as regisseur, chose Blok's second play to join his first and thereby provide an evening bill of Blok plays. His third play, *On Love, Poetry, and Government Service* (O liubvi, poezii i gosudarstvennoi sluzhbe), was developed from drafts of *The King in the Square* (summer 1906), completed in October, and published in the journal *Pereval* in April 1907. His fourth play, *The Unknown Woman* (Neznakomka), was completed November 11 and subsequently published in the journal *Vesy* (Nos. 5-7) 1907. Accepted for production in the Theater of Komissarzhevskaia, *The Unknown Woman* was prohibited by the government on the grounds that the censor "could not make out the content" because "it presented such decadent chaos" and because the author apparently depicted the Mother of God in the character of the Unknown Woman.

Since *The King in the Square* was also denied production by the censor, *The Little Show Booth,* now on the same bill with Maeterlinck's *The Miracle of Saint Anthony* (Le Miracle de Saint-Antoine), opened on December 30 under Meierkhol'd's direction, after some fifteen rehearsals (décor and costumes by Sapunov; music by Kuzmin; and performance of the central role—Pierrot—by the regisseur himself). Considered a seminal Meierkhol'd production of an outstanding play in the Russian Symbolist movement, *The Little Show Booth* has received a better-than-average share of literary, as well as performance, criticism. Biographers suggest that both the structure and style of this "strange and terrifying farce" (Chulkov) may have been inspired by the poet's disillusionment with his marriage to Liubov Mendeleeva, daughter of the chemist D.I. Mendeleev. The chief incidents in the eternal triangle (Pierrot-Columbine-Harlequin) in the play perhaps mock a simulation of events in Blok's own life, that is, his role in the life triangle of himself-his wife-Andrei Belyi.

However much Blok's own life may be mirrored, the play itself has been variously viewed in terms of political symbol, social document, existential model, literary parody, and aesthetic matrix of the major characteristics of the Russian avant-garde movement at the turn of this century. As political symbol, for example, the character Columbine represented the "longed-for" and heretofore "unrealized" constitution promised by the tsarist government following the Revolution of 1905. Critics (Kisch, Ershov, Fëdorov) have noted the parody, as well as the satiric rejection, of "mysticism" promulgated in such works as *The Death of Tintagiles* by Maeterlinck, *The Arrival* by Belyi, and *The Earth* by Briusov. In terms of recent Soviet and Western criticism, *The Little Show Booth* has been ranked significant and singular in its treatment of ambiguity (the transcendental and real, the high and low, the poetic and trivial) and of duality (Columbine, for example, is both bride—life—and death; Harlequin is Pierrot's double, the Clown struck, but not touched, by the wooden sword ·"bleeds"—not blood—but cranberry juice).

Both the playscript and the production were conceived and executed in terms of the ambiguity of the mask, the divisive concept of illusion-reality-irony, and the nature of the grotesque. The performers playing the characters were each given gestures and movements that were typifying and suggestive. For example, Meierkhol'd, playing Pierrot, developed precise gestures, in this case, flapping arms, which were repeated consistently and were associated only with Pierrot. Such performance techniques anticipated similar techniques in the effect of making strange (*Verfremdungseffekt*) popularized in plays by Bertolt Brecht. The style of both playscript and production is usually identified in the Russian and Soviet theater as exemplary of the theater of conventions (*uslovnyi teatr*) in direct contrast to the style of Naturalistic or Realistic theater. As one of the first native Russian plays written and produced in the theater of conventions, *The Little Show Booth* became a rallying cry and a model for those associated with the "new" theater in Russia (1905-ca. 1928).

The response by audience and critics to *The Little Show Booth,* performed five times in three weeks, has been described as "diverse and discrepant." One person who was there on opening night recalled, fifteen years after the event: "I have never observed—neither before nor since—such intransigent opposition and such exultation by the admirers among the spectators in the auditorium. The frenzied hissing by enemies and the sound of friendly applause blended with the clamor and the howling." The day following the opening night, Blok noted in his diary: "I came on stage 4 times. Nothing but strident hissing and applause. I bowed to both." Newspaper reviews were largely negative, calling Blok "God's fool" and his play, "*The Little Bedlam*" (Bedlamchik). When the play was performed by the company on tour to Moscow the following season, newspaper response was generally similar to that in St. Petersburg. Here and there, however, critics noted the "originality" of the play and characterized the production as a "bold and new step in art."

The Little Show Booth was revived twice by Meierkhol'd (Minsk, summer 1908; St. Petersburg, April 1914) and received production in Geneva (season 1915/16) and in Paris (season 1923/24)—both productions under the direction of Georges Pitoëff—as well as in New York (spring and summer 1923). In terms of both audience and critics, response to the New York production was negative. The Soviet correspondent reported to the *Krasnaia gazeta* (4 August 1923) "smiles, guffaws, snorts . . . and, finally, vulgar heckling." *The New York Times* denied its modernity, compared Blok's play unfavorably with productions by the Moscow Art Theater which had recently been seen on tour in the United States, and summed up Russia's "new" theater as "backward looking" (4, 10 April 1923).

In 1908 Blok published three of his first four plays in a single volume, under the title *Lyrical Dramas* (Liricheskie dramy). Drawing "no ideological, moral, or other conclusions," Blok explained in his Preface that all three plays are *lyrical* since "the experiences of an individual soul—his doubts, passions, failures, deg-gradations—are merely presented in dramatic form." The chief character in each play—unlucky Pierrot in *The Little Show Booth,* the morally inept Poet in *The King in the Square,* and the drunken Poet who squanders his vision in *The Unknown Woman*—is inevitably linked to the other two. All are different aspects of one person's soul and all indulge in the same objective: all search for "the beautiful life, free and bright, which alone can cast from their weak shoulders *lyrical* doubts, contradictions, and . . . [multiplicity of] doubles." The image of the Eternal Feminine, personified by Columbine, the Architect's Daughter, and The Unknown Woman, respectively, is actually the beautiful life they seek. Moreover, these three plays communicate a "mocking tone" which connects them with the so-called transcendental irony of Romanticism.

Blok's aims as dramatist were founded on several premises: (1) both the drama and the theater are best unified as one object in which "the word becomes flesh" in performance; (2) the theater, properly managed, can effectively educate the Russian people, almost 75% of whom were illiterate; (3) that dialogue written to be performed requires training, especially dialogue written in verse, which must be spoken in terms of its sounds and rhythms, not its content; (4) that an appropriate repertory should perhaps consist of romantic drama or melodrama, that is, plays of "great passions and stupendous events" ("O teatre," *Zolotoe runo,* Nos. 3-5, 1908) as well as the traditional masterpieces by authors such as Sophocles, Shakespeare, Molière, Goethe ("O repertuare kommunal'nykh i gosu-darstvennykh teatrov," *Repertuar,* 1919). Having played an important role in the vanguard of the Russian *uslovnyi* theater, Blok rejected much of the "new" drama and its production as early as 1908: "Maeterlinck has found small nodules in which to assemble a melody." However, Blok praised the plays of Andreev, especially his *Life of Man* (1907), and advocated the production techniques of Stanislavskii, Nemirovich-Danchenko, and the Moscow Art Theater (MAT) as exemplary of the kind of theater that would best serve his own aims as dramatist.

The year 1908 marked the period of transition for Blok as dramatist, during which he shifted from the world of the avant-garde (his first four plays) into a Symbolist universe of his own making which culminated in his major verse drama, *The Rose and the Cross* (Roza i krest, 1913, 1920). His fifth original play, *The Song of Fate* (Pesnia sud'by), was completed in April 1908, and the directors of MAT expressed an interest in producing it. Stanislavskii, in Blok's words, "passionately praised *The Song of Fate* and ordered that two scenes be altered." In August Blok sent his revised version to Stanislavskii, and after several exchanges of letters, the regisseur finally refused to produce the play, first, because the play lacked a "single harmonic aim" which could thread the parts into a complete action; second, because the new scenes were appealing in terms of their "poetry and spirit," but the characters generally disenchanted him and, in some places, clashed with "the nature of humankind." In the early stage of developing his system of acting, conceived in terms of Naturalistic or Realistic production, Stanislavskii essentially objected to characters drawn with minimal "human" character traits. Convinced that Stanislavskii was "the most talented person in

Russia," Blok was perhaps motivated to develop plays that would be accepted for production in MAT. Even though he found himself unable to change his play until 1919, since he "tenderly loved all the characters," Blok consistently turned down offers to stage it in other theaters.

If the events surrounding the creation of *The Song of Fate* marked the first phase in Blok's transition as dramatist, the second was associated with his translation of Franz Grillparzer's *Ancestress* (Die Ahnfrau, 1916), under the archaic Russian title, *Pramater'*. Completed in August 1908, the play was written for production in the Theater of Komissarzhevskaia (décor and costumes by Benois) under the direction of F.F. Komissarzhevskii (Théodore Komisarjevsky). After reading the five-act verse tragedy in the original, Blok wrote to the famous actress-manager that Grillparzer's "heroic (perhaps, even melodramatic) romanticism might be revived on the Russian stage." The task of translating a first-rate model play enabled Blok to accomplish a number of objectives: he learned how to structure a full-length play; how to endow characters with "human" character traits, motivations, actions; and (perhaps most important for Blok) he learned how to write outstanding verse intended to be spoken in a theater. With the exception of his first play and his first translation, a verse rendition of Rutebeuf's *The Miracle of Théophile,* Blok's plays were composed chiefly in prose. Acquainted with Spanish baroque drama (Grillparzer's chief inspiration had been Calderón), Blok developed variations in his Russian trochaic tetrameter, using "words as the composer of a symphony uses instruments," that gives his *Pramater'* "a supranational character" (R.B. Thompson). In short, Blok not only learned his lessons in playwriting from a master craftsman but also created an exceptional full-length verse drama that contains some of the best Russian dramatic poetry composed in this century. Moreover, when he turned to the making of his next original play, *The Rose and the Cross,* Blok had learned his lessons well enough to develop a four-act drama completely in verse whose characters were given sufficient "human" character traits, motivations, and actions to establish a firm Realistic plane on which Blok's uses of Symbolism were founded.

The Rose and the Cross, undoubtedly Blok's finest play, and perhaps the best Russian verse drama in this century, was originally conceived as a ballet, then as an opera, and finally, as a drama. Cast in medieval imagery, replete with gnostic myths, Wagnerian *leitmotifs,* and elemental forces set in Brittany and Provence, and endowed with Blok's own experience and expertise in matters intellectual and poetic, *The Rose and the Cross* was apparently inspired by Blok's omnivorous reading in medieval literature, history, and language, as well as by his acquaintance with the works of Calderón and Paul Claudel. In several notes, letters, and other materials, Blok described the framework of the play. "In the first place, it is the drama of the *person* Bertran. He is not the hero, but the intellect and heart of the drama . . . . In the second place, *The Rose and the Cross* is the drama of Izora, even though it represents only part of [her] journey [through life] ." In Blok's treatment of Bertran as protagonist, however, may be seen the essential dramatic conflict in the play. That is, Bertran is like a Claudelian hero who "comes to grips with life's incompatibilities" (Ewa Thompson), makes major discoveries that lead to decisions in his struggle to "reconcile the Rose of Joy with the Cross of Suffering" (Blok).

The play was accepted for production by MAT, and Stanislavskii gave the play more than 180 three-hour rehearsals over a three-year period (1916-1918) but eventually he denied it a public performance. Even though a number of prominent persons and theaters were prepared to stage his play—among them Tairov and the Kamernyi Theater in Moscow (1916), Aleksandrinskii and Mikhailovskii in Petrograd (1918), the Theater of F.A. Korsh in Moscow (1921)— Blok did not allow production of *The Rose and the Cross* until the last year of his life, when it was given for fifteen performances (1920/21 season) by the Kostromskoi City Theater.

Following the October Revolution, Blok continued an active involvement in theater by heading the Repertory Committee of the Theater Section in Petrograd and gave a major share of energy in getting the masterpieces into print and into production, since he believed that his first objective was the education of the Russian people. In the same period he revised his own plays and essays, wrote a short play *Ramses* (Ramzes, 1919) which is considered inferior to his other plays, and clarified his theories of drama and theater. Blok's plays are rarely produced in our age because they apparently lack that sense of urgency required for revivals. Consequently, they find their greatest attraction today in terms of dramatic literature to be read and experienced. And three of his plays, *The Little Show Booth, Pramater'*, and *The Rose and the Cross,* are exceptional and may be ranked among the finest Russian drama written in this century.

Works: *Liricheskie dramy* (Pb., 1908); *Teatr* (M., 1916); *Sobranie sochinenii*, 8 vols. (M., 1960-1965). In English translation: *The Show Booth, Dublin Magazine,* vol. I (June 1924); *The Unknown Woman, Transition,* vol. II (May, June, July 1927); *King in the Square, Slavonic and East European Review,* vol. XII (April 1934); *The Rose and the Cross, Slavonic and East European Review,* vol. XIV (April 1936); *The Song of Fate, Poet Lore,* vol. XLIV (1938); *Dialogue About Love, Poetry, and Government Service, Dublin Magazine,* n.s., vol. XXII (April-June 1947); *Puppet Show, Slavonic and East European Review,* vol. XXVII (April 1950); *Love, Poetry, and Civic Service, Poet Lore,* vol. LVII (Spring 1953), 99-110.

References: N. Volkov, *A. Blok i teatr* (M., 1926); P.N. Medvedev, *Dramy i poèmy Al. Bloka* (L., 1928); L.R. Lewitter, "The Inspiration and the Meaning of Aleksandr Blok's *The Rose and the Cross," Slavonic and East European Review,* vol. XXXV (June 1957), 428-42; Sir Cecil Kisch, *Alexander Blok: Prophet of Revolution* (London, 1960); P. Ershov, "Simvolicheskaia lirika na stsene: *Balaganchik* Al. Bloka," *Novyi zhurnal* (N.Y.), No. 67 (1962), 98-117; V.I. Bezzubov, "Aleksandr Blok i Leonid Andreev," *Blokovskii sbornik,* vol. I (Tartu, 1964); Victor Erlich, *The Double Image* (Baltimore, 1964); V.M. Zhirmunskii, *Drama A. Bloka "Roza i krest"* (L., 1964); A. D'iakonov (Stavrogin), "Aleksandr Blok v teatre Komissarzhevskoi," *O Komissarzhevskoi,* ed. K. Rudnitskii (M., 1965); George Annenkov, "The Poets and the Revolution—Blok, Mayakovsky, Esenin," *The Russian Review,* vol. XXVI, No. 2 (April 1967); R.D. Thomson, "The Non-Literary Sources of *Roza i Krest," Slavonic and East European Review,* vol. XLV (July 1967); A.B. Rubtsov, *Dramaturgiia Aleksandra Bloka* (Minsk, 1968); Ewa M. Thompson, "The Development of Aleksandr Blok as a Dramatist," *Slavonic and East European Journal,* vol. XIV (Fall 1970); E. Heier,

"Grillparzer's *Ahnfrau* in Russland: A. Blok," *Comparative Literature,* vol. XXIII (Summer 1971); A.V. Fedorov, *Teatr A. Bloka i dramaturgiia ego vremeni* (L., 1972); T.M. Rodina, *Aleksandr Blok i russkii teatr nachala XX veka* (M., 1972); R.B. Thompson, *"Die Ahnfrau* by Franz Grillparzer and *Pramater'* by Aleksandr Blok," *Germano-Slavica,* vol. I (1973); J.E. Bowlt, "Aleksandr Blok: The Poem 'The Unknown Lady'," *Texas Studies in Literature and Language,* vol. XVII (Special Russian Issue, 1975).

Eugene K. Bristow

BLUE BLOUSE, *see* Supplementary volume.

BOBINSKII, VASILII, *see* BOBYNS'KYI, VASIL' PETROVYCH.

BOBORÝKIN, PĖTR DMITRIEVICH (1836-1921). Russian novelist, playwright, journalist. Boborykin was born to the landed gentry on 15 (27) August 1836 in Nizhnii Novgorod (now Gor'kii). He studied law at Kazan University and then medicine at Derpt (Tartu) University. The acceptance of his play *The Small Landholder* (Odnodvorets, 1860) for publication in the *Biblioteka dlia chteniia* encouraged Boborykin to become a professional writer. The *Biblioteka* also began publication of his autobiographical novel *Setting Out on the Road* (V put' dorogu) in 1862, and a year later, after receiving an inheritance, Boborykin bought the journal outright, editing it until its demise in 1865. Encumbered with huge debts, Boborykin paid off his creditors over the next twenty years. He lived in a great many cities both in Russia and in Western Europe, steadily contributing his novels and dramas to a variety of Russian journals, and journalistic pieces such as his accounts of the aftermath of the Paris Commune in 1871 to Nekrasov's *Otechestvennye zapiski.* After 1890 he lived abroad, for the most part, and never returned to Russia after the Bolshevik Revolution of 1917.

Boborykin was a prolific writer: more than 20 novels, 40 short stories, and 20 plays came from his pen, in addition to a large number of newspaper articles on diverse topics, memoirs, and essays on the theater, in which he was avidly interested. Boborykin also received considerable attention for his study *The European Novel in the XIX Century* (Evropeiskii roman v XIX stoletii, 1900).

Boborykin was a polyglot and read widely in contemporary European literatures. He was avidly interested in the works of the French Naturalists, particularly Zola, and his own works display those literary features often associated with Naturalism: the stance of an objective observer, the concern with external details, the themes taken from the life of the lower and middle classes. The excesses often associated with this aesthetic in the French Naturalists, are apparent also in Boborykin's work. Contemporary critics complained of his predilection for superfluous details, and for unnecessary episodes which hamper the orderly development of the primary plot line. Russian critics objected to his dry, unemotional narrative voice, which led readers to believe that the author was uninvolved in his work.

On the other hand, Boborykin was given credit for having an unquestionable gift for observation and for rendering contemporary problems in relatively convincing works. No writer captured the atmosphere and the mood of contemporary life better than Boborykin. For this reason alone, his works may profitably be read as period pieces. Boborykin's very prolificacy places him in the tradition of those nineteenth-century giants, Balzac and Zola, who aspired to be the chroniclers of their ages.

The basic theme of Boborykin's novels and tales is the appearance and progress of the middle class in Russia. His most popular and significant novels are *Evening Victim* (Zhertva vecherniaia, 1868), *Solid Virtues* (Solidnye dobrodeteli, 1870), *Businessmen* (Del'tsy, 1872-3), *China Town* (Kitai-gorod, 1882), *Vasilii Tërkin* (1892), *The Pass* (Pereval, 1894), *The Urge* (Tiaga, 1898), and the novelette *[He] Got Smart* (Poumnel, 1890). *Vasilii Tërkin,* in particular, detailed the successful efforts of a peasant entrepreneur to acquire wealth. Boborykin also devoted some attention to the intelligentsia, beginning with *On the Wane* (Na ushcherbe, 1890), which concerns the withdrawal of the intelligentsia from social issues during the period of political "reaction" in the last decade of the nineteenth century, and ending with *The Defeated Are Not Judged* (Pobezhdënnykh—ne sudiat, 1910) and *Breach into Eternity* (Proryv v vechnost', 1911). Both of these novels deal with the mystical searching of the intelligentsia, of which Boborykin, as an adherent of the scientism of the second half of the nineteenth century, did not approve.

A moderate liberal politically, Boborykin could not align himself with the Bolshevik Revolution. Consequently, he did not return to Russia after 1917. He died in Lugano, Switzerland, on 12 August 1921. Although Boborykin was widely read in his time, his popularity quickly waned, and with the exception of *China Town* and his memoirs, none of his works have been reprinted during the Soviet period since 1917.

Works: Sochineniia, 12 vols. (Pb., 1884-86); *Sobranie romanov povestei i rasskazov,* 12 vols. (Pb., 1897); *Za polveka. Moi vospominaniia* (M.-L., 1929); *Kitai-gorod* (M., 1957); *Vospominaniia,* 2 vols. (M., 1965).

References: S.A. Vengerov, *Kritiko-biograficheskii slovar',* vol. 4 (Pb., 1895), 191-241 [contains useful bibliography, pp. 224-28]; B. Cheshikhin, *Sovremennoe obshchestvo v proizvedeniiakh Boborykina i Chekhova* (Odessa, 1899); A.M. Linin, *K istorii burzhuaznogo stilia v russkoi literature: Tvorchestvo P.D. Boborykina* (Rostov-on-Don, 1935); A.V. Lunacharskii, *Kriticheskie étiudy* (L., 1925); *Istoriia russkoi literatury,* v. 9, bk. 2 (chapter "Boborykin") (M.-L., 1956).

BOBÓ YUNÚS KHUDOIDODZADÉ (1870-1945). Tadjik poet, storyteller. Bobo Yunus was born a peasant in the village of Baldzhuan. For many years he wandered from village to village singing folk songs, telling fairy tales and legends. His repertory also included epic poems, heroic tales, variations of the folk epic *Gurguli,* and the tale "Vose's Rebellion." Bobo Yunus is also known for his epic poem "The Tale of Artilleryman Mukhamed Ibrahimov," which he wrote during World War II. He died at his birthplace in 1945.

Works: Surudhoi Bobinus (Stalinabad, 1951). In Russian translation: *Pesni Bobo Iunusa* (Stalinabad, 1950).

BOBRÍSHCHEV-PÚSHKIN, NIKOLAI SERGEEVICH (1800-1871). Russian poet, Decembrist. Born a nobleman on 21 August (2 September) 1800, Bobrishchev-Pushkin received his education at the school for the nobility affiliated with

Moscow University. He became a member of the Southern Secret Society (Iuzhnoe tainoe obshchestvo) in 1820, was arrested together with his brother Pavel for involvement in the Decembrist Rebellion and incarcerated in the Petropavlovsk Fortress in 1826.

Of little interest as a poet, Bobrishchev-Pushkin receives attention in Soviet publications because of his role in the Decembrist Rebellion. His poems "Hymn to Compassion" (Gimn miloserdiia), "Contentment and Tranquility" (Dovol'stvo i spokoistvie), "Morning in the Country" (Utro v derevne), "Immortality" (Bessmertie), were all written in adolescence and appeared along with translations from Florian, Saadi, and J.J. Rousseau, in the almanac *Kalliopa* (1816-17). His literary activity ceased soon after the trial of the Decembrists, when Bobrishchev-Pushkin became mentally disturbed. He was sentenced to twenty years exile in Siberia, but his steadily deteriorating mental condition led to his transfer to other locations in his brother's care, and final return to European Russia after the amnesty granted the Decembrists in 1856. He died on 13 (25) May 1871.

Works: Dekabristy. Poeziia, dramaturgiia, proza . . . (M.-L., 1951); *Poety-Dekabristy* (L., 1960).

References: S.A. Vengerov, *Kritiko-biograficheskii slovar',* vol. 4 (Pb., 1895), 19-20.

BOBRÍSHCHEV-PÚSHKIN, PAVEL SERGEEVICH (1802-1865). Russian poet, Decembrist. A nobleman, Bobrishchev-Pushkin was born on 12 (24) July, 1802 and was educated in the school for the nobility affiliated with Moscow University. He served thereafter as an officer on the Southern Army's Staff. In 1822 he joined the Southern Secret Society (Iuzhnoe tainoe obshchestvo) and in 1826, together with his brother Nikolai, was arrested for his involvement in the Decembrist Rebellion and sentenced to eight years at hard labor. In 1832 he was sent into an exile colony in the Irkutsk region, then transferred to Krasnoyarsk to look after his mentally ill brother Nikolai. In Siberia Bobrishchev-Pushkin took active part in the "Convict Academy" (Katorzhnaia akademiia), a religious "congregation" where he conducted philosophical disputes. In 1839 he was transferred to Tobolsk together with his brother. Espousing homeopathy, Bobrishchev-Pushkin treated the poor gratis and took great personal risks during the cholera epidemic of 1848. After the amnesty of 1856 he moved to the Tula region together with his brother. Bobrishchev-Pushkin's contributions as a writer are negligible and he receives continued attention at present because of his role as a Decembrist. Four of his fables, written in adolescence, appeared in the almanac *Kalliopa* (1817), although he apparently also wrote satirical fables later. Bobrishchev-Pushkin's lyric poetry reflects his concern for religion, in which he sought consolation during the years of exile and hard labor. He died on 13 (25) February 1865 in Moscow.

Works: Poèziia dekabristov (L., 1950); *Dekabristy. Poeziia, dramaturgiia, proza . . .* (M.-L., 1951); *Poéty-dekabristy* (L., 1960).

BOBRÓV, SEMËN SERGEEVICH (1768-1810). Russian poet. Bobrov was a graduate both of a theological seminary and of Moscow University (1785), and was an employee of the Naval Office from 1792. Bobrov's poems, first published in 1784, are didactic and religious, abound in Slavonicisms, in heavy morphological constructions and complex epithets. Praised by Admiral Shishkov, his works were later ridiculed by Pushkin, Viazemskii, and Batiushkov. In his allegories ("Tavrida") Bobrov sometimes directed satirical barbs against contemporary society. He died on 22 March (3 April) 1810 in Petersburg.

Works: Tavrida, ili Moi letnii den' v Tavricheskom Khersonise (Nikolaev, 1798); *Rassvet polnochi, ili Sozertsanie slavy, torzhestva i mudrosti porfironosnykh, branonosnykh i mirnykh geniev Rossii . . .,* 4 parts (Pb., 1804).

References: S.A. Vengerov, *Kritiko-biograficheskii slovar',* vol. 4 (Pb., 1895), 57-65. S. Brailovskii, "Semën Sergeevich Bobrov," *Izvestie istoriko-filologicheskogo instituta kniazia Bezborodko v Nezhine,"* vol. 15 (Nezhin, 1895).

BOBRÓV, SERGEI PAVLOVICH (1889-1971). Soviet Russian poet, science fiction writer, translator. A native Muscovite, Bobrov was born on 27 October (8 November) 1889 in the family of a government official. He graduated in 1913 from the Moscow Archaeological Institute and taught statistics and mathematics. Although published first in 1911, Bobrov's first significant book appeared in 1913, *Gardners over the Vines* (Vertogradari nad lozami), the publication of a Neo-Symbolist group called "Lyrika." The book reflects Bobrov's thorough knowledge and love of the poets of Pushkin's era, particularly Baratynskii and Yazykov, and a knowledge of the French Symbolists, particularly Rimbaud.

Like Symbolist Andrei Belyi, Bobrov was primarily interested in the analysis of metrics. In his most important theoretical essay, "On the Lyric Theme" (O liricheskoi teme, 1913), he asserted that rhyme would disappear from Russian verse and be replaced by assonance (which meant all departures from regular rhyme in Bobrov's definition). A poet of considerable skill himself, Bobrov sought for unusual or "proscribed" metrical effects, such as the juxtaposition of lines or entire stanzas written in differing meter.

Bobrov contributed almost a third of the poems in an important anthology of Futurist poems sponsored by Tsentrifuga, *Second Tsentrifuga Anthology* (Vtoroi sbornik Tsentrifugi, 1916). Here he wrote under nine different names (of the 25 "authors" announced as contributors). His next important work was *Diamond Forests* (Almaznye lesa, 1917), which, according to Markov, seemed already dated since it contained earlier poems not representative of Bobrov's style in 1917. Bobrov's only book of verse written in genuine futuristic style was *Lyre of Lyres* (Lira lir, 1917), in which Bobrov used a different style in each poem presumably "to show that Futurism is more than a set of literary devices" (Markov).

Although Bobrov wrote articles on Belyi and Blok and others after the Revolution, he turned to science fiction, producing the *Uprising of the Misanthropes* (Vosstanie mizantropov, 1922), the *Specification of the Iditol* (Spetsifikatsiia Iditola, 1923), and *The Finder of Treasure* (Nashedshii sokrovishche, 1931), under the pseudonym A. Orlov. Bobrov also translated works of Voltaire, Stendhal, Hugo, J. Becher and others. In the later years of his life he wrote books of popularized mathematics for young people—*The Magic Two-Horn* (Volshebnyi dvurog, 1949), and *Archimedes' Summer* (Arkhimedovo leto, 1959), which deal with the origins of higher mathematics. His last work was the novel *A Little Boy* (Mal'chik, 1966). Bobrov died in March 1971.

Works: Liricheskaia tema (M., 1914); *Novoe o stikhoslozhenii A.S. Pushkina* (M., 1915); *N.M. Iazykov o mirovoi literature* (M., 1916); *Almaznye lesa* (M., 1917); *Lira lir* (M., 1917); *Opisanie stikhotvoreniia Pushkina "Vinograd"* (Pg., 1917); *Zapiski stikhotvortsa,* 2 vols. (M., 1916-23); *Indeksy Gosplana* (M., 1925); *Pesn' o Rolande. Vol'noe stikhotvornoe perelozhenie* [Introduction by I. Érenburg] (M.-L., 1943); *Mal'chik* (M., 1966); *Evgenii Delakrua, Zhivopisets* (M., 1971).

References; I. Aksënov, S.P. Bobrov, "Vosstanie Mizantropov," *Pechat' i revoliutsiia,* bk. 6 (1923); B.E. Gusman, *100 poétov. Literaturnye portrety* (Tver, 1923).

BOBÝNS'KYI, VASYL' PETROVYCH (1898-1938). Soviet Ukrainian poet. Bobyns'kyi was born on 11 March 1898 in the village of Kristinopol in the Sokol Uezd in Galicia. The son of a railroad sentry, he studied at the gymnasium in Lvov and in Vienna. From 1923 on he took an active part in the Communist press, edited the weekly publication *Svitlo* (1925-27), for which he was harassed by the Polish government, then in control of the area. From 1927-30 Bobyns'kyi edited the journal *Vikna,* which published proletarian writers and played a significant role in the development of the revolutionary movement in Western Ukraine. Bobyns'kyi's narrative poem "Death of Franko" (Smert' Franka, 1926), which creates the striking figure of a poet-soldier, was written during Bobyns'kyi's five months' imprisonment in Lvov, and received the Ukrainian Soviet State award as one of the best literary works written on the occasion of the tenth anniversary of the October Revolution. In 1930 Bobyns'kyi became a Soviet citizen and settled in Kharkov, where he continued his literary career as a member of the organization "Western Ukraine" (Zakhidna Ukraina) and the Ukrainian Union of Proletarian Writers (VUSPP). The works of this period, such as *Narrative Poems and Pamphlets* (Poemy i pamflety, 1933) treat the theme of capitalist injustice. Bobyns'kyi translated Blok's "Twelve" into Ukrainian and the poems of such West European poets as A. Rimbaud, E. Verhaeren and J. Becher. Bobyns'kyi was illegally arrested and died in prison on 2 January 1938. He has been posthumously rehabilitated.

Works: Poezii (Kharkov, 1930); *Smert' Franka. Poema* (Kharkov, 1931); *Poezii, 1920-1928* (Kharkov, 1930); *Slova v stini. Vybrani poezii* (Kharkov-Kiev, 1932); *Revoliutsiini poety Zakhidnoi Ukrainy* (Kiev, 1958); *Vybrani tvory* (Kiev, 1960).

BODIANSKII, OSIP MAKSIMOVICH, see BODIANSKYI, OSYP MAKSYMO-VYCH

BODIÁNS'KYI, OSYP MAKSYMOVYCH (1808-1877). Ukrainian philologist and Slavist, historian and writer. Bodians'kyi was born on 31 October (12 November) 1808 in Varva, in the Lokhvitsa uezd, Poltava Province, the son of a Ukrainian priest. He graduated from Moscow University in 1834. In 1835, under the pseudonym Zaporozhets Is'ko Materynka, he published a poetic rendering of Ukrainian fairy tales, *Our Ukrainian Tales* (Nas'ki ukrains'ki kazky). In 1834 he published a review of the novelettes of H. Kvitka-Osnov'ianenko (under the pseudonym Mastak). He was a friend of N.V. Gogol, T.G. Shevchenko and M.A.

Maksymovych. In 1837-42 Bodians'kyi travelled through the Slavic countries, and from 1842 to 1868 was a professor of Slavic literatures at Moscow University. In 1848 he was reprimanded for attempting to publish a translation of a book written by the English diplomat Giles Fletcher, *Of the Russe Common Wealth* (1591). Because Bodians'kyi was a proponent of university autonomy and supported the Charter of 1863, he aroused the suspicions of the conservative professors, and their intrigues forced him to retire in 1868. Bodians'kyi was a member of the liberal wing of the Slavophiles.

Bodians'kyi's interests and scholarly studies were typical of East Slavic Romanticism and are reflected in his works: *On the Folk Poetry of the Slavic Tribes* (O narodnoi poezii slavianskikh plemën, 1837), *On the Time of the Origin of the Slavic Alphabet* (O vremeni proiskhozhdeniia slavianskikh pis'men, 1855). Bodians'kyi helped to strengthen the ties between the Russian and Ukrainian intelligentsia and the Western Slavs. He translated from the Czech the works of P.J. Šafařik, *Slavic Antiquities* (Slavianskie drevnosti, 1837-48) and *Description of Slavic Peoples* (Slavianskoe narodopisanie, 1843). In 1845-48 and 1858-77 Bodians'kyi was editor of *Chteniia Moskovskogo obshchestva istorii i drevnostei rossiiskikh* where many valuable ancient works were published, among them materials about the activities of Cyril and Methodius, the *Life of Boris and Gleb* according to the twelfth-century text, *Grammatical Study of the Russian Language* (Grammaticheskoe issledovanie russkogo iazyka) by Yurii Krizhanich, and I.V. Kireevskii's *Collection of Great Russian Songs*. Bodians'kyi died in Moscow on 6 (18) September 1877.

Works: Besides the principal works listed above are: *Lingvistika O.M. Senkovskogo* (M., 1848); *Letters:* I. *Pis'ma O.M. Bodianskogo k ottsu*, II. *Pis'ma I.P. Sakharova k O.M. Bodianskomu* (M., 1893).

References: I.I. Sreznevskii, *Na pamiat' o Bodianskom, Grigoroviche i Preise, pervykh prepodavateliakh slavianskoi filologii* (Pb., 1878); V.I. Picheta, "K istorii slavianovedeniia v S.S.S.R.," *Istorik-marksist*, No. 3 (1941); N.A. Kondrashov, *Osip Maksimovich Bodianskii* (M., 1956) [contains bibliography].

BODNÁRSKII, BOGDAN STEPANOVICH (1874-1968). Soviet Russian bibliographer, Honored Scholar of the RSFSR (1945). Bodnarskii was born on 23 June (5 July) 1874 in Radzivilov, Volyn' Province. He was Professor of the Moscow Library Institute, for six years the editor of the *Bibliograficheskie izvestiia* and from 1920 to 1930 chairman of the Russian Bibliographical Society of Moscow University. Bodnarskii was the director (1920-21) of the Russian Central (now All-Union) Book Chamber. First published in 1906, Bodnarskii was an early proponent of the decimal system of bibliografical classification. His principal work is *The Bibliography of Russian Bibliography* (Bibliografiia russkoi bibliografii). It contains a description of Russian bibliographical literature from 1903 to 1925, and for 1929. Bodnarskii died on February 24, 1968, in Moscow.

Works: Bibliograficheskii ukazatel' literatury po voprosam tekushchego momenta, c marta 1917 g. (M., 1917); *Klassifikatsiia kooperativnoi literatury po mezhdunarodnoi desiatichnoi sisteme* (M., 1922); *Bibliografiia russkoi bibliografii*, 3 vols. (M., 1918-26).

References: *Ukazatel' bibliograficheskikh trudov Bodnarskogo* (M., 1944); P.N. Berkov, "B.S. Bodnarskii kak uchĕnyi i obshchestvennyi deiatel'," *Sovetskaia bibliografiia,* vol. 46 (1957); Iu.I. Masanova, ed., *Zasluzhennyi deiatel' nauki Bogdan Stepanovich Bodnarskii* (M., 1963).

BOGATYRĔV, PĔTR GRIGOR'EVICH (1893-1971). Soviet Russian folklorist, ethnographer, literary scholar. A native of Saratov, Bogatyrĕv was born on 16 (28) January 1893. In 1918 he graduated from Moscow University with a degree in history and philology. From 1921 until 1940 he lived in Czechoslovakia, conducting ethnographic and folkloric field studies. During his student years, Bogatyrĕv was one of the co-founders of the Moscow Linguistic Circle and an adherent of the Formalist approach to literature. As early as 1920 he proposed a rigorous typology of narrative plots used in folklore, offering a model for such an approach to folk anecdotes (fabliaux) but never published it. Bogatyrĕv insisted on the relevance of the linguistic model for cultural anthropology and in particular for the science of folklore, and from the beginning of the 1930s urged a structural study of the functional transformation of ethnographic phenomena. In fact, it is Bogatyrĕv's analysis of the principle of functional hierarchy, that is, the distinction between dominant and secondary functions, which is the most significant aspect of his research (Jakobson).

Bogatyrĕv's lifelong quest was to examine and determine the nature of the "folkloric act." His focus was, consequently, rural life, which constituted for Bogatyrĕv a world of semiotic values, the central figure of which was the rustic "man-sign." He investigated such folk phenomena as peasant etiquette, folk costumes, folk theater, and the relationship between "high art" and its folkloric sources.

In an early study—"Pushkin's Poem 'The Hussar,' Its Sources and Its Influence on Folk Poetry" (1923)—Bogatyrĕv pointed out the fact that Pushkin recreated a folkloric figure in his Hussar, which then reentered folk tales and plays, newly transformed. Bogatyrĕv consistently distinguished between mere borrowing of folklore material and its creative transformation. His examples of talented individuals who have been able to transform folklore into great art are, among others, Musorgskii and Stravinskii in music, and Meierkhol'd in the theater. He concluded that "in folk art, tradition and improvisation form a dialectical unity."

Bogatyrĕv investigated the "man-sign" as it is applied to folklore in its two specific domains, theatrical acts proper in the folk theater, with their predominance of the aesthetic function, and magic acts in religious ritual, particularly as labeled and discussed in his *Actes magiques: rites et croyances en Russie Subcarpathique* (1929). His thesis was that the aesthetic and magical functions of one and the same folkloric act may be diametrically opposed, both in the folk theater and in religious ritual.

For Bogatyrĕv the folk theater was the most syncretic of the art forms and held the greatest number of possible meanings. In one of his last studies, he analyzed the tendency in the theater to give human actors the functions of puppets, or puppets the functions of human actors; and explored the question of the intermediate position which puppets occupy between theatrical and figurative art, and the relationship between puppet and puppeteer or puppet and accordianist.

After 1958 Bogatyrĕv worked as a senior research associate at the Moscow Institute of World Literature, and at Moscow University after 1964. Although a forerunner of semiotic studies, he is still largely unknown in his own homeland and in the West, where little of his stimulating and valuable work is available in translation. Bogatyrĕv died in Moscow on 18 August 1971.

Works: Cheshskii kukol'nyi i russkii narodnyi teatr (Berlin-Pg., 1923); "Stikhotvorenie Pushkina 'Gusar,' ego istochniki i ego vliianie na narodnuiu slovesnost'," *Ocherki po poetike Pushkina* (Berlin, 1923), 147-95; "K probleme razmezhevaniia fol'kloristiki i literaturovedeniia" [with R. Jakobson], *Lud Słowiański* II (Krakow, 1931), 229-33; *Funkcie kroja na Moravskom Slovensku* (Turč. sv. Martin, 1937); *Lidové divadlo české a slovenské* (Prague, 1940); *Voprosy teorii narodnogo iskusstva* (M., 1971) [contains eleven of Bogatyrĕv's papers and his own introduction]; *Souvislosti tvorby* (Prague, 1971); "O vzaimosviazi dvukh blizkikh semioticheskikh sistem," *Semeiotike. Trudy po znakovym sistemem,* VI (Tartu State University, 1973), 306-29. In English translation: "On the Boundary Between Studies of Folklore and Literature" [with R. Jakobson], *Readings in Russian Poetics: Formalist and Structuralist Views* (Cambridge, Mass., 1971), 91-93; *The Functions of Folk Costume in Moravian Slovakia* (The Hague-Paris, 1971); *Semiotics of Art* (MIT Press, 1976) [contains four of Bogatyrĕv's papers published in Prague from 1936-1940].

References: Roman Jakobson, "Pĕtr Bogatyrĕv (29.I.93-19.VIII.71): Expert in Transfiguration," *Sound, Sign and Meaning,* Michigan Slavic Contributions, No. 6 (Ann Arbor, 1976), 29-39.

BOGATYRÍ. The *bogatyri* (sg. *bogatyr'*) are the valiant and bold heroes of the oral epic poetry of old Russia, the *byliny.* Among the most popular of these heroes are Sviatogor, Mikula Selianinovich (the villager's son), Volkh Vseslav'-evich (son of Vseslav), Il'ia Muromets (of Murom), Dobrynia Nikitich (son of Nikita), Alĕsha Popovich (the priest's son), Diuk Stepanovich (son of Stepan), Churilo Plenkovich (son of Plenko), Mikhailo Potyk, and Dunai Ivanovich (son of Ivan).

It is customary to group Russian oral epic poetry into cycles which relate to specific periods of history (pre-Kievan and Kievan times, for example) or to particular localities (Kiev, Novgorod, and so forth). The cycle which is generally considered the earliest, the pre-Kievan cycle, includes the heroes Volkh Vseslav'-evich, Mikula Selianinovich, and Sviatogor, who are frequently referred to as the "Older Heroes," that is, heroes endowed with qualities which many scholars consider to be symbolic representations of the elemental powers of nature. The "Younger Heroes" are those of the Kievan cycle, heroes associated in one capacity or another with the Kievan court of Prince Vladimir. It is here that they assemble and feast, and from here that they journey forth to test their skills, to perform difficult tasks, to hunt, to slay dragons, to defend the Russian land against foreign invaders like the Tatars, the Polovtsy and Pechenegs, to collect or deliver tribute, to seek a bride, and so forth. Heroes of the Novgorod cycle (for example Sadko, Vasilii Buslaev) are not usually designated as *bogatyri.*

Over the years the names of historical personages have attached themselves to some of the heroes, just as historical place names and actual events in history have occasionally become attached to the thematic material of the *byliny*. In actual fact, however, the material that comprises the *byliny* is at most only tenuously related to historical fact.

The deeds of the *bogatyri* are narrow in scope. They consist primarily of deeds of valor, or the stuff of medieval romance—love, intrigue, infidelity. And some of these exploits are in the realm of magic. Certain of the *bogatyri* are distinguished by particular kinds of physical strength, some by wisdom, some by shrewdness, some by an excessively handsome physical appearance, some by wealth. But their exploits and adventures on the whole very frequently are indistinguishable one from another. Likewise, there may be subtle stylistic differences between the *byliny* of one oral bard and those of another, and there may also be differences in style between the *byliny* of one geographical area and another, or between one country and another, but stylistic distinctions between the *byliny* about one hero and the *byliny* about another simply do not exist. This is a feature of all oral traditional literature. It is even difficult at times to distinguish one hero from another on a descriptive level. Take, for example, physical appearance and clothing. Mikula Selianinovich is usually described as having long and curly hair, eyes as bright as those of a falcon, sable brows, a brocaded robe, shoes made of morocco leather with high heels and pointed toes. But this description fits a number of other young heroes—Dobrynia Nikitich, Alēsha Popovich, and at times even Prince Vladimir. The same is true regarding weapons, the most typical of which is a "taut bow with a bow string of silk and a tempered arrow."

One of the more popular of the "older" heroes is Sviatogor, who is gigantic in stature, endowed with superhuman and supernatural strength, and of such weight that the earth can scarcely support him. In spite of all this, however, he is faced with frequent frustration, and even a non-heroic death. One *bylina* about Sviatogor cites a particular occasion when his extraordinary strength proves insufficient: Sviatogor is unable to lift a sack belonging to a traveler whom he meets along the road. In actual fact, this sack contains the "weight of the whole world." A second incident concerns Sviatogor's death, which comes to him in a coffin or stone tomb. Once while traveling with Il'ia Muromets, these two heroes come upon a coffin or tomb, which Il'ia is the first to try for size. Since it does not fit Il'ia, Sviatogor himself repeats this action. The coffin does, indeed, fit Sviatogor, but once it is closed, neither Sviatogor nor anyone else is able to open it again. Sviatogor's great strength again fails him, and this time the results are fatal. Before dying, however, Sviatogor manages to breathe some of his strength into Il'ia, and he leaves behind for Il'ia his sword as well.

Mikula Selianinovich, another of the "older" heroes, is noted for his feats as a plowman as well as for his incredible strength. Unlike Sviatogor, however, Mikula's strength does not fail him. On one occasion Mikula is heard plowing in the fields by Volkh Vseslav'evich. So fast did Mikula plow that it took Volkh and his attendants several days on horseback to overtake Mikula. Volkh is so impressed with the plowman that he invites Mikula to accompany him on his journey. Mikula accepts the invitation, but before journeying forth asks that his plow be thrown behind a bush so that others might use it. Not even the combined strength of all of Volkh's attendants, however, is sufficient to move the plow, so

Mikula must perform this task himself, which he does with only one hand. Even Mikula's mare has strength comparable to that of her master.

Many interesting and fantastic details are associated with the "older" hero Volkh Vseslav'evich. An independent *bylina* about him presents him as a precocious youth who could already read and write by the time he was five years old. As a youth he excelled in supernatural wisdom, and as a mature hero he had the unique ability to change shape—to become animal, fish or bird at will. Volkh is a wizard *bogatyr'*, hunter, messenger, eminently successful warrior, and conqueror of divers foreign invaders.

Il'ia Muromets, frequently referred to as the "Old Cossack" or the "peasant's son," is one of the more popular of those *bogatyri* known as the "Younger Heroes," and probably the most idealized of them all. He is constantly engaged in a struggle against the enemies of Russia, who present themselves as monsters as well as human enemies. During his early life Il'ia is described as being feeble or even paralyzed, but in an encounter with Christ and some of his apostles who come to Il'ia in disguise, he is given the strength of a warrior, a prophecy that he will not die in battle, and the knowledge that he is stronger than most other heroes. Shortly thereafter Il'ia acquires two other hallmarks of a true hero of epic poetry, namely a heroic steed and a battle sword, that of the great Sviatogor. One of Il'ia's adventures, his first significant heroic act, which also proves him worthy of Prince Vladimir's trust, ends with the death of the monstrous bird-like Solovei Razboinik (Nightingale the Robber). Il'ia is also famous for his victory over the Tatar Idolishche (monster Idol) as well as the Tatar Tsar Kalin. Il'ia, however, is not always a loyal and devoted servant; he can display a fiery temper that even Prince Vladimir has difficulty assuaging. For example, on one occasion Vladimir fails to recognize Il'ia, who has come to his court in disguise. As a result Vladimir offends Il'ia by failing to offer him a place of honor at the feast table. Before Vladimir can bring Il'ia's wrath under control the Old Cossack manages to give a thorough beating to a number of Vladimir's warriors and to deface many of the churches of Kiev as well before a reconciliation takes place.

Dobrynia Nikitich, who is sometimes represented as Prince Vladimir's nephew, is another of the popular "younger" *byliny* heroes. Youthful, loyal and courteous, he is portrayed as having the ability of a diplomat and the courage and skills of the most distinguished of heroes when face to face with dragons or human enemies. And yet even his strength fails him on one occasion when, on his way back to Kiev, he encounters an Amazon who is able to overcome him and extract from him a marriage vow. Many *byliny* are sung about how Dobrynia slew a dragon. In these narratives Dobrynia is depicted as a young, untried hero who leaves home against his mother's wishes. He returns home, however, a mature hero who has encountered and overcome his first dragon and lived to tell the tale. In certain versions of this tale, Dobrynia is also called upon to rescue from the dragon's clutches Prince Vladimir's niece as well as Russian warriors whom the dragon has been holding captive for many years. Another equally popular *bylina* about Dobrynia presents him as a kind of Russian Odysseus. Dobrynia goes off to foreign lands on a lengthy and dangerous mission for Prince Vladimir, leaving behind a young wife. Before his departure, however, Dobrynia informs his wife that if he fails to return home after a certain number of years she should remarry, but he excludes his sworn brother Alĕsha Popovich from among those suitable to be her husband in the event of his death. After a number of years Alĕsha spreads word that Dobrynia is dead and even convinces Dobrynia's wife to marry him. But Dobrynia fortuitously receives news of what is about to take place, returns to Kiev in disguise, gains entry to Vladimir's court where the marriage ceremony is about to be performed and prevents the marriage. Dobrynia abuses Alĕsha verbally in some versions, while in others he punishes him physically as well.

Alĕsha Popovich, frequently referred to as bold Alĕsha, is the primary hero of few independent *bylina* plots, although he is a participant in many. One of these is about his encounter with a gluttonous, coarse dragon Tugarin. When Alĕsha fearlessly challenges the fierce, fire-breathing Tugarin, the dragon soars skyward on paper wings. Fortunately for Alĕsha, God sends rain which soaks Tugarin's wings and renders them useless. Tugarin falls to earth and Alĕsha strikes the death-dealing blow. Alĕsha is best known, however, as the sworn brother of brother of Dobrynia, the dragon slayer par-excellence of Russian oral epic poetry.

Another favorite hero of the Kievan cycle is Diuk Stepanovich, a wealthy and foppish young man from a far-off land, who on one occasion visits Prince Vladimir's court to find out for himself whether stories that he has heard of the opulence and splendor of Kiev are true. The journey to Kiev is an arduous one with many obstacles to be overcome along the way. Upon his arrival, Diuk finds conditions in Kiev inferior in all respects to those in his homeland. But Diuk is young and boastful, and he acts in such a superior and offensive manner that he is challenged by Vladimir's steward, Churilo. The first challenge concerns which of these two young heroes has the most expensive and elegant clothing. In variants sung by many oral epic bards, the description of Diuk's clothing is remarkable. In actual fact, this is one of the few instances in which the clothing of one *bogatyr'* is described in such detail that it can be distinguished from that of another *bogatyr'.* Still wishing for one more opportunity to bring Diuk's arrogance under control, Churilo challenges him to a second and final contest to see which of them can jump across the Dnepr River on horseback. Churilo loses by dramatically landing in the middle of the river. Diuk's steed, on the other hand, is able to jump across the Dnepr with ease. Diuk returns to his native land convinced that Kiev can in no way compare with the affluence and the magnificence of his homeland. Diuk is also represented as a dragon slayer in a few *byliny*.

One of the most strikingly unconventional figures connected with Vladimir's court is Churilo Plenkovich, presumably the same Churilo who challenged Diuk and who, like Diuk, is not a native of Kiev. Young Churilo, an elegantly dressed dandy who is endowed with considerable wealth and good manners, on one occasion plunders Vladimir's property. Vladimir, however, is so impressed with Churilo's unrestrained audacity that he invites Churilo to serve as his steward at court. But so distracted are the young maidens and nuns of Kiev by such a handsome youth that Vladimir is soon forced to curtail Churilo's services and send him home to old Plenko, his father.

One of the most interesting of the *byliny* concerning the *bogatyr'* Mikhailo Potyk, a popular "younger" hero of the Kievan cycle, begins with a journey to

Poland to collect tribute for Prince Vladimir. Along the way, while amusing himself by hunting geese and swans, he catches sight of a white swan, who begs him to spare her life, saying that she is Mar'ia, daughter of the King of Poland, and that she would be willing to become his bride and convert to Orthodoxy if Mikhailo would only spare her life. Thus, Mikhailo returns to Kiev with both tribute and a bride. During the betrothal ceremony Mikhailo and Mar'ia take a death vow, swearing that the one who dies first will be accompanied by the surviving member of the union into the tomb for three months. Soon thereafter Tsar Bukhar from beyond the sea comes to collect tribute from Prince Vladimir. Mikhailo is the one chosen to deliver the tribute and so he leaves Kiev to carry out his task. Upon meeting the Tsar, Mikhailo challenges him to a chess match. Tsar Bukhar accepts the challenge and stakes the tribute which Prince Vladimir owes him. Mikhailo stakes his wife Mar'ia, the white swan. Mikhailo wins the match, but in the meantime his wife dies. True to the bargain, Mikhailo returns to Kiev to accompany his wife to the grave for the three months agreed upon, which in actual fact is a ruse on Mar'ia's part that eventually leads to Mikhailo's death. Mikhailo, however, cleverly subdues a snake in the tomb and orders it to bring the "water of life" to revive the white swan, Mar'ia. Mar'ia is revived, both are rescued from the tomb, but Mar'ia is then abducted by the Prince of Lithuania. Mikhailo goes off in pursuit, disguised as a woman, but Mar'ia recognizes him, offers him a glass of wine, and turns him to stone. After many years a passer-by brings Mikhailo back to life and Mikhailo again goes off in disguise to Poland in search of Mar'ia. Again a glass of wine leads to Mikhailo's undoing. This time Mar'ia takes him to her cellar and nails him to the wall, but before the final spike is driven through his heart, Nastas'ia, the King of Poland's other daughter, takes mercy on Mikhailo, puts a Tatar in his place, and so it is the Tatar who dies instead of Mikhailo. The story ends on a happy note when Mikhailo takes Nastas'ia, who is also willing to convert to Orthodoxy, back to Kiev with him to be his bride.

Byliny about Dunai Ivanovich tell a unique tale of the suicide of a *bogatyr'*. Dunai, to whom the epithet "quiet" is frequently attached, is servant for several years to a foreign king, usually represented as King of Lithuania. The king has a younger daughter Evpraksiia and an older daughter Nastas'ia, a kind of Amazon who is in love with Dunai. Once, after excessively boasting in public of Nastas'ia's beauty, Dunai is forced to leave the service of his king. Dunai chooses to go to Kiev, where he eventually is invited to the court of Prince Vladimir. Time passes and Dunai begins to assume a more and more important role at Vladimir's court. This role reaches its culmination when Vladimir sends Dunai to serve as matchmaker for him, Prince Vladimir, and the Princess Evpraksiia, the Lithuanian king's younger daughter. Dunai performs his task successfully and sends Evpraksiia to Kiev accompanied by Dobrynia. Dunai, however, stays behind to engage a Tatar in combat, only to find out that the Tatar is none other than Nastas'ia. Dunai asks for her hand in marriage and she immediately accepts. Time passes. Again Dunai boasts, this time in the presence of Nastas'ia. But now his boasting has far graver consequences than before. It results in Dunai's piercing Nastas'ia's heart with an arrow. Before Nastas'ia dies, however, she reveals to Dunai that she is carrying his child, at which point Dunai commits suicide.

The *bogatyri* have provided Russian poets, composers and artists of the nineteenth and twentieth centuries with considerable inspiration, in particular the poems of M.Yu. Lermontov, L.A. Mei, A.N. Radishchev and A.K. Tolstoi; in the musical compositions of A.P. Borodin and N.A. Rimskii-Korsakov; and in the paintings of V.N. Vasnetsov and I.E. Repin. See also BYLINY, FOLKLORE.

Collections: Pesni, sobrannye P.N. Rybnikovym, 3 vols. (M., 1909-1910); A.M. Astakhova, *Byliny Severa,* 2 vols. (M.-L., 1938-1951); *Onezhskie byliny, zapisannye A.F. Gil'ferdingom letom 1871 goda,* 3 vols. (M.-L., 1949-1951); *Drevnie rossiiskie stikhotvoreniia, sobrannye Kirsheiu Danilovym,* eds. B.N. Putilov and A.P. Evgen'eva (M.-L., 1958); *Byliny,* eds. V.Ia. Propp and B.N. Putilov, 2 vols. (M., 1958). In English: I.F. Hapgood, *The Epic Songs of Russia* (N.Y., 1866; reprint, Westport, Conn., 1970); N.K. Chadwick, *Russian Heroic Poetry* (New York, 1964).

References: O.F. Miller, *Il'ia Muromets i bogatyrstvo kievskoe* (Pb., 1869); A. Rambaud, *La Russie épique: Étude sur les chansons héroiques de la Russie* (Paris, 1876); R. Trautman, *Die Volksdichtung der Grossrussen: Das Heldenlied,* vol. I (Heidelberg, 1935); H.M. and N.K. Chadwick, "Russian Oral Literature," *The Growth of Literature,* vol. II (Cambridge, 1936); V.Ia. Propp, *Russkii geroicheskii epos* (L., 1958).

Patricia Arant

BOGDÁNOV [pseudonym of MALINOVSKII], **ALEKSANDR ALEKSANDRO-VICH** (1873-1928). Physician, economist, politician, sociologist, philosopher, psychologist, belletrist, and critic. Little known today either within or without the Soviet Union, Bogdanov, at the time of the October Revolution, was acknowledged as one of the most learned, original, and daring men of the revolutionary intelligentsia. For three decades (1900-1930), Bogdanov's ideas were an enormously potent force in shaping the outlook of the radical intelligentsia and of the most educated workers in Russia; and for three years (1917-1920), he was the spirit behind the Proletkult.

Bogdanov was born with the surname Malinovskii on 10 (22) August 1873 in Sokolka, Grodno Province, the son of a teacher who later became a Tula school inspector. In 1891 he enrolled at the University of Moscow as a student of natural sciences. Like many of his generation, he was soon caught up in the Populist movement "to the people," and joined the radical group "the People's Will." In 1914 Bogdanov was arrested for circulating an illegal petition for revising university statutes and sent home to Tula where he was enlisted into revolutionary circles as a propagandist. About this time, at the age of twenty-two, he assumed the name Bogdanov, or "God-gifted," which conveys the image of the high calling he apparently felt was his. He became a Social Democrat in 1896. From the lectures he read in Social Democratic circles, he published *A Short Course in Economic Science* (Kratkii kurs ékonomicheskoi nauki) in 1897. Although "mutilated" by the censor, it was warmly greeted by Lenin.

In 1895 Bogdanov had begun spending part of his time in Kharkov at the school of medicine. He wrote his first philosophical book, *Basic Elements of a Historical View of Nature* (Osnovnye elementy istoricheskogo vzgliada na prirodu) in 1898.

In the fall of 1899 Bogdanov was awarded his medical degree and was promptly arrested for propaganda. He was exiled first to Kaluga and then to Vologda where he found himself among such fellow exiles as N.A. Berdiaev and A.V. Lunacharskii. These young intellectuals plunged into intense philosophical discussions which lasted several years. As a result of the Vologda discussions, Bogdanov made in his work *Empiriomonism* (1903) what has been called "the boldest and most comprehensive attempt ever made by anyone considering himself a Marxist to reconcile Marxism with modern thought." During this same period of exile, Bogdanov found time to pursue his interest in medicine while working in a psychiatric hospital.

When Bogdanov's exile was terminated in 1903, he and his friends journeyed to Switzerland to rally to Lenin's standard. From 1905 to 1909, Bogdanov served on the editorial boards of the Bolshevik press organs *Proletarii* (The Proletarian), *Vperëd* (Forward), and *Novaia zhizn'* (The New Life).

At the London Congress of the Russian Socialist Party in 1907 Lenin and Bogdanov clashed over boycotting the Duma. All cooperation between the two came to an abrupt end in June 1909, when Lenin publicly attacked Bogdanov's views in a polemic entitled *Materialism and Empiriocriticism: Critical Remarks About a Certain Reactionary Philosophy*. As a result of this attack, both Bogdanov and Lunacharskii were expelled from the Bolshevik faction.

Bogdanov and Lunacharskii then set out for the Island of Capri, where their friend Maksim Gor'kii was living. Political reaction had forced them to admit that the Russian Revolution of 1905, for which they had had such high hopes, had been a failure. They attributed this failure to the cultural unpreparedness of the proletariat. The task which they set for themselves in 1909 was to hasten its cultural development. For this purpose, they decided to open a school for Russian workers on Capri.

From the beginning the school did not limit itself, as Lenin would have liked, to politics and economics, but dealt with philosophy, natural sciences, the history of art, the theory of proletarian culture, proletarian "ideological organization," the history of the Russian State and Church, problems in revolutionary ethics, and "leftist tactics." Lenin made a bitter attack on the leaders of the school and invited the pupils to move to Paris. Some of them were won over and the school of Capri was permanently disrupted.

In 1910 the irrepressible Bogdanov, Lunacharskii, and Gor'kii, together with the historian M.N. Pokrovskii, imported a second group of Russian workers and opened the second Party school in Bologna. Among the lecturers who joined the Capri group were Lev Trotskii and Aleksandra Kollontai.

In July 1910 Bogdanov made a brief defense of himself against Lenin's attack entitled *Faith and Science* (Vera i nauka). Six months later Bogdanov quit the faculty of the school because of his dissatisfaction with a shift in the group's interest from cultural work to "emigre political squabbles."

With the outbreak of war in 1914 Bogdanov returned to Russia and was sent to Eastern Prussia as a military surgeon. During the revolutionary period 1917-1920, he was engaged in a swirl of activities. With Lunacharskii, Pokrovskii, and others, he founded in Moscow the Socialist Academy, later called the Communist

Academy. At the same time he lectured at the Proletarian University. He also served as a member of a commission to translate and publish the works of Marx and Engels. His principal activity during this period, however, was in the Proletkult, an organization founded on the eve of the October Revolution with the blessing of the Petrograd Soviet. After the Revolution, the Proletkult equipped Bogdanov with the means to disseminate his ideas of proletarian culture far and near. Although Bogdanov enjoyed in the Proletkult a position of enormous influence, he preferred to remain aloof from Party affairs.

Lenin did not at all share the notion, espoused by Bogdanov and his followers, of three independent paths to proletarian hegemony: the political, belonging to the Party; the economic, belonging to the trade unions; and the cultural, belonging to the Proletkult. In 1920 Lenin moved to discredit totally his old opponent for the ultimate purpose of putting the Proletkult under governmental and Party control.

Bogdanov abruptly quit his cultural activity. After 1920 he devoted himself to scientific research at the Socialist Academy and to teaching political economics. As ever, his consuming interest was to improve human organization. For this purpose the Soviet Government endowed him with the world's first research institute for the study of blood transfusion. The institute engaged in research, offered mini-courses to physicians, published scholarly and popular works, and prepared and distributed the necessary materials and equipment for the transfusion of blood. At Bogdanov's direction, blood banks were established throughout the Soviet Union. In 1927 he published a book entitled *The Fight for Life Capacity* (Bor'ba za zhiznesposobnost') to encourage donors.

In spring of 1928 Bogdanov fell ill as a result of an experiment he had performed on himself. He had exchanged his blood with that of a student hopelessly ill with malaria and tuberculosis. He refused all efforts to intervene medically, but kept exact records on his own condition until his death on 7 April 1928. A week later the institute was renamed in his honor, although it is now known as The Central Order of Lenin Institute for Hematology and Blood Transfusions. For a while Bogdanov's ashes were kept at the institute, but they were later transferred to the cemetery of the Novodevichii Monastery.

Bogdanov held a very high opinion of Karl Marx's role as a philosopher. Yet his great esteem for Marx did not deter him from differing with Marx whenever he felt difference warranted. The discovery of radioactivity upset the Newtonian concept of the atom as the utmost limit of the divisibility of matter, a concept to which Marx had subscribed. In the confusion surrounding this discovery, Bogdanov set out to find for Marxism a viable epistemology. Proceeding from the views of Ernst Mach and Richard Avenarius, he advanced what he called "empiriomonism," according to which physical and mental phenomena are differently organized elements in one and the same experience. The mental consists of individually organized experience, the physical of socially organized experience. Truth is whatever is "socially accepted within a given period." Truth is "a mechanism by the aid of which reality is cut up, trimmed, and tacked together." The aim of knowledge, consequently, is not to apprehend the real, but to construct a picture out of the elements of our experience.

Bogdanov's second major construction is called "tectology." Tectology shows the correlation of the different elements in nature, in society, and in the working of the human mind, and identifies the laws which are common to them all. As Western and Soviet scholars are beginning to point out, Bogdanov's tectological ideas anticipated the modern science of cybernetics and the study of systems.

In his sociology Bogdanov tried to bring Marx's theory of economics into a synthesis with the Darwinian theory of adaptation, from which angle Bogdanov's study of society was made. He insisted that the economic approach to the study of social evolution is essentially psychological, since economics presupposes the use of technology and the ability to handle tools. Ideological changes must follow and never precede technological changes.

History is a process primarily motivated by the struggle against nature. Technological and scientific advancement, along with various organizing adjustments, facilitate and insure further progress. Social retrogression may be attributed to the failure of one or another ideological form.

Bogdanov distinguished three main stages in the historical development of society. Each stage has an integrated system of economy, ideological forms, and types of thought. The first is the stage of authoritarian institutions, and religion as an authoritarian form of thought. The second, individualistic stage has an exchange economy, individualistic norms of behavior, and supports a variety of philosophic schools. Branches of science and learning multiply. At this stage individual personality, whose emergence marks the transition from authoritarian society, acquires considerable autonomy. At first this autonomy contributes to progress, but later as the strife of individual interests contradicts the unifying tendencies of the machine age, it becomes an obstacle. The victory of these tendencies will inaugurate the third main stage of history—the stage of collective self-sufficient economy and "the fusion of personal lives into one colossal whole." It groups systematically all elements for one common struggle "against the endless spontaneity of nature."

The transition to the collective society involves the problem of revolution. There is only one case when differences between elements of a social whole turn into an insolvable contradiction. This is when groups of society develop in opposite directions: one progressing toward expanding the struggle against nature and perfecting means of production, the other retrogressing toward parasitism and consuming the products of the labor of others. In such a case a revolution occurs and the progressive class takes over the direction of society, provided it has developed the necessary organizational abilities, as in the case of the bourgeoisie in the French Revolution. If the progressive class does not possess the necessary organizational abilities, the revolution will lead to retrogression and a general decline of society similar to that which marked the transition from antiquity to the Middle Ages.

On 7 November (25 October) 1917 the Bolsheviks seized power. In Bogdanov's mind, Russia was woefully unprepared for revolution. The special, proletarian culture which, according to his theory, was essential for liberating the working class, could at best be called "emerging." Aside from a few radical intellectuals, hardly anyone was aware that such a phenomenon existed. Bogdanov perceived that the political and economic achievements of the proletariat were about to be wiped out. Unless the proletariat could quickly take possession of the cultural aspect of the total struggle, a repetition of the Revolution of 1905 was inevitable.

In a mammoth surge of enthusiasm, the Bogdanov-inspired organization Proletkult took upon itself the development of proletarian culture—"the organizing of its experience as a class." It left the economic and political struggles of the new order to the trade unions and the Bolshevik Party, respectively. The Proletkult alone would be free of the "bourgeois" elements inevitable in the other two bodies; it would jealously guard its right to organize the human soul in a purely proletarian way. Only a few of the many thousands who joined the ranks of the Proletkult in the ensuing months had a clear idea of what they were doing. Bogdanov, however, had a master plan. Like the authoritarian and individualistic stages of social development which had preceded it, the new collectivistic stage would organize all experience in a way peculiar to it. Like the former stages, the new stage would organize culture in three spheres: morals, science, and art.

Confident that the factory would determine moral consciousness, Bogdanov at first refrained from setting up particular "commandments." The preceding culture had made a "fetish" out of a fixed moral code; proletarian culture would escape this. Later he issued ten new moral commandments which were apparently not self-evident from the new environment: (1) No herd-consciousness; (2) No slavery; (3) No subjectivism, neither personal nor group; (4) No "Hottentotery" (It is good if I steal; it is evil if someone steals from me.); (5) [Does not appear in text] ; (6) No idleness; (7) The goal must not be sullied; (8) Master everything: the most important goal; (9) Understand everything: the new conscience's highest ideal; (10) Pride in the collective is the mainspring of the worker's will and thought.

Bogdanov charged proletarian science with evolving concrete and practical methods of gradually eliminating the distinction between intellectual and physical labor, of bridging the gap between organizers and executors, of developing a spirit of comradeship, collectivism, and cooperation.

In 1918 Bogdanov set forth his idea of proletarian art in a small book entitled *Art and the Working Class* (Iskusstvo i rabochii klass). Although this work concerns mainly poetry, it is easy to deduce principles applicable to literature and to art in general. "Art is the organization of living images." Both the notion of "pure art" (that art should be a goal in itself) and "civic art" (that art should further progressive tendencies) must be rejected. Art organizes life completely independently of whether one assigns it civic tasks or not.

The class character of literature is not determined by the defense of one class or another; it is determined by the author's taking the point of view of a certain class. He looks at the world, thinks, and feels exactly as his class does, although he may not even suspect it. Long before anyone had heard of Marxism in Russia, people referred to Afanasii Fet's lyrics as "nobleman's poetry," because they engendered the moods, settings, forms of life and thoughts of a definite social stratum.

In a class society art can only be class art, but this does not mean that at a given moment art must belong to a single class. For example, the poetry of

Nikolai Nekrasov is a brilliant expression of the strivings and the developing thoughts and feelings of the peasantry; yet this poetry bears the marks of the urban intelligentsia to which Nekrasov belonged professionally and of the landowner's class from which he came. The proletariat does not need mixed class poetry, it needs purely proletarian poetry. This poetry is determined by the basic conditions of the working class: its position in production, its type of organization, and its historic destiny. The proletariat is "a laboring, exploited, fighting, and developing class," but it is characterized above all by "a comradely form of cooperation." One must distinguish between proletarian poetry and the poetry of proletarian soldiers. The latter's regrettable "sadistic ecstasies" on the theme of squeezing out the entrails of the bourgeois have nothing in common with the ideology of the workers' class. The proletariat is characterized indeed by militant motifs, by unrelenting hostility to capital as a social force, but not by petty spite against its individual representatives, the inevitable products of their environment.

Proletarian art should take within its scope all society and nature, universal life. The working class is achieving its ideal through battle; yet its ideal is not destruction, but a new organization of life. In contemporary proletarian poetry agitational content sharply predominates. "There are thousands of verses calling for class war and glorifying victory in it; everything else is lost." This must be changed; a part should not be the whole.

Another tendency which Bogdanov considered alien to proletarian culture is the notion that art should be "bubbling with life and ecstatic." The gamut of proletarian class feelings should not be limited. Art must above all be sincere and true, because it is an organizer of life. What and whom shall it organize, if no one believes it? "The spirit of the laboring collective is above all else—*objectivity.*"

In regard to form, "the latest is not always the most perfect." The proletariat should not turn to the organizers of collapse, such as Igor Severianin, but to the great achievers in the field of art who supported the rise and flourishing of the present obsolescent classes, to the revolutionary romantics, and to the classical writers of different times. The simplicity, the clarity, the purity of form, of the great masters Pushkin, Lermontov, Gogol, Nekrasov, and Tolstoi correspond best of all to the nature of art now being created. In sum, Bogdanov urged the development of an authentic proletarian art which would be universal and objective in content and simple in form.

After the Bolshevik victory, Proletkult supporters appeared all over Russia, but aside from the conviction that the proletariat was somehow obliged to take over the world's culture, the Proletkultists had little in common. Out of a chaos of opinions gradually emerged a partial to total acceptance of Bogdanov's theory. However, the Proletkult was never a monolith; members spoke their own minds.

Undaunted by wartime obstacles, the members of the Proletkult expended a fantastic amount of energy toward realizing their hope for a new culture. Clubs and studios for training proletarian writers, actors, and musicians were established throughout the country. About twenty Proletkult periodicals circulated; and countless works by proletarian authors were published. As the Proletkult went international in 1921, Lunacharskii, the first People's Commissar for Education, claimed that eighty thousand workers were actively participating in the movement.

While the Proletkult was scoring impressive quantitative successes, it was also arousing bitter criticism. Lev Trotskii declared that not only did proletarian culture not exist, but also that it would not exist. Unlike Trotskii, Lenin publicly denied neither the desirability nor the possibility of a proletarian culture, but from the start he had grave misgivings about the Proletkult. He regarded with intense enmity the role played in Proletkult by Bogdanov and was particularly irked by the Proletkultists' bid for cultural autonomy. At the close of 1920, Lenin moved to discredit Bogdanov. A new spokesman for the Proletkult quickly appeared in V.F. Pletnev, who emphatically approved the Proletkult's submission to Party and government control. As much as he tried, however, Pletnev was unable to rid the Proletkult of Bogdanov's influence. It continued a miscreant, falling apart bit by bit, and in 1932 it was abolished altogether.

Although the Proletkult was beset with both artistic and ideological shortcomings, one should not conclude that the influence of the Proletkult was easily erased. In spite of Lenin's attack and several official condemnations, the basic ideas of Bogdanov and the Proletkult lingered on in Soviet literature. Although "proletarian" came to mean "not of working class origin but adherence to the Party cause," the idea of a special proletarian culture was current in Russia until 1932.

It has been pointed out that Stalin's notion that writers should be "engineers of the human soul" was lifted from Bogdanov and the Proletkult. An important difference exists, however, between Bogdanov's view and Stalin's. Bogdanov believed that the writer performed this function whether or not he was aware of it, and that the assignment of special tasks to art was "a constraint, unnecessary and harmful."

Alongside Bogdanov's prodigious production of books, articles, pamphlets, and reports are two novels: *Red Star* (Krasnaia zvezda), published in 1907, and *Engineer Menni* (Inzhener Mènni), published in 1912. These novels are among the very earliest examples of Russian science fiction. Little attention has been paid to them in part because of the very low esteem in which science fiction was held in Russia until after the Second World War, and in part because since the twenties they have not been available either to Russian or Western readers. Bogdanov himself surely thought of them as means of popularizing his ideas and demonstrating the superiority of proletarian organization. The novels contain hypotheses on nuclear rockets, on the role of automation, which Bogdanov expected would change the character of human labor, and on computers. He also suggested ways of improving and lengthening human life, including the then novel notion of blood transfusion. The novels are not entirely utopian. Bogdanov repeatedly emphasizes the enormous difficulty of coping intellectually and emotionally with the demands of the future.

Principal Works: Kratkii kurs èkonomicheskoi nauki (M., 1897); *Osnovnye èlementy istoricheskogo vzgliada na prirodu* (M., 1898); *Empiriomonizm* (M., 1903-1906); *Krasnaia zvezda* (M., 1907); *Kul'turnye zadachi nashego vremeni* (M., 1911); *Inzhener Mènni* (M., 1912); *Vseobshchaia organizatsionnaia nauka*

(Tektologiia) (M., 1913-1922); *Iskusstvo i rabochii klass* (M., 1918); *Élementy proletarskoi kul'tury v razvitii rabochego klassa* (M., 1920); *O proletarskoi kul'-ture* (M., 1924); *Bor'ba za zhiznesposobnost'* (M., 1927).

References: V.L. L'vov-Rogachevskii, *Ocherki proletarskoi literatury* (M., 1927); Viacheslav Polonskii, *Ocherki literaturnogo dvizheniia revoliutsionnoi epokhi (1919-1929)* (M., 1929); Edward J. Brown, *The Proletarian Episode in Russian Literature, 1928-1932* (New York, 1953); S.V. Utechin, "Bolsheviks and Their Allies After 1917: The Ideological Pattern," *Soviet Studies,* vol. X, No. 2 (1958), 113-35; V.V. Gorbunov, "Bor'ba V.I. Lenina s separatistskimi ustrem-leniiami Proletkul'ta," *Voprosy istorii KPSS,* No. 1 (1958); Iu.N. Davydov, "Leninskaia kritika otnosheniia Bogdanova k filosovskoi traditsii," *Voprosy filo-sofii,* No. 6 (1959); Kornelii Zelinskii, *Na rubezhe dvukh epokh* (M., 1960); Iu.V. Riurikov, "Bogdanov," *Kratkaia literaturnaia éntsiklopediia,* vol. 1 (M., 1962); S.V. Utechin, "Philosophy and Society: Alexander Bogdanov," in *Revisionism: Essays on the History of Marxist Ideas* (London, 1962), 117-26; A. Selivanovskii, *V literaturnykh boiakh* (M., 1963); Dietrich Grille, *Lenins Rivale: Bogdanov und seine Philosophie* (Cologne, 1966) [includes Bogdanov bibliography]; L.M. Far-ber, *Sovetskaia literatura pervykh let revoliutsii, 1917-1920* (M., 1966); Sheila Fitzpatrick, *The Commissariat of Enlightenment: Soviet Organization of Educa-tion and the Arts under Lunacharsky, October, 1917-1920* (London, 1970); Peter Gorsen and Eberhard Knödler-Bunte, *Proletkult* (Stuttgart, 1974, 1975); Kathleen Lewis and Harry Weber, "Zamyatin's *We,* the Proletarian Poets, and Bogdanov's *Red Star,*" *Russian Literature Triquarterly,* No. 12 (1975), 253-78.

Garland E. Crouch, Jr.

BOGDÁNOV, ALEKSANDR ALEKSEEVICH [pseudonyms: VOLZHSKII, KAR-PINSKII, AZBUKI, AL'BOV, and others] (1874-1939). Soviet Russian writer. Bogdanov was born on 12 (22) April 1874 in Penza, the son of a lawyer. He be-came involved with the revolutionary movement in 1893, in 1900 joined the Social-Democrats, and in 1903 aligned himself with the Bolsheviks. He was im-prisoned for a total of six years for his political activities. Bogdanov participated in the Civil War in Siberia and in the Far East. One of the first poets to write revolutionary proletarian poetry, Bogdanov's name first appeared in 1896 and some of his verse was selected for an anthology published in Geneva in 1902, *Songs of the Struggle* (Pesni bor'by). Most noteworthy of them are "The Song of the Proletarians" (Pesnia proletariev), "The First of May" (Pervoe maia) and "The First Swallow" (Pervaia lastochka). The Revolution of 1905 is the subject of Bogdanov's tales of "There Is No Death" (Smerti net, 1908), and Fëdor Shurup" (1909-30). Bogdanov died on 10 November 1939 in Moscow.

Works: Stikhi (M., 1936); *Rasskazy* (M., 1939); *Izbrannoe* (Penza, 1951); *Izbrannoe* (Saratov, 1951); *V staroi Penze* (Penza, 1958); *Izbrannaia proza* (M., 1960).

References: L. Zhak, "Aleksandr Bogdanov–chelovek i poét," *Zvezda,* No. 8 (1960).

BOGDÁNOV, ANDREI IVANOVICH (1692/3-1766). Russian archivist, scholar of Japanese extraction. Bogdanov was born in Siberia, and in 1733 was baptized, brought to Petersburg, and enrolled in the Gimnaziia of the Academy of Sciences. Subsequently, he worked in the Academy printing house, and later as an archivist and an assistant to the librarian of the Academy. Among Bogdanov's most significant books is *A Concordance, i.e., a Harmonizing of the Forty Epistles of the Apostle Paul, as well as All the Catholic Epistles and the Apocalypse* (Simfoniia ili Konkordantsiia, t.e. soglasie na chetyredesiat' poslanii sv. apostola Pavla, a takzhe na vse sobornye poslaniia i Apokalipsis, 1737). Bogdanov began to compile a concordance of the entire Bible, but never completed the task. Important also is *A Historical, Geographical, and Topological Description of St. Petersburg from 1703 to 1751* (Istoricheskoe, geograficheskoe i topograficheskoe opisanie S.-Peterburga s 1703 po 1751 gg., 1799). In his *Attempt at a Dictionary of Russian Writers* Novikov ascribes several other works to Bogdanov: *A Logical Primer on the Production and Properties of Russian Letters* (Logicheskaia azbuka o proizvedenii i svoistve rossiiskikh bukv), *A Grammar, Conversations, and a Concise Dictionary of Japanese* (Grammatika, razgovory i kratkii slovar' iaponskogo iazyka), and, in Japanese, *Orbis Pictus*. However, none of these works was published, and the manuscripts are kept at the Academy of Sciences. In "A Review of Russian Ecclesiastical Literature," Filaret suggests that Bogdanov also translated *A Description of Japan with the History of the Persecution of Japanese Christians* (Opisanie Iaponii s istoriei goneniia na khristian iaponskikh, 1734). Bogdanov was the first in Russia to attempt to compile materials necessary for learning Japanese. He died in Petersburg in 1766.

References: N.V. Zdobnov, *Istoriia russkoi bibliografii*, vol. 1 (M., 1944); L.B. Modzalevskii, "Ob uchastii A.I. Bogdanova v sostavlenii *Kratkogo rosiiskogo letopistsa* M.V. Lomonosova," in *Lomonosov, Sbornik statei i materialov*, 2 vols. (M.-L., 1946); I.N. Koblents, *Andrei Ivanovich Bogdanov* (M., 1958).

BOGDÁNOV, NIKOLAI VLADIMIROVICH (b. 1906). Soviet Russian prose writer. Bogdanov was born on 20 February (5 March) 1906 in Kandoma (now Riazan Oblast), the son of a district doctor. His best-known novelette is *The First Girl* (Pervaia devushka, 1928; greatly revised edition, 1958). It is the story of the first girl in a rural Comsomol unit. Bogdanov writes mainly for adolescents—the novelette *The Challenge* (1931), and the novel *A Plenum of Friends*. For children he has written *The Party of Free Youngsters* (Partiia svobodnykh rebiat, 1925), *The Camp Which Disappeared* (Propavshii lager', 1925), *About the Brave and the Skillful* (O smelykh i umelykh, 1950) and others (see Bibliography). Bogdanov is the author of *Notes of a War Correspondent* (Zapiski voennogo korrespondenta, 1941-42) and sketches *In Defeated Japan* (V pobezhdennoi Iaponii, 1947).

Works: Pervaia devushka, Povest' i rasskazy (M., 1958); *Sled cheloveka* (M., 1966); *Ulybka Il'icha* (M., 1966); *Kogda ia byl vozhatym* (M., 1974); *Vechera na ukomovskikh stolakh* (M., 1975).

BOGDÁNOV, VASILII IVANOVICH (1837-1886). Russian poet. Bogdanov was born in Likhvin, Kaluga Province on 12 (24) January 1837. He graduated from Moscow University with a medical degree in 1861. A year later he moved to Petersburg to work as a doctor in the Naval Office until 1885, and from 1863 was a contributor to the satirical journal *Iskra* until it ceased publication in 1873 (under the pseudonym "Vlas Tochechkin," and others). In Bogdanov's poems, particularly in the first half of the sixties, the principal figures are the poor, the inhabitants of urban slums, and non-aristocratic intellectuals—"Conversation with a Muse" (Beseda s Muzoiu, 1863), "Our Proletariat" (Nash Proletarii, 1864), and others. Later the peasant theme became more prominent in them. In 1865 Bogdanov published in *Budil'nik* "The Volga Boatman" (Dubinushka), which became a popular folksong in the rewritten version of A.A. Ol'khin. Bogdanov's satirical works ridiculed serfdom, hypocrisy, and bribery. Events in France provided the theme for some of Bogdanov's poems, such as his expression of support for the Parisian Communards in 1871. In tendency and style, Bogdanov's poetry is close to the Nekrasov school.

Works: Sobranie stikhotvorenii (M., 1959); *Poèty "Iskry,"* 2nd ed. (L., 1955).

BOGDÁNOVA, MEDINA ISKANDEROVNA (1908-1962). Soviet Russian scholar. Born on 26 December 1908 in Bukhara, Bogdanova became a specialist in the literatures of the peoples of Central Asia, particularly Kazakhstan. She graduated from the Eastern Department of Central Asia University in 1930 and completed the Graduate Course of the Institute of Nationalities at the Central Executive Committee of the USSR in 1934. Bogdanova was one of those involved in the change of the alphabets of the Turkic peoples of the USSR from the Arabic, first into Latin and then into the Cyrillic. Bogdanova wrote the first essay on the history of Kirgiz literature in 1947, as well as articles on the folklore and the epos of the Turkic-speaking peoples. Bogdanova played a large role in the education of scholars from the national republics. She died on 6 May 1962 in Moscow.

Works: Kirgizskaia literatura (M., 1947).

BOGDANÓVICH, ANGEL IVANOVICH (1860-1907). Russian editor, critic. Bogdanovich was born 2 (14) October 1860 in Gorodok, Vitebsk Province. While still a medical student at Kiev University, he was arrested and exiled for participating in the activities of a group connected with the revolutionary "People's Will." In Nizhnii Novgorod he met V.G. Korolenko and began to contribute to several journals in the Volga region. In 1893 he moved to Petersburg and collaborated with the journal *Russkoe bogatstvo*. He became a member of the illegal group the "People's Right" (*Narodnoe pravo*). From the second half of the nineties Bogdanovich took the position of a legal Marxist. From 1894-1906 he was editor of the journal *Mir Bozhii* until it was closed in 1906, and then edited its successor *Sovremennyi mir*. Bogdanovich was most favorable toward politically liberal literature written in the realistic tradition and highly admired such writers as Korolenko, Chekhov, and Gorkii. As might be expected, he was critical of the decadent writers. He died on 24 March (6 April) 1907 in Petersburg.

Works: Gody pereloma. 1895-1906. Sbornik kriticheskikh statei. (Pb., 1908) [Includes: V. Korolenko, "A.I. Bogdanovich. Cherty iz lichnykh vospominanii"; M. Nevedomskii, "A.I. Bogdanovich kak pisatel' i redaktor *Mira Bozh'ego*"].

BOGDANÓVICH, IPPOLIT FĒDOROVICH (1743-1803). Russian poet. A member of the Ukrainian aristocracy, Bogdanovich was born on 23 December 1743 (3 January 1744) in Perevolochnaia, Poltava Province. He received his education at Moscow University. Beginning his literary career under the direction of M.M.

Kheraskov, the poet produced a variety of works during his lifetime: a collection of lyric poetry entitled *The Lyre* (Lira, 1773), the narrative poem *Absolute Bliss* (Suguboe blazhenstvo, 1765), an anthology of proverbs *Russian Proverbs* (Russkie poslovitsy, 1785), the lyric comedy *The Joy of Dushen'ka* (Radost' Dushen'-ki, 1786), the drama *The Slavs* (Slaviane, 1788), and others. Bogdanovich was also editor of the journal *Nevinnoe uprazhnenie* (Innocent Pastime, 1763), and the newspaper *Sankt-Peterburgskie vedomosti* (1775-82). Further, he translated works of J.J. Rousseau, Diderot, and Voltaire, notably his "Upon the Destruction of Lisbon."

Bogdanovich's best work is the narrative poem *Dushen'ka* (1778, complete edition, 1783), which is a free rendering of La Fontaine's novel *The Loves of Psyche and Cupid.* Bogdanovich styled the poem on a combination of features from the idyll, love song and fable to construct a variation of the mock epic. This poem is said to have helped move poetry away from the highflown style of the heroic odes. Bogdanovich died on 6 (18) January 1803 in Kursk.

Works: Sobranie sochinenii i perevodov, 2nd ed., 4 vols. (M., 1918-19); *Sochineniia* (Pb., 1848); *Stikhotvoreniia i poemy* [Introduction by I.Z. Serman] (L., 1957).

References: D.D. Blagoi, *Istoriia russkoi literatury XVIII veka,* 3rd ed. (M., 1955); I.Z. Serman, "I.F. Bogdanovich, zhurnalist i kritik," *Vosemnadtsatyi vek,* vol. 4 (M.-L., 1959).

BOGDANÓVICH, MAKSIM ADAMOVICH, *see* BAHDANOVICH, MAKSIM ADAMAVICH in Supplementary volume.

BOGOLIÚBOV, KONSTANTIN VASIL'EVICH (b. 1897). Soviet Russian literary scholar and writer. Bogoliubov was born in the village of Aleksandrovskoe, Perm Province on 11 (23) August 1897. In the twenties his literary critical articles appeared in periodicals in the Ural region. Bogoliubov also collected and published revolutionary songs in the volumes *Songs of Struggle* (Pesni bor'by, 1934) and *Songs of the Revolutionary Underground of the Urals* (Pesni ural'skogo revolutionsionnogo podpol'ia, together with M.S. Koshevarov, 1935). Bogoliubov's works are mainly concerned with the literature of the writers from the Urals, particularly with the works of D.N. Mamin-Sibiriak. In 1934 he prepared for publication the first Soviet five-volume edition of Mamin-Sibiriak's works, and in 1950 published his study *Problems of the Creative History of the Novel "Three Ends"* (Voprosy tvorcheskoi istorii romana *"Tri kontsa"*). As for other writers, Bogoliubov edited the selected works of P.I. Zaiakin-Ural'skii (1935), I.F. Kolotovkin (1936), helped prepare for publication the works of F.M. Reshetnikov (1933), A.P. Bondin (1948) and the book of memoirs *P.P. Bazhov in Recollections* (P.P. Bazhov v vospominaniiakh, 1953). Bogoliubov's fiction is devoted mainly to the history of the Urals. He wrote a biographical novelette about Mamin-Sibiriak, *Bard of the Urals* (Pevets Urala, 1939), a trilogy of historical novels about the life of the Ural miners called *Heat Lightning* (Zarnitsy, 1954), and others.

Works: Pevets Urala, 2 ed. (Cheliabinsk, 1952); *Zarnitsy* (Sverdlovsk, 1954); *Aleksei Bondarin* (Sverdlovsk, 1957); *Ataman Zolotoi* (Sverdlovsk, 1955); *Iosif Likstanov* (M., 1957); *Groznyi god* (Sverdlovsk, 1958).

References: V. Kuskov, "Pisatel', kritik, pedagog (k 60-letiiu so dnia rozh-deniia K.V. Bogoliubova)," *Ural,* No. 2 (1957).

BOGORÁZ, VLADIMIR GERMANOVICH [pseudonyms: N.A. TAN, V.G. TAN] (1865-1936). Soviet Russian ethnographer, writer, folklorist, philologist. Bogoraz was born on 15 (27) April 1865 in Ovruch, Volyn Province. After moving to Petersburg in 1880 and joining the revolutionary populists (*narodniki*), Bogoraz was arrested and imprisoned in the Peter and Paul Fortress from 1886-89. He was then exiled to the remote area of Kolyma for his membership in the revolutionary organization the "People's Will" (*Narodnaia volia*). While there he took part in expeditions for the investigation of the peoples of the Extreme North-East, mainly the Chukchi (1894-96, 1900-01). Bogoraz is one of the founders of the writing systems of the languages of the Northern peoples, the author of fundamental works on the ethnography and folklore of the peoples of North-East Asia, of text-books, dictionaries, and a grammar of the Chukchi language. In 1921 he became professor of ethnography at the Geographical Institute, then professor at Leningrad University and other institutions of higher learning. Bogoraz was one of the founders of the Committee of the North of the Presidium of the All-Union Central Executive Council (VTsIK) and the Institute of the Peoples of the North. He was also the founder and from 1932 the director of the Museum of History of Religion of the Academy of Sciences.

Bogoraz first published a poem in the mid-nineties in the journal *Russkaia Mysl',* "Melodies of Kolyma" (Kolymskie motivy, 1896), and a sketch in the journal *Russkoe bogatstvo,* "Bow-legged" (Krivonogii, 1896), and others. His book *Chukotka Stories* (Chukotskie rasskazy, 1899) placed Bogoraz in Russian literature alongside V.G. Korolenko and other liberal writers of this period who wrote of the wretched conditions in which many of the ethnic groups lived in remote areas of the Russian Empire. Bogoraz's sketches and stories are notable for their convincing depiction of the North, for their lively popular style and their folkloric quality. The ethnographic and artistic elements merge in his novels taken from the life of primitive peoples, *Eight Tribes* (Vosem plemën, 1902), and *The Dragon's Prey* (Zhertva drakona, 1909), which are remarkable for their absorbing plots. In the novel *Resurrected Tribe* (Voskresshee plemia, 1935) Bogoraz describes the rebirth of a small Northern tribe after the October Revolution. His poetic works consist primarily of patriotic and revolutionary themes. The best of them, "Song" (Pesnia), "The First of May" (Pervoe maia), "Tsusima," "Song Before Dying" (Predsmertnaia pesnia) and others, were popularized by the Bolshevik press and have now become part of the song tradition. Bogoraz died on 10 May 1936.

Works: Stikhotvoreniia (Pb., 1900); *Novoe krest'ianstvo: Ocherki dereven-skikh nastroenii* (M., 1905); *Sobranie sochinenii,* 10 vols. (Pb., 1910-11); *Rasprostranenie kul'tury na zemle* (M., 1928); *Soiuz molodykh* (M., 1928); *Sobranie sochinenii,* 4 vols. (M.-L., 1928-29); *Kolymskie rasskazy* (M.-L., 1931); *Chukchi,* 2 pts. (L., 1934-39); *Severnye rasskazy* (M., 1958); *Vosem' plemën* (M., 1962). In English: *The Chukchi of Northeastern Asia* (N.Y., 1901); *The Folklore of Northeastern Asia, as Compared with That of Northwestern America* (N.Y., 1902); *The Chukchee* (N.Y., 1904-09); "Religious ideas of primitive man, from

Chukchee material," *International Congress of Americanists, 14th Session, 1904,* vol. 1 (Stuttgart, 1906), 129-35; *Chukchee Mythology* (N.Y., 1910); *The Eskimo of Siberia* (N.Y., 1913); *Koryak Texts* (N.Y., 1917); *Tales of Yukaghir, Lamut, and Russianized Natives of Eastern Siberia* (N.Y., 1918); *Sons of the Mammoth* (N.Y., 1929); "Elements of the Culture of the Circumpolar Zone," *Annual Report of the Smithsonian Institution for 1930* (Washington, 1931).

References: Ia.P. Al'kor, "V.G. Bogoraz-Tan," and I.N. Vinnikov, "Bibliografiia étnograficheskikh i lingvisticheskikh rabot V.G. Bogoraza," *Sovetskaia étnografiia,* Nos. 4-5 (1935); D.K. Zelenin, "V.G. Bogoraz–étnograf i fol'klorist," in *Pamiati V.G. Bogoraza* (M.-L., 1937); M. Voskoboiniknov, "O poézii V.G. Bogoraza-Tana," *Na Severe Dal'nem,* No. 4 (Magadan, 1959); B.I. Kartashev, *Po strane olennykh liudei* (M., 1959).

BOGORÓDITSKII, VASILII ALEKSEEVICH (1857-1941). Soviet Russian linguist. Corresponding Member of the Academy of Sciences (since 1915). Bogoroditskii was born on 7 April, 1857. He was a follower of Baudouin de Courtenay and one of the representatives of the Kazan school of linguistics. Bogoroditskii was professor at Kazan University, later at Kazan Pedagogical Institute. He worked in the field of general linguistics, phonetics, comparative-historical grammar of the Indo-European languages, of Russian, and of Turkic linguistics. In the eighties he established the first experimental phonetic laboratory in Russia (at Kazan University) applying the experimental phonetic method to study meter in Russian poetry. Besides special monographs, Bogoroditskii also wrote many fundamental general studies in the disciplines mentioned: *Essays on Linguistics and the Russian Language* (Ocherki po iazykoznaniiu i russkomu iazyku, 1901; 4 ed., thoroughly revised, 1939); *Lectures on General Linguistics* (Lektsii po obshchemu iazykovedeniiu, 1911); *A Brief Essay on the Comparative Grammar of the Aryo-European Languages* (Kratkii ocherk sravnitel'noi grammatiki arioevropeiskikh iazykov, 1916); *General Course of Russian Grammar* (Obshchii kurs russkoi grammatiki, 1904); *Russian Grammar* (Russkaia grammatika, 1918); *The Physiology of General Russian Pronunciation in Connection with Experimental Phonetic Data* (Opyt fiziologii obscherusskogo proiznosheniia v sviazi s éksperimental'no-foneticheskimi dannymi, 1909); *A Course of Experimental Phonetics as Applied to Literary (Standard) Russian Pronunciation* (Kurs éksperimental'noi fonetiki primenitel'no k literaturnomu russkomu proiznosheniiu, 1917); *The Phonetics of the Russian Language in the Light of Experimental Data* (Fonetika russkogo iazyka v svete éksperimental'nykh dannykh, 1930); *Studies in Tatar and Turkic Linguistics* (Étiudy po tatarskomu i tiurkskomu iazykoznaniiu, 1933); *Introduction to Tatar Linguistics with Reference to Its Ties with Other Turkic Languages* (Vvedenie v tatarskoe iazykoznanie v sviazi s drugimi tiurkskimi iazykami, 1934); *Introduction to the Study of Modern Romance and Germanic Languages* (Vvedenie v izuchenie sovremennykh romanskikh i germanskikh iazykov, published posthumously, 1953). Bogoroditskii died on 23 December 1941.

Works: "Kazanskaia lingvisticheskaia shkola," in *Trudy Instituta istorii, filosofii i literatury,* vol. 5 (M., 1939).

References: S.A. Vengerov, *Kritiko-biograficheskii slovar',* vol. 4 (Pb., 1895), 167-70; I.A. Boduen de Kurtene, "Lingvisticheskie zametki i aforizmy. Po povodu noveishikh lingvisticheskikh trudov V.A. Bogoroditskogo," *Zhurnal Ministerstva narodnogo prosveshcheniia,* No. 4 and 5 (1903); G.A. Il'inskii, "Zaslugi professora V.A. Bogoroditskogo v oblasti iazykovedeniia," *Vestnik Nauchnogo obshchestva tatarovedeniia,* No. 7 (1927); P.S. Kuznetsov, "Vasilii Alekseevich Bogoroditskii," and A.N. Mironositskaia, "Bibliograficheskii ukazatel' trudov V.A. Bogoroditskogo," in *Trudy Instituta iazykoznaniia ANSSR,* vol. 2 (M., 1953); *Pamiati V.A. Bogoroditskogo* (Kazan, 1961).

BOGOSLÓVSKII, NIKOLAI VENIAMINOVICH (1904-1961). Soviet Russian scholar. A native of Kaluga, Bogoslovskii was born on 14 (27) October 1904. He graduated from Moscow University in 1925 with a degree in philology. His first literary analyses—on Esenin, A.N. Tolstoi, Briusov, Forsh and others—were published in 1925-28. Bogoslovskii's interest, however, centered on Turgenev, and, to a far greater degree on Chernyshevskii. He wrote numerous articles on Chernyshevskii's life and work, commentaries to his works, a popular biography, and a novella about the revolutionary as a young man. In 1934 Bogoslovskii published a collection, *Pushkin as Critic* (Pushkin—kritik), the first attempt to systematize the opinions of the great poet on literature. Later he compiled other collections on the same principle: *N.G. Chernyshevskii on Art* (1950), *N.V. Gogol on Literature* (1952), and *A.P. Chekhov on Literature* (1955). Bogoslovskii died on 12 October 1961 in Moscow.

Works: "Molodost' Chernyshevskogo," *Krasnaia nov',* No. 3-4 (1942; separate publication under the title *Gody iskanii,* M., 1944); *Zhizn' Chernyshevskogo* (M., 1958); *Turgenev* (M., 1959); *Komu nuzhny pëstrye përyshki?* (Yaroslavl, 1965).

References: A.B. Lunacharskii, *Stat'i o Chernyshevskom* (M., 1958), 86-87, 102; I. Sergievskii, "Pushkin—kritik," *Kniga i proletarskaia revoliutsiia,* No. 5 (1935); B. Meilakh, "Pushkin—kritik," *Literaturnyi sovremennik,* No. 1 (1935); I. Lezhnev, "Biografiia Chernyshevskogo," *Novyi mir,* No. 4 (1956); L. Nikulin, "Zametki o knige *Turgenev,*" *Oktiabr',* No. 9 (1959).

BOGRÓV, GRIGORII ISAAKOVICH (1825-1885). Russian writer of Jewish extraction. Bogrov was born in 1825 in Poltava to the family of a rabbi. He received a strict religious upbringing and secretly studied Russian on his own. In the early 1860s Bogrov wrote the first part of *Notes of a Jew* (Zapiski evreia), which are autobiographical in nature and describe the life of Russian Jewry in the 1830s and 1840s. The manuscript appealed to Nekrasov, who subsequently accepted Bogrov's completed *Memoirs* for publication in *Otechestvennye zapiski* in 1871-73. A continuation of sorts was Bogrov's *Poimannik,* which was published in *Evreiskaia biblioteka* in 1873. Moving to Petersburg, Bogrov devoted himself to literature: he published a historical novel from the time of Bogdan Khmel'nitskii entitled *Jewish Manuscript: Before the Drama* (Evreiskii manuskript. Pered dramoi, 1876), contributed to the journal *Slovo* (Word) in 1878 and collaborated with *Russkii evrei* (Russian Jew), founded in 1879 and which, to all intents and purposes, he edited for six months. Later Bogrov moved to the journal *Rassvet* (Dawn), where he published a novel from the life of the Jewish intelligentsia, *The Scum of the Century* (Nakip' veka, 1879-81, unfinished), and several tales, notable among which are "Damned" (Prokliatyi), "Good News"

(Dobrye vesti), "God's Finger" (Perst Bozhii), "Vampire" (Vampir), "Who Is To Blame?" (Kogo vinit'?), "Orthodox" (Ortodoks), and "The Girl Book Seller" (Knizhnitsa). Bogrov was forced to quit the editorial staff of *Rassvet* in 1882 because of differences of opinion on the nationality question and his participation in the Spiritual Biblical Fraternity, which formed in Elizavetgrad (now Kirovograd) in 1881. In the final years of his life Bogrov contributed two stories to *Voskhod*, "The Past" (Byloe, 1883) and "The Maniac" (Maniak, 1884). Bogrov's works have significant social interest, although artistically they suffer from excessive tendentiousness and dry rationalism. Even his best works, *Notes* and *Poimannik*, in which he tries to depict not only the personal, family, and community life of Russian Jewry, but also their social and economic way of life, are not free of these shortcomings. Even Bogrov's wide knowledge of everyday life and his subtle powers of observation do not prevent the picture from being one-sided: on the one hand, his negative attitude toward traditional Judaism and its representatives is too sharp, as is his emphasis on the belief that the people's spiritual rebirth and their radical re-education are possible only by transforming traditional religion into rational moral teachings. Tendentiousness and a failure to observe artistic norms are even more apparent in those works where Bogrov depicts an epoch with which he is less familiar. His historical novel *Jewish Manuscript* suffers from a lack of historical perspective and insipid psychological analysis. Equally unsuccessful are his attempts to render artistically the new ideological trends which arose among Jews in the 1870s and 1880s: his novel *Scum of the Century*, caricatures the progressive young generation, and the story "Maniac" underscores the chimerical nature of the ideas of Palestinism. Bogrov died in 1885 in the village of Derevki (Minsk Province).

Works: ha-Nilkad (Warsaw, 1877); *Ketav-yad 'ivri* (Petrokov, 1900); *Di kinder khaper fun Rusland* (N.Y., 1915).

References: M. Lazarev, "Literaturnaia letopis'," *Voskhod*, bk. 4 (1885); S. Vengerov, *Kritiko-bibliograficheskii slovar'*, vol. V (1897); M.G. Kogan, *Me'ereb ad areb*, vol. I, 69, 71, 75, 80, 85, 181-184; vol. II, 123-40.

BOGUSHEVICH, FRANTSISK KAZIMIROVICH, *see* BAHUSHEVICH, FRANTSISHAK KAZIMIRAVICH

BOIÁN. Russian singer-warrior of the second half of the eleventh-beginning of the twelfth centuries, who won great fame for his art. He is first mentioned in the *Lay of the Host of Igor*. The author of the *Lay* calls him the "grandson of Veles" (the Russian pagan god of cattle, but here a Slavic "Apollo"), "the nightingale of ancient times," a "prophetic" singer who lauded princes such as the old Yaroslav (the Wise), brave Mstislav, handsome Roman (Sviatoslavich). Boian's poetry inspired the troops going into battle, enkindled in warriors' hearts a thirst for glory. The name Boian became symbolic for the designation of a poet. Some scholars have denied the existence of Boian (A.N. Afanas'ev), while others have identified him with the elder Yan Vyshatich mentioned in the chronicle, with prophetic Baian, the son of King Symeon of Bulgaria, and with Grand Duke Oleg Sviatoslavich.

References: V.G. Belinskii, *Polnoe sobranie sochinenii* (M., 1955), vol. 7, 365-66; A.S. Orlov, *Slovo o polku Igoreve,* 2nd ed. (M.-L., 1946); N. Shliakov, "Boian," *Izvestiia po russkomu iazyku i slovesnosti AN SSR,* vol. 1, kn. 2 (1928).

BÓICHENKO, OLEKSANDR MAKSYMOVYCH (1903-1950). Soviet Ukrainian writer who wrote also in Russian, CP member since 1923. The son of a railroad worker, Boichenko was born on 9 (22) November 1903 in Kiev. In 1930-32 he was the Secretary General of the Central Committee of the Ukrainian Komsomol. In 1933 Boichenko became bedridden as the result of a crippling disease. Over a period of ten years Boichenko wrote two volumes of a planned trilogy *Youth* (Molodist', 1945-48), in which he described the activities of the Komsomol in the Ukraine during the twenties as a struggle to rebuild the devastated country, to defeat Ukrainian bourgeois nationalism and Trotskyism. The author drew vivid portraits of the young Komsomol members of the period. The novella was translated into Russian, Lithuanian, Bulgarian and other languages, and the dramatic version, called *With Heart's Blood,* was performed in the theaters of the Ukraine. Boichenko also wrote the books and brochures *For Lenin's Working Style* (Za Leninskii stil' v rabote, 1931), *Along Leninist Paths* (Leninskimi putiami, 1931), *New Situation: New Tasks* (Novia obstanovka—novie zadachi, 1932). Boichenko died on 30 May 1950 in Kiev.

Works: Molodist' (Kiev, 1958). In Russian translation: *Molodost'. Povest'* (M., 1946).

References: O. Savchuk, *Oleksandr Boichenko* (Kiev, 1957).

BOKONBÁEV, DZHOOMART (1910-1944). Soviet Kirgiz poet and playwright. Bokonbaev was born on 16 May 1910 in Mazar-Sai (Now the Potoktogul Region) in the family of a poor peasant. Soviet sources describe him as an ardent Soviet patriot. His works are marked by heavy ideological content. His first poem was "To the Poor Who Got Land, (1927), and his first collection of poems, *The Profits of Toil* (Ėmgek tòlu), appeared in 1933. Bokonbaev extolled the new life of the Kirgiz people in such works as "Kokosh's Eyes Are Opened (Kòkòsh kòzùn achty, 1928), "The Imprints of the Kamcha" (Kamchy tagy), and "The Heart Rejoices." He was the first to introduce into Kirgiz literature the figures of workers and miners, and to write poems about the industrial building sites of Kirgizia: "Kyzyl Kyia" (1932), "Suluktu" (1933), "Turksib" (1930-32), and others. The poet contrasted evocations of the dark past with his dedication to the Soviet system in "Destitution" (1928), "The Desert of Life" (Turmushchòlù, 1930), "Chùi Valley" (Chùi talaasy, 1930), and "My Fergana" (1932). In other poems Bokonbaev expressed a love for Lenin and the CP: "Along Lenin's Path" (1931), "Toil" and "Flourishing Life" (Gùl tarmush, 1939). The poet's principal lyrical and narrative poems from World War II are "The Spirit of the Great Lenin (Ulu Lenin Arbagy), "The Red Banner Is My Heart," "Above the Lake (Kòl ùstùndò), and "Death and Honor" (Azhal menen ar-namys). These poems combine ideological passion with lyricism.

Bokonbaev's principal works for the theater are the musical drama *Altyn kyz* (1937), the drama *Kargasha* (1939), the libretto for the operas *Toktogul* (1939) and *Aichurek* (1937), on the motifs of the Kirgiz epic *Manas* (together with K. Malikov and J. Turusbekov). Bokonbaev died in an automobile accident on 1 July 1944.

Works: Chygarmalarynyn toluk zhyinagy, 2 vols. (Frunze, 1950-54); *Tandalgan chygarmalarynyn* (Frunze, 1973). In Russian translation: *Pis'ma étikh dnei. Stikhi* (Frunze, 1942); *Komuz. Izbrannye stikhi* (M., 1947); *Izbrannoe* (Frunze, 1958).

References: B. Kerimzhanova, *Put' poèta* (Frunze, 1960); T. Mambetsariev, *Zhoomart-zhurnalist* (Frunze, 1960).

BÓKOV, VIKTOR FËDOROVICH (b. 1914). Soviet Russian poet. Bokov was born in a peasant family in Yazvitsy (now Moscow Oblast) on 6 (19) October 1914. He worked as a lathe operator and in a zoo. At the Gor'kii Literary Institute in 1938 he completed his literary training. Bokov compiled an anthology called *The Russian Chastushka* (Russkaia chastushka) in 1950. He is the author of the collections of poems *Yar-Khmel'* (1958), *Furrows of Windswept Snow* (Zastrugi, 1958), and a book of prose miniatures, *Above the Isterma River. The Notes of a Poet.* (Nad rekoi Istermoi. Zapiski poèta, 1960). The main themes of Bokov's poetry are nature and kolkhoz village life. His poems show a strong influence of the traditions of folk poetry.

Works: Lirika (M., 1964); *Viktor Bokov* (M., 1966); *Izbrannoe* (M., 1970); *Kogda svetalo* (M., 1972); *Stikhotvoreniia i pesni* (M., 1973);*Tri travy: novaia kniga stikhov* (M., 1975).

References: N. Rylenkov, "Shchedrost' poèta," *Literatura i zhizn',* No. 63 (1959); I. Mikhailov, "Shchedraia poèziia," *Neva,* No. 11 (1959); G. Levin, "Svoimi slovami," *Ogonëk,* No. 3 (1961); I. Denisova, "Vechno zhivye," *Znamia,* No. 4 (1966).

BOLEBALÁEV, OSMONKUL (1888-1967). Kirgiz *akyn* (poet-improvisor), People's Artist of the Kirgiz SSR. Bolebalaev was born a peasant on 22 August 1888 in the village of Chondaly (now Kant Raion). In his youth he wrote lyric love-songs and lyric epic songs. After the October Revolution political themes became part of Bolebalaev's songs: he extolled the Revolution, Lenin and the toil of simple people. His narrative poems *Baatyr Cholponbai* (1943), "Ashymzhan" (1949), "Poem about a Hero" (Baatyrdyn baiany, 1954), "Gul'shaiyr" (1958) were popular. Bolebalaev was a talented performer of the folk narratives *Kurmanbek* and *Kedeikan.* He died on 28 September 1967 in Frunze.

Works: Osmonkuldun yrlary (Frunze, 1936); *Gul'shaiyr* (Frunze, 1958); *Tandalgan chygarmalar* (Frunze, 1957); *Chygarmalar* (Frunze, 1960). In Russian translation: *Antologiia kirgizskoi poezii* (M., 1957).

References: S. Baikhodzhaev, *Osmonkul yrly* (Frunze, 1964).

BOLOTOV, ANDREI TIMOFEEVICH (1738-1833). Russian writer. Bolotov was born to the aristocracy on 7 (18) November 1738 in Dvorianinovo, Tula Province. In 1755 he entered military service, but retired at age 24 in 1762 to administer his estate. From 1779-97 he also managed the royal estates located in Tula and Moscow Provinces. His first publication, *Children's Philosophy, or Moral Chats Between One Lady and Her Children* (Detskaia filosofiia, ili Nravouchitel'nye razgovory mezhdu odnoiu gospozhoiu i ee det'mi, 1776-79) was intended to be useful in rearing children. Bolotov published the first agricultural journal in Russia, *Sel'skii zhitel'* (1778-79), and edited the journal *Ėkonomicheskii magazin* (1780-89), published by N.I. Novikov. Bolotov wrote the drama *Unfortunate Orphans* (Neschastnye siroty, 1781) and made numerous translations. Of all of Bolotov's enormous literary production, his memoirs won the greatest popularity. They were called *The Life and Adventures of Andrei Bolotov Described by Him for His Progeny, 1738-1793* (Zhizn' i prikliucheniia Andreia Bolotova opisannye samim im dlia svoikh potomkov 1738-1793), published in 1870-73 in the supplement of *Russkaia starina.* Bolotov's notes are a valuable source of information about the society, everyday life and manners of the second half of the eighteenth century. Among other things, they contain reactions to the peasant war of 1773-75, and to the execution of Pugachev. Bolotov's memoirs clearly reflect the world view of a serf-owner. He died on 4 (16) 1833.

Works: Zapiski Andreia Timofeevicha Bolotova (Pb., 1851); *Pamiatnik protekshikh vremen, ili Kratkie istoricheskie zapiski o byvshikh proisshestviiakh i nosivshikhsia v narode slukhakh* (M., 1875); *Zhizn' i prikliucheniia Andreia Bolotova . . . ,* 3 vols. (M.-L., 1931); *Izbrannye sochineniia po agronomii, plodovodstvu, lesovodstvu, botanike* (M., 1952).

References: M. Bolotov, "A.T. Bolotov," *Russkaia starina,* vol. 8 (1873); V. B. Shklovskii, "Kratkaia i dostovernaia povest' o dvorianine Bolotove," *Krasnaia nov',* No. 12 (1928); I. Morozov and A. Kucherov, "Bolotov–publitsist," *Literaturnoe nasledstvo,* Nos. 9-10 (M., 1933); A.A. Blok, "Bolotov i Novikov," in Blok, *Sobranie sochinenii,* vol. 11 (L., 1934); A.P. Berdyshev, *Bolotov–pervyi russkii uchĕnyi agronom* (M., 1949).

N. V. Baranskaia

BONCH-BRUÉVICH, VLADIMIR DMITRIEVICH (1873-1955). Russian revolutionary, historian, editor, one of the original members of the Social Democratic Party. A native Muscovite, Bonch-Bruevich was born on 28 June (10 July) 1873, the son of a surveyor. Enrolled at the Moscow Land-Surveying Institute, he was expelled in 1889 for having participated in student demonstrations, and in 1892 became involved in the Marxist circles. He joined the revolutionary movement in 1895 and went abroad, associating there with Lenin, whom he had met in 1894. He was imprisoned a number of times for his revolutionary activities. In Switzerland he was active in the "Liberation of Labor" group (Osvobozhdenie truda), and thereafter was active in the Social-Democratic Party. Bonch-Bruevich was in charge of the publication of Bolshevik literature in Geneva, as a staff member on Lenin's newspapers *Iskra* and *Pravda.* In 1889 he accompanied the large group of Russian sectarians, the Dukhobors, who were moving from the Caucasus to Canada. Upon his return he took up the task of publishing abroad *Materials for the History and Study of Russian Sectarianism* (Materialy k istorii i izucheniiu russkogo sektanstva) a task which he renewed in Russia proper in 1908. From 1908 to 1918 Bonch-Bruevich was in charge of the legal Bolshevik publishing house "Zhizn' i znanie," and from 1917-20 he was in charge of the Secretariat of the Council of People's Commissars. From 1920-36 he once more headed the (now cooperative) publishing house Zhizn' i znanie.

Bonch-Bruevich's literary work dates from the nineties. He compiled and published several anthologies, among which were *Selected Works of Russian Poetry* (Izbrannye proizvedeniia russkoi poézii, 1894) and *Native Songs* (Rodnye pesni, 1896). He also oversaw editions of literary-historical documents, such as the Literary Museum's publications entitled *Links* (Zven'ia) and *Chronicles* (Letopisi), and was the founder and first director (1933-39) of the State Literature Museum in Moscow. From 1945-1955 Bronch-Bruevich headed the Museum of the History of Religion and Atheism of the Academy of Sciences. Bonch-Bruevich has also written on the history of the revolutionary movement, memoirs, and stories for children.

Works: [The following titles represent works most directly related to literature and culture] : *Sokhraniaite arkhivy* (M., 1920); *Iz mira sektantov. Sbornik statei* (M., 1922); *"Zhivaia tserkov' " i proletariat* (4th ed., M, 1929); *Bol'shevistskie izdatel'skie dela v 1905-1907 gg.* (L., 1933); *Lenin i deti* (M., 1959); *O religii, religioznom sektantstve i tserkvi* (M., 1959); *Izbrannye sochineniia*, 3 vols. (M., 1959-61); *Stat'i, vospominaniia, pis'ma, 1895-1914 gg.* (M., 1961); *Vospominaniia* (M., 1968); *Izbrannye ateisticheskie proizvedeniia* (M., 1973).

References: Vladimir Dmitrievich Bonch-Bruevich, 1873-1955. Bibliografiia trudov (M., 1958).

BÓNDAREV, IURII VASIL'EVICH (b. 1924). Soviet Russian writer, member CP since 1944. Bondarev was born on 15 March 1924 in Omsk. During World War II he was an artillery officer, and in 1951 he graduated from the Gor'kii Literary Institute. His first work appeared in 1949, and his first collection of stories *On the Great River* (Na bol'shoi reke) in 1953. The novelette *The Youth of Commanders* (Iunost' kommandirov, 1956), is devoted to the life of the trainees of the Artillery School. In the novelettes *Batallions Ask for Fire* (Batal'ony prosiat ognia, 1957) and *The Last Volleys* (Poslednie zalpy, 1959), Bondarev highlighted the heroism of soldiers and officers, and the psychology of Soviet people in the war from the viewpoint of a rank-and-file participant. Vivid description, dramatic tension, a precision and subtlety of psychological analysis are the principal traits which mark Bondarev's style.

Works: Pozdnim vecherom (M., 1962); *Stil' i slovo* (M., 1965); *Goriachii sneg* (M., 1970); *Vzgliad v biografiiu* (M., 1971); *Sobranie sochinenii*, 4 vols. (M., 1973-74); *Povesti* (M., 1973). In English: *The Last Shots* (M., 1959?); *Silence* (London, 1965); *The Hot Snow* (M., 1977).

References: A. Borshchagovskii, "Zhizn' i smert' kapitana Novikova," *Druzhba narodov,* No. 10 (1959); G. Baklanov, "Novaia povest' Iu. Bondareva," *Novyi mir,* No. 7 (1959); I. Kozlov, "Vechno velikoe," *Moskva,* No. 1 (1960); K. Paustovskii, "Srazhenie v tishine," *Izvestiia* (28 October 1962); I. Zolotusskii, "Material i mysl'," *Literaturnaia gazeta* (26 November 1969); V. Sevrukh, "Talant i muzhestvo," *Izvestiia* (8 December 1969); I. Kozlov, "Vechnyi ogon'," *Literaturnaia gazeta* (10 December 1969).

BONDÁRIN, SERGEI ALEKSANDROVICH (b. 1903). Soviet Russian writer. Bondarin was born on 14 (27) January 1903 in Odessa. In 1929 he graduated from the Institute of National Economy. In 1931 his first book appeared *Dyndyp* *from the Valley of Durgup-Khotok* (Dyndyp iz doliny Durgup-Khotok), a novelette about the childhood of a Mongolian boy. Bondarin writes about children, about the formation of character in youth, exemplified in *Novel for My Son* (Povest' dlia moego syna) published in 1935. *Life on the Sea* is the subject of his novelette *Vania Zolushkin* (1957) and a number of his stories. Bondarin's forte is the psychological short story, the lyrical etude. He is particularly skillful in handling emotionally poignant detail.

Works: Piat' (M., 1935); *Tri starika. Kartiny Balkarii* (M., 1937); *Raznye vremena* (M., 1939); *Puteshestvie k gornomu perevalu* (M.-L., 1940); *My idëm v desant* (M., 1955); *Liricheskie rasskazy* (M., 1957); "Malaia zemlia," *Novyi mir,* No. 8, (1959); "Eduard Bagritskii. lz vospominanii," *Novyi mir,* No. 4 (1961); *Volny Dunaia* (M., 1961); *Grozd' vinograda* (M., 1964); *Prikosnovenie k cheloveku* (M., 1973).

References: "Pochemu ego ne znaiut?" (Pis'ma V. Shklovskogo i L. Slavina), *Literaturnaia gazeta,* No. 143 (24 October 1934); A. Drozdov, "V poiskakh zhelannogo," *Literaturnaia gazeta,* No. 41 (26 July 1939); T. Gritz, "Proza Sergeia Bondarina," *Kniga i proletarskaia revoliutsiia,* No. 11 (1939); M. Shaginian, "Dobrota," *Literaturnaia gazeta* (9 May 1964); S. Grigor'iants, "Chto polozhit' v kotomki . . . ," *Druzhba narodov,* No. 3 (1968).

BONDIN, ALEKSEI PETROVICH (1882-1939). Soviet Russian writer. Bondin was born at Nizhnii Tagil on 5 (17) August 1882 and worked for more than 30 years as a fitter in Ural factories. He was a member of revolutionary workers' circles. Bondin started his literary activity as a playwright, producing such plays as *Enemies* (Vragi, 1920), which, although formally imperfect, conveyed the revolutionary fervor and the events of the Civil War. From 1923-25 Bondin's first stories began to appear, "The Timekeeper" (Tabel'shchitsa) and "The Switchman" (Strelochnik). In *Loga* (1932-34), the first Soviet novel about the Ural workers, and in the novels that followed—*My School* (Moia shkola, 1934; *Ol'ga Ermolaeva* (1939)—Bondin set himself the task of showing the growth of class consciousness and the revolutionary tempering of the young workers, workers of the copper mine, before and after the establishment of Soviet rule. It is typical of Bondin to show a broad picture of reality and to strive for precision in dialogue, to make skillful use of popular Urals expressions and sayings. He died in the city of his birth on 7 November 1939.

Works: Sobranie sochinenii [Introduction by K. Bogoliubov] (Sverdlovsk, 1948); *Izbrannoe,* 2 vols. (M., 1957-58); *Ol'ga Ermolaeva* (Sverdlovsk, 1965); *Loga* (Sverdlovsk, 1969).

References: S. Zhislina, *Tvorchestvo A.M. Bondina* (Sverdlovsk, 1952); *A.P. Bondin: Sbornik vospominanii o pisatele* (Sverdlovsk, 1957); S.Z. Gomel'skaia, *Pisateli Urala* (Sverdlovsk, 1954); K.V. Bogoliubov, *Aleksei Bondin* (Sverdlovsk, 1957); *Russkie sovetskie pisateli prozaiki. Bibliograficheskii ukazatel',* vol. 1 (L., 1959).

BORATÝNSKII, EVGENII ABRAMOVICH, *see* BARATÝNSKII, EVGENII ABRAMOVICH.

BORDULIAK, TIMOTEI GNATOVYCH [pseudonyms: T. VETLINA, T. BONDARYSHYN] (1863-1936). Ukrainian writer. Borduliak was born in a peasant family in Borduliaki, Brody uezd (now Lvov Oblast, Ukrainian SSR) on 2 February 1863. In 1889 he graduated with a degree in theology from Lvov University. Borduliak was a teacher and priest in the villages of Galicia. He wrote stories which are "simple, genuine and warmed by kind feelings" (I. Franko) from the life of the West-Ukrainian peasantry at the end of the nineteenth century and beginning of the twentieth. He depicted peasant life with grim realism, their hunger for land, their oppression by the landowners, rich peasants, and the Austro-Hungarian authorities. In 1889 the first collection of his tales, *Dear Ones* (Blyzhni) was published in Lvov, and in 1903 *Tales of Galician Life* (Opovidannia z halyts'koho zhyttia) came out in Kiev. In his stories "Here Is Where We Shall Go, Sufferers!" (Os' kudy my piidemo, neboho! 1894), "Storks" (Buz'ky, 1896), "Ivan Brazyliets' " (1899), Borduliak tells of the hard lot of the peasant poor who were forced to emigrate to the Americas, and of their difficult lot there. "A Voyage to Hell" (Puteshestvie v ad) is the writer's grim description of these events.

Works: Opovidannia (Kiev, 1927); *Vybrani tvory* (Kiev, 1930); *Tvory* (Kiev, 1958); In Russian translation: *Rasskazy* (M., 1958).

O. Zosenko

BORIÁN, GURGEN MIKHAILOVICH (b. 1915). Soviet Armenian poet and playwright. Borian was born in Shusha on 20 June 1915, in the family of a teacher. He published his first collection of poems in 1937. Borian has produced a number of collections of poems: *The Road to the Sea* (Chanapar'h depi tsov, 1940), *The Oath of the Soldier* (Martiki erdumy, 1941), *With a Tongue of Flame* (Krake lezvov, 1943), *The Dawn* (Hrats'olki, 1945), *Erevan Dawns* (Erewanyan lowsabats', 1947); *Poems* (Banasteghtsowt'yownner, 1954), *Selected Poems* (1953). Borian also writes for children, *Children's Poems* (1942), *Bouquet* (1946), *Yes and No* (1950), and *I, You and He* (1952). His heroic drama *On the Hills* (Bardgunknerum), and his plays *Under One Roof* (Nuin kharki tak), *Remarkable Treasure* (Rashali gundz), and *The House on the Roads* (Tuny chanaparneri vra) have been staged in Armenia.

Works: Stikhi i p'esy (Erevan, 1966); *Izbrannye proizvedeniia* (Erevan, 1966) [text in Armenian]. In Russian translation: *Ognennym iazykom* (M., 1944); *Erevanskie rassvety* (M., 1948); *Pod odnoi kryshei* (M., 1959); *Dve dramy* (M., 1960).

BORISENKO, VASILII VASIL'EVICH, *see* BARYSENKA, VASIL' VASILEVICH in SUPPLEMENTARY VOLUME.

BORÍSOV, LEONID IL'ICH (b. 1897). Soviet Russian writer. Borisov was born in Petersburg on 24 May (5 June) 1897. His first novel, *Knight's Move* (Khod konêm, 1927), dealing with the fate of an intellectual who could not find his place in Soviet life, received very favorable comment from Maksim Gorkii. In his novelettes *Repairs* (Remont, 1930) and *Work* (Rabota, 1931), Borisov examines the relationship of art to life and ultimately takes the position that art cannot be autonomous. In his short novels *Very Probably* (Ves'ma vozmozhno, 1933) and

The Show is Over (Seans okonchen, 1934) Borisov dwells on themes of everyday life of the workers in the blocks of houses in pre-Revolutionary Petersburg. Borisov's collections of tales deal both with contemporary life and the past: *The Beginning of History* (Nachalo istorii, 1938), *Non-Setting Sun* (Nezakatnoe solntse, 1940), *Evening Sunset* (Vecherniaia zaria, 1941) and *Danube Waves* (Dunaiskie volny, 1947). His artist stories, "The Overcoat" (Shinel', 1938), about Gogol, "Across Dark Abysses" (Cherez bezdny tëmnye, 1939), about Nekrasov, *Evening Sunset,* mentioned above, devoted to Tiutchev, and "Maupasant" (1940), depict the lot of the artist in the last century as tragic. In his novelette *The Wizard from Gel'-G'iu* (Volshebnik iz Gel'-G'iu, 1945), devoted to A.S. Grin, and his novel *Jules Verne* (1955) Borisov subordinates biographical material to his own fiction, thus blurring the boundary line between reality and the imagination of the artist, which gives the work a romantic coloring. The novel about Stevenson, *Under the Flag of the Cathriona* (Pod flagom Katriony, 1957) and the novelette *The Golden Cockerel* (Zolotoi petushok, 1960) about the last days of Rimskii-Korsakov are in the tradition of standard literary biography.

Works: Izbrannoe (L., 1957); *Jules Verne. Pod flagom Katriony. Volshebnik iz Gel'-G'iu* (L., 1960); *Zhestokii vospitatel'* (L., 1961); *Svoi po serdtsu. Rasskazy* (L., 1963); *Shchedryi rytsar'. Tsvety i slëzy. Povesti o S. B. Rakhmaninove* (L., 1964); *Roditeli, nastavniki, poéty* (M., 1967); *Izbrannye proizvedeniia,* 2 vols. (L., 1968); *Za kruglym stolom proshlogo. Vospominaniia* (L., 1971).

References: A. Shishkina, "Deistvitel'nost' i mechta," *Zvezda,* No. 3 (1947); E. Brandis, "Leonid Borisov," *Zvezda,* No. 1 (1959).

BORN, IVAN MARTYNOVICH (?-1851). Russian writer and pedagogue. Sponsor of *The Free Society of Lovers of Literature, the Sciences and Art* (Vol'noe obshchestvo liubitelei slovesnosti, nauk i khudozhestv), in which he occupied the post of secretary and, from 1803 to 1805, that of president. In his poems "Ode of Callistratus" (Oda Kalistrata), "Ode to Truth" (Oda k istine), "On the Death of Radishchev" (Na smert' Radishcheva), "Victory" (Pobeda) and others, Born expressed liberal sentiments characteristic of members of the "Free Society" at the beginning of the nineteenth century. In 1808 with the collaboration of A.Kh. Vostokov he published *A Concise Guide to Russian Literature* (Kratkoe rukovodstvo k rossiiskoi slovesnosti), which presented a course in Russian grammar, and the theory and history of Russian literature. After 1809, having abandoned his literary activity, he settled in Tver as secretary to Prince Georg Ol'denburgskii. Later he traveled widely, served in the court of the Queen of Wuerttemberg. Born died in Stuttgart in February 1851.

References: Istoriia russkoi literatury, vol. 5, pt. 1 (M.-L., 1941); V.G. Bazanov, *Vol'noe obshchestvo russkoi slovesnosti* (Petrozavodsk, 1949) [contains extensive bibliography] ; *Poéty-radishchevtsy,* 2nd ed. (L., 1952); V. Orlov, *Russkie prosvetiteli 1790-1800-kh godov,* 2nd ed. (M., 1953).

BORNHÖHE [pseudonym for: BRUNBERG] , **EDUARD** (1862-1923). Estonian writer, the founder of the historical genre in Estonian literature. Bornhöhe was born on 17 February 1862 on the estate of Kullaaru, near the city of Rakvere.

He completed the gymnasium in Tallin as an external student and later studied for a time at Tartu University. Bornhöhe worked as a pedagogue, a journalist, and a judge. His literary activity began during the rise of the nationalist movement. His historical works are built primarily around themes of the people's struggle against oppressive barons for emancipation. In the historical novel *The Avenger* (Tasuja, 1880) Bornhöhe portrayed the Estonian peasant uprising of 1343. The novel *Villu's Struggle* (Villu võitlused, 1890) is devoted to the same events. The events of the Livonian War are recorded in his novel *Prince Gabriel, or The Last Days of the Pirita Monastery* (Vürst Gabriel ehk Pirita kloostri vümased päevad, 1893). Bornhöhe is also the author of stories and tales about contemporary city life. He died on 17 November 1923 in Tallin.

Works: Tasuja (Tallin, 1922); *Kuulsuse narrid* (Tallin, 1941); *Villu võitlused. Jutustus Eestimaa vanast ajast* (Tallin, 1946); *Ajaloolised jutustused* (Tallin, 1952); *Tallinna jutud* (Tallin, 1962); *Jutud ja reisikirjad* (Tallin, 1963). In Russian translation: *Istoricheskie povesti* (Tallin, 1959, 3rd ed., 1972).

References: E. Nirk, *Bornhöhe* (Tallin, 1961).

BORODÍN, SERGEI PETROVICH [pseudonym before 1941: AMIR SARGIDZHAN] (b. 1902). Soviet Russian writer, member CP since 1943. Borodin was born in Moscow on 8 October 1902. He graduated from the Briusov Higher Literary-Art Institute in 1926, where he specialized in folklore. In 1923-26 he participated in expeditions to Bukhara and Samarkand and has since traveled and worked in the Far East, Kazakhstan, Tadzhikistan, Armenia, the Pamirs and other places. Since 1951 he has lived in Tashkent. Borodin's first poems and sketches were published in children's journals in 1915. His novels *The Last Bukhara* (Posledniaia Bukhara, 1932), *The Egyptian* (Egiptianin, 1932), and a collection of novellas, *The Bird Expert* (Master ptits, 1934), are devoted to the life of the peoples of Soviet Central Asia. The Far East is described in his tale *The Birth of Flowers* (Rozhdenie tsvetov, 1938). In his historical novel *Dmitrii Donskoi* (1941; Stalin Prize, 1942) the struggle of the Russian people with the Tatar-Mongolian invasion is depicted. Borodin is the author of an unfinished historical trilogy *The Stars over Samarkand* (Zvězdy nad Samarkandom), consisting of *Lame Tamerlane* (1953-1954), and *Campfires of the March* (1957-1959). The novel attempts to recreate the life of the peoples of Central Asia and Transcaucasia during the era of Tamerlane's last marches at the turn of the fourteenth century. Borodin portrayed the preeminent figure of Tamerlane against the background of complex social and national relationships. Characteristic of Borodin's novels are authentic historical color and their unaffected, unstylized language. Borodin translates from Tadjik, Uzbek, Hindi and other languages.

Works: Dmitrii Donskoi (Kuibyshev, 1942); *Zvēzdy nad Samarkandom* (M., 1956); *Sobranie sochineniii,* 4 vols. (Tashkent, 1958-60); *Molnienosnyi Baiazet* (M., 1973); *Sobranie sochinenii,* 6 vols. (Tashkent, 1973-). In English: *Dmitri Donskoi* (London-N.Y., 1944). Translation into Russian: Sadriddin Aini, *Raby* (Dushanbe, 1970) [from Tadjik].

References: V. Il'enkov, "Kniga-oruzhie," *Oktiabr',* No. 9 (1942); Iu. Avaliani and L. Roizenzon, "Zametki v iazyke i stile istoricheskikh romanov S. Borodina," *Zvezda Vostoka,* No. 11 (1955); E. Starikova, "Narod—èto liudi," *Novyi mir,*

No. 7 (1956); G. Vladimirov, *Poéziia pravdy* (Tashkent, 1959); *Russkie sovetskie pisateli-prozaiki. Bio-biograficheskii ukazatel'*, vol. 1 (1959).

BORODULIN, GRIGORII IVANOVICH, see BARADULIN, RYHOR IVANA-VICH in SUPPLEMENTARY VOLUME.

BORÓLYCH, IURII IURIIOVYCH (b. 1921). Ukrainian writer living in Czechoslovakia. Borolych was born on 28 February 1921 in Velikoe Bereznoe, Transcarpathia. He studied in the Uzhgorod gimnaziium and in 1939 emigrated to the Soviet Union. During World War II he fought with Czech units against the Germans and began to write as a correspondent for military newspapers. In his stories and sketches—the collections *Darunok* (1953), *A Page of Life* (1956), *Under One Sky* (1958)—Borolych wrote of the friendship between Czechoslovakian and Soviet soldiers, and of life in Communist Czechoslovakia.

Works: Darunok. Zbirnyk opovidan' (Priashev, 1953); *Storinka zhyttia. Zbirnyk opovidan'* (Bratislava, 1956); *Pid odnym nebom. Opovidannia* (Bratislava, 1958); *Pisnia zhyttia* (Priashev, 1960); *Khoral verkhovyny: tryptykh* (Priashev, 1964); *Z ridnykh beregiv* (Priashev, 1966); *Prezydents'ka usmishka* (Uzhgorod, 1967); *Zhyly sobi . . . Povist'* (Kiev, 1969).

BOROVIKÓV, GRIGORII FĒDOROVICH (b. 1905). Soviet Russian writer, member CP since 1945. Borovikov was born in Beloglazovo (now Kirovskaia Oblast) on 6 (19) August 1905. His first book, *In the Caspian Jungles* (V Kaspiiskikh dzhungliakh, 1946), is a poetic tale about nature and the inhabitants of the Astrakhan Preserve. Many of Borovikov's tales, sketches and stories are devoted to the lands and people along the Volga. Borovikov is more successful with his treatment of nature, which he experiences deeply, than he is with his human characters.

Works: Goluboi plios (Saratov, 1947); *Glubokoe ruslo* (Saratov, 1951); *Volzhskie rasskazy* (Saratov, 1952); *Stroitel'. Dokument. Povest'* (M., 1953); *Serëzhino leto* (Saratov, 1955); *Pantushka* (Saratov, 1957); *Imenem Respubliki* (M., 1959); *Irina* (Saratov, 1959); *Liven'* (M., 1960); *Syn Dobrynina* (Saratov, 1960); *Svetlaia noch'. Rasskazy* (Saratov, 1962); *Nika* (Saratov, 1963); *Dederkoi* (Saratov, 1966); *Dal'nii veter. Rasskazy* (M., 1966).

References: G. Guliia, "Volzhskie rasskazy," *Ogonëk*, No. 40 (1952); A. Turkov, "Ob odnoi tipichnoi oshibke," *Novyi mir*, No. 9 (1951).

BOROVYKÓVS'KYI, LEVKO IVANOVYCH (1806-1889). Ukrainian poet. Borovykovs'kyi was born to the aristocracy on 10 (22) February 1806 in the village of Meliushki, Poltava Province. He received a degree from the University of Kharkov in 1830, and taught history, Latin and Russian literature in secondary school from 1830-1835, in Kursk and Poltava. Borovykovs'kyi began publishing in 1828, writing variously songs, ballads, *dumas* (Ukrainian folk ballads) and fables. The romantic ballad "Marusia" (1829) is a free rendition of the motifs of Zhukovskii's "Svetlana." In dealing with historical subjects Borovykovs'kyi treats them from the viewpoint of Russian nationalism officially acceptable during the reign of Nicholas I. His verse was published in the only volume to appear during his lifetime, *Baiky i pribaiutky Levka Borovykovs'koho* (1852). The poems touch upon ethical problems and the problems of everyday life, less frequently upon social questions. Borovykovs'kyi was also active in other literary and cultural endeavors: he was a folklorist and an ethnographer, collecting folk songs, proverbs and superstitions, he worked on a Ukrainian dictionary, and he was one of the first to translate Pushkin and Mickiewicz into Ukrainian. Not all of Borovykovs'kyi's works have survived. He died on 15 (27) December 1889 in Meliushki.

Works: Marusia [Commentary by Iv. Franko] (Lvov, 1902); *Tvory* (Kiev, 1957); *Povne zibrannia tvoriv* (Kiev, 1967).

References: N.I. Petrov, *Ocherki istorii ukrainskoi literatury 19 st.* (Kiev, 1884), 140-46; I. Franko, *Tvory v dvadtsiati tomakh,* vol. 17 (Kiev, 1955), 280-92; *Istoriia ukrainskoi literatury,* vol. 1 (Kiev, 1954), 199-201; S. Kryzhanivs'kyi, "Pershyi ukrains'kyi poet romantyk," in L. Borovykovs'kyi, *Tvory* (Kiev, 1957), 3-52.

BOROZDÍN, ALEKSANDR KORNILIEVICH (1863-1918). Russian scholar. Borozdin was born in 1863 in Petersburg and was educated at the University of Petersburg in history and philology. His Master's dissertation on Avvakum was published in 1898 *(Protopop Avvakum. Ocherk iz istorii umstvennoi zhizni russkogo obshchestva v 17 v.).* After 1896 he lectured on the history of Russian literature at the University of Petersburg. Borozdin's principal works are devoted to Russian literature of the nineteenth century and are collected in two volumes entitled *Literary Descriptions* (Literaturnye kharakteristiki, 1903-07). They contain studies of Zhukovskii, Krylov, Pushkin, Lermontov, Gogol, Granovskii, I.S. Aksakov, I.V. Kireevskii, Turgenev, and others. Borozdin is author of the work *A Book of Suffering. A.N. Radishchev's Journey from Petersburg to Moscow* (Mnogostradal'naia kniga. Puteshestvie A.N. Radishcheva iz Peterburga v Moskvu, 1906) and the articles "A.I. Gertsen and the Peasant Question," "Iu.E. Samarin and Emancipation of the Peasants," and others. He died on 6 October 1918.

Works: Pětr Velikii po ego pis'mam v 1688-1703 gg. (Pb., 1903); *Sobranie sochinenii,* 2 vols. (Pb., 1914); *A.S. Pushkin* (Pb. 1914).

BOROZDNA, IVAN PETROVICH (1804-1858). Russian poet. The son of a collegiate assessor, Borozdna was born on 27 November 1804 in the village of Medvedevo, Starodubskii District. He received his education at the Moscow University Boarding School for the Nobility, which he completed in 1823. Borozdna's first poems were printed in 1823 in *Vestnik Evropy.* And although he possessed no particular poetic gift, he contributed his verse with considerable regularity to at least ten journals and five literary almanacs between 1823 and 1844. Borozdna realized his long-standing desire to travel throughout Russia in 1834, visiting the Ukraine, Novorossiia, and the Crimea. His recollections of the trip, set down in tranquillity on his estate of Medvedevo and entitled *Sketches of the Ukraine, Odessa, and the Crimea* (Poeticheskie ocherki Ukrainy, Odessy i Kryma), were written in the form of twelve letters to Count V.P. Zavadovskii and published in Moscow in 1837. From 1836 to 1838 Borozdna, together with V.G. Benediktov, P.P. Svin'in, I.A. Goncharov, and others, placed their poetry in a hand-written journal *Podsnezhnik* (Snowdrop), intended to develop an appreciation of literature in the sons of the well-known painter N.A. Maikov. Again in 1844, together with N.M. Yazykov, S.P. Shevyrëv, and N.P. Ogarëv, he assisted in the publication of the anthology *Literaturnyi vecher,* which was issued to aid the family of the writer V.V. Passek, who had died in 1843. According to I.I. Yasinskii, whose father's house the poet often visited, Borozdna spoke wittily, beautifully, softly, courteously; however, he was vain and loved to be flattered. His verse was collected in 1828 under the title *Experiments in Verse* (Opyty v stikhakh), in 1834 in an anthology entitled *The Lyre* (Lira), which contains poems written chiefly at the end of the twenties and the beginning of the thirties, and in 1847 under the title *Shafts and Shadows* (Luchi i teni). Borozdna's works are interesting primarily as the works of an aristocratic dilettante. Almost all of his poems are marked by grandiloquence and high-flown phrases. His most successful and sincere poem is the one published in *The Lyre,* written on the death of his wife, who died in 1830. Borozdna died on 7 December 1858.

References: S.A. Vengerov, *Russkie knigi,* vol. 3 (Pb., 1898), 130; – – –, *Istochniki slovaria russkikh pisatelei,* vol. 1 (Pb., 1900), 327.

BOR-RAMÉNSKII, DMITRII PETROVICH (b. 1899). Soviet Russian writer. The son of a farm laborer, Bor-Ramenskii was born on 27 October (9 November) 1889 in the village of Sudinskoe, Osinskii uezd, Perm Province. He received his university training in philology through a correspondence training school. He began to write in 1924, but his principal works were published much later—his novels *The Pine Forest* (Ramen'e, 1940) on the struggle with sectarians, former White Guardists and kulaks against collectivization, and *In the Prikamskii Forests* (V prikamskikh lesakh, 1950), on strengthening the Prikamskii forestry collective. In the short novel *Danilo Shitov,* on the Pugachev movement in the Udmurt region, Bor-Ramenskii shows the joint efforts of the Russian and Udmurt peoples against their oppressors.

Works: Kamskii vikhr' (M., 1925); *Danilo Shitov,* 2nd ed. (Izhevsk, 1956); *Rasskazy* (Izhevsk, 1959).

References: A. Chukhlantsev "Rasskazy stareishego pisatelia Udmurtii;" *Udmurtskaia pravda* (12 April 1959); *Pisateli Udmurtii* (Izhevsk, 1963), 23-25.

BORSHCHAGÓVSKII, ALEKSANDR MIKHAILOVICH (b. 1913). Soviet Russian novelist, critic, playwright. Member CP since 1940. The son of a journalist, Borshchagovskii was born on 1 (14) October 1913 in Belaia Tserkov. His literary activity began in 1933. In 1935 he graduated from the Kiev Theatrical Institute and wrote critical articles, reviews and books on the Ukrainian drama such as *The Dramatic Productions of Ivan Franko* (Dramatychni tvory Ivana Franka, 1946), *A.M. Buchma* (1947) and *Tobilevich's Dramatic Art* (Dramaturgiia Tobilevicha, 1948). In 1953 Borshchagovskii's historical novel *Russian Flag* (Russkii flag) appeared, recounting the defense of Petropavlovsk-na-Kamchatke in 1854 and the victory of Russian forces over an English squadron. In his short novels on the workaday life of Soviet people, *Gray Gull* (Sedaia chaika, 1958), *The Island of All Hopes* (Ostrov vsekh nadezhd, 1960), in his story of the exploits of Soviet sailors in the Pacific Ocean "Missing in Action" (Propali bez vesti, 1955), in his tragic narrative, *Troubled Clouds* (Trevozhnye oblaka, 1958), about the "match to the death" between Soviet and German soccer-players in occupied

Kiev and also in his plays *My Wife* (Zhena, 1955) and *The Bear Hide* (Med-vezh'ia shkura, 1958), Borshchagovskii emphasizes the qualities of moral staunch-ness, courage and loyalty to duty in his depiction of Soviet people.

Works: Stekliannye busy (M., 1963); "Bezumstvo khrabrykh," *Zametki pisa-telia* (M., 1965); *Noev kovcheg. Rasskazy* (M., 1968); *Mlechnyi put'* (M., 1970); *Tri topolia* (M., 1974); *Gde poselitsia kuznets* (M., 1976). In English translation: *The Match of Death* (Moscow, n.d.).

References: V. Sutyrin, "Russkii flag na Tikhom okeane," *Oktiabr'*, No. 12 (1953); R. Messer, "Novoe o proshlom," *Zvezda*, No. 3 (1954); G. Boguslavskii, "Roman o slave russkogo flota," *Znamia*, No. 12 (1954); S. Vladimirov, "Prava i obiazannosti dramaticheskogo geroia," *Zvezda*, No. 5 (1960); V. Sokolov, "Po sovesti," *Novyi mir*, No. 8 (1968); L. Pozhidaeva, "Byt' chelovekom," *Zvezda*, No. 1 (1969).

BORSHCHÉVSKII, SOLOMON SAMOILOVICH (1895-1962). Soviet Russian literary scholar. Borshchevskii was born on 8 (20) July 1895 in Ekaterinoslav (now Dnepropetrovsk). His first scholarly work, *A New Character in Dostoev-skii's "The Possessed"* (Novoe litso v "Besakh" Dostoevskogo, 1918), is an analy-sis of the narrator's role in the novel. Borshchevskii's scholarship dealt mainly with the work of Saltykov-Shchedrin. His early textual research resulted in the publication of *Saltykov-Shchedrin: Unknown Pages* (Saltykov-Shchedrin. Neiz-vestnye stranitsy, 1931). Borshchevskii established that certain literary-critical and journalistic articles, which originally had appeared anonymously, were, in fact, written by Shchedrin. These works now comprise the eighth volume of Shchedrin's complete collected works (1937). The results of many years' study of the relationship between Shchedrin and Dostoevskii are gathered in his book *Shchedrin and Dostoevskii* (1956), in which the ideological struggle and constant polemic between the two writers is thoroughly examined. Borshchevskii is fa-mous as a textual critic: he prepared for publication Gertsen's *My Past and Thoughts* (Byloe i dumy, 1956-57), and directed textual work on Chernyshev-skii's complete collected works. Borshchevskii died on 14 April 1962 in Mos-cow.

Works: "Bor'ba Shchedrina za tip revoliutsionera v literature," in N. Shched-rin, *Polnoe sobranie sochinenii*, vol. 8 (M., 1937); *"Otechestvennye zapiski," 1868-1884: khronologicheskii ukazatel' anonimnykh i psevdonimnykh tekstov* (M., 1966).

References: A. Walicki, "O polemice Szczedrina z Dostojewskim . . . ," *Slavia orientalis*, No. 2 (1958).

A.A. Belkin

BÓRSHOSH-KUM'IÁTS'KYI, IULII VASYL'OVYCH (b. 1905). Soviet Ukrain-ian poet. Borshosh-Kum'iats'kyi was born on 8 July 1905 in the village of Velikie Kom'iaty (today the Vinogradov Raion in Transcarpathia), the son of a peasant. He was educated at the Uzhgorod Teachers' Training College in 1924 and worked as a teacher. A collection of poetry for children, *Vesnianni kvity*, appeared in 1928, followed by the anthologies *Z moho kraiu* (1929), *Kraina dyv* (1934) and *Z nakazu rodu* (1938), which deal with themes of the struggle of labor in the pre-Soviet period and the lack of workers' rights. After the reunification of Transcarpathia with the Ukrainian SSR, Borshosh-Kum'iats'kyi wrote *Dvi doli* (1948) and *Na Vysokii polonyni* (1956), about the new Soviet life. His *virshi* have been translated into German, Hungarian, Czech and Slovak.

Works: V Karpatakh svitae (Prague, 1935); *Grai, trembito (Biografichna dovidka)* (Kiev, 1958); *V orlinomu leti* (Uzhgorod, 1961); *Shovkova kositsia. Poezii* (Uzhgorod, 1971). In Russian translation: *Igrai, trembita* (M., 1962).

BÓRUTA, KAZYS (1905-1965). Soviet Lithuanian writer. The son of a peasant, Boruta was born on 6 January 1905 in the village of Kulokai (now Kapsukas Raion), and educated at the Universities of Kaunas and Vienna. He was one of the initiators of the anti-Fascist periodical *Trečias frontas* (The Third Front). Boruta was imprisoned in the thirties by the Lithuanian government, and once again by the Russians, after the takeover of the Baltic states at the end of World War II.

First published in 1921, Boruta's first book of verse, *Allo,* appeared in 1925. Three more collections of lyric poems followed: *Lithuania of the Crosses* (Kryžiu Lietuva, 1927), *Daily Bread* (Duona kasdieninė, 1934), and *Verses and Poems* (Eiles ir poemos, 1939). In his novel *Wooden Marvels* (Mediniai stebuklai, 1938) the tragic fate of an artist from the people is depicted. In the short novel *Baltaragis's Windmill* (Baltaragio malūnas, 1945) Boruta used motifs from Lithuanian folk tales. He wrote a book of children's tales *The Sky Is Falling* (Dangus griuva, 1955). His documentary novel *Heavy Monuments* (Sunkūs paminklai, 1957) tells of the Lithuanian sculptor Gribas, who was shot by the Germans. Boruta died on 9 March 1965 in Vilnius.

Works: Tarptautiniu žodžiu žodynas (Kaunas, 1936); *Mediniai stebuklai* (Kaunas, 1938); *Baltaragio malūnas* (Chicago, 1952); *Šiaurės Kelionės* (Vilnius, 1957); *Jurgio Paketurio klajonės su visokiais pavojais . . .* (Vilnius, 1963); *Neramūs arimai* (Vilnius, 1970); *Rinktiniai raštai* (Vilnius, 1970); *Saulės parnešti išejo* (Vilnius, 1973). In Russian translation: *Nebo rushitsia, ili Byli-nebylitsy, v kotorykh uchastvuiut zveri i ptitsy* (1959); *Tiazhelye pamiatniki* (M., 1961); *Vetra vol'nogo volia* (M., 1967). In English: *Whitehorn's Windmill* [dramatic adaptation of *Baltaragio malūnas*], in *The Golden Steed* (Prospect Heights, Ill., 1978).

References: Lietuvių Literatūros istorija, vol. 3, pt. 2 (Vilnius, 1965); and vol. 4 (1968).

BORZÉNKO, SERGEI ALEKSANDROVICH (b. 1909). Soviet Russian writer, CP member since 1942. A native of Kharkov, Borzenko was born on 19 June (2 July) 1909 in Kharkov in the family of a medical assistant. He worked as a metalworker and electrician, and in the thirties began to publish in newspapers. Borzenko fought in the Second World War, working for several months behind enemy lines on special missions. For participation in the capture of Kerch Strait, Borzenko was awarded the order of Hero of the Soviet Union. He is the author of tales and stories about the Second World War: *Landing in the Crimea* (Desant v Krym, 1944), *Obeying the Laws of the Fatherland* (Povinuias' zakonam otechestva, 1954), and a cycle of sketches on war-torn Korea, *Korea in Flames* (Koreia v ogne, 1951) and *Korea's Courage* (Muzhestvo Korei, 1953). As a journalist

Borzenko succeeds in conveying the fresh impressions of a direct participant in these events. At the same time his tales and stories suffer from superficiality.

Works: Zhizn' na voine (M., 1958); *Kakoi prostor*, book 1 (M., 1958); *Frontovye byli* (M., 1959); *Povesti* (M., 1959); *Kosmicheskie bogatyri* (M., 1964); *Pervyi kosmonavt, Iu.A. Gagarin* (M., 1969); *Samorodok Rossii, S.M. Budënnyi* (M., 1970).

References: A. Sakhnin, "Koreia v ogne," *Znamia*, No. 5 (1951); A. Chakovskii, "To, a chëm ne zabudet mir," *Znamia*, No. 9 (1954); V. Gavrilenko, "Na shirokii prostor," *Oktiabr'*, No. 2 (1959); M. Iunovich, "Ot nashego voennogo korrespondenta . . .," *Znamia*, No. 5 (1967).

BÓTKIN, VASILII PETROVICH (1811-1869). Critic of art, music, literature and student of economics and philosophy; close friend or associate of almost all leading writers, literary critics, and literary editors from the late 1830s through the 1860s. Botkin was born on 27 December 1811 in Moscow, the eldest son in a family of 14 children, some of whom achieved illustrious careers in medicine and art. Botkin was educated into two worlds: into English and German literary and philosophical studies at the Kriazhev Pension (one of the best private schools in Russia); and into the economic realities of managing a large commercial enterprise by his father, who owned a major tea-importing company in Moscow. An awareness of the financial, industrial structure that constituted, outwardly at least, the basis of nineteenth-century civilized progress, and a sensitivity to the poetry of life—expressed by man's creative response to nature and imagination—remained lifelong balancing counterparts in Botkin's world view. He eschewed writing formally for publication but deluged his friends with hundreds of letters. Consequently, most of his critical work was conducted privately and, similarly, most appreciation for and comments about his critical sensibility are found in letters from his correspondents. The major exception, critically, is his article on A.A. Fet, written in 1857. To the public, Botkin's reputation was that of a feuilletonist whose *Letters on Spain* (1847-49, 1851) became a sourcebook for poets and social scientists and a guidebook for travellers through many more decades.

Trained from an early age in French, German and English, Botkin was a true polyglot and eventually learned all the major Western European languages. He read Western literatures and philosophies avidly and after the mid-1830s became associated with a group of students at Moscow University who were interested in German idealist philosophy and Romanticism (Botkin himself was not a student there). Initially he met the ex-student and current newspaper critic Vissarion Belinskii, who was to become the most influential social and literary critic of the century, and through him he met the former or actual students who constituted the Stankevich Circle. Botkin was considered by them to be one of the best interpreters of the new philosophical and aesthetic theories that were developing in the West. He read and understood the German Romantic writers and idealist philosophers probably as well as anyone, and he acquired a similar familiarity with the writers of Young Germany, the French utopian socialists, especially Saint-Simon, and even Engels.

However much he may have been influenced by whatever school of thought he happened to be studying, Botkin did not become an adherent or partisan of any of them. His liberal outlook was expressed primarily by his constant desire to read the very latest writings of any new school of thought; his Westernist outlook was manifested by his lifelong immersion in European cultural achievements, whether in music, art, architecture, philosophy, history, literature or criticism, and by his lifelong penchant for lengthy and frequent sojourns in Europe. Behind his liberalism and Westernism lay his businessman's conservative acceptance of government and society as the necessary conditions for the growth and profit of industry and commerce, without which a nation would not progress.

Initially Botkin seems to have combined business and pleasure on his many journeys about Russia and Europe, performing a merchant's tasks and a tourist's sightseeing. It also seems that by the time of his lengthy stay abroad in 1843-1846 he was more of an expatriate who had a very comfortable income sent him by his father. By the mid-1850s Botkin withdrew from tea-business matters (after his father's death), leaving the managing of the firm to his younger brothers. Throughout his life he lived as a rich man who did not have to work; his apartments, travels, entertainings, and assistance to friends exemplify his wealth and generosity.

Botkin's status in Russian literature is, for us, largely hidden from view but was for his contemporaries of singular importance. He possessed a most unusual ability to perceive the essence of a work, its structure, intent, style, devices, and strengths as well as weaknesses. Moreover he had the keenest insight not only into the cognitive component factors of art—inspiration, originality, sincerity, truth—but also into the physical means of expressing the poetry of an art—medium, genre, technique, performance. Added to this was his enormous knowledge of the history of art and literature. It was to this man that his friends turned for advice and criticism. For example, Belinskii's correspondence with Botkin was by far his most voluminous, if family letters are excluded from consideration. The extent of Botkin's assistance to Belinskii is a matter of controversy. Botkin's contemporaries took it for granted that he contributed to the sections on Romanticism in Belinskii's series of articles on Pushkin. Nearly one-third of Belinskii's second article, "Karamzin and His Merits," (*Otechestvennye zapiski*, XXX, No. 9, 1843) is an incorporation of Botkin's essay "On Romanticism." Current Soviet scholarship denies such an important dependence by Belinskii, while admitting Botkin's influence over Belinskii's intellectual development (Egorov). The internal evidence of the passage in question suggests that if Botkin did not actually compose it, his notes provided Belinskii the necessary data for writing it. The Turgenev-Botkin correspondence is even more voluminous and was printed in a separate volume in 1930. It shows that Turgenev was very sensitive to Botkin's critiques of new works and incorporated Botkin's thoughts or suggestions into revised versions. Botkin's incisive understanding of a new work was equal to Dostoevskii's, for Turgenev stated that they alone had understood what he attempted in the characterization of Bazarov in *Fathers and Sons*. Tolstoi, during the mid-1850s, referred to Botkin, Druzhinin, and Annenkov as his "literary triumvirate."

Botkin's early printed works (1836) were travel accounts and reviews of books as widely diverse as the stories of E.T.A. Hoffman, and a government foreign trade report. By 1836 he was writing his first reviews of concerts, operas, and exhibits, as well as an article on Mozart. Frequently during the 1840s he translated articles, especially about Shakespeare, but also about Spanish literature, German literature and philosophy, and French history. Botkin's discussions of philosophy in 1842 employ a distinctly Hegelian terminology: "In the dialectical process of time, falsehood destroys itself and gives an even greater impulse to truth"; and again, "The subject of philosophy is . . . not only an absolute that is manifested in the historical passage of time, and consequently contains in itself the moment of destruction and passage into a higher form, but is also an absolute that is divorced from time and space" ("On the *History of Ancient Philosophy* of Karl Sederholm" [1890, II, 394, 397]). The following year Botkin managed to include a cursory paraphrase and much abbreviated summary of the beginning of Friedrich Engels' 1842 pamphlet *Schelling and Revelation* as the introduction to his article "German Literature in 1843" (*Otechestvennye zapiski,* Jan., Feb., Apr., 1843). His reliance upon Hegelian conceptual terminology and upon post-Hegelians like Engels did not last much longer. In 1843 his marriage and separation shortly thereafter, and the resulting three-year-long stay in Western Europe changed his primary concerns from the latest German philosophical developments to the less abstract pursuits of travel and literature.

In 1847 Botkin began the serial publication in the *Sovremennik* (Contemporary) of his *Letters on Spain,* based both on his trip to Spain in 1845 and on various reference and travel books which he might or might not mention by name. The *Letters* made him fairly well known to a wider public than had earlier been aware of his reviews and articles. He presented an enormous amount of detail about Spaniards and their way of life: hundreds of Spanish words and expressions; hundreds of lines from Spanish songs and epic poems (all presented in Spanish with his translation); and he debunked the prevalent Romantic idealized views of the Spanish countryside and flora. The letters incorporated historical surveys, summaries of religious, political, economic, and provincial developments, current events, and descriptions of the everyday things a tourist is bound to see: bullfights, museums, churches, castles, and inns. The essence of the *Letters'* value lies in Botkin's impersonal writing. He lost the earlier philosophical narrowness of interpreting history and facts, and now admitted openly that his old philosophy did not explain everything after all: "truly it is difficult not to have doubts about that so-called eternal perfectibility, especially when you see that in place of the [Arab] civilization, now disappeared, there prevails savagery, ignorance, and fanaticism!" ("Cordova," 1976, 50).

Botkin's published literary criticism consists of two articles, one on the poetry of his old friend Nikolai Ogarëv ("Second-Ranked Russian Poets: N.P. Ogarëv," *Sovremennik,* Feb. 1850), and the other on that of Afanasii Fet ("The Works of A.A. Fet," *Sovremennik,* Jan. 1857), whom he had then not yet met, but who was to become his close friend and brother-in-law. In both he praised their avoidance of "abstract ideas" or thoughts, which he equated with the "abstract conception of humanity that German scholars so love to formulate." He had abandoned almost completely the Hegelian and post-Hegelian philosophical interpretations that captured his imagination during his twenties and, in fact, was so concerned by the general lack of any current theory of aesthetics that he preceded the Fet review with a lengthy formulation of aesthetic theory. Botkin was prompted to present his theory by the publication in 1855 of Chernyshevskii's dissertation, *The Aesthetic Relation of Art to Reality,* which he viewed as a well thought-out attempt to provide such a theory, but in which he abhorred the definition of art as a "surrogate for reality." In the Preface to the Fet article, Botkin argued against the utilitarian concept of art and artist that the more radical Russian critics, including Belinskii and Chernyshevskii, had espoused: "The true poet is filled with an instinctive urge to express the inner life of his soul. This instinctive, involuntary act constitutes the prime condition of poetic creations that are challenged by every kind of positive worldly practical goal belonging to the prosaic sphere and opposed to involuntary expressions of the soul that are poetic by substance and essence. Such an involuntary outpouring of the soul has only one purpose: to express by any menas—music, painting, sculpture, or word—the soul's feeling, outlook and thought, not for any social instruction (that is, there is no worldly purpose), but only to express the feelings, outlooks, and thoughts that are spilling from the artist's soul. This outpouring serves as the basis of the aesthetic theory with the very confusing name, 'Art for art's sake'; in other words, the theory of free creativity, in contrast to a utilitarian theory that seeks to subvert art to the service of practical goals" (1890, II, 361-2). Botkin acknowledged at the time the influence of Carlyle's theories of poetic creativity. Nevertheless Botkin's main ideas of a spontaneous outpouring of the soul had been expressed even earlier in the 1850 review of Ogarĕv, and his insistence on "free" creativity as a necessity for true art is contained in his *Letters on Spain* ("Cordova," 1976, 52).

After the Fet review Botkin wrote and translated very little for publication, concentrating rather on correspondence with friends. He remained what he had been basically all his life—a Romantic, convinced that an artist creates intuitively, instinctively, persuaded that art must express eternal ideas, not the social ideas of the moment. At the same time his desire for an accurate portrayal of reality in literary works was accompanied by an insistence on the artist's possession of "outlook" and "poetry": "Pisemskii has much talent in portrayal and local color, a poverty in outlook on life, and a lack of poetry—in short, all his former qualities and failings" (Letter No. 51 to Turgenev dated 2 Jan. 1857). He was apolitical but can be called conservative regarding the basic order of society, and liberal regarding gradual reforms. An urbane gentleman, sophisticated connoisseur of the arts, lifelong student of philosophy and economic theory, Botkin joined the finest intellectual achievements of the century with hedonistic gratifications in his personal life. He died on 10 October 1869 after a two-year illness.

It is hazardous to estimate the influence Botkin exerted on his contemporaries, or even to define its scope. This is inherently so since he sought a condition of artistic freedom that by its very nature predicates variety, originality and imaginative interpretation. His abhorrence of dogmatism, however, can be joined to his expectation that "eternal" human values and ideas form the innate essence of art. Additionally, one must consider his catholic scholarly interests and his intensive pursuit of the latest world intellectual developments. The composite, then, is of a man who wanted to keep Russian culture from becoming provincial, from being isolated in its temporary preoccupation with certain aspects of social reality. He brought world culture into his life and probably infected his closest associates. During the 1850s his closest associates among the major fiction writers were Turgenev and Tolstoi, both of whom were very much aware of world culture and its current developments. Botkin may have influenced them by reinforcing existing aspects of their intellects or by providing new interpretations of their work or by serving to define their developing artistic natures. In any event, it seems fair to define Botkin's role in Russian literary culture as that of the counterpoise to the utilitarians like Chernyshevskii and Dobroliubov, as a critic whose definition and subtlety of opinion were valued for their perceptiveness and incisiveness. He rounds out, critically, the literary picture, complementing poets like Fet, novelists like Tolstoi and Turgenev, editors like Druzhinin, and playwrights like Ostrovskii.

Works: Pis'ma ob Ispanii (Pb., 1857; L., 1976) [The 1976 edition contains valuable notes and supplementary materials, making it the best book on Botkin's work yet published] ; *Sochineniia*, 3 vols. (Pb., 1890-93); Vassili Botkine, *Lettres sur l'Espagne* (Paris, 1969); N.L. Brodskii, ed., *V.P. Botkin i I.S. Turgenev*, "Academiia" (M.-L., 1930) [81 letters from Botkin, 1851-1869] ; Afanasii A. Fet, *Moi vospominaniia* (M., 1890; rept. Munich, 1971) [Contains 79 letters from Fet] .

References: V.E. Cheshikhin-Vetrinskii, "V.P. Botkin, Biograficheskii ocherk," in *V sorokovykh godakh* (M., 1899), 129-95; N.I. Prutskov, "V.P. Botkin i literaturno-obshchestvennoe dvizhenie 40-60-kh gg. XIX st.," *Uchĕnye zapiski*, Groznyi State Pedagogical Institute, No. 3 (1947), 47-148; M.P. Alekseev, *"Pis'ma ob Ispanii* V.P. Botkina i russkaia poéziia," in *Uchĕnye zapiski Leningradskogo universiteta*, No. 90 (1948), 131-65 [Reprinted in *Ocherki istorii ispano-russkikh literaturnykh otnoshenii XVI-XIX vv.* (L., 1964), 171-206] ; B.F. Egorov, "V.P. Botkin—Literator i kritik," in *Uchĕnye zapiski Tartuskogo universiteta*, No. 139 (1963), 20-81; No. 167 (1965), 81-121; No. 184 (1966), 33-43: Edmund Kostka, "A Trailblazer of Russian Westernism," *Comparative Literature*, vol. XVIII (1966), 211-24; V. Kantor, *"Pis'ma ob Ispanii* V.P. Botkina," *Voprosy literatury*, No. 6 (1977), 279-87; G.A. Genereux, "Botkin's Collaboration with Belinskij on the Puškin Articles," *Slavic and East European Journal*, vol. XXI, No. 4 (1977), 470-82.

Important related materials: P.V. Annenkov i ego druz'ia (Pb., 1892); N.V. Izmailov, ed., *Turgenev i krug "Sovremennika"* (M.-L., 1930); P.S. Popov, ed., *Pis'ma k A.V. Druzhininu, 1850-1863* (M., 1948).

George Genereux

BOTSÍEV, BORIS TIMOFEEVICH (1901-1944). Soviet Ossetian poet, one of the founders of Ossetian poetry. Botsiev was born on 10 September 1901 in the village of Tib into the family of a poverty-stricken mountaineer. He worked as a farm-laborer, delivery man and newspaper vendor in Vladikavkaz, then graduated from the Communist University of the Workers of the East in Moscow. In his novel *Broken Chain* (Sast raekhys, 1935) Botsiev depicts the difficult life of the Ossetian peasantry before the October Revolution and their struggle for freedom. Soviet workers *(Girl Kolkhoz Worker, Safirat, An Evening of Dance)* and patriot-heroes *(Three Girls, Death of a Brave Lad)* are the subjects of Botsiev's verse. Many poems are devoted to the Communist Party and the heroes of the Civil and Second World Wars (*Song of Ordzhonikidze,* the poems "Partisan Bibo," "Courageous Khadzy myrza," 1942, and others). Several of his poems became popular songs. His *Pilots' Song, Children's Song,* and a fairy tale in verse, *The Man and the Lion* (1939), are written about and for children and young people. Botsiev died on 20 July 1944.

Works: Amdza vgataama poemata (Ordzhonikidze, 1941); *Ravzarst uatsmysta* (Dzaudzhikhau, 1947); *Amdzavgata ama poemata* (Ordzhonikidze, 1958).

References: Niger, "Botsity Baron sfaldystady tykhkhai," *Makh-Dug,* No. 5-6 (1938); Kh. Ardasenty, "Botsity Baron," *Makh-Dug,* No. 5 (1945); T. Epkhity, "Botsity Baron poetikon dasnyiady takhkai," *Makh-Dug,* No. 9 (1959).

BOUTS-RIMÉS (literally, "rhymed ends"). A form of literary play called in Russian *"burime,"* which involves writing a poem, often humorous, using a given set of unusual and meaningless rhymes. Often bouts-rimés also must be on a given theme. The form arose in France in the early seventeenth century. In Russia V.L. Pushkin, D.D. Minaev, and A.A. Golenishchev-Kutuzov were famous for their ability to compose bouts-rimés. Examples can be found in N.F. Ostolopov's *Dictionary of Ancient and Modern Poetry* (Slovar' drevnei i novoi poėzii, 1821). In 1914 the Petersburg journal *Vesna* (Spring) held a contest for the best bouts-rimés.

References: N.N. Shul'govskii, *Zanimatel'noe stikhoslozhenie* (L., 1926).

BOVÁ KOROLÉVICH. A hero of the Russian magical folk tale. Surmounting various obstacles, Bova Korolevich performs heroic deeds, manifests miraculous bravery and attempts to win the beautiful tsarevna Druzhevna. The character Druzhevna is the embodiment of love and devotion.

The Russian tale of Bova Korolevich goes back to the chivalric romance of Buêves d'Hanstone, which arose in France during the time of the Crusades and was disseminated throughout Europe. In the sixteenth century the tale was translated from an Italian edition into Serbian and then into Belorussian. This text is the source of several Russian drafts of the tale in the seventeenth century. The tale was already popular in an oral version by the sixties and seventies of the sixteenth century. The figure of Bova Korolevich has been firmly established in Russian folklore and popular literature since the eighteenth century. In the popular literature of the nineteenth and the beginning of the twentieth centuries, Bova Korolevich often figures among the favorite heroes of the Russian epic: Il'ia Muromets, Ivan-tsarevich. Popular tales of Bova Korolevich appeared in hundreds of editions from the end of the eighteenth century until the beginning of the twentieth century in Russia and the Ukraine. Tales of Bova Korolevich have entered the repertoire of modern Russian, Ukrainian and Karelian storytellers and folk tale narrators (M. Korguev, M. Kriukova, G. Sorokovikov and others). One of the literary reworkings of Bova Korolevich's tale in Russia, *Bova, an*

Heroic Tale in Verse (Bova, povest' bogatyrskaia stikhami, about 1798-99), was written by A.N. Radishchev, who introduced civic motifs into it (destruction of the country by noblemen and bureaucrats, libertinism of the nobility, etc.). The same figure attracted Pushkin's attention; under the direct influence of Radishchev he began to write the poem *Bova* (1814), several drafts of which have been preserved.

References: V.P. Adrianova-Peretts and V.F. Pokrovskaia, *Drevne-russkaia povest'*, fascicle 1 (M.-L., 1940); V.D. Kuz'mina, "Povest' o Bove-koroleviche v russkoi rukopisnoi traditsii XVII-XIX vv.," *Starinnaia russkaia povest'* (M.-L., 1941); V.D. Kuz'mina, "Frantsuzskii rytsarskii roman na Rusi, Ukraine i Belorussii ('Bova' i 'Piotr zlatye kliuchi')," *Slavianskaia filologiia. Sbornik statei 2* [IV Mezhdunarodnyi s'ezd slavistov] (M., 1958); – – –, *Rytsarskii roman na Rusi* (M., 1964), 17-132.

BOVSHÓVER, IOSIF [pseudonym: BASIL DAHL] (1873-1916). Yiddish poet. Bovshover was born in Liubavichi, Mogilëv Province. While still a boy, he ran away from home, worked for a miller, and at age 18 emigrated to America. In New York Bovshover worked in a factory where he read his revolutionary poems to fellow-workers, for which he was dismissed. His poems and articles appeared in American anarchist publications (under the pseudonym Turbov) and in the London anarchist newspaper *Arbeiter Freund*. Bovshover attained great technical mastery in his work, far superior to the poetry of other Jewish revolutionary poets (Vintshevskii and Edel'shtat). He introduced into Yiddish poetry the traditions of Walt Whitman and Emil Verhaeren. His poetry was popular among Jewish readers in America, Poland, and Lithuania. Among his works is a translation into Yiddish verse of Shakespeare's *Merchant of Venice* (1899). The labor publishing house Freie Arbeiter Stimme produced his *Selected Works* in 1911, and in 1918 a collection of *Selected Poems* (Geklibene Lider) appeared in Petrograd. It is said to have had some impact on the development of Soviet Jewish poetry. Bovshover became mentally ill in 1899 and spent the last sixteen years of his life in mental hospitals. He died in 1916.

Works: Lider un gedikhte (London, 1907); *Gezamelte Schriften* (N.Y.[?], 1911); *Bilder un gedanken* (n.p., 19); *Lider un dertseylungen* (Kiev, 1939). In English translation: *To the Toilers, and Other Verses* (Berkeley Heights, N.J., 1928).

References: Z. Reizen, *Leksikon fun der idisher literatur, presse un filologie*, vol. 1 (Vilno, 1926); E. Fininberg, *Idische Literatur* (Kiev, 1928); S. Lastik, "Iosif Bovshover, 1873-1915," in his *Mitn ponim tsum morgn* (Warsaw, 1952).

BRÁGIN, MIKHAIL GRIGOR'EVICH (b. 1906). Soviet Russian writer, member CP since 1931. Bragin was born on 10 (23) December 1906 in the village of Krasnopol'e (now Kalinin Raion of the Belorussian SSR). In 1928 he joined the Soviet Army and in 1934 graduated from the Military Academy. He is the author of a biography, *Commander Kutuzov* (Polkovodets Kutuzov, 1941), and two books of sketches of the Second World War, *The Great Battle at Stalingrad* (Velikoe srazhenie pod Stalingradom, 1943) and *From Moscow to Berlin* (Ot Moskvy do Berlina, 1947), depicting events in which the author participated.

Bragin's historical biographies are dedicated to N.F. Vatutin, *Path of a General* (Put' generala, 1953) and A.P. Shilin, *Path of a Lieutenant* (Put' leitenanta, 1957).

Works: In English translation: *Field Marshal Kutuzov: A Short Biography* (M., 1944).

References: Iu. Sevruk, "Uroki istorii," *Novyi mir,* Nos. 11-12 (1941); V. Picheta, "Velikii polkovodets," *Znamia,* Nos. 1-2 (1942); E. Tarle, "Mikhail Bragin 'Ot Moskvy do Berlina,' " *Znamia,* No. 7 (1947);V. Koroteev, "Kak leitenant Shilin stal dvazhdy Geroem Sovetskogo Soiuza," *Novyi mir,* No. 2 (1958).

BRAGÍNSKII, IOSIF SAMUILOVICH (b. 1905). Soviet Russian Orientalist, editor, CP member since 1925, Corresponding Member of the Academy of Sciences of the Tadzhik SSR (1951), Honored Scientist of the Tadzhik SSR (1955). Braginskii was born on 5 (18) June 1905 in Baku. He completed the Moscow Institute of Oriental Studies in 1931. His works are many and varied, and deal with the cultural history of the Central Asian peoples, the classics of Tadjik and Persian literature (Rudaki, Firdawsi, Hafiz, Kamol Khudzhandi, and others), with general theoretical problems of the development of Eastern literatures, the development of Soviet Tadjik literature, and the study of Tadjik folklore. Braginskii is the chief editor of the journal *Narody Azii i Afriki* (The Peoples of Asia and Africa), and administers scholarly projects.

Works: Tadzhikskaia poéziia (Stalinabad, 1949); *Iz istorii tadzhikskoi narodnoi poézii* (M., 1956); *Ocherki iz istorii tadzhikskoi literatury* (Stalinabad, 1956); *Zhizn' i tvorchestvo Sadriddina Aini* (M., 1959); *Persidskaia literatura; kratkii ocherk* (M., 1963); *12 miniatiur* (M., 1966); *Iz istorii persidskoi i tadzhikskoi literatur. Izbrannye raboty* (M., 1972); *Problemy vostokovedeniia: aktual'nye voprosy vostochnogo literaturovedeniia* (M., 1974). In English translation: *Central Asia and Kazakhstan in Soviet Original Studies* (M., 1968).

References: Iosif Samuilovich Braginskii (Dushanbe, 1966) [Materialy k biobibliografii uchěnykh Tadzhikistana].

BRAMBEUS, BARON, *see* SENKOVSKII, O.I.

BRANT, LEOPOL'D VASIL'EVICH (dates unknown). Russian writer, journalist. The son of an officer, Brant served in the army in the communications corps. For thirty years he was a member of the staff of Bulgarin's *Severnaia pchela* where his critical feuilletons appeared over the initials "Ya.Ya.Ya." In addition Brant contributed to several other journals and newspapers, including *Biblioteka dlia chteniia* and *Russkii invalid.* Brant's most noteworthy books beyond his journalism are a collection of tales entitled *Remembrances and Sketches of Life* (Vospominaniia i ocherki zhizni, 1839),*Petersburg Critics and Russian Writers: Some Thoughts on the Contemporary State of Russian Literature in Relation to Criticism* (Peterburgskie kritiki i russkie pisateli. Neskol'ko myslei o sovremennom sostoianii russkoi literatury v otnoshenii k kritike, 1840), an overview of Russian literature in French, *Aperçu rapide de la littérature russe* (1844), *The Aristocratic Woman, a True Story of Recent Times* (Aristokratka, byl' nedavnikh vremën, 1843), *A Few Words on Russian Periodical Publications* (Neskol'ko slov o periodicheskikh izdaniiakh russkikh, 1842), and *Life as It Is* (Zhizn', kak ona est', 1843), the diary of an unknown in three parts.

References: V.A. Vasil'ev, "L.V. Brant," *Russkaia starina,* No. 5 (1883); S.A. Vengerov, *Russkie knigi,* vol. III; *Sochineniia V. Belinskogo,* part 6 (M., 1882), 385-392; V.I. Shenrok, "Otzyvy sovremennikov o *Perepiske s druz'iami* Gogolia," *Russkaia starina,* No. 11 (1894); A.V. Starchevskii, "Vospominaniia starogo literatora," *Istoricheskii vestnik* (August, 1891).

BRAUN, FËDOR ALEKSANDROVICH (1862-1942). Russian philologist, Germanist. In 1885 Braun graduated from the University of Petersburg with a degree in history and philology. Trained by A.N. Veselovskii, the founder of Russian comparative literary studies, Braun wrote a work on Beowulf (1885). From 1900 to 1920 Braun was professor of Western European literature at the University of Petersburg. He is well-known for his linguistic, literary-critical, historical and ethnographic studies of the reciprocal influence of Germanic and Slavic cultures: *Discoveries in the Field of Gotho-Slavic Relations* (Razyskaniia v oblasti goto-slavianskikh otnoshenii, 1899), *A Swedish Runic Inscription, Found on the Island of Berezan* (Shvedskaia runicheskaia nadpis', naidennaia na ostrove Bere-zani, 1907). He also wrote critical articles for the collected works of Shakespeare and Byron. After the October Revolution Braun was director of the Historico-Philological Institute and participated in the planning of revisions in teacher education. Sent to Germany in 1920 to conduct scholarly research, Braun made the decision not to return to the USSR. In 1923 he received a professorship at the University of Leipzig.

Works: Die letzten Schicksale der Krimgoten (Pb., 1890).

References: Biograficheskii slovar' professorov i prepodavatelei imperator-skogo S.-Peterburgskogo universiteta, 1869-1894, vol. 1 (Pb., 1896); V. Buzeskul, *Vseobshchaia istoriia i ee predstaviteli v Rossii v XIX i nachale XX v.,* part 2 (L., 1931); S. Platonov, I. Krachkovskii and S. Ol'denburg, "Zapiska ob uchënykh trudakh professora F.A. Brauna," *Izvestiia Akademii Nauk SSSR* (1927), 1517-20; T.J. Arne, "In memoriam professor F. Braun," in *Fornvännen* (Stockholm, 1942), 375-77.

BRAUN, NIKOLAI LEOPOL'DOVICH (1902-1975). Soviet Russian poet. A native of Parakhino, Tula Province, Braun was born on 2 (15) January 1902 in the family of a teacher. In 1929 he graduated with a degree in literature from the Leningrad Pedagogical Institute, and since 1932 has been a teacher of literature. Braun began to publish in 1924. His first collection of poems, *World and Master* (Mir i master, 1926), is marked by the poet's attempt to determine his place in life by a search for his "own voice." Braun's various collections—*New Circle* (Novyi krug, 1928), *Sortie into the Future* (Vylazka v budushchee, 1931), *Loyalty* (Vernost', 1936), *Links* (Zven'ia, 1937), *Naval Glory. Poems. 1941-1944* (Morskaia slava. Stikhi. 1941-1944, 1945), *Valleys of My Homeland* (Doliny Rodiny moei, 1947), *Earth in Blossom* (Zemlia v tsvetu, 1955) and others—are characterized by Soviet sources as dealing with nature, the Homeland and its history, and an exaltation of love and friendship. Braun has also written the long poems *Munich* (Miunkhen, 1933) and *Youth* (Molodost', 1960).

Works: Stikhotvoreniia (M., 1958); *Novaia lirika. 1955-1957* (L., 1958); *Izbrannoe,* 2 vols. (L., 1972).

References: N. Molchanov, "Istoriia odnoi temy," *Molodaia gvardiia,* No. 5 (1934); Z. Kedrina, "Nikolai Braun," *Literaturnoe obozrenie,* No. 4 (1941); Vs. Rozhdestvenskii, "Nikolai Braun," *Zvezda,* No. 7 (1959); Z. Shteinman, "Nemerknushchaia iunost'," *Literatura i zhizn',* No. 119 (7 Oct. 1960).

BRÁZHNIN, IL'IA [pseudonym for PEISIN, IL'IA YAKOVLEVICH] (b. 1898). Soviet Russian writer, member CP since 1942. Brazhnin was born on 4 (16) February 1898 in the city of Staritsa, Tver Province. He studied literature at the University of Petrograd. Brazhnin has been a reporter, feuilletonist and editor, and has written various kinds of fiction. His first novels, *The Leap* (Pryzhok, 1928) and *Cruel Step* (Zhestokaia stupen', 1930), portray the life of Soviet youth in the twenties. Most significant among Brazhnin's pre-war works is the two-volume work *My Generation* (Moë pokolenie, 1937) and *Friends Meet* (Druz'ia vstrechaiutsia, 1940), about young men and women of the pre-Revolutionary years. their attitudes towards the Revolution and their role in it. His historical novel *Blue Leaves* (Golubye listki, 1957), whose central figure is N.I. Kibal'-chich, portrays the revolutionary People's Will (Narodnaia volia) movement and the murder of Alexander the Second. Brazhnin is the author of military sketches, *Winged Soldiers* (Krylatye voiny, 1942), a play, *Wings* (Kryl'ia, 1948), and stories for children, *Five of Them* (Ikh piatero, 1931), *Riushka* (1935), *A Country Sought After* (Strana zhelannaia, 1955), and others. Brazhnin translated N. Kotliarevs'kyi's *Aeneid* from the Ukrainian (published 1953).

Works: Sovsem nedavnee (M., 1959); *Sila sil'nykh* (L., 1960); "Kak mimolëtnoe viden'e," *Zvezda,* No. 9 (1960); *On zhivët riadom. Dasha Svetlova* (L., 1962); *Iuzhnaia tetrad': Zapiski voennogo korrespondenta* (L., 1967); *V Velikoi Otechestvennoi* (M., 1971); *Siren' na Marsovom pole. Malen'kie romany* (L., 1972); *Sumka volshebnika* (L., 1973).

BRIÁNTSEV, GEORGII MIKHAILOVICH (1904-1960). Soviet Russian writer, member CP since 1926. Briantsev was born in Aleksandriiskaia, Stavropol Krai, on 23 April (6 May) 1904. He served in the Soviet Army from 1925 to 1950. During the Second World War he was head of a unit directing partisan detachments, and was himself twice behind enemy lines on special missions. Briantsev's first book, *You Won't Get Away From Us* (Ot nas nikuda ne uidësh', 1948), is a collection of stories about the partisans. The danger and difficulties in the work of Soviet intelligence agents are the principal content of Briantsev's exciting tales and stories. In his last books, *It Was in Prague* (Ėto bylo v Prage, 1955) and *On Thin Ice* (Po tonkomy l'du, 1960), Briantsev attempted to break with the cliches of adventure literature, to come to grips with great historical events and to develop characters more thoroughly. He died on 27 December 1960 in Moscow.

Works: Po tu storonu fronta (Tashkent, 1949); *Tainye tropy* (M.-L., 1953); *Sledy na snegu* (M., 1954); *Klinok ėmira* (Tashkent, 1959); *Konets osinogo gnezda* (M., 1960); *Goluboi paket* (Tashkent, 1961); *Povesti* (M., 1964). In English: *On Thin Ice* (Washington, D.C. 1964).

References: L. Mikhailova, "Ėto bylo v Prage," *Oktiabr',* No. 9 (1956); G. Vladimirov, "Pisatel' geroicheskoi temy," *Zvezda Vostoka,* No. 8 (1950); G. Vladimirov, "Bol'she zaboty o masterstve," *Zvezda Vostoka,* No. 1 (1952).

BRÍGADERE, ANNA (1861-1933). Latvian playwright, prosaist, poetess. Her most important contributions to Latvian literature are her fairy-tale plays and her autobiographical trilogy.

Brigadere was born on 1 October (19 September) 1861 on the Baḷḷas farm in the Kalnamuiža district, Zemgale, where her father worked as foreman. Brigadere tried to emulate her father's religiosity, authority, unselfishness, helpfulness, and love for nature and work in her own life and her literary works. Her mother knew a wealth of folk songs, fairy tales, legends, and other folklore which deeply affected Brigadere's works. Brigadere received only four years of formal education, 1871-75; from then on she studied on her own. Necessity forced her to work at a variety of jobs—as a shepherdess in childhood, as a seamstress in Ventspils in 1877-79, as a clerk in a grocery store in Riga, as a governess in 1882-84 for some aristocratic wealthy German and Russian families in Moscow and Yaroslavl. In 1885 she successfully completed a formal one-year course in tutoring and received her diploma in Riga, where she worked as governess until 1897, at the same time continuing to study independently. Brigadere was especially fascinated with Tolstoi, Goethe, Schiller, Shakespeare, Ibsen and Björnson.

Having published her first story in 1893 and having her first play performed at the Riga Latvian Theater in 1897, Brigadere became a full-time writer with the financial support of her brother, Jānis Brigaders, then a well-known actor and later a book publisher. At her brother's home in Riga she came in close contact with the cultural elite of the period: R. Blaumanis, J. Jaunsudrabiņš, A. Baltpurviņš, K. Strāls, J. Rozentāls, D. Akmentiņa, J. Skaidrite, J. Duburs, and other prominent writers, artists, and actors. Brigadere published other stories (some written in German) and plays, wrote poetry after the turn of the century, became editor of the feuilleton section and the humorous-satirical section of the journal *Latvija* (after Blaumanis' death) in 1908-09, and the literary editor of the annual *Daugavas kalendārs* from 1915-1933 (annual retitled *Daugavas Gada Grāmata* in 1921) first in Moscow, then in Riga.

When Latvia became an independent state in 1918, Brigadere returned home. There she worked on stories, sketches, plays, poems, and her novel *In the Flaming Ring* (Kvēlošā lokā, 1919), which is particularly nationalistic. She wrote her autobiographical trilogy (1926-32), dealing with observations from early childhood to adolescence, in her summer home Sprīdīši (in Tērvete), which had been awarded to her in 1922 by the Latvian government in recognition of her literary contributions. She died there on 24 June 1933, and was buried in the national cemetery, Meža kapi, in Riga.

Brigadere's *Tom Thumb* (Sprīdītis, 1903) the most important of three fairy-tale plays, was the first Latvian play in this genre. Written in only nine days, the play became immediately popular and has remained so over the years. It has been performed also on Russian, Estonian, Lithuanian, Finnish, Hungarian, and English stages and a 1925 opera by J. Mediņš was based on it. An intermingling of reality and fantasy, *Tom Thumb* is based on various Latvian fairy-tale motifs and deals with the orphan Sprīdītis, his childhood friend Lienīte, and his harsh stepmother, with whom he experiences various conflicts, so that he decides to seek his luck in the world. Finally he returns home, having become wiser, and is reconciled with them. Folkloric materials are an integral part of the characters, language, and content of the play, as is the use of satire.

In *Princess Gundega and King Redbeard* (Princese Gundega un karalis Brusubārda, 1912), the latter stoops as beggar to conquer the haughty, selfish princess, who must endure suffering and perform hard work in order to change through inner growth. The play contrasts the opulence of the court with the humble abodes of the peasants. Brusubārda (similar to Barbarossa) is one of Brigadere's most noble and positive male characters. In most of her other works she is mainly concerned with the portrayal of female characters through contrast, which at times is rather black and white. *Maija and Paija* (1921), another children's play in the folklore genre, contrasts the positive aspects of the industrious, purehearted stepdaughter (Maija) with the negative aspects of the lazy, shallow, real daughter. Maija's willingness to sacrifice herself for the rather lazy farmhand Varis, so that he could be freed from the power of the devil and overcome his laziness, again stresses that it is a blessing to suffer and carry another's burden, that good will conquers evil, that a person grows through work and suffering—religious and ethical themes that fascinated Brigadere all her life. Related to these folklore plays is the dramatic fantasy *Lolita's Wonderbird* (Lolitas brīnumputns, 1927; J. Kalniņš' opera, 1932) dealing with a father's three sons and a phoenix-like bird.

But Brigadere also wrote several important realistic plays. Among them is her first larger play, *At the Crossroads* (Ceļa jūtis, 1906), which under the original title *Father's Sin* (Tēva noziegums), had been censored in 1899 because "it destroyed family principles and respect for parents." Brigadere based her realistic play *Raudup's Widow* (Raudupiete, 1914) on the cruel female character in Blaumanis' short story by the same name.

The author's autobiographical trilogy (1926-32) is a realistic account of people whom Brigadere had observed in her childhood and youth. They are small portrayals of life, united by the common theme of the inner growth of the main characters. Part I, *God, Nature, Work* (Dievs, daba, darbs), is a deliberately naive presentation of Anna's childhood observations of nature and people. Part II, *In Harsh Winds* (Skarbos vējos), shows Anna as an eight-year-old with more critical observations of life as a shepherdess and later as a student, touching on some social problems of farmhands and their families. Part III, *Stone Enclosure* (Akmeņu sprostā) treats Anna's years as seamstress with her sister in Jelgava, and her struggle to support herself and further her education. The novel describes and deplores the shallowness of those Latvians who imitated German ways instead of maintaining their Latvian traditions.

Many of Brigadere's stories portray city life, while others characterize conditions on the farmsteads, the lifestyle of German landlords and Russian aristocrats. These stories are distinguished by their graphic description and vivid dialogue, and by their skillful analysis of the characters of positive and negative women, of children and youth. Brigadere stressed nobility and purity of heart, and opposed laziness, shallowness, haughtiness as well as materialistic considerations in marriage and social position.

At the turn of the century Brigadere started writing poetry concerning the inner life of women, nature, and recollections of childhood. This genre is not her strongest, however. Her one novel, *In the Flaming Ring* (Kvēlošā lokā, 1919), denounced the Soviet intruders into Latvia after its declaration of independence in 1918 as bloodthirsty barbarians, and extolled those fighting for Latvian independence.

Works: Dzejas (Riga, 1913); *Paisums* (Riga, 1922); *Raksti*, 10 vols. (1929-39); *Pasaku lugas* (Riga, 1956); *Stāsti un noveles. Izlase* (Riga, 1958).

References: Biografiska dzeja [autobiography], vol. II of *Raksti;* Arveds Švābe, *Latvju enciklopēdija*, IV (Stockholm, 1950); *Latviešu literatūras vēsture*, IV (Riga, 1957); *Latviešu literatūras darbinieki* (Riga, 1965).

Arvids Ziedonis, Jr.

BRIK, OSIP MAKSIMOVICH (1888-1945). Russian critic, literary theoretician. Brik was born in Moscow on 16 January 1888 to a prosperous middle-class Jewish family. His father was a diamond and coral merchant who travelled extensively in eastern Russia; his mother, a well-educated member of the intelligentsia. In his youth Brik often travelled with his father to the eastern regions of Russia, an activity which he continued throughout his life.

A voracious reader, Brik's performance as a gymnasium student was brilliant. His eloquence, keen wit, magnetic personality and formidable intellectual powers inspired envy and hatred, or admiration and worship. No one who knew Brik ever remained indifferent to him. Snobbery and pretense were instinctively alien to his character. He drew people to himself, regardless of social class or origin, by speaking to their concerns and interests.

When Brik was still at the gymnasium, he became engrossed in the political problems of the day. He read all the works of Marx, Engels and the Russian revolutionary democrats, formed his own Marxist discussion circle, and in 1905 took part in demonstrations against the autocracy, which led to his expulsion from the gymnasium. Without ever completing secondary school, Brik passed the entrance examinations for the Law Faculty at Moscow University in 1906. Brik chose that field because he was not required to attend lectures and classes, thus providing him more time to devote to politics. Although Brik graduated with a degree in law in 1910, he never practiced law during his life, but did apply his legal knowledge during his service with the Cheka in the revolutionary years 1918-1921.

In 1905 Brik met Liliia Yurievna Kagan, the daughter of a prominent Jewish family. She was then a thirteen-year-old student, and her interests were mainly in painting, sculpture, dance and ballet. Their personalities apparently complemented each other. In any event, Lilia's interest in Brik was essentially intellectual. Their marriage in 1912 made Brik an object of envy, since, even though not particularly attractive himself, he had married a most charming, cultured and beautiful woman, eventually considered a Beatrice of her age.

Three years after their marriage, the Briks made the acquaintance of the young Futurist poet Vladimir Maiakovskii, and subsequently became permanently associated with him. This association was of the most profound significance not only for the three of them, but also for the history of Russian literature. First, it inspired some of the most moving lyric poetry of this century, dedicated largely to Liliia Brik. Second, it resulted in Brik's brilliant Formalist studies of poetic sounds, rhythm and syntax, and in the formation of the Society for the Study of Poetic Language, known by the Russian acronym OPOIAZ. Brik was, as will be seen, the principal organizer of this movement. Third, the association rescued Maiakovskii from suicide, with which he had been obsessed prior to his meeting with the Briks. The major source of Maiakovskii's despondency at the time was his feeling that his poetic talent was unrecognized and misunderstood, a feeling which he never really overcame during his lifetime; and this feeling was not without justification or objective reasons. Finally, and perhaps most importantly, this association made Maiakovskii one of "the most original Russian poets of all time . . . ." In other words, Maiakovskii, as we have come to know him in Russian literature, would have been a very different kind of poet without the Briks; indeed, Osip Brik to a certain degree shaped and directed Maiakovskii's art from 1915 to his suicide in 1930.

Maiakovskii's early poetry, which Brik published at his own expense, led Brik to pose fundamental questions about the nature of poetry: How was it made, organized, or better, how was it *produced?* What were its basic ingredients, the secret and mystery of its charm, its characteristic formal components? In particular, what comprised the captivating qualities of Pushkin's poetry? Why was Pushkin's poetry so unique, and why was the poetry of those who consciously tried to imitate his poetry, in both form and content, so dull, pale and undistinguished by comparison? In order to answer these questions and solve the enigma of Pushkin, Brik, with no more background and training than a former "passive" interest in poetry or literature, plunged into the poetic world of Pushkin, Lermontov and Yazykov, a world which he mastered with consummate ease.

Brik's 1916 study of the sound patterns or "sound repetitions" ("Zvukovye povtory") in the poetry of Pushkin and Lermontov added a new critical dimension to the understanding of poetic "laws." Brik boldly challenged the traditional notion of poetry as the "art" or "language of images" and asserted that sound patterns were closely related to semantic levels in poetry and to its musicality. These patterns (or repetitions) were not arbitrarily appended to rhyme and alliteration, but existed intrinsically as a "complex product of the interaction of the general laws of euphony." Rhyme and alliteration were merely "external manifestations" of those laws and did not exhaust "the instrumentation of poetic language."

In his analysis of Pushkin's and Lermontov's poetry, Brik discovered that the repetitious patterns of a consonant and of consonantal clusters, enclosed by various vowels, in different parts of poetic lines engender a "musical" effect. He noted that the "acoustical significance" of repetitious combinations of vowels, consonants and consonantal groupings lay in the following scheme: (1) accented vowels, which impart assonance; (2) stressed consonants, which impart alliteration; (3) unstressed consonants, which constitute the sound patterns or repetitions; (4) unaccented vowels, which provide the general sound background because of their ability to form definite sound combinations in view of their weak acoustical complexion. Brik concluded his study by drawing an analogy between a poem and a painting: in the latter, the "central figures" were its most obvious distinctive aspect, but which did not comprise its totality. Similarly in a poem:

its instrumentation was a unified whole, consisting not only of "central assonances," but also the totality of its "sound" structure, or material.

When Brik was working on the sound patterns in Pushkin's poetry, Maiakovskii suggested to him that he discuss his research with a young literary critic, Viktor Shklovskii, a passionate admirer of Futurist poetry. Liliia Brik also suggested that her childhood friend, Roman Jakobson, a brilliant philologist, also join the discussion. Thereafter, other promising philologists participated: Lev Yakubinskii, Evgenii Polivanov, Boris Eikhenbaum, Boris Kushner. Subsequent meetings were held at the Brik apartment, where philological papers and reports were read aloud for critical discussion.

The Society for the Study of Poetic Language (OPOIAZ) was thus founded in the Brik apartment, which became a vital, creative meeting ground for literary and linguistic discussions. The circle of friends expanded to include not only philologists and Futurist poets, but also artists and novelists, and later, film directors, critics, actors, actresses, musicians, political commissars and, interestingly enough, Chekists (members of the secret police) with a certain thirst for culture.

After the papers of the linguistic scholars were discussed and refined, Brik collected them for publication at his own expense. In 1916 the first issue of *A Collection of Essays on the Theory of Poetic Language* (Sbornik po teorii poéticheskogo iazyka) was published. A year later Brik published another collection of Formalist essays, once again at his own expense. These publications marked a major reaction against a deeply ingrained "civic" approach in Russian literary criticism, which viewed literary works almost exclusively as an expression of social, political and biographical determinants. The aim of the essays was to formulate a specific set of principles or laws that govern the *linguistic* creation or production of poetic works. For these Formalist scholars the essential ingredient in poetry was language, its role, structure, organization and function, and they pointed the way to new and pregnant possibilities in the theoretical study of literature and poetry in general. Their approach ultimately led to some of the most penetrating formalistic studies in the history of Russian literary criticism.

Brik's publication of the essays had important implications. His aim was to link Formalism to Futurism. He regarded the former as a theoretical offshoot of the latter. He believed that Futurist poetry functioned as a laboratory for additional linguistic studies for Formalist scholars, because it provided the critical insights into the formal evolution of poetry and into the nature of poetic language. This also shaped his views in important ways. First, a literary society such as OPOIAZ served a symbiotic function between literary practice and theory, a view which he never abandoned and vigorously sought to propagate after 1917. The intensity of his polemical struggle to do so is largely unintelligible without reference to his interest in the Formalist analyses, which he continued to support even when Formalism became ideologically unacceptable in the mid-twenties. Finally, his own linguistic research shaped his view of the writer, artist and poet as a craftsman, an artificer, a producer who applies his skills to his particular craft, and later, to definite social and cultural problems. For Brik, the artist was the active, creative, independent "filter" of the social and cultural imperatives of his age. In the history of literary criticism, Brik is one of the very few who successfully synthesized Formalism and Marxism.

After 1917, Brik formed a shortlived alliance between the Russian artistic avant-garde and the Bolshevik regime. He became a key figure in the Department of Fine Arts in the People's Commissariat of Education, which directed the art life of the country during the revolutionary years; and it was during those years that Russia witnessed one of the most flourishing periods of creative activity, despite the social and political turmoil. Brik was also an editor of the newspaper *Iskusstvo kommuny* (The Art of the Commune), the principal organ of the radical Futurists and avant-garde artists.

In 1920 Brik, together with Vasilii Kamenskii, founded the Institute of Artistic Culture, which formulated theoretical principles for artistic workshops, particularly the Higher Artistic-Technical Workshops. Almost all the major avant-garde artists were connected with the Institute until 1924, when it disintegrated because of organizational conflicts with the Academy of Artistic Sciences, with which it was associated.

In 1923 Brik and Maiakovskii founded the Futurist-Formalist journal *Lef* (The Left Front of Arts) and when *Lef* ceased publication in 1925, the two men created *Novyi Lef* (The New Left Front of Arts, 1927-28).

Throughout the nineteen-twenties Brik was a principal spokesman of the artistic and literary avant-garde. His theory of the "social commission" (sotsialnyi zakaz) was widely recognized and discussed in the late twenties. The theory involved a client-producer relationship from an "artistic" vantage, by which an artist consciously and independently fulfills the cultural, social and class needs or demands of his time. But the commission also provided the opportunity for formal experimentation, to create the artistic forms adequate to the fulfillment of the commission. The theory had significant implications: "artistic" production was considered similar to other forms of production or work, since it was basically a function of craft or skills, and not essentially the expression of political ideology. nor did it mean the imposition of any "tendency" in fulfilling the commission. Put differently, the artist was not so much a creative, spiritual entity above society as he was a worker integrally related to the normal processes of production.

After Maiakovskii's suicide in 1930, there was some pressure toward diminishing the poet's status and his contributions to Russian literature. Brik immediately began an active campaign to promote Maiakovskii's memory, writing about 200 articles on the poetry, emphasizing its political value, and editing a number of editions of his works. This campaign culminated in a personal appeal to Stalin in 1935, written by the Briks, to which the dictator's now-famous reply was: "Indifference to his memory and his works is a crime." The reputation which Maiakovskii enjoys even today can be seen to be in significant measure due to Brik's efforts.

Brik's critical role in the formation of Russian Formalism, his pioneering studies of poetic sound repetitions and of the relationship between poetic syntax and rhythm, his successful efforts to find a place for Maiakovskii in Soviet literature—these are some of his enduring contributions to that literature.

Works: "Zvukovye povtory," in *Sbornik po teorii poėticheskogo iazyka* (Pg., 1916); "Drenazh iskusstvu," *Iskusstvo kommuny,* No. 2 (1918); "Khudozhnik i kommuna," *Izobrazitel'noe iskusstvo,* No. 1 (1919); "V poriadke dnia," in *Iskusstvo v proizvodstve* (Moscow, 1921); "Shkola Konstruktivizma," *Zaria Vostoka* (August 12, 1923); "Za chto boretsia *Lef,* " *Lef,*No. 1 (1923); "Nasha slovesnaia rabota," *Lef,* No. 1 (1923); "Nepoputchitsa," *Lef,* No. 1 (1923, also published separately, Moscow, 1925); "Tak-nazyvaemyi formal'nyi metod," *Lef,* No. 1 (1923); "Fotomontazh," *Zaria Vostoka* (September 21, 1924); "Fakt protiv anekdota," *Vecherniaia Moskva* (October 14, 1925); "Kino v teatre Meier-khol'da," *Sovetskii ėkran,* No. 7 (1926); "Foto i kino," *Sovetskoe kino,* No. 2 (1926); "Predislovie," in Boris Arvatov, *Sotsiologicheskaia poėtika* (Moscow, 1926); "Za novatorstvo," *Novyi Lef,* No. 1 (1927); "Blizhe k faktu," *Novyi Lef,* No. 2 (1927); "Ritm i sintaksis," *Novyi Lef,* Nos. 3, 4, 5, 6 (1927); "My—futuristy," *Novyi Lef,* No. 8-9 (1927); "Uchit' pisatelei," *Novyi Lef,* No. 10 (1927); "Protiv tvorcheskoi lichnosti," *Novyi Lef,* No. 2 (1928); "Kommentarii k Maiakovskomu," in *Maiakovskii: Sochineniia,* 1 (M., 1928); "Ne teoriia, a lozung," *Pechat i revoliutsiia,* No. 1 (1929); "Poėt V.V. Maiakovskii," in *Shkol'nyi Maiakovskii* (M., 1929); "Maiakovskii—khudozhnik," in *Vladimir Maiakovskii* (M., 1938); "Maiakovskii i muzyka," *Sovetskaia muzyka,* No. 4 (M., 1938); "Kartina vyshla na ulitsu," *Znamia,* No. 12 (1942); *Potomok Chingis-Khana* [film scenario based on the novel of I. Novokshonov] (1928).

References: Roman Jakobson, Postscript to "Two Essays on Poetic Language," in *Michigan Slavic Materials,* No. 5 (Ann Arbor, 1964); Victor Erlich, *Russian Formalism: History and Doctrine* (The Hague, 1965); A. Dymshits, "O.M. Brik," in his *Zven'ia pamiati* (M., 1968); Vladimir Markov, *Russian Futurism: A History* (Berkeley, 1968); Edward J. Brown, *Mayakovsky: A Poet in the Revolution* (Princeton, 1973); Vahan D. Barooshian, *Russian Cubo-Futurism, 1910-1930* (The Hague, 1974); – – –, *Brik and Mayakovsky* (The Hague, 1978).

Vahan D. Barooshian

BRIÚSOV, VALERII YAKOVLEVICH (1873-1924). Russian poet, theoretician, critic, translator, leader in the Russian Symbolist movement. Born 1 (13) December 1873 in Moscow, Briusov was the grandson of a former serf turned cork merchant on his father's side and an amateur littérateur on his mother's. His father Yakov Kuz'mich, who wrote some poems and stories in his youth, and his mother Matrěna Aleksandrovna Bakulina raised him in a "progressive" atmosphere influenced by the revolutionary and utilitarian ideals of the sixties—he was free to read anything but fairy tales or religious works. Briusov's interest in literature began very early; as a child he wrote poetry and began a novel and a journal. While attending Kreiman's gymnasium from 1884 to 1890 he had scholastic and family difficulties and went through a period of rebellion, but he did put out a handwritten journal *(Nachalo)* with a friend and took an interest in Roman history, which was later reflected in his fiction. At the age of sixteen he published an article on horse racing in a sporting magazine. In the fall of 1890 he entered L.I. Polivanov's gymnasium and became more interested in his studies, particularly mathematics, a lifelong avocation, and Russian literature. His industriousness was evident even in his youth: he claimed to have written two thousand poems between June 1890 and April 1891. He entered the historico-philological department of Moscow University in 1892.

In 1892-1893 he became interested in the works of the French Symbolists and began translating Mallarmé. He saw in Symbolism or Decadence, as it was also called, not only exciting aesthetic possibilities, but opportunities for himself in the role of the leader of the Russian school, which he then diligently set out to create:

> I must find a guiding star in the fog. And I see it:
> it is Decadence. Yes! Whatever one may say—it is false
> or it is funny—it is going forward, it is developing, and
> the future will belong to it, particularly when it finds
> a worthy leader. And that leader shall be I!

In 1894, together with his friend A.A. Lang (known by the pseudonym A. Miropol'skii), he brought out the first installment of *Russian Symbolists* (Russkie simvolisty), a collection of translations and imitations of French models of poetry. In the Preface he declared a new art which would "hypnotize the reader" and evoke a certain mood. The work received considerable attention; almost all the critics condemned it, although there were a few words of praise for some of Briusov's poems. Vladimir Solov'ëv found it very offensive and added that if Briusov were a grown man, "any literary hopes are out of place." The second installment appeared about seven months later, including poems under several pseudonyms by the editor, and also received bad reviews—Solov'ëv called one of Briusov's poems "diseased." The third installment appeared in 1895, after Briusov's translations of Verlaine's *Romances sans paroles,* and included Briusov's notorious one-line poem "O, cover thy pale legs." Despite the negative tone of most of the reviews, Russian Decadence and Briusov as its self-appointed leader had become a *cause célèbre.* Briusov had also become acquainted with other poets such as Aleksandr Dobroliubov, Vladimir Gippius, and, most importantly, Konstantin Bal'mont.

The titles of Briusov's first two collections of his own poetry reflect his Europeanism. *Chefs d'oeuvre* (1895) featured characteristically Decadent themes of eroticism and perversity designed to shock the bourgeoisie and reflected Baudelaire's influence. *Me eum esse* (1897), although more purely lyric and less strikingly Modernist, was also greeted negatively. It contains poems affirming the noble calling of the poet, among them the well-known "To the Young Poet" (Yunomy poètu) which reflects his characteristic aloofness, isolationism, and extreme individualism, which sometimes made his dealings with others difficult. His brashness and attempts to create a sensation had made enemies, and he reported that the journals were closed to him for several years. Even periodicals which published works by other Modernist poets often considered Briusov too radical.

After traveling to Germany in 1897, where he received inspiration for his later novel *The Fiery Angel* (Ognennyi angel), Briusov married Ioanna Matveevna Runt. She remained with him until his death, despite his several infidelities, and edited and published some of his works posthumously.

In 1898 Briusov contributed an article on Tiutchev to *Russkii arkhiv* (Russian Archive), whose editor Pëtr Bartenev was impressed with Briusov's scholarship and began a fruitful association with him, publishing his first article on Pushkin. Briusov officially became secretary at *Russkii arkhiv* two years later and worked there for several years. Briusov's *On Art* (O iskusstve, 1899) articulated his view of art as communication with the soul of the artist and his aesthetic individualism, which he elaborated in later theoretical works. He contributed to several journals during this period, apparently being considered "rehabilitated" in part through his association with Bartenev. He received his degree from the university in 1899, an extremely erudite man with a knowledge of ancient languages, world history, and philosophy, and thereafter devoted himself even more exclusively to journalistic activities and writing poetry. In 1899 some of his poems appeared in *Book of Meditations* (Kniga razdumii).

Through Bal'mont, Briusov met S.A. Poliakov and Yu. Baltrušaitis. In 1900 the publishing house Skorpion was founded by Poliakov, giving the Modernists of both Decadent and mystical persuasion a forum for their works. Skorpion published Briusov's collection *Tertia Vigilia* (1900), which was his first real critical success and is often considered the beginning of his maturity as a poet. It included both narrative poems and lyrics and his first urban cycle "The City" (Gorod), as well as poems incorporating major historical figures. It was generally more sober and restrained than his earlier mannerist Decadence. The poem "I" (Ya) contained the characteristic line "But [I] myself loved only combinations of words," reflecting his overriding concern with poetic language.

Briusov was also active in an editorial capacity at Skorpion, helping to organize such works as the almanac *Severnye tsvety* (Northern Flowers), which included works by Chekhov, Bunin, Z. Gippius, and others, and Briusov's own article "Truths" (Istiny). He also contributed to *Mir Iskusstva* (World of Art) and was active in literary circles, becoming a member of the literary commission of the Moscow Literary-Artistic Circle in 1902 (and later its chairman). Admiration for Briusov's editorial and journalistic abilities led Merezhkovskii and Pertsov to invite him to be secretary of the journal *Novyi put'* (The New Way), which first appeared in 1903. However, the basic differences between Merezhkovskii's Neo-Christian mysticism and Briusov's Decadence and interest in questions of craftsmanship and technique soon led to a parting of the ways.

Briusov was an impressive figure, deliberately presenting an eccentric image, with an air of mystery which led Andrei Belyi to call him "madness, tightly buttoned in a frock coat" and the "black magician." In addition to his journalistic activities, Briusov assiduously proselytized on behalf of the new poetry, making French models available through translations and introductory articles, and served as mentor to younger poets such as Belyi and Blok. His personal influence was so great that he was sometimes described as "hypnotizing" his co-workers and proteges, an impression reinforced by the fact that he was more respected than liked.

In 1903 Briusov's fourth collection of poetry, *Urbi et orbi,* was published. It was very well received and had a great influence on Belyi and Blok, who called it "almost a work of genius." In this collection Briusov experimented boldly with rhyme and rhythm, including *vers libre* from the French Symbolists and *chastushki* from Russian folk culture. It also included "Ballads." The theme of the city is further developed, together with his usual erotic themes tinged with sadism and necrophilia.

Briusov was also a prolific contributor to several journals on literary subjects and the occult and continued to publish on Pushkin and his era. From 1904 on, however, his activities centered around Skorpion's new journal *Vesy* (The Scales), which provided at least a temporary rallying point for all Symbolists and became the most influential periodical of the era. Briusov was the unofficial editor and claimed to have read every line in editing and in proof and to have rewritten several articles nominally contributed by others, in addition to contributing articles under pseudonyms and under his own name, such as the introductory "To Our Readers" and the article "Keys to Mysteries" (Kliuchi tain) in the first issue. *Vesy* originally contained only critical articles, but later also accepted original literary works. It published articles by Viacheslav Ivanov, Rozanov, and Merezhkovskii, poems by Blok, Gippius, Sologub, Kuzmin, and Gumilёv, and prose by Briusov, Belyi, Sadovskii, Ėllis, and Remizov, among others, as well as translations. *Vesy* was thus the main organ of Symbolism from 1904 until 1909 and Briusov was its unquestioned leader. His influence is reflected in its European and particularly Belgian-French flavor, with an emphasis on criticism and poetic theory and on poetry rather than prose. It published many works from French contributors, including René Ghil, and reviews of contemporary European literature, offering encouragement to young and often controversial European poets, and translations, particularly from Verhaeren, whom Briusov met in 1908, and Maeterlinck. It thus functioned not only as a forum for the Russian Symbolists of all varieties but as a means of introducing European models and keeping abreast of the latest developments there. Briusov himself made repeated trips to Europe throughout his life and published in European journals.

The unity of the Symbolists was short-lived, however; about 1904-1905 the division between the "older" generation, called Decadents, and the "younger" generation of Symbolists began to be felt. The Decadents, including Bal'mont and Briusov, were distinguished from those Symbolists such as Blok, Viacheslav Ivanov and later Belyi, by their lack of interest in mysticism and metaphysics, as discussed below. The polemics increased with the appearance of several rival journals (such as *Zolotoe runo* [Golden Fleece] and *Apollon)* and publishing houses. Despite personal differences between Briusov and Belyi over Nina Petrovskaia, they continued to work together at *Vesy* and basically adopted the same theoretical stance until its demise in 1909.

Briusov's fifth collection of poetry, *Stephanos* (Venok, dated 1906), is generally considered the height of his poetic achievement and added to his reputation as a leading poet. It, too, was particularly admired by Belyi and Blok. It exemplifies Briusov's "classicist" and "Parnassian" side, his precision and elegance, and includes some of his best-known poems such as "Pale Horse" (Kon' bled) and "The Coming Huns" (Griadushchie gunny). It contains some of his most successful experiments with rhyme and meter, including free verse. The erotic themes have tragic overtones here and the view of the city in the section "The Present" (Sovremennost') is apocalyptic. The cycle "Eternal Truth of Idols" (Pravda vechnaia kumirov) is one of the best embodiments of his interest in myth and history.

Briusov's first collection of short fiction, *Earth's Axis* (Zemnaia os', 1907), is built around the interplay of fantasy and reality, with no clear dividing line between the two. It includes works dealing with the city of the future, such as "Republic of the Southern Cross" (Respublika iuzhnogo kresta), in which the inhabitants of the futuristic polar city, which is protected from the elements and electrically illuminated during the long polar night, are stricken with an epidemic of *mania contradicens* which causes them to do the opposite of what they intend and leads to catastrophe. It also deals with madness ("In the Mirror"[V zerkale]), perverse erotic themes ("Sisters") and Roman history ("Rhea Silvia"). As in most of his fiction, he displays a taste for adventure and the exotic, and the book is characteristically eclectic, containing varied stylistic experiments. Another collection of "stories and dramatic scenes," *Nights and Days* (Nochi i dni), with female eroticism as its central theme, was published in 1913 and other short fiction was published posthumously.

Briusov's first novel *The Fiery Angel* (Ognennyi angel), which first appeared in *Vesy* in 1907-1908 and was later published by Skorpion, is set in Cologne in 1534. Like his other fiction, it emphasizes adventure and displays his erudite knowledge of other times and mores, in this case, the role of the occult in sixteenth-century Germany. The narrator, Ruprecht, becomes involved with a young woman named Renata, who had seen the "fiery angel" Madiel in her childhood and encountered him in human form in the person of Graf Heinrich von Otterheim, with whom she lived briefly and whom she now seeks with Ruprecht's aid. In the course of the search, he studies magic and seeks advice from the occultist Agrippa von Nettesheim and his pupil Johann Weyer (both historical figures). After several adventures such as a duel between Heinrich and Ruprecht and a stormy relationship between Ruprecht and Renata, counterbalanced by his visits to the childish Agnes, Renata leaves. Ruprecht meets Faust and Mephistopheles, and later encounters Renata in a nunnery, where she is accused of demonic possession and condemned and, refusing Ruprecht's offer of help, dies with a sense of absolution. Sergei Prokof'ev later created an opera based on this story.

Briusov's earlier works were reissued as *Paths and Crossroads* (Puti i pereput'ia, 1908). He continued to be active in literary circles, to contribute to journals, and to write, but early in 1909 he left *Vesy* and in the fall of 1910 went to *Russkaia mysl'* (Russian Thought), where he headed the literary criticism section for two years. Briusov had not taken an active part at *Vesy* during his last days there; within a year it closed down. The heyday of Symbolism was over. Briusov felt that the struggles to introduce freedom in form and theme had been successful and that it was time to consolidate and elaborate on what had gone before, as was evident in his sixth collection of poetry, *All Melodies* (Vse napevy, 1909), which contained the famous injunction "To the Poet" (Poètu). This poem reworks and refines his usual erotic, historic, and urban themes and displays his technical virtuosity in the use of repetitions, "difficult" and recondite rhymes, and verbal instrumentation. His interests were not exclusively centered on Symbolism as a partisan school, but on literary freedom in general and its future developments. Having sided with the "clarists" against the "mystics," he was also receptive to new poetry such as that of Gumilĕv and sympathetic to Acmeism, which was in some ways an outgrowth of his own work. His attention turned more and more to Russian poets such as Tiutchev, Baratynskii and Pushkin and to Latin poets, especially Virgil.

During this period Briusov also published *Mirror of Shadows* (Zerkalo tenei, 1912), which includes his well-known poem "To my Native Language" (Rodnomu iazyku) and is essentially a reworking of his earlier themes and verbal experimentation, *Distant and Close Ones* (Dalĕkie i blizkie, 1912) on his fellow poets, his memoirs *Outside My Window* (Za moim oknom, 1913), and the idiosyncratic *Poems of Nelly* (Stikhi Nelli, 1913), written in the guise of the romantic memoirs of a woman poet, which had a great influence on Igor' Severianin.

Briusov's novel *Victory's Altar* (Altar' pobedy) appeared in *Russkaia mysl'* in 1911-1912. The title refers to the altar of the goddess Victory which once stood in the Senate but was removed by the Christian emperor Gratianus; the work is set in fourth-century Rome and presents the struggle between decaying paganism and Christianity through the eyes of young Decimus Junius Norbanus. Although Briusov's knowledge of the period is evident, the novel is not very successful.

Briusov spent the first months of World War I at the front as a war correspondent for *Russkie vedomosti* (Russian News). His eighth collection of poetry, *Seven Colors of the Rainbow* (Sem' tsvetov radugi, 1916) included enthusiastically patriotic verses. It is generally considered part of the decline of Briusov's poetic achievement which continued through the rest of his career. He continued to translate prolifically, however, working on his never-completed translation of the *Aeneid* (published in part posthumously). He also became interested in Armenian culture and, having learned the language in less than a year, lectured on Armenian poetry and was editor, compiler, and major translator of *Armenia's Poetry* (Poëziia Armenii, 1916) and author of *Chronicle of the Historical Fortunes of the Armenian People from the Sixth Century B.C. to Our Times* (Letopis' istoricheskikh sudeb armianskogo naroda ot VI veka do R.Kh. po nashe vremia, 1918).

Briusov accepted the 1917 Revolution enthusiastically and played an active role as administrator and teacher under the new regime, in addition to continuing to write poetry. He became a member of the Communist Party, an act which was never forgiven by many of his former colleagues who had emigrated and regarded him as a political opportunist. In fact, however, Briusov seems never to have had any firm political beliefs and ideals and he was essentially continuing his devoted work as littérateur and organizer. He was active in Narkompros (The People's Commissariat for Education) from 1917 on, serving as manager of its Division of Scientific Libraries in 1918-1919, in the State Publishing House, and at the Institute of Art and Literature; he organized LITO (the Literary Division of Narkompros) in 1920.

His continuing interest in poetic technique is evident in works such as *Experiments in Metrics and Rhythm, Euphony and Harmonies, Strophe and Forms* (Opyty po metrike i ritmike, po evfonii i sozvuchiiam, po strofike i formam, 1918) and in works on poetic theory: *A Short Course on the Science of Verse* (Kratkii kurs nauki o stikhe, 1919) with its introductory article "The Poet's

Trade" (Remeslo poèta), *Treatise on Versification* (Osnovy stikhovedeniia, 1924), and "Synthetics of Poetry" (Sintetika poèzii) in *Problems of Poetics* (Problemy poètiki, 1925), which he edited.

During this period he also wrote dramatic pieces and screenplays, served as editor of an edition of Pushkin's collected works (which was not completed), and contributed critical and theoretical articles to journals such as *Pechat' i revoliutsiia* (The Press and Revolution). He published several more poetry collections: *Last Dreams* (Poslednie mechty, 1920); *In These Days* (V takie dni, 1921) and *Moment* (Mig, 1922), in which he glorifies the Revolution; *Distances* (Dali, 1922), which includes his unsuccessful attempts at "scientific poetry"; *Horizon* (Krugozor, 1922), a selection of his earlier lyrics; and *Mea* (1924). *Distances* and *Mea*, in particular, show the influence of the Futurists and the cosmism of the proletarian poets. He continued to be active in organizations, participating in *Dom Pechati*, which gave many authors an opportunity to read their works during those years of paper shortages. He became a professor at Moscow State University, teaching courses on ancient Greek literature, Imperial Roman literature, and contemporary Russian literature, and also taught at the Literary-Artistic Institute. His feverish activity on behalf of literature was rewarded by an All-Russian Celebration of his fiftieth birthday in 1923, including speeches by Lunacharskii and other dignitaries. He died of pneumonia and pleurisy on 9 October 1924.

Briusov's importance as a literary figure in the era of Symbolism is undeniable. In addition to his original works, he was an indefatigable translator of works of European literature and proselytizer of Western literature in Russia. His interests were wide-ranging, from the Greeks and Romans to the latest developments in French and Belgian poetry. He also remained open to new cultural experiences, as evidenced by his discovery of and interest in Armenian poetry. His translations from the French and Belgian Symbolists evoked mixed reactions, critics sometimes suggesting that his understanding of them was superficial and his translations and "imitations" incompetent, particularly in his early efforts as a translator. However, many of his translations were considered masterpieces—his translations from Verhaeren's work are excellent (E. Verhaeren, *Stikhi o sovremennosti,* 1906; *Poèmy,* 1923). His translation of part of the *Aeneid,* which he worked on during much of his lifetime, was obviously a labor of love and what was published was very successful. He published a wide variety of translations, including, for example, Maeterlinck's *Péléas et Mélisande* (1907), D'Annunzio's *Francesca da Rimini* (1908, with V. Ivanov), Oscar Wilde's *The Ballad of Reading Gaol* (1915), Verlaine's *Romances sans paroles* (1894) and *Collected Verse* (1911), and Goethe's *Faust I* (1928), as well as the collections *French Lyric Poets of the 19th Century* (Frantsuzskie liriki XIX veka, 1909), *French Lyric Poetry* (Frantsuzskaia lirika, 1922), and the Armenian anthology.

He also wrote several stories and longer prose works: for example, the novel *Dasha's Engagement* (Obruchenie Dashi, 1915) and his two novels mentioned above, as well as experimental pieces such as the "psychodrama" *Wayfarer* (Putnik, 1911), theatrical works, diaries, memoirs, and letters. He contributed innumerable articles on the occult, topical subjects, literary theory, history, and criticism, one of the most interesting of which is an article, "Burnt to Ashes" (Ispepelennyi, *Vesy* No. 4, 1909), on Gogol as fantasist. His work appeared in *Vesy* and other Russian journals, and in foreign periodicals, such as his annual review of Russian literature for the English *Athenaeum,* and several contributions to French periodicals. He was especially interested in Tiutchev and Pushkin and his contemporaries, writing scholarly articles on them and editing their work—for example, the collected works of Karolina Pavlovna in 1915 and Pushkin's *Gavriliiada* in 1917. One of his more controversial efforts was his "reworking" and his completion of Pushkin's *Egyptian Nights* (Egipetskie nochi, 1917), which most critics, including Viktor Zhirmunskii, found very unlike Pushkin and regarded the increased exoticism and emotionalism and use of repetitions and exclamations in an elevated pathetic style as evidence of Briusov's Romanticism of theme and style, despite his taste for the classical. Another critic noted the paradoxical combination of "mathematical exactitude" of language and the Romanticism and emotionalism of Briusov's own verse, finding it almost antithetical to Pushkin.

Besides Briusov's translations, editing, and articles on European and nineteenth-century Russian poetry, the younger Symbolist poets and those who followed felt his influence through his innovations and experiments in poetic technique, which represented Briusov's attempt to free verse from outdated conventions. He made a great contribution as a pioneer in the shift from the strict meters of syllabo-tonic verse to tonic verse, which Blok in particular developed further, experimenting with *dol'niki* (used only sporadically before Briusov) and *vers libre.* His work with popular forms such as *chastushki* was also developed further by poets who followed, such as Maiakovskii. He made use of odd juxtapositions and introduced metaphors in unexpected contexts, although he was more conservative than the younger poets in his less frequent use of developed metaphors. Like the other Symbolists, he often employed the devices of repetition and parallelism. He also experimented with vocal instrumentation and was influential in his attempts to break away from strict and conventional rhyme, experimenting with the rhyming of morphologically different words and with polysyllabic, rare and recherché, truncated, and compound rhymes and various forms of imperfect (*netochnyi*) and imparisyllabic (*neravnoslozhnyi*) rhyme. In this field, too, his experiments were solidified and further developed by others. Like many of the other Symbolists, he showed a propensity toward an abstract lexicon and the use of foreign words and archaisms.

Briusov's major themes often reflect French influences: aestheticism and artificiality, the quest for sensation, eroticism and amorality, flirtation with death, isolation, extreme individualism, and exoticism. They are often presented in a cultivatedly extreme manner designed to shock, particularly in *Chefs d'oeuvre,* in which Baudelairean themes are especially evident. Briusov played an important role in introducing the theme of the city in Russian poetry (influenced most of all by Verhaeren), which was to be especially fruitful for Blok. It has been suggested, indeed, that the two essential factors in defining Briusov's role are his link with French Decadence and the urban character of his work. His interest in the city of the future is also evident in his short fiction. Although tinged with admiration for the city's technological grandeur and artificiality, his urban vision is often dark and even apocalyptic. In the dramatic scene "Earth" (Zemlia, in *Earth's Axis,* 1907), the inhabitants of a domed city of the future wish to see the sun again, but when the dome is finally opened, they all die because the atmosphere has long ago disappeared. He also deals frequently with historical and mythological themes, as in the case of the historical settings and personages of his fiction and in the cycle "Eternal Truth of Idols" (Pravda vechnaia kumirov, *Stephanos,* 1906), in which the figures of Anthony and Cleopatra, Theseus and Ariadne, and Orpheus and Eurydice appear. Belyi called him the "poet of marble and bronze." Perhaps related to this monumental aspect of his work are his patriotic poems and glorifications of the Revolution. The theme of loneliness and isolation also plays a central role in his work, sometimes with overtones of melancholy, but more often with a characteristic sense of aloofness and superiority.

This aloofness is clearly embodied in his view of the role of the poet, enunciated most strikingly perhaps in his injunctions "To the Young Poet" (Iunomu poètu, *Me eum esse,* 1896): " . . . sympathize with no one,/ But love yourself boundlessly./ . . . worship art only,/ heedlessly, without goal . . . ." Again, in "To the Poet" (Poètu, *Vse napevy,* 1907), Briusov wrote the famous lines, "Perhaps everything in life is but a means/ To brightly singing verses,/ And you, from carefree childhood/ Seek combinations of words." The poet must be "proud as a banner" and "sharp as a sword" and be a "cold witness of everything," a detached, superior being. Briusov did not disdain hard work as part of the metier of poet, evidenced by his tireless experimentation with poetic techniques and insatiable search for knowledge and his line "Forward, my dream, my faithful ox!"

Briusov also made clear his views of the essence of poetry itself. Influenced by the French, he felt that the task of Symbolism was "to create a new poetical language, to work out poetic media anew" and stressed the new and original: "The Symbolist should be afraid of the banal more than of anything else." Symbolist poetry was not the Bearer of the Word, a means to some metaphysical revelation, but communication: "in enjoying a work of art, we communicate with the soul of the artist." A moment of experience is transmuted into poetry. His position has therefore been called "aesthetic individualism." His disagreements with the second generation of Symbolists such as Viacheslav Ivanov, Blok, and, somewhat later, Belyi, with their mystical bent, and his sympathy for the "clarists" are clear in the polemics in *Apollon* in 1910 between Ivanov and Briusov in his article "On Slave Speech: In Defense of Poetry" (O rechi rabskoi. V zashchitu poèzii): "Symbolism *wanted to be and always was only art* . . . . Art is autonomous; it has its own methods and its own aims . . . ." Throughout his life Briusov maintained his interest in the integrity and freedom of art, not only in the Symbolist "school" narrowly construed, but in all poetic developments.

Briusov and Belyi were the most articulate theoreticians among the Symbolists. Although their specific formulations were vehemently attacked by the Futurists and Formalists, their contribution in renewing interest in poetic language, techniques and "instrumentation" was important. Indeed, Briusov took an active interest in the work of the Futurists.

Although his coldness and aloofness may have alienated Briusov from many of his contemporaries and made him personally unpopular, particularly among emigres who considered him a traitor for his support of the Revolution, most respected his ceaseless work in behalf of literature, which led Marina Tsvetaeva to call him, albeit somewhat sarcastically, a "hero of labor." Belyi, despite his personal differences and eventual ideological split from Briusov, admitted the debt which the younger poets owed him: "Valerii Briusov is the first among contemporary poets . . . . He gave us models of eternal poetry. He taught us anew to become aware of verse . . ." and called him "our slogan, our banner, our commander in the battle with routine and vulgarity." Blok wrote: "I considered, consider, and will consider Briusov my closest teacher after V. Solov'ëv," an influence evident both in poetic technique and urban orientation.

In addition to this major role as mentor to the younger poets, as teacher and popularizer of European culture, and his own original work, Briusov devoted himself to the organization of literary activities and to the cause of supporting and furthering literature in Russia with immense energy, before and after the Revolution. His activities for Narkompros and teaching activities were a logical outgrowth of his earlier role as leader. The scope of his dedicated efforts as teacher, editor, poet, and critic is phenomenal. His work at Skorpion and *Vesy* was particularly important, both in his editorial activities and as a contributor. His literary criticism was usually perceptive and articulate. In his journalistic activities he also found the means to encourage new developments in poetry, such as the work of Gumilëv, which he reviewed favorably (and may be considered to have influenced through his own poetry). Although his poetic works may, with few exceptions, be considered less significant than those of many of the poets whom he influenced, his role as dedicated man of letters and indefatigable organizer and teacher can scarcely be overestimated.

Works: Russkie simvolisty, vols. I and II (M., 1894), vol. III (M., 1895); *Chefs d'oeuvre* (M., 1895); *Me eum esse* (M., 1897); *Tertia Vigilia* (M., 1900); *Urbi et orbi* (M., 1903); *Stephanos. Venok* (M., 1906); *Zemnaia os'* (M., 1907); *Puti i pereput'ia,* 3 vols. (M., 1908-1909); *Ognennyi angel* (M., 1908-1909); *Vse napevy* (M., 1909); *Dalëkie i blizkie* (M., 1912); *Zerkalo tenei* (M., 1912); *Altar' pobedy* (Pb., 1913); "Avtobiografiia," in S.A. Vengerov, ed., *Russkaia literatura XX veka* (M., 1914); *Za moim oknom* (M., 1913); *Stikhi Nelli* (M., 1913); *Sem' tsvetov radugi* (M., 1916); *Egipetskie nochi* (M., 1917); *Opyty po metrike i ritmike, po evfonii i sozvuchiiam, po strofike i formam* (M., 1918); *Kratkii kurs nauki o stikhe* (M., 1919); *Poslednie mechty* (M., 1920); *V takie dni* (M., 1921); *Mig* (Berlin, 1922); *Krugozor* (M., 1924); ed., *Problemy poètiki* (M., 1925); *Izbrannye proizvedeniia,* 3 vols. (M., 1926-1927); *Dnevniki* (M., 1927); *Iz moei zhizni* (M., 1927); *Neizdannye stikhi* (M.-L., 1928); *Izbrannye stikhi* (M., 1933); *Neizdannaia proza* (M., 1934); *Neizdannye stikhotvoreniia* (M., 1935); *Stikhotvoreniia* (M., 1943); *Izbrannye stikhotvoreniia* (M., 1945); *Stikhotvoreniia* (L., 1952); *Stikhotvoreniia* (Minsk, 1955); *Izbrannye sochineniia,* 2 vols. (M., 1955). In English: *The Fiery Angel* (London, 1930; repr. London, 1975); "In the Mirror," in *A Bilingual Collection of Russian Short Stories,* vol. II (N.Y., 1965); "A Sonnet to Form," *The Republic of the Southern Cross,* and "Now When I Have Awakened," in *The Silver Age of Russian Culture* (Ann Arbor, 1975).

References: V. Zhirmunskii, *Valerii Briusov i nasledie Pushkina* (Pg., 1922); N.S. Ashukin, *Valerii Briusov v avtobiograficheskikh zapiskakh, pis'makh, vospominaniiakh sovremennikov i otzyvakh kritiki* (M., 1929); D. Maksimov, *Poėziia Valeriia Briusova* (L., 1940; rev. as *Briusov: Poėziia i pozitsiia,* 1969); Georgette Donchin, *The Influence of French Symbolism on Russian Poetry* (The Hague, 1958); N.S. Gornitskaia, "Briusov–kritik," *Istoriia russkoi kritiki,* v. II (M., 1958); F.D. Reeve, "*Vesy:* A Study of a Russian Magazine," *Slavonic and East European Review,* No. 37 (1958); V. Setschkareff, "The Narrative Prose of Brjusov," *International Journal of Slavic Linguistics and Poetics,* No. 1 (1959); Konstantin Mochul'skii, *Valerii Briusov* (Paris, 1962); Alexander Schmidt, *Valerij Brjusovs Beitrag zur Literaturtheorie* (Munich, 1963); *Briusovskie chteniia 1963 goda* (Erevan, 1964); F.D. Reeve, "Dobroljubov and Brjusov: Symbolist Extremists," *Slavic and East European Journal,* No. 8 (1964); Victor Erlich, "The Maker and the Seer: Two Russian Symbolists," *The Double Image* (Baltimore, Md., 1964); T.J. Binyon, "Bibliography of the Works of Valery Bryusov," *Oxford Slavonic Papers,* XII (1965); Danylo Struk, "The Great Escape: Principal Themes in Valerij Brjusov's Poetry," *Slavic and East European Journal,* No. 12 (1968); *Briusovskii sbornik* (Stavropol, 1974); Martin P. Rice, *Valery Briusov and the Rise of Russian Symbolism* (Ann Arbor, Mich., 1975); Pierre Hart, "Myth and History: Brjusov's 'Rhea Silvia,' " *Slavic and East European Journal,* No. 20 (1976); Brigitte Flickinger, *Valerij Brjusov: Dichtung als Magie. Kritische Analyse des "Feurigen Engels"* (Munich, 1976).

Kathleen Lewis

BRĪVZEMNIEKS, FRICIS [pseudonym for: TREULANDS, FRICIS] (1846-1907). Latvian folklorist, publicist, poet, and public figure. The son of a village artisan, Brīvzemnieks was born on 20 October (1 November 1846) in Rokaiži Volost (now Aizpute Raion). He lived for a long time in Moscow and wrote for Slavophile publications. In the 1870s, under the direction of the Russian Society of Anthropology and Ethnography, Brīvzemnieks led an expedition into Latvia and compiled the first scholarly anthologies in Russian of Latvian folk songs, entitled *Anthology of Anthropological and Ethnographical Materials* (Sbornik antropologicheskikh i ėtnograficheskikh materialov, 1873), proverbs and sayings, in *Materials on the Ethnography of the Latvian Tribe* (Materialy po ėtnografii latyshskogo plemeni, 1881), and tales and legends, in *Latvian Tales: An Anthology of Materials on Ethnography* (Latyshskie skazki. Sbornik materialov po ėtnografii, 1887), as well as the first anthology of Latvian tales in Latvian: *Our Folk Tales* (Mūsu tautas pasakas, 1887). He has translated works by Russian authors into Latvian. Brīvzemnieks died on 2 (15) September 1907 in Ropaži, near Riga.

Works: Raksti, 4 vols. (Riga, 1909-14).

BRÓDELE, ANNA (b. 1910). Soviet Latvian writer, playwright. The daughter of a forester, Brodele was born on 16 September 1910 in the village of Tauroga, Lithuania. In 1927 she began to publish poems and stories. Brodele was sentenced to four years' imprisonment in 1932 for participation in Communist activities. After Latvia was made a Soviet republic she worked in editorial offices. She studied at the Gor'kii Literary Institute in Moscow. During the Second World War Brodele wrote the plays *Duty* (Pienākunis, 1942), *Don't Let Them Leave* (Nelaujcet aiziet, 1943), *An Unfulfilled Idea* (Nepiepildītā, ideja, 1944) and others. In the post-war years the plays *Spring in Upesciema* (Upesciema pavasaris, 1948), *Schoolmaster Straume* (Skolotajs Straume, 1948), *Golden Cornfield* (Zelta druva, 1949), *Fervent Hearts* (Dedzīgās sirdis, 1951) and others were written. Soviet sources characterize the contents of these plays as an exposure of remnants of the capitalist past and the growth of the kolkhoz workers' consciousness. In the tale *Marta* (1950), Brodele depicts the struggle of Latvian workers for Soviet power. Her novels *With the Heart's Blood* (1955) and *Fidelity* (Uzticiba, 1960) are devoted to kolkhoz life.

Works: Izlase (Riga, 1960); *Mana trauslā meitene* (Riga, 1964); *Klusā pilsētina* (Riga, 1967); *Tas ir mans laiks* (Riga, 1969). In Russian translation: *Vesna v sele Rechnom. P'esa* (M.-L., 1949); *Uchitel' Straume* (M.-L., 1949); *Marta* (M., 1952); *Krov'iu serdtsa* (M., 1960); *Vernost'* (M., 1962).

References: Latyshskie sovetskie pisateli. Biograficheskie spravki (Riga, 1948); *Ocherk istorii latyshskoi sovetskoi literatury* (Riga, 1957).

BRÓDSKII, IOSIF ALEKSANDROVICH [JOSEPH BRODSKY] (b. 1940). Russian poet and critic, in emigration since 1972.

Brodskii was born in Leningrad on 24 May 1940 of Russian-Jewish parents. His father, a photo-journalist, served in the Navy during the Second World War; his mother worked as a translator. Both are now retired, and live in Leningrad. During the war, largely in the care of his grandparents, Brodskii lived through the German blockade of the city. He attended public schools in Leningrad through the eighth grade, leaving in 1955 to pursue his education on his own. It proceeded along two lines concurrently: close contact with other poets, writers, and translators, primarily from Leningrad; and extensive independent reading in Russian, European, British, and American literature, Russian religious and philosophical thought, Greek mythology, the poets of the classical world, and— beginning in 1963—the Old and New Testaments. In 1958 he began to write poetry and soon thereafter to display extraordinary gifts as a verse translator. He tried to gain admission to the studios of Natal'ia Grudinina and Gleb Semenov, but both refused him. Grudinina came to Brodskii's defense during his trial in 1964, saying that she had been mistaken in not recognizing his talent earlier; Semenov recognized it, but realized that he would never make an "official" poet out of Brodskii.

Brodskii worked at various jobs in Leningrad factories and laboratories, and on geological expeditions to the Far North (White Sea region) (1957), the Far East (1958), and the South (Caspian Sea region) (1959 or 1960). (Brodskii's poems to the memory of Fedia Dobrovol'skii go back to the latter summer.) Professor E.G. Etkind, an outstanding theoretician and practitioner of poetic translation, welcomed Brodskii to his informal translation workshops. In 1960 Brodskii met Anna Akhmatova (1889-1966) and knew her well during the last five years of her life. She encouraged him and on several occasions expressed her high opinion of his work. Her influence on Brodskii was very great, though it took the form of inspiration and guidance rather than that of a direct influence on his style. She shaped his future in two important ways. First, she was a living tie with the great Russian lyric tradition that reaches back in a continuous line to the first half of the eighteenth century. From 1961 on, in his *choice* of form, Brodskii writes within the tradition. (In working from traditional forms, however, he has developed them in ways that are quite untraditional.) And second, Akhmatova knew English and American poetry and encouraged Brodskii's already awakened interest in it. In addition, her special veneration of Dante, parallel to Mandel'shtam's, found a strong response in Brodskii.

He began to study Polish in 1956 under the impetus of the lively cultural ferment which accompanied the "Polish October." By the end of the 1950s he was reading some of the best modern Polish Poets (Norwid, Herbert, Miłosz) and translating Gałczyński. Polish also served as a bridge to twentieth-century Western writers unavailable in Russian translation but then being published in translation in Poland (Kafka, Faulkner, Proust, and Virginia Woolf).

In January 1964 Brodskii was arrested and, in February and March, tried and condemned as a "social parasite." The trial was an attack, with Brodskii as its victim, on all those outside the "official ranks" of poetry and indeed on literature itself. Professors Etkind, Grudinina, and Admoni spoke vigorously on his behalf as witnesses for the defense; among those who expressed their support for him during the trial were Akhmatova, Kornei Chukovskii, and Dmitrii Shostakovich. Brodskii was sentenced to five years' administrative banishment from Leningrad, and ordered to work on a state farm in the Arkhangelsk region of northern Russia. The sentence was commuted the next year, however, and Brodskii was allowed to return to Leningrad in November 1965. While he was in exile, an American publisher issued the first collection of his poetry: *Shorter and Longer Poems* (Stikhotvoreniia i poémy, 1965). Brodskii was not involved in its preparation, but it remains important for the study of his earliest verse, much of which is unavailable elsewhere.

By the time Brodskii returned to Leningrad he could read English well and was writing in his own fully developed "metaphysical" style. The years 1965 to mid-1972 represent his mature Leningrad period. During this time he wrote most of the poems included in his second book *A Halt in the Wilderness* (Ostanovka v pustyne, 1970), as well as many of those included in his third book *The End of a Wonderful Epoch* (Konets prekrasnoi epokhi, 1977) and the first eight poems of his fourth book, *A Part of Speech* (Chast' rechi, 1977). He worked on translations from English: Donne, Marvell, Behan's *Quare Fellow,* Stoppard's *Rosencrantz and Guildenstern Are Dead.* A few of his translations were published in Moscow, and four of his own poems appeared in print in Leningrad in *Molodoi Leningrad* (1966), and *Den' poèzii* (1967).

In June 1972 Brodskii became an involuntary exile from his native country. After brief stays in Vienna and London, he settled in the United States; he has been a permanent resident since July 1972 and a U.S. citizen since October 1977. Since September 1972 Brodskii has been poet-in-residence and special lecturer at the University of Michigan; during leaves of absence from Michigan he has taught at Queens College, New York, and the Five Colleges (Amherst, Smith, Mt. Holyoke, Hampshire, and the University of Massachusetts), and Columbia's

Russian Institute. He has given numerous poetry readings in the United States, Canada, Mexico, Western Europe, and Greenland, and his poetry has been translated into at least a dozen languages. He is a member of the Bavarian Academy of Fine Arts and the American Academy of Arts and Sciences as well as the editorial board of the Russian-language journal *Kontinent,* published in Paris. In 1977/78 he was a Guggenheim Fellow in poetry; in May 1978 Yale University conferred upon him the degree of Doctor of Letters *honoris causa.*

Brodskii dedicated some of his early poems to such fellow Leningrad poets as Gleb Gorbovskii, Evgenii Rein, and Anatolii Naiman. He learned from many of them (Vladimir Ufliand, for example, whose irony, like Brodskii's, has a tender rather than an angry or bitter edge); and they in turn, as well as younger poets (Oleg Okhapkin, for example), learned from Brodskii. They wrote in different styles, but all of them were committed to the common task of working to revive and restore Russian poetic culture, which the Stalinist era had reduced to impoverishment. The language of poetry had to be brought to life again. This involved both reinvigorating the language and retrieving lost riches. It meant breaking up standard phrases and learning to write a line of verse one word at a time. Brodskii's work has been a major contribution to this effort. Among his gifts is an ear for what is serviceable in poetic contexts, whether it be postwar Soviet slang or an archaism from the seventeenth or eighteenth centuries. The language of Brodskii's poetry is at once bookish and colloquial, and at all times has the robustness of spoken speech.

Brodskii's earliest poems (1958-1960), such as "The Monument" (Pamiatnik), with its climactic final line:

> "Postavim pamiatnik lzhi"
> (We'll build a monument to lies)—

are generally short and dominated by simple declarative sentences. They are written in a "free" verse line with neither a fixed length nor fixed rhythm, and with only occasional rhymes. They assert, rather than question; they lay down axioms, often with ingenious development of a basic metaphor ("Verbs" [Glagoly], "Fish in Winter" [Ryby zimoi]). Their language is plain and direct without any ornamentation; they aim not at achieving musical or poetic effects but at establishing basic values.

Since then Brodskii's work has grown rapidly in complexity and scope without straying from what is an essentially continuous vision. He is concerned with some of the central problems of the human spirit in the twentieth century; in his choice of forms, and in the way his imagination is grounded in the history and mythology of the Western tradition, he is a modern descendant of classicism. The result is a very human, sometimes difficult "metaphysical" poetry in which both the poet and his audience "are adjured by the poem to rethink their existence" (Arthur Cohen).

Brodskii's work between 1961 and 1964 includes impressive achievements in the song and other shorter lyric forms: "A Christmas Ballad" (Rozhdestvenskii romans, 1962), "Enigma for an Angel" (Zagadka angelu, 1962), "Songs of a Happy Winter" (Pesni schastlivoi zimy, 1963), his interesting and very unconventional sonnets, and many others. But this period is characterized best by a turning to the long poem, and by radical experimentation with inherited verse forms. In the long poem Brodskii has found almost unlimited freedom to experiment, and he has used this freedom to explore new possibilities for his verse. Formally, he began from traditional models of the iambic line (Pushkin, Akhmatova), and in rhythm and phrasing his earliest iambic pentameters are very close to them, as in the long poem "The Procession" (Shestvie, 1961). But that same year he began to experiment with techniques that bring the line into sharp relief, or in the opposite direction, tend to efface it. The result in either case is something quite different from standard Russian verse. The former led him to the verse of the two major long poems of this period, "Isaac and Abraham" (Isaak i Avraam) and "Elegy for John Donne" (Bol'shaia élegiia Dzhonu Donnu), both written in 1963. This verse tends toward a maximum possible density of stressed syllables, which in Russian is formally very difficult to achieve because it requires the use of predominantly one- and two-syllable words. Yet Brodskii manages to do it, and the result is a completely new iambic music with a sense of maximum fullness in the line.

Thus, in the "Elegy . . ." Brodskii squeezes *nine* Russian words into a single line of iambic pentameter:

> tak beden, gust, tak chist, chto v nikh—edinstvo
> (so poor, so pure and dense, that all seems one).

What is thus described is a line of John Donne's poetry. Speaking directly to Donne, Brodskii creates a line of his own with *ten* Russian words:

> I Ad ty zrel—v sebe, a posle—v iavi
> (And you glimpsed Hell, first in your dreams, then waking).

In "Isaac . . ." Brodskii exhibits a stunning transformation of the word *kust,* 'bush,' into the word *krest,* 'cross,' a process which takes place (in Isaac's dream) painfully, letter by letter, symbolizing the conversion of a part of nature into the altar upon which Isaac is to be sacrificed. The name "Isaac" becomes a kind of acronym, formed from the first, the last, or the first and last, letters of the words I ('and'), SnovA ('again'), zhertvA ('victim'), and Krichit ('screams'):

> I SnovA zhertvA na ogne Krichit:
> Vot to, chto "Isaak" po-russki znachit.
> (The victim wrItheS upon the flAme And sCreams:
> This is what "Isaac" comes to mean in Russian.)

At the other end of the spectrum from his dense single lines are Brodskii's experiments with mobile intonational breaks, begun in this period but fully worked out only after 1965. In this type of line Brodskii uses a very high frequency of enjambments, and long sentences, with complex syntax, spilling over from line to line and even from one stanza to the next. An extreme case is the 28-line poem "On the Death of a Friend" (Na smert' druga, 1973), the first sentence of which occupies *20* long anapestic pentameter lines. At the same time Brodskii began during this period to experiment in different, but equally original ways with the anapest. Continuing these experiments through the sixties, Brodskii has developed out of the traditional iambic and anapestic meters verse forms that bear his own individual signature.

The Polish poets, especially Gałczyński, were a catalytic influence on Brodskii, showing him new ways of broaching a subject indirectly, letting the poem follow its own absurd logic through verbal jokes and even intellectual clowning, and at the same time allowing the subject to retain whatever serious implications it might have. "Two Hours in an Empty Tank" (Dva chasa v rezervuare, 1965) and "A Letter in a Bottle" (Pis'mo v butylke, 1965) are extended examples of Brodskii's wit in this vein.

English was a second and more important influence on his work. It gave him access to the great English lyric tradition from the sixteenth to the twentieth centuries, especially Donne, Marvell, Eliot, Frost, Wallace Stevens, Dylan Thomas, and W.H. Auden. Brodskii's genius has found a home in their company. His "Verses on the Death of T.S. Eliot" (Stikhi na smert' T.S. Eliota, 1965), a poem Akhmatova particularly admired, was modelled closely on a poem by Auden entitled "In Memory of W.B. Yeats (d. Jan. 1939)." Of the poet's death, Brodskii declares: "It was not God, but only time, mere time/that called him." God would have summoned the poet only if his creative work had been completed. But this was not the case with Eliot; his body had simply worn out. The gravesite is evoked in two powerful lines:

> I tuch plyvut po nebu korabli.
> No kazhdaia mogila—krai zemli.

> (And ships of cloud swim slowly heavenward.
> But each grave is the limit of the earth.)

The poet's immortality is secured not only by posterity but also by the world of nature. Addressing Eliot directly, Brodskii asserts:

> Pamiat'—esli ne granit—
> oduvanchik sokhranit.

> (If you're not recalled by stone,
> puffball drift will make you known.)

Brodskii found his closest tie of kinship with the "metaphysical" poetry of John Donne (1573-1631). Donne's lyric style is discursive, dramatically expressive, richly metaphorical, and intellectually complex. In content it is a poetry of the heart and mind together, in which no line of separation stands between love and philosophy or between the sacred and the profane. Brodskii has incorporated all this into his own style. Indeed, he adds to Donne's "conceit"—death stringing heaven and earth together, like beads, on the thread of a human soul—the "Russian" element of falling snow, thus creating the strikingly original image of snowflake-needles that stitch body to soul and earth to heaven. Of the "sleeping" John Donne Brodskii writes:

> Like some great bird, he too will wake at dawn;
> but now he lies beneath a veil of white,
> while snow and sleep stitch up the throbbing void
> between his soul and his own dreaming flesh.

Brodskii's mind is always focussed upon the present. But he makes forays into history and myth, seeking affinities with our own age, constructing and speaking through masks that show the single Janus-face of past and present. The concerns are contemporary, but the objects of the poet's "intuitive synthesis" (to use Brodskii's own expression) are often drawn from the past. Examples are the Russian eighteenth century, as in "Epistle to My Verses" (Poslanie k stikham, 1967); a generalized Garden of Eden, as in "Almost an Elegy" (Pochti élegiia, 1968); the heroic age in Greece, as in "To Lycomedes on Scyros" (K Likomedu, na Skiros, 1967) and "Odysseus to Telemachus" (Odissei Telemaku, 1972); the founding of the Roman Empire, as in "Aeneus and Dido" (Ènei i Didona, 1969); and the point of transition from the Old to the New Testament, as in "*Nunc Dimittis*" (Sreten'e, 1972). Brodskii is a learned man, but not a "learned poet": the aim is not scholarly interest or a desire to make historical commentary. It is, rather, to show that the present is contained in the past, for it is that unbroken tie with our past, contact with our origins, fidelity to our spiritual and cultural legacy that we in the twentieth century need if we are to possess ourselves whole.

Two main currents may be discerned in Brodskii's use of historical and mythological themes, though they are not separable because they constitute a single whole which is the heritage of Western man. But that whole has its polarities in Brodskii's work. One current looks back to origins. Here are the Greek, Christian, and Old Testament themes, and, in Russian terms, the theme of St. Petersburg in the eighteenth century; Brodskii associates the latter with Derzhavin (1743-1816), the greatest Russian poet of that age. Origins are characterized by love, miracle, wholeness, a sense of life's sacred character. The other current measures the distance from origins. Its historical image is the Roman or Romano-Byzantine Empire. Here Brodskii explores the themes of man and the state; service, and the meaning of service; betrayal, faith-breaking, the lie. The immediate present is an ambiguous middle ground. An example is "A Halt in the Wilderness" (Ostanovka v pustyne, 1966), a poem in blank verse on the subject of the razing of a Greek church in Leningrad to make space for the construction of a glass-and-steel concert hall. It shows Brodskii as a man of common sense, but also as a moralist and an ironist; it looks back to Russia's Christian origins, and measures its present distance from them with dismay and misgiving.

Perhaps the central theme developed during this period is the theme of *razluka,* parting, a traditional lyric theme of considerable complexity in the work of poets who have influenced Brodskii (Baratynskii, Akhmatova, Donne). Brodskii has developed it in his own, original way. "Stanzas" (Strofy, 1968) and "Refusing to catalogue all of one's woes" (Otkazom ot skorbnogo perechnia, 1967) are valedictions modelled on Donne, but their treatment of the theme is Brodskii's own. It is a love theme; its central image is a woman whom the poet loves. Parting from her prefigures the final parting, which is death. The longest of these poems is "Adieu, Mademoiselle Véronique" (Proshchaite, madmuazel' Veronika, 1967). It shows very clearly that in Brodskii's work the sacred and the profane cannot be separated. This is a love poem about a man and a woman; it is also a Christian poem about suffering. For parting is the moment when the tie with love, miracle, and wholeness is broken. This shows its essential elegiac character. At the same time it affirms, with wit and spirit, the worth and the meaning implied by that loss.

Brodskii's most ambitious poem written in Leningrad is doubtless *Gorbunov and Gorchakov* (1965-1968). Technically, it is the most formidable challenge

Brodskii has set himself. Each of its 14 sections contains 100 iambic pentameter lines, arranged, as a rule, in 10 stanzas of 10 lines each, with the same two rhymes alternating throughout the entire stanza. These obsessively repeating rhymes give it a formal quality in keeping with the setting of the poem, a hospital for madmen. It is mostly a discussion between two inmates of the hospital, a kind of philosophical dialogue, not Socratic but Dostoevskian: "Gorbunov, the humane, half-crazy dreamer about mushrooms and the sea, and his tormentor, the *seksot* [informer] Gorchakov, are really two facets of one anguished consciousness," and section V, "Song in the Third Person," is "a kind of monument to the ritual of denunciation" (Clarence Brown). That Gorbunov and Gorchakov are "two facets of one . . . consciousness" is perhaps true at one level; but at another level, they are quite distinct. The name "Gorbunov" suggests the Russian word for "hunchback," *gorbun;* Gorbunov is a kind of spiritual cripple, beaten down and tormented by the world. "Gorchakov" suggests the Russian word for "bitterness," *gorech';* Gorchakov is a bitter man, who embitters the lives of others. He reports to the hospital psychiatrists the heterodoxies which Gorbunov has dreamed (and confided to him) and is rewarded with a promise of "release at Easter time." Gorchakov thus emerges as a Judas figure and Gorbunov as a Christ figure, betrayed and crucified.

All literature, Brodskii has said, is about "what time does to human beings," as manifested in loss, separation, deformity, madness, old age, and death. Poetry, for Brodskii, is a way—in the end, the only way—of enduring the "horrors and atrocities of existence" (to quote a Nietzschean expression favored by the thinker whom Brodskii most admires, Lev Shestov). As Brodskii put it in the 1976 poem "York," dedicated to the memory of his friend and mentor W.H. Auden:

> Subtract the greater from the lesser—Time from the man—
> and you get, as a remainder, words, which stand
> out against their white background more clearly
> than a man's body does while he lives . . . .

The prospect of exile into a foreign culture and language is terrifying for a poet, since it threatens to reduce the "remainder" of his not-yet-written poetry. In his first major poem written in exile, called simply "1972," Brodskii gives a stark list of what he is losing:

> volosy, zuby, glagoly, suffiksy
> (my hair and teeth, my verbs and endings)

—in other words, the total control of his native language which a poet must retain. There was no fear of such loss, of course, in the poems of "domestic" exile written in Orenskaia in 1964-65. Then Brodskii felt himself "buried alive," threatened with "a shadow of mindlessness," he was "without memories, with only an inner noise," "nearly deaf" and "nearly blind" ("New Stanzas to Augusta" [Novye stansy k Avguste, 1964]). Both kinds of exile involve suffering, loss, separation; but permanent exile in a foreign country adds the threat of silence in the sense of "non-speaking" (molchanie).

Fortunately, Brodskii's poetic voice is still strong, and his formal inventiveness still fresh. "1972" is written entirely in triple dactylic rhymes of the kind he calls "destructive." Each rhyme-position has a rigidly associated symbolic level.

That associated with the first position is moral-spiritual-intellectual; with the second, emotional-psychological; with the third, biological-physical. For example, the triple slant-rhyme: *"trusosti/trudnosti/trupnosti"* refers to diverse aspects of the phenomenon of suicide. The first is moral cowardice, the second emotional difficulty, the third the physical condition of deadness (literally "corpseness," a Brodskian coinage), of being an inert thing. The three-step structure of the dactylic rhyme itself ($/\smile\smile$) is a kind of iconic representation of this descending semantic movement. This is a formal device of striking originality and power.

The connection made in "Gorbunov and Gorchakov" between life and speech, on the one hand, and death and silence, on the other—"Life is but talk hurled in the face of silence"—is continued and deepened in *"Nunc Dimittis"* and in a series of powerful poems written in the mid-1970s: "The Butterfly" (Babochka, 1973), "Cape Cod Lullaby" (Kolybel'naia Treskovogo Mysa, 1975), and "December in Florence" (Dekabr' vo Florentsii, 1976), the last being Brodskii's "Dante" poem. Other important "Italian" poems are "The Lagoon" (Laguna, 1973), "The Torso" (Tors, 1973), and "San Pietro" (1978). The theme of speech and silence is combined in these poems with a theme which has come increasingly to preoccupy Brodskii, the absurdity of existence and the absurd "Hell" of Nothingness into which death plunges us.

But Brodskii remains a moralist, for whom absurdity is not the final word. "[E]ven after the Absurd," he has written, "one has to live, to eat, drink, . . . betray or not betray one's neighbor." It was in this sense that he wrote, in "To Lycomedes on Scyros":

> When all is said and done, a murder is
> a murder. And we mortals have a duty
> to take up arms against all monsters.

In addition to poetry written in Russian, Brodskii has, since his exile, produced: two poems in English (on the death of W.H. Auden and of Robert Lowell); Russian verse translations from the Lithuanian of Tomas Venclova and the Polish of Czesław Miłosz; a Russian prose translation of George Orwell's "Shooting an Elephant"; penetrating critical essays on Akhmatova, Mandel'shtam, Cavafy, Montale, and Miłosz (Brodskii wrote the last three of these directly in English); an engaging memoir of his Leningrad childhood; an essay on Stalin and Stalinism, review-essays on Solzhenitsyn's Gulag Archipelago and Dolgun's *An American in the Gulag;* forewords to works by Andrei Platonov and Osip Mandel'shtam and to a volume of *Modern Russian Poets on Poetry.* A number of Brodskii's prose writings are collected in the forthcoming volume *Less than One.*

Works: Stikhotvoreniia i poémy (Washington-N.Y., 1965); *Ostanovka v pustyne* (N.Y., 1970); *Konets prekrasnoi épokhi: Stikhotvoreniia 1964-1971* (Ann Arbor, Mich., 1977); *Chast' rechi: Stikhotvoreniia 1972-1976* (Ann Arbor, Mich., 1977); *V Anglii* (Ann Arbor, Mich., 1977). Translations into English: *Joseph Brodsky: Selected Poems* [Introduction by George L. Kline, Foreword by W.H. Auden] (London and N.Y., 1973); *A Part of Speech* (N.Y., 1979); *Less than One* (N.Y., 1980) [a collection of essays].

References: Pierre Emmanuel, "A Soviet Metaphysical Poet," *Quest,* 52 (1967), 65-72; Ernst Pawel, "The Poetry of Joseph Brodsky," *Midstream,* XIV,

No. 5 (1968), 17-22; Milica Nikolić, "Mutni govor Josifa Brodskog," Preface to Josif Brodski, *Stanica u pustinji* (Belgrade, 1971), 5-37; Stephen Spender, "Bread of Affliction," *New Statesman* (14 December 1973), 915; Susan Jacoby, "Joseph Brodsky in Exile," *Change*, V, No. 3 (1973), 58-63; Kees Verheul, "Iosif Brodsky's 'Aeneas and Dido,' " *Russian Literature Triquarterly*, No. 6 (1973), 490-501; Victor Erlich, "A Letter in a Bottle," *Partisan Review*, XLI (1974), 617-621; Rosette C. Lamont, "Joseph Brodsky: A Poet's Classroom," *Massachusetts Review*, XV (1974), 553-577; Richard D. Sylvester, "The Poem as Scapegoat: An Introduction to Joseph Brodsky's *Halt in the Wilderness,*" *Texas Studies in Literature and Language*, XVII (1975), 303-325; Kees Verheul, "Het persoonlijke konflikt van Iosif Brodski," in *Verlaat debuut* (Amsterdam, 1976), 53-58; V. Alloi, "Proryv v beskonechnost' (chitaia stikhi Iosifa Brodskogo)," *Vremia i my*, No. 8 (1976), 147-158; A. Losev "Niotkuda s liubov'iu: Zametki o stikhakh Iosifa Brodskogo," *Kontinent*, No. 14 (1977), 307-331; Henry Gifford, "The Language of Loneliness," [London] *Times Literary Supplement* (11 August 1978).

Bibliography: George L. Kline, comp., "A Bibliography of the Published Works of Iosif Aleksandrovich Brodsky" in Fred Moody, ed. *Ten Bibliographies of 20th Century Russian Literature* (Ann Arbor, Mich., 1977), 159-175. (This bibliography, originally published in 1971, is partially updated by the editor).

George L. Kline and *Richard D. Sylvester*

BRÓDSKII, NIKOLAI LEONT'EVICH (1881-1951). Soviet Russian literary scholar. Brodskii was born on 15 Nov. 1881 in Yaroslavl. He was not only a graduate of Moscow University (1904), but returned to teach there, first as privat-docent, and then as professor. He taught general courses in Russian literature and special seminars in many institutions of higher learning in Moscow and other cities. An eminent lecturer and pedagogue, Brodskii devoted much attention to the education of teachers and researchers, and to the methodology of teaching literature in Soviet schools. Brodskii's first work was published in 1904. Beginning his scholarly activity as an adherent of the cultural-historical school, Brodskii, even before 1917, protested against the lack of ideological content in literature (his article "Has Belinskii Been Debunked?" Razvenchan li Belinskii?, 1914). After the October Revolution, Brodskii did much to aid the development of Marxist literary criticism. His scholarly works are devoted mainly to the study of the connections between the development of Russian social thought and nineteenth-century Russian literature. Brodskii's numerous works on Belinskii, Gertsen, the Slavophiles, Westernizers, Chernyshevskii, Dostoevskii, and the development of Russian theater from the eighteenth to the twentieth centuries are well known. Brodskii was among the founders of the scholarly study of Turgenev's writings and author of *I.S. Turgenev's Undertakings. (Materials for a History of His Artistic Work)* (Zamysly I.S. Turgeneva [Materialy k istorii ego khudozhestvennogo tvorchestva], 1917), *I.S. Turgenev and His Work on the Novel "On the Eve"* (I.S. Turgenev v rabote nad romanom *Nakanune,* 1922), and *Belinskii and Turgenev* (1924). Under his editorship a number of historico-literary collections appeared: *Turgenev and His Time* (Turgenev i ego vremia, 1923), *I.S. Turgenev* (1940), *Dostoevskii's Career as a Writer* (Tvorcheskii put' Dostoevskogo,

1924) and others. Brodskii is author of a popular scholarly biography of Aleksandr Pushkin (1937), of elaborate commentaries for the novel *Eugene Onegin*. Finally Brodskii produced a fundamental work in 1945 on Lermontov's early years (up to 1832), based on extensive and as yet unstudied materials, which attempts to encompass broadly the social and literary problems of Lermontov's time. Brodskii died on 5 June 1951 in Moscow.

Works: Turgenev i russkie sektanty (M., 1922); *A.S. Pushkin.* [Vol. 1:1814-1832] (M., 1945); *V.G. Belinskii* (M., 1946); *"Borodino" Lermontova* (M., 1947); *I.S. Turgenev* (M., 1950); *"Evgenii Onegin," roman Pushkina* [Commentary], 4th ed. (M., 1957); *Izbrannye trudy* (M., 1964).

References: "Nikolai Leont'evich Brodskii. 1881-1951," [Nekrolog] , *Literatura v shkole,* No. 5 (1951).

BRODSKY, JOSEPH, *see* BRODSKII, IOSIF ALEKSANDROVICH

BRÓŬKA, PIATRUS' USTSINAVICH (b. 1905). Soviet Russian Belorussian poet, People's Poet of Belorussia (1962), member CP since 1940, Corresponding Member of the Belorussian Academy of Sciences (since 1953), Deputy of the 5th and 6th Supreme Soviets. Broŭka was born on 12 (25) June 1905 in Putilkovichi (now Ushachi Raion, Vitebsk Oblast) in a peasant family. After 1924 he worked in the Komsomol and was chairman of an agricultural council. He graduated from Belorussian State University in 1931. His first major work, in 1932, is the long poem *Over Mountains and Steppe* (Praz hory i step) in which the stern, heroic spirit of the Civil War is communicated. In search of a poetic style, Broŭka passed from a certain rhetorical quality and over-simplification in his early work to the creation of concrete images and pictures of Belorussian landscapes, to the revelation of the spiritual world of the men and women working for a socialist transformation of the village. His long poem *Katerina* (1938) chronicles the passage of a woman farm-laborer from crushing poverty to the happy life of an important kolkhoz member. Among other poems on these themes are "1914," "The Gardener" (Sadovnik), "Grandfather Taras" (Ded Taras), "Poles'e." During the Second World War Broŭka worked in the frontline and partisan press. His long poem *Belorussia* (Belarus', 1943) and the poems "To the Belorussian Warriors" (Baitsam-belarusam), "Kastus' Kalinovskii," "To Work, Belorussians!" (Budzem seiats', belarusy!, 1943) are depictions of heroic Soviet soldiers and Belorussian partisans and their unlimited devotion to the Soviet Union. Besides this heroic-epic theme, Broŭka also employs lyrical and folklore motifs, as in *Nadia-Nadeika* and *Two Maples* (Dva klěna). Collective farm labor and the friendship of various Soviet nationalities are the principal themes of his long poem *Bread* (Khleb, 1946), in which collective farms are rebuilt and restored by veterans of the Soviet Army, and of the poems "Brother and Sister" (Brat i siastra, 1946), "Narodnae dziakui" (1946), "The Meeting" (Vstrecha, 1943), and "Thoughts about Moscow" (Dumy pra Masku, 1946), all of which were awarded State Prizes in 1947. A poetic response to social and international events from an ideological viewpoint is to be found in his collection *The Road of Life* (Doroga zhizni, State Prize, 1951). Brouka is author of the long poems *Liasy* *naddzvinskiia* (1953), *Always with Lenin* (Zausody z Leninym, 1956) and a collection of verse *And the Days Pass*... (A dni idut ..., 1961, Lenin Prize, 1962). Warmth, sincerity and rich poetic language typify Broŭka's best works. His novel *When Rivers Flow Together* (Kali zlivaiutstsa reki, 1957) concerns the construction of a hydroelectric station on the border of three republics and points up the friendship of Belorussians, Lithuanians and Latvians. Broŭka's works are distinguished for their highly national coloring. They have been translated into many of the languages of the Soviet Union and Eastern Europe. Brouka wrote the librettos for the operas *Mikhas' Podgornyi* and *Girl from Polesye* (Devushka iz Poles'ia). He translated into Belorussian works by Shevchenko, Maiakovskii, P.G. Tychina, A.T. Tvardovskii, and M.V. Isakovskii.

Works: Vybranyia tvory (Minsk, 1947); *Tsvĕrdymi krokami* (Minsk, 1954); *Zbor tvoraŭ,* 2 vols. (Minsk, 1957); *Dalioka ad domu* (Minsk, 1960); *Vershi i poĕmy* (Minsk, 1966); *Mizh chyrvonykh rabin* (Minsk, 1969). In Russian translation: *Doroga zhizni* (Minsk, 1950); *Stikhotvoreniia i poĕmy* (M., 1955); *Kogda slivaiutsia reki* (M., 1958); *Stikhotvoreniia i poĕmy* (M., 1959); *Petrus' Brovka* (M., 1966); *Izbrannye proizvedeniia* (M., 1969); *Pishu o serdtse chelovech'em* (M., 1974).

References: N. Perkin, *Tvorchasts' Petrusia Broŭki* (Minsk, 1952); N.S. Perkin, "Petrus' Brovka," in *Ocherki istorii belorusskoi sovetskoi literatury* (M., 1954) 305-25; R. Biarozkin, "Piatrus' Broŭka," in his *Poeziia praŭdy* (Minsk, 1958); S. Gorodetskii, "Piatrus' Brovka," *Literaturnaia gazeta,* No. 24 (1 May 1939); E. Mozol'kov, "Stikhi o Belorusii," *Izvestiia,* No. 67 (21 March 1945); – – –, "Doroga v svetloe zavtra," *Pravda,* No. 90 (31 March 1951); N. Pylenkov, "Odnotomnik P. Brovki," *Literaturnaia gazeta,* No. 31 (13 March 1956); E. Mozol'kov, "Petrus' Brovka," in his *Poiushchaia zemlia* (M., 1965); *Piatrus' Broŭka. Bibliiahrafichny davednik* (Minsk, 1965); M. Isakovskii, *Sobranie sochinenii,* vol. 4 (M., 1969), 90-97.

BROVKA, PĔTR USTINOVICH, *see* BROŬKA, PIATRUS' USTSINAVICH.

BRŎVMAN, GRIGORII ABRAMOVICH (b. 1907). Soviet Russian literary critic, member CP since 1942. Brovman was born 1 (14) August 1907 in the small town of Kalarash, Province of Bessarabia. In 1931 he graduated with a degree in philology from Moscow University and began to publish in the same year. During the Second World War he wrote sketches about life at the front: *From a Front-line Diary* (Iz frontovogo dnevnika, 1943), *War's Everyday Life* (Budni voiny, 1943), *Night Take-off* (Nochnoi start, 1945) and others. He is the aurhor of a book on V.V. Veresaev's life and works, and of critical articles on modern literature: *The Writer and Life* (Pisatel' i zhizn', 1936), *Literary Notes on a Contemporary Theme* (Literaturnye zametki o sovremennoi teme, 1938), *Portrait of a Hero* (Oblik geroia, 1947), *Books Engendered by Life* (Knigi, rozhdennye zhizn'iu 1958), *The Life Situation of a Hero* (Zhiznennaia pozitsiia geroia, 1960) and others.

Works: V.V. Veresaev. Zhizn' i tvorchestvo (M., 1959); *Problemy i geroi sovremennoi prozy: kriticheskoe obozrenie* (M., 1966); *Talant i napravlenie* (M., 1971); *Trud, geroi, literatura* (M., 1974).

References: Iu. Babushkin, "Ocherki zhizni i tvorchestva V. Veresaeva," *Voprosy literatury,* No. 4 (1960); L. Plotkin, "Monografiia o Veresaeve," *Novyi mir,* No. 5 (1960).

BRUNBERG, EDUARD, see BORNHÖHE, EDUARD.

BRUSHTÉIN, ALEKSANDRA YAKOVLEVNA (1884-1968). Russian children's writer, prose writer and playwright. Born in Vilnius on 12 (24) August 1884 in the family of a Russianized Jewish doctor, Brushtein studied at the Russian Girls' High School in Vilnius, combining her studies with teaching at evening and Sunday schools for adults. She continued working as a teacher in St. Petersburg where she attended the Bestuzhev Courses (the most prestigious higher educational institute for women), graduating from the School of History and Philology.

Her literary activity dates from 1901 when she began publishing verse, articles and translations. From 1906, for over ten years, she was a prominent member of two illegal organizations, the "Political Red Cross" and the "Group for the Assistance of Political Prisoners in the Shlisselburg Convict Jail." After the 1917 Revolution she campaigned for the establishment of adult educational courses, herself organizing 173 schools of literacy.

Her play *May,* published in 1922, was performed at the Petrograd Theater of New Drama. *Gavrosh* (Gavroche, 1925), based on V. Hugo's novel *Les Misérables,* established her reputation as a children's dramatist. Her subsequent close and lengthy association with children's theaters led to her writing about 60 plays for children. A number of these are dramatised versions of famous works of world literature, including *Don Quixote* (co-author B. Zon, 1926), *Uncle Tom's Cabin* (Khizhina diadi Toma, first version, 1927), and *Little Dorrit* (1948). Other plays deal with the life of Soviet schoolchildren, such as *Seven of Us* (Nas semero, 1937).

One of her most successful plays was *Blue and Pink* (Goluboe i rozovoe, first performed in 1936, published in 1939), which depicts the experiences of schoolgirls in a pre-Revolutionary high school. Widely performed, it successfully combines the precepts of Soviet dramaturgy with features of pre-Revolutionary "gimnasium (high school) literature." Criticism of the old educational system is balanced by nostalgic reminiscence of the turn-of-the-century high school stmosphere.

Among other plays which can be singled out are the anti-Fascist *To Be Continued* (Prodolzhenie sleduet, 1933), a romantic play *Tristan and Isolde* (1947), and a drama about Pablo Neruda *Sorrow of My Land* (Pechal' moei zemli, co-author O. Savich, 1955).

The fifties marked a change in Brushtein's literary endeavors. In 1952 she published a book of memoirs *Pages of the Past* (Stranitsy proshlogo) about theatrical life in Russia at the turn of the century. Later works include her autobiographical trilogy—*The Road Goes off into the Distance* (Doroga ukhodit v dal', 1956), *At the Hour of Dawn* (V rassvetnyi chas, 1958), *Spring* (Vesna, 1961)—which was written expressly for children and brought out by a children's publishing house. However, the growing interest in literary memoirs during the post-Stalin decade ensured its popularity among adult readers as well.

Brushtein's memoirs do not display any profound insight into historical events: they are written wholly from a position of acceptance of the Revolution. At the same time her prose gives a sympathetic portrayal of the pre-Revolutionary intelligentsia and a sensitive concern for moral dilemmas, traits which distinguish it from the mass of literature produced during the Stalin period. She writes in a traditional, lucid, narrative style, and although she has a clear educational purpose in mind, she avoids overt didacticism. Brushtein's ability to recreate the atmosphere of student life and the life of the intelligentsia during the late nineteenth century and early twentieth century remains one of her more enduring achievements. Stylistically and thematically her prose most resembles that of Paustovskii, whose memoirs appealed to a similar group of readers.

Although almost completely blind during the last years of her life, Brushtein continued working on a story about the Second World War entitled *My Grandchildren, Grandchildren . . .*, which was interrupted by her death in Moscow on 20 September 1968.

Works: P'esy (M., 1956); *Doroga ukhodit v dal'* (M., 1956); *V rassvetnyi chas* (M., 1958); *Vesna* (M., 1961).

References: O. Ziv, "V te dalëkie gody," *Znamia,* No. 11 (1956); *Sovietskie detskie pisateli. Bibliograficheskii slovar' (1917-1957)* (M., 1961); L. Razgon, "Glazami nashego vremeni," *Narodnoe obrazovanie,* No. 12 (1961); L. Lebedeva, "Sviaz' vremën," *Novyi mir,* No. 2 (1962); A.M. Turkov, *Ot desiati do devianosta* (M., 1966).

Michael Ulman

BRUSÍLOV, NIKOLAI PETROVICH (1782-1849). Russian writer. The son of a landowner, Brusilov was born in 1782 in Orlov Province. In 1790 he entered the Corps of Pages, transferred into the army in 1796, and in 1798 changed to the civil service. Brusilov served with the rank of state-secretary in the office of P.S. Molchanov until his appointment in 1820 as governor of Vologda Province, where he served until 1834. Retiring in that year, Brusilov moved to Petersburg, where he lived until his death on 27 April 1849. Brusilov occupies a place among the minor literary figures of the beginning of the nineteenth century. Among Brusilov's literary works are a translation of Louis Sebastien Mercier's comedy in three acts, *The Inhabitant of Guadeloupe* (Gvadelupskii zhitel', 1800), the novella "The Old Man, or The Vicissitudes of Fate" (Starets, ili prevratnost' sud'by, 1803), *Poor Leander, or An Author without Rhetoric* (Bednyi Leandr, ili avtor bez ritoriki, 1803), *My Journey, or The Adventures of One Day* (Moë puteshestvie, ili prikliucheniia odnogo dnia, 1803), and *The Fruits of My Leisure* (Plody moego dosuga, 1805). All of Brusilov's original work is imitative, chiefly of Karamzin, with whom Brusilov shared many views and convictions. According to the author himself, the desire to imitate was often the main reason for writing a work; consequently, his works have all the traits of Sentimentalism, the prevailing literary taste of the period. In 1805 Brusilov published *Zhurnal rossiiskoi slovesnosti* (The Journal of Russian Literature), whose contributors included the best writers among the members of the Free Society of Lovers of Literature: I.N. Pnin, Benitskii, A. Izmailov, N. Ostolopov, N. Grech, and I. Pokhvisnev. Since members of the Society not only pursued historical and literary interests, but were absorbed in social issues, their collaboration (especially that of Pnin and Benitskii) also left a mark on the journal and introduced a social dimension into it. However, most of the original and translated prose in the journal belonged to Brusilov himself. Of the questions discussed in *Zhurnal,* the one most often dwelt on by Brusilov was gallomania, which, in his eyes, had caused the decline of contemporary Russian literature. Although he was an enthusiastic champion of the reforms of Tsar Alexander I, Brusilov rarely touched upon the question of serfdom, and, indeed, he was inclined to idealize peasant life. In his "Letter on the Theater" (Pis'mo o teatre) he urged building a theater for the common people with a special repertoire for its educational value; and he urged that women be given higher education. Brusilov also published critical reviews in the journal, but he displayed no real critical gift. In December 1848, several months before his death, Brusilov wrote his absorbing and substantial *Memoirs* (Vospominaniia), which were published in *Istoricheskii vestnik* in 1893. These memoirs contain many interesting facts and observations about the reigns of Catherine II and Alexander I. Brusilov also wrote two articles on numismatics, and two articles on the so-called Varangian question, "A Historical Discussion of the Beginning of the Russian State" (Istoricheskoe rassuzhdenie o nachale russkogo gosudarstva), in which Brusilov's Slavophile sympathies are expressed, and "Guesses at the Cause of the Normans' Incursion on the Slavs" (Dogadki o prichine nashestviia normanov na slavian).

References: [Obituary] , *Severnaia pchela,* No. 94 (1849); [Bibliography of Brusilov's works] , *Severnaia pchela,* No. 101 (1849); F.N. Fortunatov, "Pamiatnye zapiski vologzhanina," *Russkii arkhiv* (1867), 1689; V.F. Botsianovskii, Preface to Brusilov's *Memoirs, Istoricheskii vestnik,* No. 4 (1893); N.N. Bulich, *Ocherki po istorii russkoi literatury s nachala XIX v.,* vol. 1 (Pb., 1902).

BRÚTANE, VALJA (b. 1911). Soviet Latvian poetess. Brutane was born 15 (28) January 1911. She began to publish in 1945. Author of the verse collections *Gardens are Blossoming* (Dārzi plaukst, 1950) and *Rustle, My White Birches!* (Salciet, mani balti bērzi!, 1956). Translates work of Russian classical and Soviet literature into Latvian.

Works: Rasa (Riga, 1965); *Atmiņu gaismā* (Riga, 1967); *Uz Līgatni man brauciet līdz* (Riga, 1969); *Tiešums. Dzeja* (Riga, 1970). In Russian translation: *Vsia zolotaia listva; stikhi* (Riga, 1971).

BRÝKIN, NIKOLAI ALEKSANDROVICH (b. 1895). Soviet Russian writer, CP member since 1917. Brykin was born 19 (31) December 1895 in the village of Daratniki (now Yaroslavl Oblast). He participated in both the Civil and Second World Wars. Having begun his literary work in 1920, Brykin's first book of sketches, *In the New Village* (V novoi derevne), appeared in 1925. The transformation of the village in the course of the socialist revolution became the main theme of his creative work. Brykin strove to pass from individual studies and sketches to broad pictures revealing the life of the Soviet peasantry in his stories "People of the Hollows" (Liudi nizin, 1927), "Steel Mamai" (Stal'noi Mamai, 1934), and the novel *Land in Captivity* (Zemlia v plenu, 1930). From 1937 to 1939 Brykin published sketches and stories taken from the life of frontier guards—

"On the Border" (Na granitse), "At the Outpost" (Na zastave), "On Patrol" (V dozore)—and, together with Vl. Nedobrovo, wrote the film scenario for *The Defense of Petrograd* (Oborona Petrograda). In 1957 Brykin's novel *Redemption* (Iskuplenie) appeared, dedicated to the peasantry during the Civil War. His memoirs recalling the village during the first years of Soviet rule were published in 1958. The first book of his novel *On the Eastern Front of Change* (Na Vostochnom fronte peremeny, 1960), which concerns the events preceding the October Revolution, was printed in the journal *Neva.*

Works: Bol'shie dni (L., 1927); *Muchnye koroli* (L., 1931); *Zolotoi potok* (M.-L., 1932); *Provintsial'naia ideia* (L., 1935); *Oborona Petrograda* (L., 1939); "Pravda novogo veka," *Neva,* No. 6 (1958).

References: N. Slepnev, "Brykin N., 'Stal'noi Mamai,' " *Zvezda,* No. 6 (1934); E. Maimin, "Novyi roman N. Brykina," in the almanac *Na beregakh Velikoi,* No. 10 (Pskov, 1958).

BRYL, YANKA (b. 1917). Soviet Belorussian writer. Bryl was born in Odessa on 4 August 1917, the son of a railroad worker. In 1922 the family returned to their native village of Zahor'e, Stoŭbtsy district, Western Belorussia, which was part of Poland before World War II. After completing seven years' formal education, Bryl worked full-time on the family farm. He continued his education privately, avidly reading the classics in Belorussian, Polish and Russian literatures. In 1939 Bryl was called up into the Polish army and in September of the same year was taken prisoner by the invading German army. Successful in his second attempt to escape from a German prison camp, the writer returned to Belorussia in the fall of 1941 and from late 1942 fought with the Soviet partisans until the German army had been driven out of Belorussia. Bryl settled in Minsk towards the end of 1944, where he has held, among others, the posts of Deputy of the Supreme Soviet of the BSSR and Secretary of the Union of Writers of the BSSR. He has been a member on the editorial boards of several Belorussian publications, such as *Vozhyk* (Hedgehog), *Maladosts'* (Youth) and *Polymia* (Flame). He has been awarded the USSR State literary prize, the Yakub Kolas prize, Soviet orders and medals, and Polish literary prizes. Among the latter is a medal for his contribution to Polish literature, namely for his translation into Belorussian of works by such Polish writers as Kruczkowski and Iwaszkiewicz, and his studies on Polish literature in general.

The beginning of Bryl's varied and multifaceted career dates back to 1938, when his lyrical poem "The Last Ice Floes" (Aposhniia kryhi) was published in the Belorussian journal *Shliakh moladzi* (The Path of Youth) printed in Vilnius. His other poems appeared in Belorussian journals in Poland before World War II. However, he became known to Soviet readers as a prose writer only in the postwar years following the publication of his collections *Short Stories* (Apaviadanni, 1946) and *Nioman Cossacks* (Niomanskiia kazaki, 1947). The works describe life in the West Belorussian village and partisan warfare against the German army in his native area. His prize-winning novelette *The Dawn in Zabalotstse* (U Zabalotstsi dnee, 1950) deals with the introduction of collectivization and the socialist way of life in Western Belorussia. Bryl's other novelettes include *The Last Meeting* (Aposhniaia sustrecha, 1959) and *Nizhniia Baiduny* (1975). His numerous short stories, many written for children, appeared in separate collections, such as *Stained Glass Window* (Vitrazh, 1972), as did his lyrical short sketches, in the collection *A Handful of Sun Rays* (Zhmenia sonechnykh promniaŭ, 1955).

The novel *Birds and Nests* (Ptushki i hniozdy, 1963) may be considered his highest literary achievement. The work is partly autobiographical. Ales' Rune-vich, the main character, spends his childhood and youth, like the writer, in a West Belorussian village, is captured by the Germans, and after his escape fights with the partisans. Bryl also co-authored, with A. Adamovich and U. Kalesnik, the historical novel *I Am from a Fiery Village* (Ya z vohniennai vioski, 1973), which details the tragedy of the brutal destruction of thousands of Belorussian villages by the Germans.

Finally, Bryl is well known as a translator of Russian, Ukrainian and Polish writers into Belorussian, while his own works have been translated into Russian, Polish, Ukrainian, Lithuanian, Latvian, Czech, Slovak, French, English, Spanish and other languages.

Before World War II, Bryl, like most West Belorussian writers, published only poems because they were the most effective means of expressing his opposition to a Polish government bent on suppressing Belorussian culture. He imitated the poems of Maksim Tank, the famous Belorussian poet, but he was also influenced by the great classic authors of Belorussian (Bahdanovich, Kolas and Kupala), Polish (Mickiewicz, Prus, Słowacki, Sienkiewicz and Orzeszkowa), and Russian (Pushkin, Lermontov, Tolstoi, Chekhov and Gor'kii) literatures. This period is very important, since the writer's personality and literary technique were in pro-cess of formation.

After the War Bryl turned exclusively to prose, particularly short stories. Many of his stories may well be defined as poems in prose because of their highly lyrical nature. He does not limit himself to any particular form of lyrical prose. First-person narration is used both in those cases in which the author is identified with the hero, as in the short story "In the Family" (U siam'i), and in those in which he is distinct from the hero, as in "Because of True Joy" (Dzelia zapraŭ-dnai radastsi). Bryl's short sketches, novelettes and a major part of his novel *Birds and Nests* are also written in lyrical prose.

Since Bryl chose lyrical prose, characterized by a subjective description of reality, he prefers heroes with strong emotions and a tendency towards reflection and self-analysis. The emphasis is not so much on action and its consequence as on the hero's psychological and spiritual state, his inner conflicts and their final resolution. The hero's world, however, is not narrow because it is described in its relationship with society and outside reality. Bryl's use of nature represents the familiar notion of "pathetic fallacy": nature not only reflects the hero's feelings and the state of his soul, but also seems to participate in events.

In his portrayal of people Bryl pays little attention to external attributes. Rather he stresses their psychological and spiritual states and qualities. The op-posite is the case in his satirical portraits, such as his caricatures of German sol-diers in *Birds and Nests*.

Historical perspective can hardly be perceived in the majority of his works, since Bryl fuses past and present. At the beginning of the novelette *Nizhniia*

Baiduny, for instance, one is under the impression that the author intends to write a history of his native village. However, it soon becomes evident that Bryl is presenting a gallery of deft portraits of his fellow villagers, drawn with appealing humor. He does not follow any chronological order, intermingling present and past and speculating about the future.

The style and language in Bryl's works are rich, colorful and expressive. Bryl draws on the inexhaustible treasure of Belorussian folklore, especially when he describes the peasants or simple people who are its true preservers. The vocabulary is carefully selected; Bryl prefers to use adjectives with multiple meanings and precise and expressive verbs. From a prosodic point of view, Bryl's prose resembles free verse. Rhythm can be detected in the description of nature, the hero's inner monologue and the writer's meditation on people and events. Bryl's aesthetic views have been collected in the volume *Reflection and Word* (Rozdum i slova, 1963).

Bryl excels in the genre of short story and is rightly regarded as the dean of Belorussian short story writers. He has also contributed to the development of Belorussian lyrical prose, initiated by the great writers Kuzma Chorny and Yanka Kolas. Bryl can be compared favorably to such Soviet writers as Olga Berggol'ts, Vladimir Soloukhin and Ion Drutse, and has many traits in common with the famous Russian writers Mikhail Prishvin and Konstantin Paustovskii.

Works: Apaviadanni (Minsk, 1946); *Niomanskiia kazaki* (Minsk, 1947); *Zbor tvoraŭ,* 2 vols. (Minsk, 1960); *Ptushki i hniozdy* (Minsk, 1963); *Zbor tvoraŭ,* 4 vols. (1967-68); *Adzin dzen'. Apaviadanni. Apovests'. Narys* (Minsk, 1968); *Vitrazh. Apaviadanni* (Minsk, 1972); "Nizhniia Baiduny: Apovests'," *Polymia,* No. 10 (1975), 61-114.

References: N. Vatatsy, *Ianka Bryl': Bibliiahrafichnyia pamiatki chytacha* (Minsk, 1957); S. Maikhrovich, *Ianka Bryl'* (Minsk, 1961); Iu. Kane, *Ianka Bryl'* (M., 1964); L. Huseva, "Apovestsi Ianki Brylia," *Vestsi AN BSSR. Seryia hramadskikh navuk,* No. 1 (1965), 113-20; – – –, *Ianka Bryl'–mastak* (Minsk, 1968); U. Kalesnik, "Perad pershai staronkai," *Polymia,* No. 10 (1968), 214-21; D. Buhaioŭ, "Shmatfarbny paetychny svet," *Polymia,* No. 1 (1970), 186-96; V. Vitka, "Zapavetnaia labaratoryia pis'mennika," *Polymia,* No. 2 (1971), 230-37; V. Osotskii, "Po pravu liubvi . . . shtrikhi k portretu Ianki Brylia," *Druzhba narodov,* No. 6 (1972), 256-68; "Ianka Bryl'," *Styl' pis'mennika* (Minsk, 1974); A. Adamovich, *Zdaliok i zblizku* (Minsk, 1976), 559-97; "Ianka Bryl'," *Istoriia belorusskoi sovetskoi literatury* (Minsk, 1977).

John Sadoŭski

BUBENNÓV, MIKHAIL SEMĔNOVICH (b. 1909). Soviet Russian writer, CP member since 1951. Bubennov was born 8 (21) November 1909 in the village of Vtoroe Polomoshnevo (presently Altai Krai) in a peasant family. He has taught school in Siberia and Tataria since 1927, the year in which he began to publish. His first story, "Roaring Year" (Gremiashchii god, 1932), is devoted to the organization of a commune in an Altai village. In his collection of stories *In the Spring Flood* (V polovod'e, 1940) and his tale *Immortality* (Bessmertie, 1940) the Civil War is rendered in vivid scenes. The novel *White Birch* (Belaia bereza, vol. 1, 1947; State Prize, 1948; vol. 2, 1952) recreates the events of the Second

World War. The central figure of the novel is a soldier who undergoes a spiritual maturation during the arduous days of retreat in 1941. Together with the heroism of the people and the country, symbolized in the lyric image of the white birch, Bubennov depicts the treachery of deserters. In the second book of the novel, the influence of the "theory" of conflictlessness *(beskonfliktnost')* is apparent; the realism and dramatic quality in the narration of the battles around Moscow is noticeably weakened. The novel *Eagle's Steppe* (Orlinaia step', 1959) is written in heroic style of the young people who subjugate virgin lands.

Works: Stremnina (M., 1970); *Izbrannye proizvedeniia*, 2 vols. (M., 1973). In English translation: *The White Birch* (M., 1949).

References: M. Shkerin, "Poéma o novom cheloveke," *Oktiabr'*, No. 5 (1948); N. Kalustova, *M.S. Bubennov* (Baku, 1956); A. Orekhovskii, "Krasivyi chelovek," *Molodaia gvardiia*, No. 8 (1960); V. Survillo, "Na putiakh romantiki (Stat'ia tret'ia)," *Novyi mir*, No. 7 (1960); Iu. Mostkov, "O krasote zhizni i literaturnykh 'krasivostiakh,' "*Sibirskie ogni*, No. 7 (1960); *Russkie sovetskie pisateli-prozaiki, Biobibliograficheskii ukazatel'*, vol. 1 (L., 1959).

BUCHINSKAIA, NADEZHDA ALEKSANDROVNA, *see* TEFFI, NADEZHDA.

BÚDDE, EVGENII FEDOROVICH (1859-1929). Russian linguist, Corresponding Member of the Academy of Sciences (since 1916), Professor at Kazan University. Budde was born 13 (25) December 1859. His special interests were problems of dialectology and the history of the Russian literary language, but he also concerned himself with questions of methodology. His theoretical views stem from the teachings of F.F. Fortunatov. Budde's studies of Russian literature include works on Pushkin, Belinskii, Gogol, Chekhov, and folk literature. Budde died in 1929 in Kazan.

Works: K dialektologii velikorusskikh narechii. Issledovanie osobennostei ria-zanskogo govora (Warsaw, 1892); *K istorii velikorusskikh govorov. Opyt istoriko-sravnitel'nogo issledovaniia narodnogo govora v kasimovskom uezde Riazanskoi gubernii* (Kazan, 1896); *O literaturnykh mneniiakh Pushkina* (Voronezh, 1896; reprt., 1960); *Opyt grammatiki iazyka Pushkina*, 3 fascicles (Pb., 1904; Ann Arbor, Mich., 1960); *Lektsii po istorii russkogo iazyka*, 2nd ed. (Kazan, 1913); "Ocherk istorii sovremennogo literaturnogo russkogo iazyka (XVII-XIX vv.)," *Éntsiklopedia slavianskoi filologii*, fascicle 12 (Pb., 1908); *Osnovy sintaksisa russkogo iazyka* (Kazan, 1913) [off-print].

References: S.S. Vysotskii, "Raboty E.F. Budde o riazanskikh govorakh v svete novykh dannykh," *Biulleten' dialektologicheskogo sektora Instituta russ-kogo iazyka*, fascicle 6 (1949).

"BUDÍL'NIK" [lit., "Alarm Clock"], a satiric journal with cartoons published from 1865 to 1871 in Petersburg and in Moscow from 1873 until 1917, at first twice a month and then weekly from 1866. N.A. Stepanov, an artist and satirist of liberal views, was founder and editor of *Budil'nik* until 1877. Subsequent editors were A.I. Utkin, N.G. Kicheev, N.V. Nevrov, A.D. Kurepin, and V.D. Levinskii. During the sixties such liberal poet-satirists as G.N. Zhulev, D.D. Minaev, L.I. Pal'min, writers A.I. Levitov and N.N. Zlatovratskii published in *Budil'-nik*. In the seventies and later, the humor and satire in *Budil'nik* became less socially trenchant. From 1881-1887 A.P. Chekhov contributed to *Budil'nik* chiefly under the pseudonym of "A. Chekhonte."

BÚDNY, SYMON (*ca.* 1530-1593). Belorussian religious figure (follower of Socinian), translator. Budny was born in the early 1530s in the village of Budy in Mazowsze, Poland. He received his education at Krakow Academy, where he was won over to the ideas born of the intellectual ferment of the Reformation. Renowned as a man of superior education and persuasive in argument, Budny was invited by Mikołaj Radziwiłł of Vilno to assume the position of pastor of a Calvinist church around 1552 in the city of Kletsk. Beginning in 1562 Budny, together with Matvei Kavechinskii and Vavrzhinets Krzhizhkovskii, published various religious works in Belorussian, Polish and Latin. There is some indication that Budny may have published the Gospels in Belorussian as early as 1560. The first book which was printed in the printing house in Nesvizh, however, was *On a Sinner's Justification Before God* (Pra apraŭdanne hreshnaha chalaveka perad Boham, 1562), followed by the Arian Catechism and the Psalter, all in Belorussian. In 1570 Budny published the entire Bible in Polish, and a second edition in 1572. Soon thereafter Budny abandoned Calvinism and became a fervent advocate of the teachings of Socinian and the doctrine of antitrinitarianism, working, for the most part, in Lithuania. A Catholic church council was held in 1582, at which Budny was ordered to abandon his heretical ideas (that Christ was not God, that His birth was not a sacrament/mystery) under pain of harsh punishment. Budny did so, and little is known of his biography subsequent to his renunciation. Many of his works were destroyed by the Catholic church as heretical tracts. Like his predecessor Frantsysk Skaryna, Budny was a pioneer in the development of book publishing in Belorussia.

Works: O urzedzie miecza używajadem 1583 (Warsaw, 1932).

References: N. Merczyng, *Szymon Budny jako krytyk takstów biblijnych* (Krakow, 1913); A.F. Korshunaŭ, "Symon Budny" in *Khrestamatyia na starazhytnai belaruskai literatury* (Minsk, 1959); Ia.I. Poretskii, *Simon Budnyi—peredovoi belorusskii myslitel' XVI v.* (Minsk, 1961); *Iz istorii filosofskoi i obshchestvenno-politicheskoi mysli Belorussii* (Minsk, 1962), 40-82; S.A. Padokshyn, "Budny, Symon," in *Belaruskaia savetskaia entsiklapediia,* vol. 2 (1970), 453-4.

BUDOGÓSKAIA, LIDIIA ANATOL'EVNA (b. 1898). Soviet Russian writer. Budogoskaia was born on 10 (22) November 1898 in Warsaw. Writing mainly for children, she appeared in print in 1929 with the book *Tale of a Red-Headed Girl* (Povest' o ryzhei devochke), which purports to be a high school girl's diary from pre-Revolutionary years. At the center of the story is the unusual fate of a girl with a strong and fiery character. In *Tales of a Lantern* (Povesti o fonare, 1936), which treats Soviet school life, Budogoskaia emphasizes the connection between teaching and life and the students' moral education by contrasting the figures of two instructors. The action of her tale "The Sentry" (Chasovoi, 1947) occurs in a Leningrad hospital during the blockade in the Second World War. Budogoskaia contrasts those who "work according to conscience" to those employees who rob the hospital, and urges the necessity of a conscientious attitude toward one's duty. Among her short books for very young children are *Little Zeros* (Nulevki) and the tale "Nurses" (Sanitarki, 1931).

Works: Povest' o ryzhei devochke, 2nd ed. (M.-L., 1939); *Chasovoi,* 3rd ed. (L., 1961).

References: Ia. Rykachev, "Povest' o ryzhei devochke L. Budogoskoi," *Detskaia literatura,* Nos. 1-2 (1940); L. Chukovskaia, "O knigakh zabytykh ili nezamechennykh," *Voprosy literatury,* No. 2 (1958).

BUGAEV, BORIS NIKOLAEVICH, *see* BELYI, ANDREI.

BÚILO, KANSTANTSYIA ANTONAŬNA [pseudonym of KALECHYTS, KANSTANTSYIA ANTONAŬNA] (b. 1898). Soviet Belorussian poetess. Builo was born in Vilnius on 30 December 1898 (11 January 1899), in the family of a forest warden. She graduated from teachers' courses in Vilnius and became a village teacher. Her first collection of verse, *Barrow Flower* (Kurgannaia kvetka, 1914), appeared under the editorship of Ya. Kupala. Builo's artistic vision was influenced by the realistic elements in the poetry of Yakub Kolas. She sketched the burdensome life of the Belorussian peasantry and called for social and national liberation. The heroic feats of the Russian people provide the themes of her poetry during the Second World War and the post-war period. These poems appeared in the collections *Dawn* (Svitanne, 1950) and *By a Forest Lake* (U bliasku zor, 1968).

Works: Vybranyia tvory (Minsk, 1954); *Na adnoŭlenai ziamli; vershy* (Minsk, 1961); *Vybranae* (Minsk, 1968); *Mai* (Minsk, 1965); "Pa proidzenym shliakhu," in *Piats'dzesiat chatyry darogi* (Minsk, 1963); *Vybranae* (Minsk, 1968). In Russian translation: *Pishu tebe: stikhi* (M., 1971).

References: S. Maikhrovich, "Kanstantsyia Antonaŭna Buila," *Polymia,* Nos. 8-9 (1946); N. Taras, "Piasniarka rodnai ziamli," *Polymia,* No. 2 (1968).

BUK, VILLEM (1879-1941). Soviet Estonian writer. Buk was born on 25 March 1879 in Tartumaskii Uezd, in the family of a blacksmith. A teacher by training, he received his advanced education in Kaarepere. Buk joined the revolutionary movement and was arrested several times in 1907-09 and 1915-17. He began his literary activity during the 1905 Revolution and in the same year published a book of stories, *Three Great Worries* (Kolm suurt muret), taken from the life of village workers. His story "The Stone Book" (Kivine raamat, 1911) is written as the diary of a political prisoner. Buk worked in the editorial offices of the Estonian Bolshevik newspaper *Kür.* He published a series of articles and brochures on the life of the workers of Narva: "One Forgotten Estonian City" (Uks unustatud Eesti linni, 1912). In 1913 he published the long poem *Lina.* Buk participated in preparations for the revolution and fought in the ranks of the Red Army. Remaining in the USSR, he worked as a teacher and has lived in the city of Kalinin since 1934. Buk's book of verse *The Thaw* (Sula, 1926) contains his best early work, in addition to poems on the October Revolution. He died in July 1941.

Works: Sula (L., 1926). In Russian translation: *Antologiia èstonskoi poèzii,* vol. II (M.-L., 1959).

References: Eesti proletaarne kirjandus (Tallin, 1951).

BUKÉEV, SHANGEREI (1847-1920). Kazakh poet. Bukeev was born to the Kazakh aristocracy in 1847 in Western Kazakhstan (Bukei Orda). After completing a gymnasium in Astrakhan, Bukeev served as a justice of the peace and received a title in the Russian nobility. His love lyrics speak of woman's dignity and praise her beauty and mental qualities. Bukeev wrote memorable panoramic sketches in which he reflected Kazakh life and customs of the period. He was an adherent of the "art for art's sake" aesthetic. The lyric poetry of the anthology *The Poet* (Shaiyr, 1911) is a poetry of moods and philosophical meditations and is distinguished by its elegance of form. The Russian poet Aleksandr Fet influenced Bukeev's work to some extent. Bukeev translated Lermonotov's poem "The Fugitive" into Kazakh. He died in 1920 in a steppe village in the Akbajai area.

Works: Ölender zhinaghy (Alma-Ata, 1934). In Russian translation: *Pesni stepei. Antologiia kazakhskoi poezii* (M., 1940).

References: Kh. Zhùmaliev, "Shenġerei," in *Qazaq ădebieti,* part 2 (Alma-Ata, 1946); Z. Akhmetov, "Shăngerei aqyn," *Izvestiia AN Kazakhskoi SSR. Seriia filologii i iskusstvovedeniia,* fasc. 3/10 (1959); *Qazaq ădabietining tarikhy,* vol. 2, book 2 (Alma-Ata, 1961).

BUKHÁRIN, NIKOLAI IVANOVICH (1888-1938). Marxist theoretician, official of the Russian Communist Party, and leader of "the right opposition." Bukharin was born on 27 September (9 October) 1880 in Moscow, the son of two educators. His father, a mathematics graduate of Moscow University, took charge of Nikolai's pre-school education. He instilled in his son a lifelong appreciation of literature and art, and taught him to read and write before entering school. After achieving consistently high grades in primary school, Bukharin was enrolled in a classical gymnasium in Moscow, the curriculum of which was solidly based upon the study of languages and literatures. Bukharin was eventually able to speak French and German well, and possessed a good reading knowledge of English.

While he was becoming acquainted with world literature, Bukharin was also becoming aware of philosophy and politics. At a young age he had lost his family's staunch belief in Orthodoxy and had become convinced of the necessity for a new socio-political order in Russia. Marxism answered Bukharin's desire both for political action and a world view which explains isolated phenomena as part of a harmonious whole.

Bukharin's participation in the disorders of 1905 was apparently limited to enthusiastic student meetings and propaganda work, but in the following year he formally joined the Bolshevik wing of the Russian Social Democratic Labor Party. During the 1906-10 period Bukharin worked as a Party organizer among students and workers in Moscow. At the same time, after completing the gymnasium course with distinction and passing the entrance examinations, he was admitted to Moscow University as an economics student in the fall of 1907.

Bukharin was elected to the Moscow City Committee of the Bolshevik Party and as a result attracted more attention from the police. He was first arrested in 1909 but was released within a few months. In 1910 he was again arrested and, after six months in Moscow jails, was exiled to Onega in 1911. In that same year he escaped from his place of exile and went to Germany, beginning a six-year period as a political refugee.

During his years as an emigre, Bukharin became well-known as a Marxist theoretician. After spending a year in Germany and visiting Lenin in Krakow for a short time, Bukharin settled down in Vienna in order to study and write. He attended classes at the University of Vienna, gathered materials for future writings, and took part in Bolshevik political activities. *The Economic Theory of the Leisure Class* (Politicheskaia ékonomika rant'e, 1919) established Bukharin's reputation as a Marxist economist, and *Imperialism and the World Economy* (Mirovoe khoziaistvo i imperializm, 1923) brought attention to his analysis of the contemporary socio-political situation and his strategy for pursuing a proletarian revolution in light of that situation. In addition to these major works, a series of articles in journals kept his name before the public during the war years.

During this period of intellectual activity Bukharin frequently changed his place of residence. At the outset of World War I he was expelled from Austria as an enemy alien and went to Switzerland, where Lenin had also settled. Bukharin and Lenin had several disagreements, among them the role of the state after the revolution and the role of nationalism among colonial peoples. Bukharin moved to Scandinavia in 1915, took part in socialist anti-war agitation, and in 1916 left for the United States, where he spent five months in New York as editor of *Novyi mir* (New World). Among his collaborators on the Russian-language socialist newspaper was Lev Trotskii, who arrived in New York a few months after Bukharin.

In March 1917 Bukharin returned to Russia through Japan. He went to his native city of Moscow, and in July was named to the Central Committee of the Bolshevik Party on the eve of his 29th birthday. He also became editor of *Pravda,* a post which he held until 1929 with one short interruption. He continued to rise in the Party hierarchy, becoming in 1919 both a candidate member of the Politburo and a member of the Executive Committee of the Communist International (Comintern). In 1924 he became a full member of the Politburo.

During this time Bukharin continued to publish his theoretical works, including *The ABC of Communism* (Azbuka kommunizma, co-authored with E. Preobrazhenskii, 1920), and *Historical Materialism* (Teoriia istoricheskogo materializma, 1923). The former book, extremely popular in the Soviet Union and translated into many languages, was a popularized introduction to Marxism, while the latter was Bukharin's attempt to reconcile Marxism with the newly-emerging social science of sociology. For this latter work, Bukharin was labelled "the sociologist of the proletariat."

After opposing Lenin on the Brest-Litovsk treaty at the conclusion of World War One, Bukharin eagerly supported the New Economic Policy (NEP), which Lenin had initiated in 1921. After Lenin's demise in early 1924, Bukharin emerged as the main spokesman of NEP.

The death of Lenin triggered not only a struggle for Party leadership, but also a full debate on the immediate future of the Soviet state. Trotskii and his allies wished to pursue a program of rapid industrialization and collectivization of agriculture, a process which would have heavily favored industry at the expense of agriculture. Bukharin, on the other hand, wished to attain these goals at a much slower pace in order to allow both areas to grow as evenly and as smoothly as possible. With Stalin's support, Bukharin's point of view was victorious; Trotskii and his supporters were either expelled from the Party or demoted to minor positions.

In 1928, however, Stalin changed course with the introduction of the first Five Year Plan, which was an adaptation of Trotskii's proposal. After months of acrimonious debate, Bukharin was branded a "right deviationist" and expelled from the Politburo in November 1929. He also lost his positions with the Comintern and *Pravda*. During 1930-33 he held the comparatively minor positions of Director of Research for the Supreme Economic Council and the Commissariat of Heavy Industry.

In 1934 Bukharin was demoted to candidate member of the Central Committee, but he was also appointed chief editor of *Izvestiia*, a post which he retained until his final downfall in 1937. He was also allowed to give a major address at the First Congress of the newly-formed Union of Writers in 1934. One of Bukharin's last official tasks was to collaborate in drafting the Soviet Constitution of 1936, which remained in force until 1977.

In early 1937 Bukharin was arrested as Stalin's purges grew in scope and as Bukharin's criticism of Stalin's policies grew more vocal. After a trial which gained international notoriety for its variety of false charges and because of the stature of the defendant, Bukharin was executed on 14 March 1938.

Although Bukharin's fame rests mainly upon his political activity and contributions to Marxist theory in the areas of economics and sociology, his influence upon early Soviet literature was extremely important, although of short duration. Bukharin's education, both at home and at school, enabled him to develop a sensitivity to literature which was not shared by many of his colleagues within the Bolshevik leadership. In addition, his desire to reconcile Marxism with new developments (for example, with sociology in *Historical Materialism*) saved him from a dogmatism that considers Marxism a perfect system with answers for all questions.

This latter trait characterized Aleksandr Bogdanov, an innovative Marxist philosopher and ideological opponent of Lenin. Although he disagreed with most of Bogdanov's positions, Bukharin did accept the basic concept of proletarian literature which Bogdanov propagated through his Proletkult studios during the Civil War. Bukharin, however, strongly disagreed with Proletkult's desire for independence from the Party and with Proletkult's methods of creating a proletarian literature.

The idea of proletarian literature was based upon the assumption that each ruling class creates its own culture. When the working class comes to power, therefore, it also should develop a new culture, just as the bourgeois social order had created its cultural forms.

The foremost opponent of proletarian literature was Trotskii, who believed that the proletariat could not possibly create its own culture. In *Literature and Revolution* (1923) Trotskii stated that the transition period from the dictatorship of the proletariat to the classless society would be too brief to allow an entirely new culture to develop. In addition to this basic objection, he pointed to the backwardness of the Russian masses as further proof of his contention. According to Trotskii, the problems of literacy, elementary hygiene, and subsistence would have to be conquered before a proletarian literature could develop.

Bukharin, on the contrary, assessed the progress of the new Soviet state more realistically and foresaw a lengthy transition during which the proletariat would be able to create a new culture. This period would be so lengthy that the problems caused by the backwardness of the masses would be eliminated, freeing them to devote attention to the development of new cultural forms. Thus, Bukharin and Trotskii's political differences were reflected in their disagreement concerning the possibility of a proletarian literature.

The question was complicated by demands, issued in the name of proletarian literature, for ideological purity in Soviet letters. Various groups of writers and critics (such as Left Front of the Arts [LEF] and On Guard [Na postu]), each believing itself to possess the correct Marxist approach to literature, worked to deprive non-proletarian writers of access to publishing houses. Since this latter group represented the bulk of literary talent in the Soviet Union at that time, such a denial would have spelled the end of literature of high quality in Russia.

As these demands grew more vocal and as charges and countercharges were issued, the leadership of the Communist Party felt compelled to intervene with a statement concerning the future development of Soviet literature. Bukharin is considered by many to be the author of that statement, "The Policy of the Party in the Field of Imaginative Literature" (O politike partii v oblasti khudozhestvennoi literatury). The decree, published in *Pravda* and *Izvestiia* on July 1, 1925, reflected Bukharin's opinion that a proletarian literature would evolve as the transitional period progressed. It also reflected, however, Bukharin's contention that the new literature could evolve only through freedom for writers of various persuasions to publish, even non-Party and non-proletarian writers. Bukharin felt that young proletarian writers could learn from the "fellow travellers," as non-Party writers were called during the twenties, and as the former group learned their craft and began to issue good literature, the importance of the latter group would diminish. Bukharin also believed that as the transitional period progressed, non-Party writers would feel more at ease with the new sociopolitical situation and begin to reflect the positive aspects of Soviet life.

In the meantime, the decree provided that non-Party writers not be pressured by the Party or proletarian literary groups; otherwise, literary production would come to a virtual halt. Bukharin had criticized the proletarian literary organizations on previous occasions for issuing manifestoes and engaging in polemics, but not writing literature of high quality. Until that literature is produced, the proletarian literary organizations would not receive the support of the Party. Both fellow travellers and members of proletarian literary organizations viewed the resolution favorably, the former citing the decree's tolerance towards them, and the latter hailing its call for an eventual proletarian literature.

Bukharin's position in this controversy reflects his general thinking during NEP. Just as agriculture and industry were to develop together at a slow, smooth pace, neither expanding at the expense of the other, so all groups of writers should be allowed to publish without interference by the Party. Bukharin felt that literature and the economy would "grow into socialism" rather than leap forward with dramatic steps. Bukharin's victory in this dispute coincided with his victory over Trotskii in the political arena, and these twin victories began the enduring official connection between politics and literature in the Soviet Union. The 1925 Resolution may have been intended to be benevolent toward fellow travellers, but it also marked the beginning of Party interference in literature.

In 1928 the Party Resolution on literature was not officially rescinded, but the introduction of the first Five Year Plan signalled a dramatic shift in literary politics as well as in economic direction. Just as Bukharin's economic policies were criticized as "right opportunism" and discontinued in favor of a proletarian literature which would emphasize ideological education at the expense of literary quality. During the same period Bukharin was attempting to outmaneuver Stalin on economic and political issues; hence his influence on literature was minimal.

In 1934 the First Congress of the Union of Soviet Writers was held in Moscow. Although Bukharin had just been relegated to candidate membership on the Central Committee, he had also been appointed editor of *Izvestiia* and consequently began to play a more active, although still limited, role in Soviet literary matters. At the Congress Bukharin delivered a major address on Soviet poetry, entitled "Poetry, Poetics, and the Problems of Poetry in the U.S.S.R." (Poeziia, poetika i zadachi poeticheskogo tvorchestva v S.S.S.R.). Bukharin called for higher artistic quality and an end to propaganda verse, praising the lyrics of Boris Pasternak as examples of a high literary standard, and criticizing Vladimir Maiakovskii's political poetry as an unsuitable model for young Soviet poets.

Bukharin also issued a plea for a new art which would surpass the achievements of the past. He believed that a socialist culture should be superior to past cultural phenomena because socialism was superior to previous social orders. He feared that the bureaucratization of literature would ruin the promise of artistic quality which Soviet letters had shown during the twenties.

In his speech Bukharin once again called for freedom of competition in the literary arena as the only way to assure a literature of high artistic quality. Delegates to the Congress reacted favorably, giving Bukharin loud applause at the points in his speech where he opposed Stalin's literary policy of the previous six years.

Bukharin's suggestions were not taken seriously. Literature continued under the firm control of Party ideologues, who criticized Bukharin for demoralizing writers and for advocating a literature without social themes. Most of the prominent non-Party delegates to the Congress soon became victims of Stalin's purges.

Bukharin's interest in literature extended to writing critical essays on Goethe, Heine, Briusov, Esenin and a number of other literary figures. He was also helpful to individual authors, such as Osip Mandel'shtam and Panteleimon Romanov, who ran afoul of Soviet political and literary authorities.

In the final analysis, however, Bukharin's primary contribution to Soviet letters was his sympathetic and understanding attitude towards literature while he wielded political power. His direct influence allowed the liberal attitude of the twenties to continue as long as it did, and his thoughts on the subject, contained in his speeches and writings, stand as an alternative to Socialist Realism, which became the official literary doctrine of the Soviet Union.

Works: Proletarskaia revoliutsiia i kul'tura (Pg., 1923); "O politike partii v khudozhestvennoi literature," *K voprosu o politike RKP(b) v khudozhestvennoi literature* (M., 1924); "O formal'nom metode v iskusstve," *Krasnaia nov'*, No. 3 (1925); "Proletariat i voprosy khudozehstvennoi politiki," *Krasnaia nov'*, No. 4 (1925); *Etiudy* (M.-L., 1932); *Poéziia, poétika i zadachi poéticheskogo tvorchestva v SSSR* (M., 1934). In English: *Culture in Two Worlds* (N.Y., 1934); "Poetry, Poetics, and the Problems of Poetry in the U.S.S.R.," in *Problems of Soviet Literature* (M.-L., 1935), 185-258.

References: Herman Ermolaev, *Soviet Literary Theories* (Berkeley, 1963), especially 44-48; Robert Maguire, *Red Virgin Soil* (Princeton, 1968); Stephen Cohen, *Bukharin and the Bolshevik Revolution* (N.Y., 1973).

Bibliography: Sidney Heitman, *Nikolai I. Bukharin: A Bibliography* (Stanford, 1969).

Philip G. Maloney

BUKINISTÍCHESKAIA KNIGA (French *bouquiniste*—a dealer in old books). An old or second hand book named thus because a new edition of the same book, as yet untouched by the reader, could be on sale side by side with it. It is this which differentiates the second hand book from the antiquarian, for which there are no new, unused copies. Among the antiquarian books are extremely rare (at times single copy) editions of Gutenberg, the Venetian printer Aldo Manuzio, and the Dutch printers, the Elsevier brothers; in Russian there are Old Slavonic books, editions from the time of Peter I, early editions of the classics, old almanacs and journals, the works of forgotten authors of the past, old scientific books, travel descriptions by the "Russian Columbuses," early illustrated editions, popular folk books, etc. The most significant of these books are sometimes republished today, at times by photolithography, in order to convey an idea of the character of the original. Using this method, in 1935 the publishing house Academia issued A.N. Radishchev's *A Journey from Petersburg to Moscow,* originally published in 1790 and immediately suppressed by the censor. The publishing house of the USSR Academy of Sciences issued facsimile editions of A.I. Gertsen and N.P. Ogarev's newspaper *Kolokol* (The Bell). Rare manuscripts and books with autographs, engravings and lithographs are also objects of the antiquarian book trade.

The homeland of second hand and antique book trade is Germany, where as early as 1564 the first catalogs of old and antiquarian books were printed and sold at the fairs in Leipzig and Frankfurt-on-Main. Paris, London, Amsterdam and other European capitals became subsequent centers of such trade, while in Russia the sale of such books arose toward the end of the eighteenth century. The first bookseller and antiquarian in Russia was Ignatii Ferapont.

In Paris, scattered along the banks of the Seine, are the second hand booksellers' shops more than once poetically described by Anatole France, by Charles Nodier and George Duhamel. Second hand bookdealers often appeared in Russian works such as P.I. Mel'nikov-Pecherskii's *On the Mountains* (Na gorakh) and N.A. Nekrasov's *Three Points of the Compass* (Tri strany sveta).

The most prominent antiquarian booksellers before the Revolution periodically issued catalogues of their stock (P.P. Shibanov, V.I. Kolchkov, N.V. Solov'ev, and others). During the Soviet period such catalogues have been issued by the second hand bookstores of "International Book," the USSR Academy of Sciences, and several Moscow and Leningrad bookdealers. Specialized journals dedicated to book collection once existed: *Russkii bibliofil* (Russian Bibliophile, 1911-16), *Sredi kollektsionerov* (Among Collectors, 1921-24), and *Izvestiia knizhnogo magazina T-va M. Vol'fa* (M. Vol'f's Bookstore News, 1897-1917). The Soviet secondhand book trade renders great assistance to publishers; by obtaining old books and putting them into circulation again, it effectively doubles and triples the number of books available in original editions. Considering the tremendous demand for books in the USSR, in the face of which even mass editions are insufficient, such assistance from secondhand dealers becomes an important social and cultural undertaking. In alloting the purchase and sale of antiquarian books, the needs of government book depositories and museums are satisfied first, as well as those of individual scholars, historians, writers, literary scholars and numerous book collectors and specialists of all professions who are establishing private libraries.

The sale of old as well as antique books is carried out in special secondhand stores and book stalls.

References: K. Kalaidovich, *Izvestie o drevnostiakh slaviano-russkikh i ob Ignatii Ferapontoviche Ferapontove, pervom sobiratele onykh* (M., 1811); *Materialy dlia istorii russkoi knizhnoi torgovli* (Pb., 1879); D.V. Ul'ianinskii, *Sredi knig i ikh druzei,* part 1 (M., 1903); N.A. Rubakin, *Sredi knig,* 3 vols., 2nd ed. (M., 1911-15); *Iz zapisnoi knizhki A.P. Bakhrushina (Kto chto sobiraet?)*(M., 1916); I. Lazarevskii, *Sredi kollektsionerov,* 2nd ed. (Pg., 1917); P.P. Shibanov, "Antikvarnaia knizhnaia torgovlia v Rossii," in *Knizhnaia torgovlia* (M.-L., 1925); A.G. Mironov, *Bukinist Konstantin Zakharovich Nikitin* (M., 1925); N.I. Sveshnikov, *Vospominaniia propashchego cheloveka* (M.-L., 1930); N. Smirnov-Sokol'-skii, *Rasskazy o knigakh* (M., 1959); F. Shilov, *Zapiski starogo knizhnika* (M., 1959).

BÚKOV, EMILIIAN NESTEROVICH (b. 1909). Soviet Moldavian writer, CP member since 1950. Bukov was born 26 July (8 August) 1909 in the city of Novaia Kiliia, southern Bessarabia, in the family of a gardner. He finished the Khazhdeu Lyceum in Kishinĕv and graduated with a degree in literature and philosophy from the University of Bucharest. As a member of the Rumanian Communist Youth League he actively participated in underground revolutionary work. Bukov contributed to leftist Rumanian journals, published articles on Russian literature, and was among the greatest admirers of Maiakovskii's poetry. His collections of verse—*Work Is in Full Swing* (Clocotul muncii, 1932), *The Sun's Speech* (Discusul soarelui, 1937), *China* (1938)—constitute a harsh attack on capitalist society while expressing the poet's enthusiasm for the revolutionary movement and his optimism for the future of the working class. Bukov writes in praise of socialism in such collections as *I See You, Moldavia* (1942), *Spring on the Dniestr* (1944), *My Country* (1947), *The Stories Grow* (1952), *Poems* (1954), and the novel in verse *The City of Reut* (Orashul Reut, 1956). His fairy tale in verse "Andriesh" enjoys great popularity. Bukov is the author of a play, *The Danube–Troubled Waters* (1956, staged under the title *The Seething Danube,* 1957). His works are translated into many languages of the USSR and the Soviet bloc countries.

Works: Opere alese (Kishinev, 1954); *Poezii* (Kishinev, 1958); *Magistral'* (Kishinev, 1969); *Sochineniia* (Kishinev, 1969) [text in Moldavian]. In Russian translation: *Stikhotvoreniia i poëmy* (M., 1955); *Izbrannye stikhi i poëmy* (M., 1960); *Iskry serdtsa: novelly, rasskazy, miniatiury* (Kishinev, 1965); *Kalei loskom, rasskazy* (M., 1968); *Moi V'etnam* (Kishinev, 1968); *Krylo vetra. Stikhi* (M., 1970); *Stikhotvoreniia* (M., 1972).

References: S. Chibotaru, *Emiliian Bukov* (Kishinev, 1959) [bibliography]; V. Koroban, "Emiliian Bukov," in *Literatura sovetike moldoveniaske (ocherkul)* (Kishinev, 1960); E. Zlatova, "Emiliian Boukov," *La littérature sovietique,* No. 4 (1955).

BULAKHÓVS'KYI, LEONID ARSENOVYCH (1888-1961). Soviet Russian-Ukrainian linguist, Honored Scientist of the Ukrainian SSR (1941). Bulakhovs'-kyi was born on 14 April 1888 in Kharkov. He taught at Kharkov and Perm Universities until 1921, after which time he lived in Kharkov and Kiev. A member of the Ukrainian Academy of Sciences (1939) and a Corresponding Member of the Academy of Sciences of the USSR (1946), Bulakhovs'kyi served as the director of the A.A. Potebnia Institute of Linguistics of the Ukrainian Academy of Sciences after 1944. Bulakhovs'kyi's works deal with various problems of Russian and Ukrainian linguistics, Slavic linguistics, and teaching methodology. Drawing on Ukrainian, Russian, Bulgarian, Czech and other Slavic languages, Bulakhovs'-kyi reconstructed the Old Slavic accentual system and made various discoveries in the history of stress and length in individual Slavic languages: *An Accentual Commentary on the Polish Language* (Aktsentologicheskii kommentarii k pol'-skomu iazyku, 1950), *An Accentual Commentary on the Czech Language* (Aktsentologicheskii kommentarii k cheshskomu iazyku, 3 vols., 1953-56), *Bulgarian as a Source for the Reconstruction of the Old Slavic Accentual System* (Bolgar-skii iazyk kak istochnik rekonstruktsii drevneishei slavianskoi aktsentologicheskoi sistemy, 1958). Bulakhovs'kyi devoted much effort to the study of related problems in Ukrainian, such as *The Question of the Origin of the Ukrainian Language* (Pytannia pokhodzhennia ukrains'koi movy, 1956), *Ukrainian Literary Accentuation* (Ukrains'kyi literaturnyi naholos, 1943), and the orthography and punctuation of contemporary Ukrainian. His interests also extended to the history of the Russian literary language: *Russian Literary Language of the First Half of the Nineteenth Century* (Russkii literaturnyi iazyk pervoi poloviny XIX veka, 2 vols., 1941-48). Bulakhovs'kyi is the author of many textbooks for use at the university level on linguistics and the Russian literary language. He has also written monographs on Ukrainian linguistics: *From Historical Commentaries on Ukrainian* (Z istorychnykh komentariiv do ukrains'koi movy, 1946-52). Bulakhovs'kyi died on 4 April 1961 in Kiev.

Works: Uchenie I.V. Stalina o iazyke i zadachi sovetskogo iazykoznaniia (Kiev, 1951); *Narysy z zahal'noho movoznavstva,* 2nd ed. (Kiev, 1959); *Vybrani pratsi* (Kiev, 1975-).

References: Leonid Arsenovych Bulakhovs'kyi (Kiev, 1959) [contains bibliography]; V.I. Borkovskii, "Semidesiatiletie L.A. Bulakhovskogo," *Voprosy iazykoznaniia,* No. 2 (1958); I.K. Beloded, "Leonid Arsen'evich Bulakhovskii," *Izvestiia AN SSSR. Otdelenie literatury i iazyka,* fasc. 2, vol. XVII (1958); I.K. Beloded, *L.A. Bulakhovskii* (Kiev, 1968).

BULGÁKOV, MIKHAIL AFANAS'EVICH (1891-1940). Russian novelist and dramatist, famous during his lifetime as the author of the play *The Days of the Turbins* (Dni Turbinykh). His importance as a novelist was recognized only in 1966 with the publication of his *Selected Prose* (Izbrannaia proza). In this same year the Soviet journal *Moskva* published a censored version of his novel *The Master and Margarita* (Master i Margarita), a work which was an immediate sensation, and established Bulgakov as one of the major novelists of the Soviet period.

Bulgakov was born in Kiev on 3 (15) May 1891, into the family of a professor of theology. Many of his relatives were physicians, and Bulgakov chose medicine as his first profession despite a childhood attraction to literature and drama. He received his medical degree from Kiev University in 1916 and, like the hero of his *Notes of a Young Doctor* (Zapiski iunogo vracha, written between 1924 and 1927), served his medical apprenticeship in ignorant rural areas, where he got his first good look at the life of the Russian peasant. He returned to Kiev in 1918 and lived through one of the worst years of the Civil War there. The Bulgakov family belonged to the intelligentsia, and its sympathies were with the White cause in the beginning. By war's end two of Bulgakov's brothers had emigrated to France, and Bulgakov had considered it himself.

Bulgakov dated the beginning of his literary career as 1919, when he traveled to the Crimea and began publishing in the local newspapers. In the Caucasian town of Vladikavkaz he staged his first plays and served his literary apprenticeship. After struggling to feed himself and his wife, Bulgakov finally left the Caucasus for Moscow, where he felt his literary career might be able to support him.

Like so many other writers of the time, Bulgakov spent his first years in Moscow writing feuilletons. He edited an industrial newspaper for a while, and in general managed to live on his work for some thirty different newspapers, including the famous satirical paper *The Whistle* (Gudok), where Il'f and Petrov, Kataev and Olesha also got their start.

In 1922 Bulgakov began the series of feuilletons for the Berlin emigre newspaper *Nakanune,* which led to the publication of his first book. In 1925 *Diaboliad* (D'iavoliada) came out, a collection which included one of his most famous stories, *The Fatal Eggs* (Rokovye iaitsa). In this same year he wrote a novelette which was rejected everywhere, and to this day has not been published in the Soviet Union, *The Heart of a Dog* (Sobach'e serdtse).

The most important work of these years was the novel *White Guard* (Belaia gvardiia), part of which was published in 1925 in the journal *Rossiia.* This was the work which Bulgakov loved the most, the story of a family in Kiev torn between loyalty to the tsarist regime and the Bolsheviks during the crucial year 1918-19. The authorities closed down the journal *Rossiia* before the rest of the novel could come out, but even in its unfinished form, it attracted the attention of the Moscow Art Theater. The theater asked Bulgakov to turn his novel into a play, which, as it happened, he had already begun to do. Bulgakov's prose and drama must be considered together if one wishes to understand his development as a writer, since themes and characters often migrate from one work to another. Thus began a new stage of Bulgakov's career.

The years 1925 to 1929 could be called Bulgakov's theater period, as the writer turned out play after play, all of which were controversial but successful, when they were passed by the censorship and allowed to be staged. His first play was the incredibly popular dramatization of *White Guard,* entitled *The Days of the Turbins* (1925), followed by the grotesque comedy *Zoia's Apartment* (Zoikina kvartira, 1926). In 1928 he wrote *Flight* (Beg), a play about emigration and return to Russia, banned before it could be produced. The next play to be staged was *The Crimson Island* (Bagrovyi ostrov, written in 1927), a comedy-allegory of the Revolution.

Attacks on Bulgakov had begun with his first play, which was seen by the critics as being too sympathetic a portrayal of the White enemy, despite the fact that by the end the characters are welcoming the Bolsheviks. Bulgakov was labeled an "internal emigre," and his past as a White sympathizer was held against him. Yet no matter how vicious the attacks of the critics became, the public continued to flock to his plays, which were genuinely entertaining as well as being notorious. But by 1929 the censorship, far more important than the critics, refused to pass his works, and he became virtually unemployable in the theater— the one place he wished to work. Bulgakov's career as a playwright was over.

On 28 March 1930 Bulgakov sent his now-famous letter to Stalin, asking permission to go abroad, since, as he complained, the country did not wish to make use of him as a writer. Written four days after Maiakovskii's suicide by a playwright who was extremely famous at the time, the letter prompted Stalin to call Bulgakov and assure him that something would be done to get him work in the theater.

After a short stint at a small theater, Bulgakov was offered a place at his beloved Moscow Art Theater, where he stayed until 1936, adapting and translating works by other authors. And even though there was little chance of production or publication, he continued to work at his own plays and prose. No playwright in the history of Russian drama, with the exception of Ostrovskii, was so deeply involved with all aspects of theater life. From 1925 to 1936 Bulgakov was a playwright, an adaptor, a director, and even an actor. Part of the great success that *The Days of the Turbins* enjoyed is attributable to Bulgakov's personal direction of the actors. He was a writer who could act out all of his characters, from the pose of the body to the pattern of intonation. For most of his life, Bulgakov's friends came from the theater world, not the literary one.

In 1928, just before the most serious attacks began, Bulgakov had begun a tale called "The Consultant with a Hoof," which eventually became the novel *The Master and Margarita.* This early variant, along with a novel entitled *Theater,* was burned by the author in early 1930, just before he wrote the letter to Stalin. But after he was again working for the theater, Bulgakov returned to the novel and continued to work on it until his death.

In 1931 he finished a play with a science fiction theme of the world destroyed in a devastating war, perhaps a foreshadowing of World War II. Entitled *Adam and Eve* (Adam i Eva), this play has never been published or produced in the Soviet Union.

Bulgakov's fortunes took a sudden turn for the better in 1932 when the ban on *The Days of the Turbins* was lifted, although the other plays were still proscribed. In this year another play, *Molière* (also known as *Cabal of Hypocrites),* was accepted for production by the Art Theater, which Bulgakov saw as a sign that he might again become a working playwright.

Bulgakov adapted several works during these years: Molière's *Le Bourgeois gentilhomme,* and Gogol's *Dead Souls.* He began a biography of Molière, which was rejected in 1933 as being too colorful and too artistic by the editors to whom he submitted it.

In the next two years, while he continued to work on *The Master and Margarita,* Bulgakov wrote three plays which remained unproduced during his lifetime, although two of them became successful after his death. *Bliss* (Blazhenstvo, 1934) is a time-travel play about life in the future seen through the eyes of people transported from the present. *The Last Days* (Poslednie dni, 1935, also known as *Pushkin*) is the story of the events surrounding the death of Pushkin, although the poet himself never appears as a character. *Ivan Vasilievich* (1935), a companion play to *Bliss,* brings Ivan the Terrible to Moscow of the thirties.

Bulgakov left the Moscow Art Theater in 1936 to work as a librettist for the Bolshoi Theater. This break was due to the unpleasantness surrounding the staging of *Molière.* The play had been accepted for production in 1932, but was not performed until 1936. Stanislavskii interfered with the production and demonstrated, to Bulgakov at least, that he misunderstood the play completely. After negative reviews, the play was cut from the repertory after a run of only seven nights. It is hardly coincidental that Bulgakov began at this time to write a satire of the theater world in general, and Stanislavskii in particular, in a work which he called *Theatrical Novel* (Teatral'nyi roman, 1936, known in English as *Black Snow*). However, Bulgakov abandoned it in favor of work on more pressing projects.

After completing an adaptation of *Don Quixote* in 1938, Bulgakov was approached by some of the Art Theater people with a request that he write a play about Stalin, in honor of his sixtieth birthday jubilee. He complied with the play *Batum* (1938), but the project ended when Stalin decided that a play about his youth was not needed. Bulgakov wrote the play under duress, presumably convinced that it would in some way help his widow after his death. For as early as 1937 he had been aware that he had neurosclerosis—the disease his father had died of—and he decided to do only those things which were vital to him, chiefly *The Master and Margarita.* In 1939 Bulgakov went blind and abandoned work on everything but *The Master and Margarita,* dictating the final corrections to his wife. On March 10, 1940, at the age of 49, Bulgakov died in his Moscow apartment.

Bulgakov was one of the Soviet writers like Fedin and Leonov who clearly continued the traditions of nineteenth-century Russian literature. His basic theme is that of the intelligentsia and its struggle to preserve its humanistic ideals in the face of the stern demands of the new Soviet society.

Bulgakov's earliest important prose work was "Notes on the Cuffs" (Zapiski na manzhetakh, 1922), a fragmentary autobiographical account of his years in the Caucasus and his early days in Moscow. It is a highly original work, modern in its laconicism and striking imagery, which combine to convey the atmosphere of the early years after the Revolution when families were scattered and professions were abandoned.

The Notes of a Young Doctor is also an autobiographical work, but here the echoes of nineteenth-century literature are very strong: Chekhov and Pushkin (themes, character types, allusions), as well as Tolstoi, whose "Snowstorm" and "Master and Man" are paralleled in Bulgakov's "Blizzard" (from *Notes of a Young Doctor*).

These two early works show that the experimental style as well as the more realistic, traditional one were present from the start of Bulgakov's career. In the collection *Diaboliad* we find much that is typical of the prose of the twenties: fantasy, stylistic grotesquerie, plot twists and parody. But there is also much that is directly derived from the previous century. The title story of the collection, for example, belongs to the tradition of Russian stories about little men and civil servants begun by Gogol and continued by Dostoevskii in *The Double*. In their isolation and fear of their superiors, as well as their madness, they are direct descendants of the earlier characters. But Bulgakov also took from Western literature: in the famous story *The Fatal Eggs* he writes a variation on the theme of Wells' *The Food of the Gods*. In this story giant reptiles begin to destroy Russia until a frost kills them. The efforts of a scientist to control the growth and spread of the reptiles are frustrated by state interference, a theme that occurs again and again in Bulgakov's science fiction plays and stories. His ability to make the fantastic seem real, and the ordinary fantastic makes Bulgakov's story more powerful than Wells'.

Another work which deals with the use and misuse of science is *Heart of a Dog,* which, like *The Fatal Eggs,* is both comic and serious. A transplant operation which gives a dog the pituitary and testicles of a criminal produces unexpected results. The operation has clear parallels with the Revolution, and the point is made that you cannot induce real change in a man or a nation by the use of violence, and that putting the proletariat in positions of power does not mean that they will automatically develop the ability to handle that power. Like *The Fatal Eggs* this story is an impressive feat of the imagination.

Bulgakov himself felt that all of these early works were far less important than the novel *White Guard*, which many consider the best Soviet Civil War novel. The novel conveys the apocalyptic atmosphere of the Civil War, mixing comic, lyrical, and terrifying moments with great dexterity. The novel's fascination lies partly in its absorbing characters, and partly in the author's ability to create plot interest, presenting mysteries which are explained at unexpected points of the narrative. Like Belyi's *Petersburg,* the *White Guard* is also a novel about a city: the monuments, streets, and the physical setting of Kiev play an important role in the novel. The citizens of this city speak in anonymous dialogues about the events that are frightening them, and they are the voice of the city itself.

The chaotic atmosphere is mirrored in the style of the novel. Landscapes take on a phantasmagoric quality, the word "misty" is repeated throughout the novel until all events seem to take place in a dream. Dreams, semi-conscious states and delirium recur. Narration is fragmented through time and space leaps, by bits and pieces of conversation and by transitions from the mind of one character into that of another. The great mixture of stylistic levels, which also typifies *Master and Margarita,* ranges from formal rhetoric to negative similes and imagery from folk literature, to the use of Ukrainian.

As in other works, Bulgakov consciously uses the literature of the nineteenth century as a reference point. Here Tolstoi and Dostoevskii, Chekhov and Gogol are used for their ideas of history as well as specific episodes. Scenes from *War and Peace* and *The Brothers Karamazov* are paralleled, and the epigraph is taken from another work about civil disorder—Pushkin's *The Captain's Daughter.*

In this work the Turbin family represents the intelligentsia who chose the wrong side in the Civil War simply because they had always believed in the Tsar. Gradually the horrors of the Civil War and the White and partisan atrocities make them see the bankruptcy of their cause, and ultimately they retire from the battle to await the arrival of the Bolshevik army.

It was all very well to show how a family of White Guardists eventually comes to see that their cause is doomed, but to show them so sympathetically, to evoke the coziness of their beloved apartment was to risk being called an apologist for the White cause. The problem was that Bulgakov had used all of his talent to summon up a way of life that no longer existed, the world of the pre-Revolutionary intelligentsia. His characters were based on his family and friends, and his love for them shows through his evaluation of the wrongness of their politics.

The Days of the Turbins is a considerably edited and censored version of the novel *White Guard,* in which characterization is the principal aesthetic virtue. But in *Flight* Bulgakov felt free to use the panoramic effects natural to him, and many of the themes from *White Guard* recur here as he follows the fates of the Whites who went into emigration. In *The Crimson Island* the theme of the Revolution and exile appear again, but here they are lampooned. *The Crimson Island* is connected with another interest of Bulgakov's as well: life backstage in a theater, and the battle with the censors, both of which appear in *Theatrical Novel* ten years later. Similarly, in the satire on Moscow under NEP, *Zoia's Apartment,* we find characters in an apartment house that resemble the inhabitants of the Moscow of *The Master and Margarita.*

Besides characters and situations, the plays and prose share larger concerns. One of Bulgakov's main interests is the relationship between the artist (or his analogue, the scientist), and the institutions that control his work. The scientist in *The Fatal Eggs,* for example, collides with government interference; Pushkin in *Last Days* is destroyed in part by the attitude of the Tsar; Molière is overwhelmed both by the power of the church and by Louis XIV. This idea receives its ultimate realization in *The Master and Margarita,* as Pilate decides not to save Yeshua—another artist figure—because he is afraid of the Emperor Tiberius.

In his last novel Bulgakov brings together all of these themes and styles. Here is the romantic, lyrical author of *White Guard,* the mocking satirist of *Heart of a Dog* and *The Fatal Eggs,* the penetrating observer of literary life in *Theatrical Novel,* the creator of the tragic *Last Days* and *Molière.* All of the Bulgakovian motifs are found here: the ignorance of the common people, the philistinism of the city folk, the prevalence of spies, acts of violence and retribution, bureaucrats, the housing problem, writers, the theater, love stories, the nature of justice, the artist versus the state, and, most of all, the problem of guilt and expiation.

The Master and Margarita, Bulgakov's masterpiece, is an immensely complex tour de force. There are essentially three interwoven strands of narration. One is the story of the writer, the Master, who is discouraged and broken when his novel is attacked by the critics because its subject is Pontius Pilate. In the end, like Faust, he is saved by his beloved, Margarita, but not before he has suffered prison and a crippling loss of faith in himself. This strand is both a love story and a meditation on the nature of absolution. The second strand is the comic portrayal of the destruction wrought by the devil Woland, who has arrived in Moscow posing as a travelling magician. The devil and his band, which includes the talking cat Behemoth, wind through various levels of Moscow society of the twenties and thirties, exposing crimes which range from the petty to the terrible. The magical group first encourage and tempt people, and then punish them for succumbing to their worse natures. The third strand is the story of Pontius Pilate, presented as a narrative, a dream, and parts of the Master's novel; but all of these different authors have the same style. The separate strands begin to interweave and finally come together in the figure of the Master himself, who, loved by Margarita and helped by Woland, finally sees his hero, Pilate, freed from the torment of guilt.

Pilate represents the highest level of evil in the novel. He is guilty of what is labeled the worst sin—cowardice. Pilate's blind obedience to the emperor, despite his own recognition that Yeshua is harmless, is what causes his centuries of suffering. Yeshua himself tries to make Pilate see the transient nature of earthly power, saying that although it may be true that his life hangs by a thread, it is not Pilate who has strung that thread, and it can only be cut by the one who suspended it.

As satire in the truest, darkest sense, the novel catalogues many other levels of evil, and the truly horrible crimes of the poisoners and murderers who attend Satan's ball are paralleled by the acts committed by the Muscovites who live in the Russia of the thirties: writers write what they do not believe, friends denounce friends, citizens are caught in their own avarice, ignorance and lies.

Time and again the novel demonstrates the consequences of evil acts, even trivial ones. One man's decision, by force of cause and effect, can affect the lives of many: a critic writes a vicious review of the Master's book, a neighbor reads the review and decides to denounce the Master, who is then imprisoned. Two thousand years earlier a procurator of Judea reviews a case and decides that the accused is indeed guilty of speaking against the emperor. A high priest chooses to let a murderer go free so that the philosopher Yeshua will be crucified. The acts of these men are interdependent, Bulgakov implies, and generate effects felt down to the present day.

For most of the characters in the novel, political morality is the only morality. When interpretation of what is politically moral changes, these characters must change with them. But in the novel, as opposed to the real life Bulgakov saw around him, men who stifle their consciences are punished—by Woland.

The Master and Margarita insists again and again, as did *White Guard,* that earthly power is fleeting, that one may die at any moment and that all allegiances to state or empire come to nothing. The empire crumbles and is remembered only by historians. Political fashions come and go, but the concepts of good and evil remain the same. In the end the fame of the madman Yeshua far exceeds that of the Emperor Tiberius.

Whatever the theme, Bulgakov's characters consistently try to assert their humanity in the face of force—whether physical or psychological. The political rules of their time—whether France under Louis XIV, Judea under the Romans at the time of Christ, or Moscow under Stalin—say that ethics and humanistic ideas are out of place, but the characters refuse to abandon these ideas, even when confronted with the threat of destruction.

Bulgakov referred to himself as a mystical writer, in that he believed that there is more to the world than common sense and dogma can explain. In his major works we find a belief in justice, but it is a justice that must come through a supernatural force, or after death. Yet Bulgakov's writing is moved by the desire for justice here and now, and his most powerful satire comes from the frustration of that desire. This concern can be seen in the biblical second epigraph to his first novel: ". . . and the dead were judged out of those things which were written in the books according to their works . . . ."

Works: D'iavoliada (M., 1925) [Contains *Diavoliada, Rokovye iaitsa, Kitaiskaia istoriia, Pokhozhdeniia Chichikova, No. 13—Dom El'pit-Rabkommuna*]; *P'esy* (M., 1962) [Contains *Dni Turbinykh, Beg, Kabala sviatosh, Poslednie dni, Don Kikhot*]; *P'esy* (Paris, 1970) [Contains *Adam i Eva, Bagrovyi ostrov, Zoikina kvartira*]; *Izbrannaia proza* (M., 1966); *Belaia gvardiia, Teatral'nyi roman, Master i Margarita: Romany* (M., 1973) [This edition contains the most complete text to date of *Master and Margarita* and has not yet been translated into English.]; *Neizdannyi Bulgakov* (Ann Arbor, 1977) [Contains letter and the play *Batum.*]. All of the major works have been translated into English, principal recent editions of which are: *Adam and Eve, Russian Literature Triquarterly,* No. 1 (Fall 1971), 164-216; *Black Snow: A Theatrical Novel* (N.Y., 1967); *A Country Doctor's Notebook* (London, 1975) [Contents: "Baptism by Rotation," "Black as Egypt's Night," "The Embroidered Towel," "The Speckled Rash," "The Steel Windpipe," "The Blizzard," "Morphine," "The Vanishing Eye," "The Murderer"]; *Diaboliad and Other Stories* (Bloomington, Ind., 1972) [Contents: "The Adventures of Chichikov," "A Chinese Tale," *The Fatal Eggs,* "No. 13. "The Elpit-Rabkommun Building," "A Treatise on Housing," "Psalm," "Four Portraits," "Moonshine Lake," "The Raid," "The Crimson Island"]; *The Early Plays of Mikhail Bulgakov* (Bloomington, Ind., 1972) [Contents: *A Cabal of Hypocrites, The Crimson Island, Days of the Turbins, Flight, Zoia's Apartment*]; *Russian Literature Triquarterly,* No. 15 (1976) [Special issue on Bulgakov. Contents: "The Red Crown," "Moscow in the Twenties," "The Capital in a Notebook,"

"The Inspector General with a Booting-out," "Song of Summer," "The City of Kiev," *Last Days (Pushkin)*] ; "Glimpses of Our Capital," *Living Age* (March 31, 1923), 769-71; *The Heart of a Dog* (N.Y., 1968); "I Dreamed a Dream," *Soviet Literature*, No. 12 (1975), 137-45; *The Life of Monsieur de Molière* (N.Y., 1970); "Lord Curzon Day in Moscow," *Living Age* (July 14, 1923), 60-62; *The Master and Margarita* (N.Y., 1967) [The Ginsburg translation is more accurate; the Glenny translation more complete] ; *White Guard* (N.Y., 1971). For a more detailed listing of all of Bulgakov's works, see E. Proffer, *An International Bibliography of Works by and about Mikhail Bulgakov* (Ann Arbor, 1976).

References: Vladimir Lakshin, "Mikhail Bulgakov's *The Master and Margarita,*" *Soviet Studies in Literature,* vol. 2 (1969); M. Chudakova, "Arkhiv M.A. Bulgakova," *Zapiski otdela rukopisei,* fascicle 37 (M., 1976); E. Proffer, *Mikhail Bulgakov* (Ann Arbor, 1979).

Ellendea Proffer

BULGÁKOV, VALENTIN FËDOROVICH (b. 1886). Russian memoirist and writer. Bulgakov was born on 13 (25) November 1886 in the town of Kuznetsk (now Kemerovo Oblast). Beginning his literary activity in 1904, he studied history and philology at Moscow University from 1906 to 1910, when he became Lev Tolstoi's personal secretary. Understandably, Bulgakov shared Tolstoi's moral views. In 1911 he published his diary entitled *The Last Year with Lev Tolstoi* (U Tolstogo v poslednii god ego zhizni), which contains a detailed account of everything he saw and heard on Tolstoi's estate, Yasnaia Poliana. He subsequently republished the diary in 1918 and 1920, expanding and revising it with each edition. In the latest (1960) edition he strove to give an especially exact and objective description of the great writer's character and his environment. From 1923 to 1948 Bulgakov lived in Prague, but returned to the USSR in 1949, where he worked at the Tolstoi Museum in Yasnaia Poliana.

Works: Khristianskaia ètika. Sistematicheskie ocherki mirovozzreniia L.N. Tolstogo (M., 1917); *Lev Tolstoi i nasha sovremennost'* (M., 1919); *Opomnites', liudi—brat'ia! Istoriia vozzvaniia edinomyshlennikov L.N. Tolstogo protiv mirovoi voiny 1914-18 gg.* (M., 1922); *Tolstoi—moralist* (Prague, 1922); "Zamolchannoe o Tolstom," in *Kovcheg* (Prague, 1926); *L.N. Tolstoi v poslednii god ego zhizni* (M., 1960).

BULGÁRIN, FADDEI VENEDIKTOVICH [TADEUSZ BUŁHARYN] (1789-1859). Novelist, critic, publisher, and journalist. Although Bulgarin achieved considerable success in Russian letters, he was a Pole, born at Pieryszew in the Province of Minsk. He is an enigmatic and controversial figure in the history of Russian literature, intensely hated during his lifetime and sorely treated in criticism and scholarship to this day. His achievements, some of dubious worth, some of great importance, are many: popular author of historical and moral-didactic or picaresque novels; influential critic and aggressive polemicist; prolific writer of sketches, surveys, travel accounts, military stories, memoirs, literary and historical essays, and moral-didactic precepts; determined, albeit not respected, historian; satirist and comic writer; interpreter and transmitter for Russians of European cultural developments; powerful editor, publisher, and journalist. Together with two other "foreigners" in Petersburg, N.I. Grech (German, Gretsch) and O.I. Senkovskii (Józef-Julian Sękowski, a fellow Pole), he established a monopoly in Russian publishing from the early 1820s into the 1850s, using his journals and political newspaper *Severnaia pchela* (Northern Bee, 1825-57) as a base for both power and profit.

Bulgarin is inevitably discussed as an arch-conservative who spoke in an unofficial but nevertheless real voice for the government of Nicholas I, and is even believed to have been an agent for the Third Section, the Tsar's secret police apparatus. In fact, he was identified with both liberals and conservatives, aristocrats and plebeians, official Russians and dissenters, anti-Polish Russians and anti-Russian Poles, Catholics and Orthodox. Which is to say that he was an opportunist—an adroit seeker after his own best interests, a man without principles other than commercial. And though he eventually alienated all sides, ending his life in isolation and ill-repute, he meanwhile achieved unprecedented financial success for himself and helped make literature, journalism, and publishing commercially viable in Russia.

Bulgarin established his duplicitous character at an early age. Although his father, a Polish nobleman, was exiled to Siberia as a supporter of Tadeusz Kosciuszko in 1794, his mother succeeded in enrolling him in the Corps of Noble Land Cadets in St. Petersburg, thus ensuring him the education of a Russian nobleman. He himself claimed in his *Memoirs* (Vospominaniia, 1846-49) that he was so thoroughly Russified as to forget his native language, and he regularly attended Orthodox services, even singing in choirs, while never surrendering his Catholicism. He served from 1806 to 1811 as a cornet and lieutenant under the command of Grand Duke Konstantin, fighting against the French at Friedland and the Swedes in Finland. He curried favor successfully, but ruined his career by writing scurrilous satires on his superiors and Konstantin. Imprisoned for a while at Kronstadt and then discharged in 1811, he returned to Poland where he nimbly switched sides by joining a Polish regiment of Uhlans which subsequently saw action in Napoleon's Italian and Spanish campaigns. Although he attempted to deny his participation in the Moscow campaign, he did in fact fight against his former comrades-in-arms. Taken prisoner in France in 1813 and pardoned in 1814 under the terms of a treaty of amnesty for Poles, he soon turned up again in Petersburg as a self-proclaimed Russian patriot.

Bulgarin's life between 1814 and 1820 is obscure. He seems to have been active in Petersburg, but also became prominent in Vilno, a center for the education of promising Poles who could be sent to positions of influence in the Russian Empire. He became a practicing lawyer at this time, and he is known to have written poetry and short prose pieces in both Polish and Russian as early as 1816. His Russian career began in 1820 when he became acquainted with Grech and was invited to help edit the latter's influential journal *Syn otechestva* (Son of the Fatherland). Following Grech's suggestion, he wrote a "Short Survey of Polish Literature" (Kratkoe obozrenie pol'skoi slovesnosti) which was greatly appreciated by information-starved Russians. In a very short time he became known among Petersburg *literati* and flattered his way into the homes of such men as N.M. Karamzin, V.A. Zhukovskii, A.F. Voeikov, P.A.

Viazemskii, A.S. Griboedov, A.A. Bestuzhev, and K.F. Ryleev. His critical articles, polemics, prose works, and other literary productions of the early 1820s identified him strongly with progressive and liberal circles, and he worked closely with the Decembrists Ryleev and Bestuzhev. But he was also careful not to alienate conservative forces and held a post in the Ministry of Public Education under the patronage of the reactionary "literary old-believer" Admiral A.S. Shishkov.

In 1822 Bulgarin, acting as both editor and publisher, brought out the first issue of his own journal *Severnyi arkhiv* (Northern Archive), devoted to articles on Russian and general Slavic history, foreign travels, and Russian literature. From 1823 to 1824 he published *Literaturnye listki* (Literary Leaflets) as an outlet for the original literary works he was able to attract to, but not find room for, in *Severnyi arkhiv,* and from 1826 to 1827 he published *Detskii sobesednik* (Children's Conversationalist) for the moral edification of young Russians. His most worthwhile almanac was *Russkaia Taliia* (Russian Thalia, 1825-26), a result of his love the the theater, composed almost entirely of his own critical articles, reviews, translations, and biographical sketches of leading singers, actors, and dancers of the day. A not insignificant accomplishment of *Russkaia Taliia* was the first publication of a portion of Griboedov's masterpiece *Woe from Wit.* In 1820 *Severnyi arkhiv* and Bulgarin's other journal interests were combined with Grech's *Syn otechestva.* Although the Grech-Bulgarin monopoly did not lack for competition, they in fact collaborated closely with some publications such as Bestuzhev and Ryleev's literary almanac *Poliarnaia zvezda* (1823-25), controlled or financed others (Senkovskii's *Biblioteka dlia chteniia,* founded in the early 1830s), and exerted political or commercial influence over others (N.A. Polevoi's journal *Moskovskii telegraf,* 1825-34). Their only significant competition in the 1830s was Pushkin's *Sovremennik,* founded in 1836 to publish the literary aristocrats, long since alienated from Bulgarin.

Bulgarin's greatest notoriety and financial success came from *Severnaia pchela,* the only privately published newspaper at the time. Although the *Severnaia pchela* demonstrated good liberal intentions during its first year (1825), Bulgarin had already begun to disassociate himself from people and ideas distasteful to the government, and the failure of the Revolt of 14 December 1825 marks the beginning of his reputation as an arch-conservative mouthpiece for the policies of Nicholas I. Many of his friends and literary allies disappeared from the literary scene (Ryleev, Bestuzhev, Kiukhel'beker, Prince A.I. Odoevskii), and others were compromised by their sympathies with the Decembrists (Griboedov, Viazemskii). Right after the revolt several issues of the newspaper were coopted by the government for its report of the affair, and in the summer of 1826 other issues were coopted to print the findings of the committee of investigation and the announcements of the sentencing and execution of the rebels. Bulgarin was himself already under suspicion for his contacts with Polish dissenters at Vilno and elsewhere, and his close relationships with many of the Decembrists now brought him into serious jeopardy. It was only the testimonies of Ryleev and Bestuzhev that cleared him of complicity in the conspiracy; and he was able to continue his publishing activities only due to the fortuitous intervention on his behalf of Count A.Kh. Benkendorf (Benckendorf), chief of the new Third Section.

Given these drastic changes in Russian conditions, to say nothing of Bulgarin's insecure position as a foreigner, it is little wonder that the *Severnaia pchela* became pro-autocracy in its reportage and ultra-patriotic in its policies. Published thrice weekly, it printed official government announcements, military postings, accounts of cultural events, reviews of Russian and foreign works in history, literary criticism, short prose pieces, and poetry. Its political reports were a prominent and closely watched feature, and it leaned heavily to foreign reportage. It favored the sensational—Bulgarin boasted that a report of a rumor of war could boost his circulation by 2,000 overnight—and it offered authentic reports from battlefields in the Caucasus, Persia, Turkey, the Mediterranean, and other troubled spots around the Empire and the world. Bulgarin never lost an opportunity to praise Russian military glory, and he took a strong stand against the Polish Rebellion of 1830-31. Many of the newspaper's stories were planted, no doubt, and its reportage was not only slanted, but highly unreliable. Bulgarin's access to privileged government information amazed Russians and raised suspicions about his relationship to Benkendorf and other official Russians. At its height the *Severnaia pchela* enjoyed a circulation of 10,000, and few educated Russians could drink their morning coffee without it.

Bulgarin wrote a considerable body of fiction, divided between novels and a variety of shorter prose genres. In the early years of his career he was admired somewhat for his lively military stories, which were featured in the prestigious *Poliarnaia zvezda,* and for his accounts of his exploits in Italy and Spain. He was an incorrigible name-dropper, and these works, together with his travel accounts biographical sketches, and *Memoirs,* are valuable sources if only because he managed to meet so many famous persons, from the tsars of Russia to (he claimed) Napoleon. Among the more interesting short prose works, most of which were written between 1816 and 1827, is "Plausible Fantasies, or A Journey About the Earth in the Twenth-Ninth Century" (Pravdopodobnye nebylitsy ili puteshestvie k sredotochiiu zemli, 1825), one of his major moral-didactic works. Bulgarin's moral-didactic works—in fact, most of his works—are too moralistic and simplistic to be read today, and it is likely that even in their time they appealed only to the most unsophisticated reader. "A Journey to the Center of the Earth," for example, is a crude allegory of three populations at the center of the earth—the Ignorances of the Land of Ignorance, the Swine-People of Swineland, and the Light People of the Land of Lightenment. As if fearing he had not made his point, the author concludes with an explanation.

Bulgarin's greatest success as a fiction writer came from his novels. During his lifetime he wrote five, the first of which, *Ivan Vyzhigin* (1829), was Russia's second bestseller. So successful was the novel that it was translated into eight languages and was even published—another first—in Philadelphia in 1832 as *Ivan Vejeeghen. Vyzhigin* is essentially a picaresque novel with a strong didactic element. Gogol was influenced by the novel's satirical pictures of corrupt provincial officialdom, and by such character types as the brash, boorish landowner. From *Pëtr Ivanovich Vyzhigin* (1831), a sequel, Gogol borrowed the petty government official, crushed alike by fate and society, thus giving Bulgarin a place in the development of the key Russian character, the Petty Clerk. Bulgarin's second novel, *Dimitrii the Imposter* (Dimitrii samozvanets, 1829), was his first attempt to write a historical novel. Although it was preceded in time and exceeded in success by Mikhail Zagoskin's *Iurii Miloslavskii, or The Russians in 1612* (1829), it gave Bulgarin claim to precedence among the soon fast-growing school of Russian Walter Scotts. The novel is not devoid of lively narrative skill, but it is perhaps more important for the wealth of documentation which comprises its bulk. That Bulgarin was more properly a historian than a fiction writer is indicated further by the superior quality of his non-fictional biography *Suvorov* (1843). Bulgarin's two other novels are *Mazepa* (1833-34) and *The Memoirs of Titular Councilor Chukhin* (Pamiatnye zapiski tituliarnogo sovetnika Chukhina, 1839). Neither work enjoyed the success of the others.

Well known in Russian literary history is the controversy between Bulgarin and Pushkin. When *Dimitrii the Impostor* appeared in print, Pushkin realized from a liberal borrowing of ideas from his *Boris Godunov* that it must have been Bulgarin who in 1826 recommended to Nicholas I, Pushkin's personal censor, that the drama be re-written as a historical novel *a la* Walter Scott. This incident, combined with the delay of the publication of *Boris Godunov* until 1831 and Bulgarin's well established campaign of sniping at Pushkin's works, led to a feud which continued until Pushkin's death. Bulgarin is even treated as a chief participant in the persecutions which drove Pushkin to despair and, indirectly, to his death. But the controversy has not been fully studied, and Bulgarin's guilt, particularly the charges that he plagiarized *Boris Godunov* and other works by Pushkin, is not conclusively established. It is a fact, for example, that Pushkin was indebted to Bulgarin for access to the historical materials on which both *Boris Godunov* and the historical verse tale *Poltava* (1828) were based. Bulgarin helped both Pushkin and Ryleev with their respective verse works on the Mazepa theme, and he provided many Russians with such materials. It was Bulgarin who first translated the Polish-Ukrainian genre known as the *duma*—a short poem dramatizing a hero of the national past—and Ryleev, the Russian master of the gnere, was indebted to Bulgarin for his awareness of its literary potential. It is true that many of Bulgarin's literary works, critical articles, and historical works are paraphrases or even direct translations of European works. But this was still accepted practice in the early nineteenth century, and much work remains to be done to establish just who borrowed from whom, and under what conditions.

Whatever the eventual findings regarding this and Bulgarin's other controversies, it is evident that he brought his troubles upon himself. For all his deftness as an intriguer, he seems simply to have been unable to resist challenging any literary person or development that offered financial or literary competition. His usual *modus operandi* was to bide his time until he had the power of public opinion or political circumstances on his side, but he was such an aggressive polemicist that he sometimes acted hastily. His first move to establish his authority—and his boldest—came as early as 1822 when he succeeded in pitting the eminent Polish historian Joachim Lelewel against the powerful N.M. Karamzin's *History of the Russian State* in his own *Severnyi arkhiv*. The result was a long, bitter debate for and against Karamzin in the pages of every Russian journal over the next three years. In short time Bulgarin felt strong enough to take on V.A.

Zhukovskii, another powerful literary figure but a comparatively safe target in that Zhukovskii's early Romantic verse was already the subject of more mature Romantic criticism. Curiously, Bulgarin scrupulously avoided taking part in the major debate of the 1820s—the question of Romanticism—but in the course of the 1820s and 1830s he mounted campaigns of careful but unrelenting criticism of Pushkin's *Eugene Onegin,* the Romantic Idealist literary almanac *Mnemozina* (Mnemosyne, 1825), of V.K. Kiukhel'beker and V.F. Odoevskii, N.A. Polevoi's claim to authority as a historian, the historical novels of most of the other Russian Walter Scotts, and a wide variety of other literary developments of the time. Bulgarin was a chief cause of the intense polemics which mark Russian literary criticism of the 1820s. And although he was able to flatter or financially induce many of his opponents back into the fold of his publications when he needed them, he was by the early 1830s one of the most hated men in Petersburg.

He is hardly the complete villain he has been made to seem in Russian and Soviet scholarship, however. He never forgot his debt to Ryleev and Bestuzhev, for example. He personally cared for Ryleev's widow and children, and he helped revive the literary career of the exiled Bestuzhev under the name Marlinskii that dominated Russian prose of the 1830s. He was instrumental in alleviating the consequences of Griboedov's involvement in the Decembrist conspiracy, and he helped many of the fallen Decembrists in personal ways and by publishing their works anonymously after 1825. He was initially reluctant to associate himself with the visiting Adam Mickiewicz, but he eventually overcame his fears and sponsored the Polish poet in Petersburg society. Later he did much to enable Mickiewicz to return to Poland. And though he was perhaps unkind to Karamzin, the campaign he mounted against the historian was on the issue of Lelewel's "democratic," "plebeian" interpretation of history versus Karamzin's conservative, "autocratic" interpretation. One result of the campaign was to make Lelewel's *History of the Polish People* acceptable in Russia, to say nothing of the publication of N.A. Polevoi's *History of the Russian People.* Above all, he made literature a financially worthwhile activity for Russians—this is undoubtedly his major contribution.

It may very well be true that Bulgarin was an agent for the Third Section. Pushkin likened him in an epigram to the notorious French double-agent Vidocq, and the rumors of his secret connection to Benkendorf were given credence in Petersburg society for the reason that he had good access. The charge was made public in the memoirs of A.V. Nikitenko, who cited Count D.N. Bludov as his source (*Notes and Diary,* 1904-5), and the question was extensively explored by the historian M.V. Lemke in his study of the censorship, *The Nicholaevian Gendarmerie and Literature of the Years 1826-1855.* These sources are not free of enmity, however, and it has to be stressed that the available evidence is not conclusive. Moreover, despite Bulgarin's repulsive behavior, he was not devoid of a few positive human qualities, and he did make a substantial contribution to Russian literature. It is clear that his political position was without respect, even without the overt label of police spy. It is equally clear that he was a mediocre writer. But the record remains in need of an objective examination, and his complex and contradictory legacy promises a great deal of knowledge about the literature and society of his time.

Works: Sochineniia (Pb., 1827-28); *Polnoe sobranie sochinenii,* 7 vols. (Pb., 1839-44); *Vospominaniia,* 6 vols. (Pb., 1846-49).

References: N.I. Grech, *Zapiski o moei zhizni* (Pb., 1886); A.V. Nikitenko, *Zapiski i dnevnik,* 2 vols. (Pb., 1904-05); M.V. Lemke, *Nikolaevskie zhandarmy i literatura 1826-1855 gg* (Pb., 1909); Walter Schamschula, *Der russische historische Roman vom Klassizismus bis zur Romantik* (Meisenheim am Glan, 1961); J. Striedter, *Der Schelmenroman in Russland: Ein Beitrag zur Geschichte des russischen Romans vor Gogol'* (Wiesbaden, 1961); Frank Mocha, *Tadeusz Bułharyn (Faddej V. Bulgarin) 1789-1859: A Study in Literary Maneuver* (Rome, 1974).

Gilman H. Alkire and **Lauren G. Leighton**

BUŁHARYN, TADEUSZ, *see* BULGARIN, FADDEI VENEDIKTOVICH

BÚLICH, NIKOLAI NIKITICH (1824-1895). Russian literary critic. Bulich was born 5 (17) February 1824 in Kurgan. In 1845 he graduated from the Department of Philosophy at Kazan University, where he served as professor of Russian literary history from 1854, and rector from 1882 until 1885. Bulich first appeared in print in 1854 with the work *Sumarokov and Contemporary Criticism* (Sumarokov i sovremennaia emu kritika), in which detailed information on Russian satirical journals of the second half of the eighteenth century is also gathered. He is the author of articles on Lomonosov, Karamzin, Pushkin and Zhukovskii, and works on the history of Kazan University: *From the First Years of Kazan University* (Iz pervykh let Kazanskogo universiteta, 2 vols., 1887-91). Bulich died on 24 May (5 June) 1895 in the village of Yurtkuli, Kazan Province.

Works: Znachenie Pushkina v istorii russkoi literatury (Kazan, 1855); *Biograficheskii ocherk N.M. Karamzina i razvitie ego literaturnoi deiatel'nosti* (Kazan, 1966); *Ocherki po istorii russkoi literatury i prosveshcheniia s nachala XIX veka,* 2 vols. (Pb., 1900-05).

References: Za sto let. Biograficheskii slovar' professorov i prepodavatelei imp. Kazanskogo universiteta (1804-1904) (Kazan, 1914).

BÚLICH, SERGEI KONSTANTINOVICH (1859-1921). Russian linguist and specialist in Russian philology. Bulich was born on 27 August (8 September) 1859 in Kazan. A disciple of Baudouin de Courtenay, he was as a professor at Petersburg University (1886) and was an instructor, later director, of the Higher Women's Courses there. Bulich became the first supervisor (1899) of the University's Experimental Phonetics Center (now the Laboratory of Experimental Phonetics). He often contributed to encyclopedic dictionaries—for example, to Brokgaus-Efron's *Encyclopedic Dictionary* he contributed more than one thousand entries on linguistics. Bulich also wrote biographical sketches on Russian Romantic composers, such as G.N. Teplov, N.A. Titov, and A.E. Varlamov. Several of his studies are devoted to the role of music in the life of Russian writers and their contribution to the development of Russian musical culture: "Pushkin and Russian Music" (Pushkin i russkaia muzyka, 1900), "A.S. Griboedov as Musician" (1911), and "M.Yu. Lermontov and Russian Music" (1913). Bulich died in 1921 in Petrograd.

Works: Zaimstvovannye slova i ikh znachenie dlia razvitiia iazyka (Warsaw, 1886); *Lektsii po russkomu iazyku* (Pb., 1892-94); *Tserkovnoslavianskie elementy v sovremennom literaturnom i narodnom russkom iazyke,* part 1 (Pb., 1893); *Ocherki istorii iazykoznaniia v Rossii,* vol. I (Pb., 1904); "A.S. Griboedov—muzykant," *Polnoe sobranie sochinenii A.S. Griboedova,* vol. I (Pb., 1911); "M.Iu. Lermontov i russkaia muzyka," *Polnoe sobranie sochinenii M.Iu. Lermontova,* vol. V (Pb., 1913).

References: V.A. Bogoroditskii, "Kazanskaia lingvisticheskaia shkola, (1875-1939)," *Trudy Moskovskogo instituta istorii, filosofii i literatury,* vol. V (1939).

BÚNIN, IVAN ALEKSEEVICH (1870-1953). Russian writer, first Russian to receive the Nobel Prize (1933). Born into the gentry on 22 October 1870 in Voronezh, Bunin in earliest childhood witnessed the increasing impoverishment of his family, which ultimately led to its complete ruin. In 1884, after four years at Elets Gymnasium, Bunin left school and resumed his education at home under the guidance of his older, extremely well educated brother, Yulii. He already showed a deep interest in literature and at Yulii's urging sent a poem "Over S.Ya. Nadson's Grave" (Nad mogiloi S.Ya. Nadsona) to the magazine *Rodina,* which was printed in 1877. Thus Bunin started his long, sixty-six-year literary career. Encouraged by his first literary success, he continued to write poetry and short stories on rural life, also printed in *Rodina.* Bunin realized how poor the quality of these first experiments was: "It seemed to me, there was no writer who had begun as poorly as I did" (Autobiographical Notes, 1950).

The year 1889 was crucial in Bunin's life. He left home, carrying into the "wide world" a thorough knowledge of the Russian countryside and its small-town people, an acute sensitivity to nature, a mastery of the Russian language and Russian literature, and a knowledge of French and English, self-taught. After three months of travels Bunin started to work as assistant editor for the newspaper *Orlovskii vestnik* (Orël Messenger).

The period when Bunin lived in Orël was closely tied with the name of a girl, Varvara Pashchenko, with whom he fell in love. Bunin rather faithfully depicted this affair with "Lika" (Varvara's nickname) in the "Fifth Book" of *The Life of Arsenev* (Zhizn' Arsen'eva, 1952). While Bunin lived with Lika in the Ukraine he formed his passion for Tolstoyism which, fortunately, resolved itself in later years into merely respectful admiration for Tolstoi's art.

In January 1894 Bunin went to Moscow to see Tolstoi. The journey was beneficial in two ways: Bunin was cured of Tolstoyism, and he wrote a beautiful verbal portrait of Tolstoi. As a matter of fact it was Tolstoi himself who advised Bunin not to take "plain living" too seriously, saying that one can live a simple life without being a Tolstoyan.

Bunin's romance ended at Lika's initiative in autumn 1894. This was a heavy blow from which Bunin never recuperated fully, as some of his notes indicate. In 1898 Bunin met Anna Tsakni. The extraordinary beauty of this twenty-year-old Russian-Greek girl struck him. She was, as Bunin put it, his "pagan passion." They married in the fall of 1898 and settled down in Odessa, but it soon turned out that Bunin and Anna had no common interests. The birth of their son in 1900 (he died five years later) did not improve their deteriorating relations, and their marriage ended in separation. In 1907 Bunin began to share his life with Vera Nikolaevna Muromtseva, and in 1922 they legalized their common-law marriage. She was a faithful companion in Bunin's long and turbulent life and wrote a valuable biography on the early years of her husband's life, *The Life of Bunin, 1870-1906.*

During the period 1895-1909 Bunin continued writing prose and poetry. His first collection of stories *To the Edge of the World* (Na krai sveta) appeared in 1897 and a book of his poems, *Under the Open Sky* (Pod otkrytym nebom), followed in 1898. In the same year he also published his translation of Longfellow's *The Song of Hiawatha,* for which he was awarded the Pushkin Prize by the Russian Academy of Sciences in 1903, an honor which he received twice more in later years. In 1909 the Russian Academy elected Bunin one of its twelve members.

Between 1907 and 1914 Bunin traveled to the Far East—Ceylon and India—to Turkey, Palestine, Africa, Greece, and Italy. On the island of Capri he lived near Gor'kii, meeting with him frequently and reading his own stories at Gor'kii's literary gatherings. While it can be stated without exaggeration that Bunin's relations with Chekhov were unblemished by discord, his eighteen-year acquaintance with Gor'kii was of quite a different character. Their friendship, the sincerity of which is doubtful, had its peak about the time Bunin wrote his *The Village* (Derevnia, 1910) and ended seven years later in complete enmity. Bunin wrote later that Gor'kii "ceased to exist" for him.

The October Revolution did not surprise Bunin. Like others, he intuitively felt the oncoming catastrophe, the end of "traditional Russia." But nonetheless, he admitted that "reality surpassed all his expectations." Bunin left Moscow in May 1918 for Odessa, then still independent of the Soviets. His participation in the Volunteer Army (White) was limited to editing a local newspaper *Nashe slovo* (Our Word). Before the final occupation of the city by the Red Army, Bunin and his wife decided to emigrate. It was a tiny, shabby, old Greek ship under the French flag, *Patras,* upon which they embarked in Odessa on 26 January 1920 to sail for Constantinople. Thus, as Bunin put it later, "having drunk the cup of indescribable sufferings and vain hopes to the very dregs," he and his wife left Russia and settled down in France, dividing their lives between Paris and the Maritime Alps.

On 9 November 1933 Bunin became the first Russian to receive the Nobel Prize for literature. His acceptance speech was preceded by a brief remark by Professor Wilhelm Nordenson of the Caroline Institute in which he characterized the laureate's art: "You have, Mr. Bunin, thoroughly explored the soul of vanished Russia, and in doing so, you have most meritoriously continued the glorious traditions of the great Russian literature. You have given us the most valuable picture of Russian society as it once was, and well do we understand the feelings with which you must have seen the destruction of the society with which you were so intimately connected. May our feelings of sympathy be of some comfort to you in the melancholy of exile."

Prior to World War II Bunin selected and corrected his works for an edition put out by the Petropolis Publishing House in Berlin (1934-1936). During the

Second World War Bunin lived in Grasse near Nice. Like many others, he endured the moral and physical privations of the war, with the result that in 1942 he "became lean and looked even more like a Roman patrician." Despite hunger and cold he never degraded himself by any kind of collaboration with the Nazis, whom he hated as much as he hated the Bolsheviks. His diaries attest to his attitude to Hitlerism and Bolshevism.

From about 1947 Bunin began to suffer from severe attacks of respiratory disease. He died on 8 November 1953 in Paris, working on a book about Chekhov. He was buried in the Russian Orthodox cemetery in Ste. Geneviève des Bois near Paris, far from his beloved Russia, from his beloved "fields, fields, a boundless ocean of cornfields."

Interestingly, Bunin's sixty-six-year literary career can be divided into two equal parts: thirty-three years in Russia and thirty-three years in exile. Similarly, about one-half of his literary output belongs to the time he lived in Russia and the other half to his years in exile. As for quality and significance, his works in emigration are, in the opinion of many critics, even superior to his works in pre-Revolutionary Russia.

Having started his literary career as a poet, Bunin wrote verse throughout his life and completed his last poem, "The Night" (Noch', 1952) shortly before his death. Early critics who were hostile toward "Modernism" evaluated Bunin's poetry favorably because of its conservative character, and paid more attention to it than to his prose. Already in 1895, shortly after Bunin met Briusov, the latter wrote in a note to Balmont: "Although Bunin is not a Symbolist, he is a genuine poet." Much as it would have been a real asset for Briusov and his confreres to have this "genuine poet" in their camp, Bunin sensed the unnaturalness of such an alliance and looked for a chance to discontinue it. Bunin was, after all, one of the last products of the gentry culture and felt close bonds with the soil. He was not comfortable among the Symbolists, the first-born sons of Russian urbanism and the representatives of the *fin de siècle* atmosphere. Symbolism's decadence, its cultivation of abnormal, artificial, and neurotic subjects were for Bunin its most obvious and unbearable traits. And this caused the break.

Emotions in Bunin's poetry are well-hidden, as illustrated in his poem, "I entered her room at midnight hour . . ." (Ia k nei voshël v polnochnyi chas . . ., 1898). Only occasionally are they exposed in his fleeting remarks, in distant allusions, or more often in lyrical endings to purely descriptive poems, "The blue sky opened . . ." (Raskrylos' nebo goluboe . . ., 1901). At times Bunin's poems lack even such endings, and lyricism itself is totally absent from such lyrics as "Calabrian Shepherd" (Kalabriiskii pastukh, 1916). And here lies the cause of his deceptive "coolness." Actually there is no coolness in the poet himself, rather there is a sort of excessive modesty. One can assume almost with certainty that Bunin's poetry would be quite different if it were not for his hatred for "decadence." From time to time, however, his emotions are beyond his control, and it can be seen that they can even be strong, deep, and spontaneous, as in, "Flowers, and bumblebees, and grass, and cornspikes . . ." (I tsvety, i shmeli, i trava, i kolos'ia . . ., 1918).

These poems fall well within existing traditions. Bunin was not interested in searching for new poetic techniques. He did not introduce new meters into

Russian versification, and he ignored Briusov's experimentation with form and never checked "harmony through algebra," as the latter did. The difference between Bunin and the Symbolists lies primarily in his aloofness from the Symbolist world view, from Balmont's, and *mutatis mutandis,* Blok's vaguely emotive "music."

Many themes in Bunin's poetry are concurrent with those of his prose. Strange as it may seem, there are only a few poems about the Russian peasant—"A Country Beggar" (Derevenskii nishchii, 1887), for example—the theme so frequent in his stories. The "civic" subjects, exemplified in "Giordano Bruno" (1906), are as scarce as they are in his prose, but love and death occupy a considerable place. The love poems recollect past love rather than describe the present: "We met by chance, at a street corner . . ." (My vstretilis' sluchaino, na uglu . . ., 1915). Furthermore, with few exceptions, Bunin's poems about love lack that erotic element which is often present in his stories. The reader does not find any love scenes, outbursts of passion, and unexpected and fatal meetings. Everything looks as if it were in the distant past, as if it were the product of pure memory. The reminiscences of "her," or "first love," and of a "beautiful woman" are associated with nature.

The theme of death is less common. Bunin speaks about the mystery of human existence or non-existence after death. The oblivion associated with death frightens Bunin as much as physical disappearance from this world, a fear he expresses in the poem "Without a name" (Bez imeni, n.d.).

Along with the poems based on historical, biblical, and mythological topics, there is a rich collection of Bunin's poems about his own country. Russia looks in Bunin's verbal picture like I. Levitan's Russian landscape, which is drawn with the most gentle, pastel colors ("Russian Spring" [Russkaia vesna], 1905). The sadness of the Russian countryside corresponds to the general mood of Bunin's poetry. Russian nuances of "sadness" (*pechal', toska, grust',* etc.) are the key words in his poems, and because of his constant use of these nouns (or their adjectives) Bunin gained the reputation as a poet of "twilight moods" in such poems as "In the Steppe" (V stepi, 1889-97).

Nature occupies a pivotal place in Bunin's poetry. As early as 1907 Blok observed: "There are not many people who know and love nature as well as Bunin does." In Bunin's handling of landscape there is less external variety, but more internal richness and meditation. As in his prose, man in Bunin's poems is not an outsider who only contemplates nature and plays a role of supernumerary; he is rather an organic part of it.

Credit must be given to Bunin as the translator of Longfellow's *The Song of Hiawatha,* Tennyson's *Lady Godiva,* Byron's *Cain, Manfred,* and *Heaven and Earth,* and a score of smaller poems of Leconte de Lisle, Coppée, Asnyk, Mickiewicz, and Shevchenko. Bunin's translation of *The Song of Hiawatha* is the only full translation of the poem into Russian. It is considered by Russian specialists in poetic translation as unsurpassed. The poem has been rendered into Russian very close to the original trochaic tetrameter; it conveys perfectly its general mood and local color, and is light, poetical, and sonorous.

Bunin's early prose was written between 1892-1909. During these years peasants, small landowners, and small town people are the main protagonists of his short stories. There are elements in his early writings which should have pleased the Populists and their adherents, such as Bunin's attention to the year of famine in "To the Edge of the World" (Na krai sveta, 1895), to peasant psychology, in "Kastriuk" (1895), to peasant poverty, in "News from Home" (Vesti s rodiny, 1893), and to peasant submissiveness to his fate, in "Meliton" (1901). Another story, "The Pines" (Sosny, 1901), did not escape Chekhov's attention. He read the story and in a letter to Bunin of January 1902 wrote: " 'The Pines' is very new, very fresh, and very good; only it is too concentrated, like a condensed broth." Thus Chekhov was perhaps one of the first who noticed the compressed style of Bunin's writings. Among the better known stories of this period is "Antonov Apples" (Antonovskie iabloki, 1900), in which "Bunin used, at least ten years earlier than Proust, the Proustian device of the 'intermittence du coeur' by causing the peculiar scent of a particular kind of apple to recall in the mind of the protagonist all the forgotten memories of the past life of his family and himself" (Poggioli).

Bunin's sketches, "travel poems" as he called them, occupy an important place among his prose writings. Appearing initially in various newspapers and journals from 1907 to 1911, they were published under a common title, *The Temple of the Sun* (Khram solntsa, 1917). Bunin visited Constantinople, the Middle East, and Egypt. His memory went back to ancient times, for antiquity always attracted him. While on the sea the author gave himself to meditation—a leitmotif of the whole collection. Bunin sang a hymn to the sun, the source of life, the antithesis of death. Decay, ruins, desolation were the keynotes which constantly recur in the description of Istanbul. In the sketch "Judea" (Iudeia, 1910), while visiting historical and holy places, Bunin meditated on the simple, primitive, real life led by the people many centuries ago on the shores of Jordan. He shudders at the mere thought that Jesus Christ lived there as an ordinary man "lean, sunburnt, with sparkling black eyes, with the dark-purple wispy arms and thin feet burnt by the heat of the sun." The climax is reached in the sketch "The Temple of the Sun" (1909), when Bunin travels through Syria, "a country of fabulous tribes, Adam's birthplace, sanctuary of the Sun." The stress is on the word "sun," which makes the reader think not only of the Temple of the Sun in Baalbek but of all the works included in this cycle.

The years 1909-1912 in Bunin's literary career are often characterized as a period of gloom. In the preface to his book, *In Spring, in Judea, Jericho's Rose* (Vesnoi v Iudee. Roza Ierikhona, 1953), Bunin stated clearly that his popularity began with *The Village* (Derevnia, 1910): "It was the beginning of a whole series of my works in which I vividly painted the Russian soul, its bright and dark aspects. In Russian criticism and among the Russian intelligentsia, where, because of their ignorance of the people [narod] or due to political considerations, the people were almost always idealized, my 'merciless' works provoked heated, hostile comments."

According to Gleb Struve *The Village* is not a novel, for in it "there is no plot, almost no development." In his view it is "a large fresco, a diptych, picturing Russian village life during the first Revolution (1904-1905)." Moreover, Bunin subtitled *The Village* a "poem" (*poèma*), the Russian meaning of which denotes not only an epic poem or poetic narration in elevated style, with lyrical digressions and ornamental language, but also any literary work of vast proportions— vast in scope of theme, in grandeur and serenity. The epic quality of *The Village* is found immediately in the two meanings of the title: "village" and "countryside." *The Village* is not only the settlement of Durnovka, but a symbol of all rural Russia; as the old peasant Balashkin says: "Russia, all Russia is but a village—fix this well in your mind!" In the criticism of *The Village,* which mainly concentrated on its socio-economic and political content, its literary value was usually barely mentioned, if not neglected altogether. Local color in *The Village* is richly employed in the form of dialecticisms, and the characters' speech is constantly interspersed with words and expressions indigenous to Orël Province. Nature description plays a paramount role in *The Village,* and since Bunin's intention was to show the village in an unappealing light, he used the color grey to convey the depressing atmosphere of hopeless penury and the senselessness of life. Even the last name of one of the characters is Seryi ('Gray'). In *The Village,* as in many other works, Bunin shows his extraordinary faculty for rendering in words the senses of sight, hearing, smell, taste, and touch.

After *The Village* Bunin enlarged the peasant theme, using it in a series of short stories in which the verisimilitude, the emotionally-charged, yet controlled narration matched the mastery of form. They are perfectly balanced, rhythmical, and show a great striving for Flaubertian *impassibilité.* Among these masterpieces are "A Night Conversation" (Nochnoi razgovor, 1912), "The Cricket" (Sverchok, 1911), "Zakhar Vorob'ëv" (1912), "Ignat" (1912), and "The Merry Farmstead" (Veselyi dvor, 1912).

Another poem in prose, *Dry Valley* (Sukhodol, 1912), dates from this period. Purportedly the saga of "the fall of the house of Khrushchev," it is actually the veiled biography of the Bunin clan. The structure of *Dry Valley* is difficult to define. The principal storyteller is a former serf girl Nataliia, but at times the author takes an omniscient point of view, and then, again, he hands over the narration to a pair of young people who identify themselves as "we" or "my sister and I." *Dry Valley,* preceded by "Antonov Apples" and followed by *The Life of Arsenev,* is central to a family chronicle in depicting the patriarchal mode of life among the landed gentry in a state of decay, impoverishment, moral degradation, and even physical degeneration. *Dry Valley* must be regarded, first of all, as a very successful attempt to recapture the "time past" of Russian rural life. Secondly, there is a symbolic image in it: the peasants dredge ponds in the bed of an old river. But these ponds dry out without a fresh water supply. Similarly the Khrushchev clan is doomed to extinction without an admixture of fresh blood. "To us," says the narrator, "Dry Valley was only a poetical monument of the past." The language of this novelette from beginning to end is subtly crafted. Its realistic simplicity is permeated with spirituality and colored with symbolism. The concrete, visible, colorfully sketched Dry Valley is closely interwoven with the unreal, ethereal, symbolic patrimonial estate. The seemingly chaotic form of narration—the abundance of digressions and repetitions—is actually in perfect accordance with Nataliia's disordered memories. The establishment of mood of *Dry Valley* is based on the narrator's intuition and insight, and its verbal art is often a matter of musical sonority.

Variety characterizes the themes of Bunin's short stories encompassing the years 1912-1920. In a letter of 18 May 1913 Bunin himself defined the character of his writings: "love stories, 'gentry' and even, if you wish, 'philosophical' stories. But again the peasant will be in the first place—or rather not the peasant in the narrow sense of the word, but the peasant's soul, the Russian, Slavic soul." The most notable of these stories that touch the inmost recesses of the Russian soul are: "A Prince among Princes" (Kniaz' vo kniaz'iakh, 1913), showing a peasant who calls himself prince because of his accumulated wealth, and an impoverished gentry family arguing about the sense of life; "The Last Day" (Poslednii den', 1913), the theme of which is the sale of an estate to a newly rich city dweller and the killing of the hunting dogs by their former owner; "I Say Nothing" (Ia vse molchu, 1913), in which a son of a formerly wealthy peasant becomes a beggar, a holy fool, out of his own inexplicable desire; and "John the Weeper" (Ioann rydalets, 1913), which unveils the strange relations between a holy fool and a tyrannical old prince.

Love is the theme of the tragic story, "By the Road" (Pri doroge, 1913), in which Bunin thoroughly analyzes the awakening of sexual feeling in a young peasant girl, and all its complications that lead to crime and insanity. "The Grammar of Love" (Grammatika liubvi, 1915) is a romantic episode about a true, unforgettable love, while "The Last Rendezvous" (Poslednee svidanie, 1913) deals with love's disenchantment. "Light Breathing" (Lĕgkoe dykhanie, 1916), about the shooting and killing of a charming young girl, is among the world's finest short stories—it is written with grace and lightness, as the heroine's carefree and enjoyable life was lived.

Bunin's travels found their reflections not only in his travelogues but also in some stories with foreign and urban settings. Among the better known are "Brethren" (Brat'ia, 1914), an exotic tale of first love of a Singhalese rickshaw boy; "The Dreams of Chang" (Sny Changa, 1919), where the whole life of a Russian sea captain is seen through the eyes of his dog, Chang; "The Son" (Syn, 1916) set in Algiers, a "case history" of love, murder, and failure to commit suicide; "Thieves' Ears" (Petlistye ushi, 1917), a powerful study of criminal perversity with an unforgettable description of nocturnal St. Petersburg; "The Gentleman from San Francisco" (Gospodin iz San Frantsisko, 1915), perhaps Bunin's best known work in the West. This is a story about the change in attitude toward an American millionaire taking a European pleasure trip, cut short by sudden death on Capri. The story attracted the attention of many critics who saw in it the direct influence of Tolstoi (Borras, Kryzytski). Indeed the second part of the story reveals some similarity with Tolstoi's "Death of Ivan Il'ich" in the way in which the living look on the phenomenon of death: none wish either to see or understand the great mystery of death and refuse to accept death as such. In their hostility toward the "unpleasant episode" that spoiled a whole evening, they clearly demonstrate the revulsion of the living to the dead.

The Revolution interrupted the normal development of Bunin's literary career. When he started to write again in France, he published some works that touched upon the Revolution and post-Revolutionary years in Russia. While still in Odessa, Bunin had written a diary which he published in the mid-twenties in installments in *Vozrozhdenie* (Paris), and later included it in his Petropolis edition under the title *Cursed Days* (Okaiannye dni, 1935). This important work is an eyewitness account of Bunin's last three years in Russia and reflects the instability and chaos in the nation during the Revolution and the Civil War. Bunin's hatred of the Revolution, anarchy, and mob rule is a leading motif of the notes. They abound in historical digressions, psychological observations about the Russian people and mankind in general, quotations from Russian and foreign writers and historians, and portraits of contemporaries, drawn mostly in an unfavorable light. Bunin published two more stories treating revolutionary themes in 1924 in *Sovremennye zapiski* (Paris) and, in the thirties, a cycle of ultra-short stories, "miniatures," under the common title *Wanderings* (Stranstviia), a remarkable account of life in Russia during the NEP period (1921-30). However, since Bunin had left Russia in 1920, he took the factual material used in *Wanderings* from letters from Russia and from stories told by recent refugees. The language was the main protagonist in the collection. Bunin adapted his language and style to the constantly alternating descriptions now of contemporary Russia and now of the past. Bunin inserted little episodes from the ugliness of the present to intensify the contrast with the beauty of the past. Some of these miniature stories are "politically" tinted and, along with *Cursed Days,* have never been published in the Soviet Union.

Love and death are again the subject of a novelette *Mitia's Love* (Mitina liubov',1925). Despite its hackneyed, old-fashioned plot, the story is spellbinding. The entire affair is filtered through Mitia's perceptions, so that Mitia is, consequently, the main character, although nature is another, ever-present protagonist. Mitia's early, happy days of love as well as his agony are inseparably linked with nature, which is ever-beautiful, now seemingly triumphant or sad, but always indifferent to human affairs. Like many other stories (such as "By the Road") *Mitia's Love* shows the gradual awakening of sex, first in infancy, childhood and early adolescence, up to Mitia's mature love for Katia. Learning of her unfaithfulness, Mitia commits suicide. Apart from excellent psychological analysis of first youthful love and its implications, *Mitia's Love* is a very fine work aesthetically. Bunin skillfully combines the overwhelming ripening of the summer with the process of Mitia's steadily growing love for Katia. Nature and Mitia's unbridled excitement form an organic whole, merge into one indivisible unit.

With *Mitia's Love* Bunin came back to literature, and a year later published another novelette, *The Elagin Affair* (Delo korneta Elagina, 1926). Although it is fiction, the story is very close to the real facts of the murder of a Polish actress by an officer in the Russian hussars, Elagin. It treats the same theme as "The Son": a love affair, the subsequent murder of the woman by her lover at her request, and the lover's unfulfilled promise to commit suicide afterwards. Bunin turned the case into an exciting novelette, a psychological study of the lovers, with the author's own analysis of the affair and conclusion independent of the official version.

The longest and perhaps most important of all Bunin's works is *The Life of Arsenev,* the first chapters of which began to appear as early as 1927 in the Parisian Russian newspaper *Rossiia.* After many revisions it came out as a book in 1952. The classification of this book as to genre is a problem which led

Paustovskii, an ardent admirer of Bunin's art, to say that *"The Life of Arsenev* is neither a short novel, nor a novel, nor a long short story," but "is of a genre yet unknown." A great majority of critics (for example, Stepun, Colin) state that the book is Bunin's autobiography with only slight modifications; the minority (K. Zaitsev) are inclined to agree with Bunin himself and define the book as "a biography of a contrived person." This kind of theoretical definition is significant because it facilitates the understanding of how and why the book was written. Bunin achieves the simplest and, at the same time, the most profound picture which art can provide by showing the very process of seeing, the process of intellectual contemplation, rather than by philosophizing about facts as seen by the author.

Love and death are Bunin's favorite themes. They run throughout his works (including *Life of Arsenev*) and fuse inseparably, for love to Bunin is a blessed yet tragic phenomenon. Long-lasting love seems unattainable for his heroes; happy is he who catches a glimpse of it. Bunin loves youth, strength, and beauty—they are absolutely necessary elements for that love which is the happiest state in human life. Old age, weakness, and ugliness are impediments to love and are the last steps before that unknown, enigmatic, and horrible thing which is called death—the end of earthly human existence and hence the end of man's eternal pursuit of happiness, his striving for love. Bunin's fear of death is the logical consequence of his extraordinary attachment to life, which, in turn, can give man the happiest moment he can dream of, that is, the blessed state of being loved and the propensity to love. And this is why so many of Bunin's stories deal with death.

The Life of Arsenev unites these basic themes: death, love, and the theme of Russia. Acknowledging his sensitivity to death, Arsenev exploits every opportunity not only to mention its existence in the world, but also to linger over the description of a dead body, its transformation, the impression which it makes upon the living, and the burial rituals. As in *Mitia's Love,* the awakening of sex in Arsenev goes back to his childhood. Gradually Arsenev progresses from very youthful infatuation with a girl of the same age to his first sexual experience with a young married woman, and, finally, to a passionate love for Lika. Many passages demonstrate that Bunin's realistic approach to love and sex has no parallel among nineteenth-century Russian writers, and although his clarity of expression and thought are on a level with such great predecessors as Turgenev and Tolstoi, with whom Bunin is often compared, his frankness of presentation does not fit within the framework of their writing. The background of Arsenev's life is Imperial Russia, with the exception of the last few pages of the "Fourth Book." Indeed, in *The Life of Arsenev* a countless number of people parade before the reader's eyes and dozens of microcosmic events and episodic figures flash across the pages of the book. Arsenev's unstable and restless nature urges him to wander through Russia and enables him to observe the country. The wintry landscape of its northern regions is contrasted with the hot summer days in the south, and the warm spring drizzle with the frost that "splits the earth several feet down." Arsenev's range of interests is wide—now he examines eagerly "a little russety cornbeetle, entangled in the spikes," now he pauses to describe a Roman Catholic church when he visits Vitebsk. Although many characters among the peasants, the small townpeople, and the intelligentsia are familiar from Bunin's other works, nevertheless one feels in this work more warmth toward them and a more humane attitude toward their weaknesses.

The first six of the thirty-six stories which comprise *Dark Avenues* (Tëmnye allei, 1946), including the title story, were written in the late thirties, the rest during the second World War. Bunin himself considered *Dark Avenues* his best book "in the sense of compactness, verve, and literary artistry in general." The number of protagonists is usually reduced to two, while the love theme provides the uniting link between the stories. Only a few of them have a meaning deeper than the mere recounting, however masterful, of this or that love episode. After publication of this collection Bunin was quite unjustly accused of senile eroticism and even pornography. In *Dark Avenues* Bunin often describes naked faminine bodies rather than sexual acts, arguing that an author has "every right to be bold in his literary descriptions of love and character, even as painters and sculptors are always expected to render faithfully what they see, but vulgar souls will see only vulgarity even in what is beautiful and terrible." Furthermore, it should not be forgotten that a certain degree of eroticism was always present in Bunin's works, beginning with *Dry Valley* through "By the Road," "Ignat," "Light Breathing," *The Elagin Affair, Mitia's Love,* and *The Life of Arsenev.* There is not much difference in the description of Liubka's passion and her giving herself to the merchant in "Ignat" (1912) and the love scene from "Antigona" (Antigona, 1940) in *Dark Avenues,* which is probably the most shocking to Victorian tastes. From the point of view of style the stories in *Dark Avenues* are samples of complete artistic mastery. There is not a single superfluous word in them. Bunin's use of colors results in a marvelous plasticity of images—everything lives, is easily remembered, stands vividly before the reader's eyes. The collection reveals Bunin's keen psychological insight and his deep understanding of the feelings of men and women in love.

Two non-fictional books belong to Bunin's literary heritage: *The Liberation of Tolstoi* (Osvobozhdenie Tolstogo, 1937) and *Memories and Portraits* (Vospominaniia, 1950). In constructing his book on Tolstoi Bunin aimed at proving the impossibility of rendering a harmonious, architecturally unified picture of such a man as Tolstoi and his philosophy. Bunin presents the aged Tolstoi in terms of externals, and speaks with animation about the "flesh" in Tolstoi's works, qualities characteristic of Bunin himself. Despite all these sensuous aspects, Bunin's picture of Tolstoi turns out somewhat more spiritual, subtle, and compassionate, less extravagant and one-sided than those given, for example, by Gor'kii, Merezhkovskii, and V. Solov'ëv. At the age of eighty, already sick and overstrained, Bunin published his *Memories and Portraits,* a subjective book of loose sketches about his contemporaries. In spite of his extremely biased opinions, it reads interestingly and furnishes a key to a more complete understanding of Bunin. In these reminiscences Bunin's wrath fell especially heavily upon Esenin, Bal'mont, Blok, Briusov, Babel, Khlebnikov, and Maiakovskii. He wrote affectionate feuilletons about his idols Tolstoi and Chekhov, portrayed Shaliapin and Rakhmaninov in a friendly manner, highly priased Ertel, gave fair treatment to Kuprin, and on a few pages again returned to the horrors of the October Revolution.

It is neither his themes nor his ability to offer keen psychological analysis that makes Bunin one of the greatest writers of the twentieth century. Bunin is unsurpassed by any of his contemporaries or even by the great writers of the nineteenth century in his language, style, and ability to create mood. Bunin's language was often called "impeccable," which prompted him to say that he spoke "ordinary Russian and that's all." And this is the point. "Ordinariness" and naturalness without carelessness and stiltedness are the characteristic features of his language. Striving for brevity and compactness, Bunin shows an unmatched facility to find the precise word and phrase and to write in such a laconic, compressed manner that a page may be reduced to a paragraph. The general mood of each story differs considerably. Bunin not only presents to the reader, for example, an oriental mood or the coolness of Russian winter, but also makes him feel the atmosphere, which is often more important than the plot itself. The effect of such a story is suggestive, evocative, and stimulating. No matter how much Bunin is involved with the main theme of the story, he never fails to find a striking simile, to use onomatopoeia, to render sense impressions, and to pay attention to detail. Nature serves not merely as background, but figures as an intrinsic part of his narratives. It lives with the heroes. Sometimes it follows their joys and sorrows, their happiness and suffering, their love and hatred, but usually it is serene, unresponsive, and totally indifferent to man's small affairs.

The purity of language, the sharpness of the imagery, and the lack of didacticism—all these are attributes of the high verbal mastery inherent in Bunin's artistry. He is the last product of the "classical" period of Russian realism. His works are sublime models of Russian and world literature.

Works: Sobranie sochinenii, 11 vols. (Berlin, 1934-36); *Osvobozhdenie Tolstogo* (Paris, 1937); *Vospominaniia* (Paris, 1950); *Sobranie sochinenii,* 5 vols. (M., 1956); *Stikhotvoreniia* (L., 1961); *Povesti, rasskazy, vospominaniia* (M., 1961); *Sobranie sochinenii,* 9 vols. (M., 1965-67) [This Soviet edition has a number of cuts and omissions]; *Izbrannoe* (M., 1970); *Stikhotvoreniia, rasskazy, povesti* (M., 1973); *Pod serpom i molotom* (London, Ontario, 1975); *Okaiannye dni* (London, Ontario, 1977); *Ustami Buninykh,* I (Frankfurt/M, 1977) [Bunin's and his wife's diaries] ; *Poslednee svidanie, Izbrannoe* (Minsk, 1978). In English: *The Village* (N.Y., 1923); *The Gentleman from San Francisco and Other Stories,* trans., D.H. Lawrence (N.Y., 1923); *Mitya's Love* (N.Y., 1926); *The Well of Days* (N.Y., 1933) [English title of *The Life of Arsenev*] ; *The Dreams of Chang and Other Stories* (N.Y., 1935); *Dark Avenues and Other Stories* (London, 1949) [Not all stories from *Tëmnye allei* included] ; *Shadowed Paths* (M., n.d.) [This collection of the late fifties contains the "Fifth Book" of *The Life of Arsenev* entitled *Leka*] ; *The Gentleman from San Francisco and Other Stories,* trans. Olga Shartse (M., 1963); *The Gentleman from San Francisco and Other Stories,* trans. B.G. Guerney (N.Y., 1964); *The Elaghin Affair and Other Stories* (N.Y., 1969); *Velga* (N.Y., 1970).

References: V.N. Muromtseva-Bunina, *Zhizn' Bunina: 1870-1906* (Paris, 1958); F. Stepun, *Vstrechi* (Munich, 1962); A. Sedykh, *Dalekie, blizkie* (N.Y., 1962); V. Afanas'ev, *I.A. Bunin, Ocherk tvorchestva* (M., 1966); G. Kuznetsova, *Grasskii dnevnik* (Washington, 1967); A. Baboreko, *Materialy dlia biografii s 1870 po 1917* (M., 1967); O. Mikhailov, *Ivan Alekseevich Bunin, Ocherk tvorchestva* (M., 1967); A. Volkov, *Proza Ivana Bunina* (M., 1969); A. Ninov, *M. Gor'kii i Iv. Bunin. Istoriia otnoshenii. Problemy tvorchestva* (L., 1973); I.P. Vantenkov, *Bunin–povestvovatel' (rasskazy 1890-1916 gg.)* (Minsk, 1974); *Literaturnoe nasledstvo*, vol. 84 (M., 1973). *In English:* S. Kryzytski, *The Works of Ivan Bunin* (The Hague-Paris, 1971); J.B. Woodward, "Eros and Nirvana in the Art of Bunin," *The Modern Language Review*, 65 (1970); D.J. Richards, "Bunin's Conception of the Meaning of Life," *Slavic and East European Review*, 119 (1972).

Serge Kryzytski

BÚNINA, ANNA PETROVNA (1774-1828). Russian poetess. Bunina was born on 7 January 1774 in the village of Urusovo, Riazan Province. Although her early education was quite limited, Bunina took a great interest in a literary career in 1802 and began studying the sciences, foreign languages, and Russian literature. Bunina's first literary adviser was her nephew, the poet B.K. Blank. She translated Abbot Charles Batteux's *Principes de littérature* in abbreviated form, which was published "with a supplement on Russian versification" under the title *The Rules of Poetry* (Pravila poézii, 1808). In 1809 Bunina brought out a collection of verse entitled *An Inexperienced Muse* (Neopytnaia muza). The collection was met by the critics with sympathy, and it caught the attention of Empress Elizaveta Alekseevna, who awarded Bunina a yearly pension. In 1810 Bunina published a long didactic poem "On Happiness" (O schastii) in four parts. When the Society of Lovers of Russian Literature was formed a year later, Bunina was selected as an honorary member, along with two other women writers, Princess E.S. Urusova and A.A. Volkova. In the same year Bunina issued a new collection of verse, *Rural Evenings* (Sel'skie vechera), which enjoyed great success. Verses were written in her honor, and she was named the "Russian Sappho." In 1812 Bunina published a second volume of the *Inexperienced Muse,* in which many of the poems praised the fate of those who had fallen at the Battle of Borodino. A great patriotic poem in 1814 entitled "A Song to Aleksandr the Great, Conqueror of Napoleon and Restorer of Kingdoms" (Pesn' Aleksandru Velikomu, pobediteliu Napoleona i vosstanoviteliu tsarstv), which earned her the good will of the Tsar. Bunina died on 4 December 1828 and was buried in Urusovo.

Works: Sobranie stikhotvoreniia (Pb., 1819-21).

References: D.M. Khmyrov, "Russkie pisatel'nitsy proshlogo vremeni," *Rassvet,* vol. XII, No. 11 (1861), 213-28; D. Mordovtsev, *Russkie zhenshchiny novogo vremeni. Zhenshchiny deviatnadtsatogo veka* (Pb., 1874), 46-58; A.V. Arsen'ev, *Slovar' pisatelei srednego i novogo perioda russkoi literatury (1700-1825)* (Pb., 1887); N. Golitsyn, *Bibliograficheskii slovar' russkikh pisatel'nits 1759-1859 gg.* (Pb., 1889).

BURÉNIN, VIKTOR PETROVICH (1841-1926). Russian poet and publicist. Burenin was born on 7 (19) March 1841 in Moscow. Graduating from an architectural institute in 1859, Burenin started his literary career two years later as a correspondent for Gertsen's *Kolokol* (The Bell). Beginning in 1862 he published satirical feuilletons, parodies, poetry, and translations under several pseudonyms, including "Vladimir Monumentov." From 1863 to 1865 he contributed most actively to the journal *Iskra* (The Spark), but he also published in *Sovremennik* (The Contemporary), *Otechestvennye zapiski* (Notes of the Fatherland), *Budil'-nik* (The Alarm Clock), and others. In poems such as "Sabbath on Bald Mountain, or Journalism in 1862" (Shabash na Lysoi gore, ili Zhurnalistika v 1862 godu, 1863), "A Well-Intended Poem" (Blagonamerennaia poéma, 1863), "Phantoms" (Prizraki, 1864), and "Public Opinion" (Obshchestvennoe mnenie, 1871), Buren-in criticized, among others, well-intended liberals, landowners advocating serf-dom, conservative journals, and the poets of "pure art." In 1864 Burenin wrote the poem "In Memory of N.G. Chernyshevskii" (Pamiati N.G. Chernyshevskogo), published only in 1920. He translated works by Henri Auguste Barbier, Thomas Hood, Lord Byron, Victor Hugo, and Heinrich Heine. In the mid-1870s Burenin broke with the leftist journals and joined the editorial staff of the Black Hundred newspaper *Novoe vremia* (New Time), where he wrote feuilletons and critical articles of a conservative stance, chiefly under the pseudonym "Count Aleksis Zhasminov." Burenin is also the author of numerous plays, tales and stories. The following anthologies appeared in separate editions: *Sketches and Parodies* (O-cherki i parodii, 1874), *The Past* (Byloe, 1880), *Arrows* (Strely, 1881), *Critical Sketches and Pamphlets* (Kriticheskie ocherki i pamflety, 1884), and *Songs and Caricatures* (Pesni i sharzhi, 1886). Burenin died in Leningrad on 15 August 1926.

Works: Sochineniia, 5 vols. (Pb., 1912-17); *Poety "Iskry,"* vol. I (L., 1933), vol. II (L., 1955).

References: N.K. Mikhailovskii, "Pis'ma postoronnego . . .," *Polnoe sobranie sochinenii*, vol. V (Pb., 1908); – – –, "O g. Burenine," *op. cit.*, vol. VI (Pb., 1909); B. Glinskii, *Sredi literatorov i uchënykh* (Pb., 1914), 56-101.

BURIÁK, BORYS SPYRYDONOVYCH (b. 1913). Soviet Ukrainian writer, crit-ic, literary scholar, CP member since 1945. The son of a railroad worker, Buriak was born on 6 August 1913 in Rubezhnoe (now Lugansk Oblast). He graduated from Kiev University in 1939 with a degree in philology. First appearing as a crit-ic in 1937, Buriak devoted his works to the history of Soviet Ukrainian literature and the formation of Socialist Realism in the Ukraine. He is the author of the novel *Taras Zhurba* (1951) and collections of sketches on foreign countries.

Buriak served in the Second World War, afterwards joining the editorial staffs of the journals *Molod'*, *Rad'ians'kyi L'viv*, and the publishing house "Vil'na Ukraina" (1949-51), and chief editor of the Dovzhenko Film Studio. He also is a member of the criticism section of the Ukrainian Writers' Union.

Works: V sim'i shchaslyvii. Literaturno-krytichni narysy (Lvov, 1949); *Litera-turni portrety* (Lvov, 1952); *Navkolo Evropy* (Lvov, 1957); *Obraz nashoho su-chasnika. Literaturno-krytichni statti* (Kiev, 1960); *Iakiv Kachura, zhyttia i tvor-chist'* (Kiev, 1962); *Khudozhnii ideal i kharakter* (Kiev, 1967); *Nauka, litera-tura, geroi. Rozdumy. Polemika* (Kiev, 1969); *Khudozhnik i zhyttia* (Kiev, 1973). In Russian translation: *Sluzhenie narodu. Ocherki o zhizni i tvorchestve S. Tu-dora, A. Gavriliuka, Ia. Galana, P. Kozlaniuka* (M., 1955).

BURIAT LANGUAGE, *see* SUPPLEMENTARY VOLUME.

BURIAT LITERATURE, *see* SUPPLEMENTARY VOLUME.

BURLIÚK, DAVID DAVIDOVICH (1882-1967). Perhaps the most exuberant and most controversial figure in the avant-garde movement of twentieth-century Russian culture. Nicknamed the "Father of Russian Futurism," Burliuk embodied its extreme contradictions: he was iconoclastic and sentimental, vulgar and sophisticated, innovative yet conservative. Like many of his colleagues within the Russian avant-garde (Elena Guro, Vasilii Kamenskii, Vladimir Maiakovskii, and others), Burliuk worked in various disciplines—painting and poetry, theory and rhetoric. Burliuk's artistic endeavors were experimental and unpredictable, although, ultimately, Burliuk should be remembered for his theoretical tracts, especially in the context of the visual arts, rather than for his pictures and verse.

Burliuk was born on 22 July 1882 near Kharkov in the Ukraine. David was the eldest of six children, all of whom manifested literary or artistic talent: Vladimir Burliuk (1886-1917) was a painter of deep sensibility, especially in his use of color (cf. his portrait of the poet Benedikt Livshits of 1911); Nikolai Burliuk (1890-1920) was a poet of originality, although he wrote comparatively little. The artistic propensity of the Burliuk family was encouraged by the mother, Liudmila Iosifovna (née Mikhnevich, 1861-1923), whose brother, Vladimir Mikhnevich acquired some renown as the author of popular stories. Liudmila herself was a painter and contributed to a number of exhibitions including the two Salons organized by David's friend Vladimir Izdebskii in Odessa in 1909-1911.

Burliuk's education was uneven and the exact sequence of his enrollments at various gymnasia and art schools has yet to be established. Sources mention that Burliuk studied at art schools in Kazan and Odessa in 1898-1901 before travelling to Munich in 1902 and then to Paris in 1904. During the mid-1900s Burliuk contributed to a number of conventional and unconventional exhibitions, such as the Spring Exhibition at the Academy of Arts in St. Petersburg, the Moscow Association of Artists and the Exhibition of Paintings in Kharkov. But of particular importance was his participation in the exhibitions called the Wreath (Venok, Moscow, 1907), Wreath-Stephanos (Venok-Stefanos, St. Petersburg, 1908) and the Link (Zveno, Kiev, 1908), at which several members of the emergent avant-garde were represented, including Ekster, Lentulov and Malevich. In 1909 Burliuk graduated from the Odessa Art School and in 1911 entered the Moscow Institute of Painting, Sculpture and Architecture, from which he was expelled in 1913 along with Maiakovskii. From 1912 onwards Burliuk was the Futurist of Futurists, organizing lectures and group activities, publishing copiously, compiling manifestoes and, in general, endeavoring to shock the bourgeoisie. Paradoxically, Burliuk was a dedicated family man and his marriage to Marusia Viazemskaia in 1912 proved to be a long and fruitful one.

With the death of his father in 1916, Burliuk and his family moved to the Urals. Early in 1918 Burliuk was again in Moscow where he co-founded *Gazeta futuristov* with Kamenskii and Maiakovskii. Later that year Burliuk crossed Siberia to Vladivostok and, for a few weeks, participated in the Siberian Futurist group called Tvorchestvo, consisting of Nikolai Aseev, Nikolai Chuzhak, Sergei Tret'iakov and others.

In 1920 Burliuk arrived in Japan with the artist Viktor Pal'mov, and, for the next two years, organized exhibitions, gave lectures, wrote poetry. In September 1922 Burliuk arrived in the United States and settled in New York City. In 1925 he welcomed Maiakovskii to the East Coast, although by then it was clear that, however deep Burliuk's socialist sympathies, he (Burliuk) was already alien to the new Soviet culture. During the 1920s and 1930s Burliuk was very active in the emigre colony, participating in various literary, artistic and political enterprises, including the journal and group *The Pilgrim's Almanac.* He also made valuable contacts with the New York art world including Alfred Barr, Jr., and Katherine Dreier, and he continued to propagate his own literary and artistic ideas. In 1930 Burliuk established his own journal, *Color and Rhyme,* an eccentric melange of memorabilia, old and new poems, reproductions of Futurist works and lyrical descriptions of family life in New York and Hampton Bays (Burliuk's Long Island *dacha*). Creative as a poet, painter and theorist until the end, Burliuk died in Southampton Hospital, Long Island, on 15 January 1967. He is survived by his two sons, David and Nicholas.

As a literary figure, Burliuk occupies an indeterminate position in the Russian hall of fame. Much of his prolific poetry has little originality and reflects even less critical discernment—a defect resulting from deliberate iconoclasm as much as from ignorance of linguistic and literary rules. The apparent stylistic innovations in Burliuk's poetry were often paraphrases of earlier cliches, especially from the Symbolist era (to which Burliuk seemed fatefully drawn); often Burliuk's syntactical ellipses and omissions made his texts incomprehensible. In emigration Burliuk was not averse to reediting and restructuring previous poems, so that a poem or painting dated 1910 in *Color and Rhyme* cannot always be regarded as authentic. In this inclination to redate and antedate works of art, Burliuk was certainly not alone—Larionov, Maiakovskii and Malevich were no less guilty of mild deceptions.

Although Burliuk began to write poetry in the late 1890s and wrote prolifically throughout the 1900s, his verse and prose sketches lacked discipline and organization and, at best, derived from the Russian Symbolists. His poem "Summer" (Leto, 1911), for example, with its constant repetition of the consonant "l" is an obvious copy of Bal'mont's *"Landyshi liutiki. Laski liubovnye."* However, in December 1911 Burliuk made the acquaintance of the poet Benedikt Livshits at Ėkster's studio in Kiev just after Burliuk had published the miscellany *A Trap for Judges* (Sadok sudei, 1910). Livshits later described this memorable meeting in his memoirs: "We began to talk about poetry. Burliuk was totally unfamiliar with French poetry. He had vaguely heard of Baudelaire, Verlaine and maybe Mallarme. Taking the little volume of Rimbaud from my pocket . . . I began to read my favorite pieces. Burliuk was amazed. He had not even suspected that such riches were stored in that little book" (Polutoraglazyi strelets, p. 25).

At that time Burliuk's father was managing Count Mordvinov's estate at Chernianka in the Ukraine, an area that had once carried the Greek name of Hylaea. Paradoxically, this ancient outpost of classical Greece gave its name, in turn, to one of the most audacious Futurist groups, that is, *Gileia* (Hylaea), supported by David and Vladimir Burliuk, Khlebnikov, Kruchĕnykh, Livshits and Maiakovskii during 1912-1913. It was also paradoxical that Chernianka, seat of the closely-knit, patriarchal Burliuk family, should have nourished David Burliuk, the radical and iconoclast, although as Livshits stated, there were certain extreme, boisterous elements peculiar to Chernianka that later "spilled over" into Russian Futurism: "In Chernianka everything took on Homeric proportions. The number of rooms . . . the number of servants . . . the amount of food . . . The monstrous piles of edibles which filled the separate ham larders, sausage, milk and various other kinds of larders made one think about the very essence of this phenomenon . . . . It would have been ridiculous to assume a serious tone in Hylaea, that most earthly of earths. 'Low' style held complete sway . . . ." (Polutoroglazyi strelets, pp. 45, 59). There is a direct poetical extension of this gustatory environment in some of Burliuk's verse, for example, in "Each one of us is young, young/And in his belly has a hell of a hunger" (1913).

In later years, Burliuk and Kamenskii put the "official" birthdate of Russian Futurism as 1910 with their publication of *Sadok sudei,* even though this can scarcely be regarded as an avant-garde collection and was conservative compared to the previous and concurrent Italian Futurist manifestoes. However, *A Trap for Judges* paved the way for other, more audacious publications engineered by Burliuk, sometimes at Chernianka. *A Slap in the Face of Public Taste* (Poshchechina obshchestvennomu vkusu), *A Trap for Judges II* (1913), *Prayer Book of Three,* (Trebnik troikh, 1913), *Sickly Moon* (Dokhlaia luna, 1913), *First Journal of the Russian Futurists* (Pervyi zhurnal russkikh futuristov, 1914) were a few of the anthologies in which Burliuk was involved. Burliuk contributed poems and theoretical statements to these miscellanies and, to a considerable extent, he influenced editorial policy. Thanks to his diligence and insistence, Burliuk coordinated or patronized at least twelve Futurist collections during 1912-1915, and he played an effective part in the propagation of Khlebnikov, Kruchĕnykh, Maiakovskii and others. Indeed, perhaps Burliuk should be remembered for his patronal rather than for his literary services; certainly, his organizational talent was exceptional. Burliuk not only compiled Futurist booklets, he also arranged Futurist lectures, including the famous grand tour of 1913-1914 in which Kamenskii and Maiakovskii, as well as Burliuk travelled through Kharkov, Odessa, Kazan, Saratov and other cities proclaiming the Futurist cause to a bewildered and often indignant audience. During this tour the Futurist heroes sometimes suspended a grand piano upside down above the stage, sometimes they spilled tea on the first rows of the audience, sometimes they recited their poetry in cacophonic unison. In Tiflis the curtain went up to reveal "Maiakovskii in the middle in a yellow vest, Kamenskii on one side in a black cloak covered in brilliant stars, Burliuk on the other side in a dirty-pink jacket . . . ." (S. Gints, p. 105). Such theatrical antics, flagrant anti-aestheticism and blatant disregard of the established order anticipated the Dada happenings by at least two years.

In his literary and artistic achievements, Burliuk's style was eclectic. Lacking a sound and comprehensive education, Burliuk functioned like a sponge, imbibing ideas and images without strict selective criteria. Consequently, Burliuk's poetry might appeal by its unexpected conglomeration of images—"The pregnant man appeals to me/He looks great beside the Pushkin Monument" (1914), or it might repel by its banality—"Still dark, but the sailors arise/Still dark, but their boats are afloat." While playing a vital organizational role in the Futurist move-ment, Burliuk failed to organize his own literary talent and juggled constantly with poetic elements that, more often than not, were incompatible and incon-sistent. Burliuk used formal devices—palindrome, catachresis, internal rhyme, typographical rearrangement, omission of punctuation—but not in the coordin-ated way of Kamenskii or Kruchĕnykh; he resorted to primitivist imagery, but without the philosophical reasoning of Khlebnikov; he used unusual assonance and alliteration, but rarely attained the musical integration of Maiakovskii. Still, among the hundreds of poems that Burliuk composed, a handful deserve atten-tion, especially those that present a lapidary, cruel, dislocated scenario: for ex-ample, "Kill all the calves/And appease your appetites" (1914). One can under-stand why Burliuk entitled his article on modern Russian art in *Der Blaue Reiter* (1912) "Die 'Wilden' Russlands" ("The 'Wild Men' of Russia").

For all the vulgarity and naivete of Burliuk's poetry, the sheer force of the man's literary talent reflects the vigor and energy germane to the Russian Futur-ist movement as a whole. Lines such as

"A beard. . . .A good guy?	"Boroda. . . .A dobr?
No wickednesses. The shadow	Net zol. Ten'
of vines. . . .And vice	loz. . . .I porok
Vice is a greasy box in smetana"	Porok. . .zhirnyi korop v smetane"

Boroda (1914?)

could have been written only in the Futurist heyday of 1912-1915. All the more depressing, therefore, that Burliuk attempted to soften his natural crudity by applying hackneyed poetical metaphors. He was especially guilty of this in emi-gration, and his journal *Color and Rhyme* carries pearls of adolescent banality such as "Oh, why without desire I live?/Why do I die as I live?/Why coming to life will I die?/Oh, why am I—but I?" ("Scaffold").

Much of the above criticism can also be directed at Burliuk's painting, a sub-ject that goes beyond the scope of this essay. Of greater importance and in-fluence, however, were Burliuk's theoretical and analytical discussions. Burliuk was partly responsible for the compilation of important declarations of new artistic principles, not least *A Slap in the Face of Public Taste* (1912) with its famous line "Throw Pushkin, Dostoevskii, Tolstoi, et al., et al., overboard from the Ship of Modernity" and the untitled manifesto in *A Trap for Judges II* (1913) proclaiming "We have disrupted syntax . . . . We have destroyed punctua-tion . . . ." Despite the awkward, ungrammatical prose, Burliuk's elucidations of key concepts such as *faktura* (texture) and Cubism were important to the general development of the Russian Futurist movement. His essay on texture, published in *A Slap in the Face of Public Taste,* provided an explanation of this phe-nomenon in formal terms and, at the same time, represented one of the first Russian endeavors to reduce the art of painting to an exact science: "The Plane of a picture can be (A) Even, and (B) Uneven . . . . Structure of a picture's sur-face, I Granular, II Fibrous, III Lamellar . . . ." ("Faktura"). Burliuk's essay on

Cubism, also published in *A Slap in the Face of Public Taste,* discussed the aims of modern art in general rather than French Cubism in particular, and pointed toward the manifestoes on abstract art that Larionov, Malevich and others would publish in 1913-1916: *"Painting* is colored space. Point, line and surface are elements of spatial forms . . . ." ("Kubizm"). In 1912-1913 Burliuk was deeply interested in the question of abstraction both in painting and in poetry and he gave a number of public lectures on the new aesthetic. In emigration Burliuk continued to theorize, issuing two so-called *Radio-Style Manifestoes* in 1926 and 1927, interpreting reality (again) as "nothing but colored space." In 1930 Burliuk published an abstruse reinterpretation of Futurist poetry under the title *Entelekhizm* to mark the twentieth anniversary of the birth of Russian Futurism. Until his death Burliuk used *Color and Rhyme* as the vehicle for the dissemination of his exotic ideas. Few read them and even fewer understood them.

Works: "Die 'Wilden' Russlands," *Der Blaue Reiter* (Munich, 1912); *Galdiashchie 'Benua' i novoe russkoe natsional'noe iskusstvo* (Pb., 1913); "Vladimir Davidovich Burliuk," *Soiuz molodëzhi* [SPb.], No. 3 (1913), 35-38; *Lyseiushchii khvost. Izbornye stikhi 1907-1918* (Kurgan, 1918); "Ot laboratorii k ulitse (Ėvoliutsiia futurizma)," *Tvorchestvo* [Vladivostok], No. 2 (1920); "Literatura i khudozhestvo v Sibiri i na Dal'nem Vostoke (1919-1922 gg.)," *Novaia russkaia kniga,* No. 2 (1922); *Burliuk pozhimaet ruku Vul'vort Bil'dingu* (N.Y., 1924); *Marusia-san* (N.Y., 1925); *Voskhozhdenie na Fudzi-san* (N.Y., 1927); *Morskaia povest'* (N.Y., 1927); *Po Tikhomu okeanu* (N.Y., 1927); *Oshima* (N.Y., 1927); *Desiatyi Oktiabr'* (N.Y., 1928); *Tolstoi i Gor'kii* (N.Y., 1929); *Ėntelekhizm* (N.Y., 1930); *1/2 veka* (N.Y., 1932); *Color and Rhyme,* Nos. 1-60 (N.Y., 1930-1966).

References: E. Gollerbakh, *Iskusstvo Davida Burliuka* (N.Y., 1930); – – –, *Poėziia Davida Burliuka* (N.Y., 1931); I. Postupal'skii, *Literaturnyi trud D. Burliuka* (N.Y., 1931); K. Dreier, *Burliuk* (N.Y., 1944); V. Markov, *Russian Futurism* (Berkeley, 1968) [Especially Chapter 2] ; V. Barooshian, *Russian Cubo-Futurism* (The Hague, 1974) [Especially Chapter 3] ; John E. Bowlt, *Russian Art of the Avant-Garde: Theory and Criticism, 1902-34* (N.Y., 1976), pp. 8 *et seq.;* B. Livshits, *The One-and-a-Half Eyed Archer* (Newtonville, Mass., 1977); *David Burliuk. Years of Transition, 1910-1931* (Southampton, N.Y., 1978) [Catalog of exhibition at the Parrish Art Museum] ; Kazuo Yamawaki, "Bururyukku to Parimofu: Roshia mirai-ha no gaka to Nihon" [Burliuk and Pal'mov: Russian Futurists and Japan], *Pilotis* [Hyogo, Japan], No. 28 (1978), 4-5, No. 29 (1978), 4.

John E. Bowlt

BURNÁSH, FATKHI [pseudonym of BURNASHEV, FATKHELISLAM ZAKIROVICH] (1898-1946). Soviet Tatar playwright, poet, journalist, CP member since 1919. Burnash was born on 1 (13) January 1898 in the village of Bikshik (now the Chkalov Raion of the Chuvash ASSR) and studied in a madrasah (mosque school) at Kazan. He is the author of more than twenty plays. Among his pre-Revolutionary works, the romantic tragedy *Takhir and Zukhra* (1918) and the drama *Young Hearts* (Iash' iöräklär, 1919) were widely known. Burnash's talent as a writer and a public figure flowered after the October Revolution.

He organized and edited a series of Tatar newspapers and journals and contributed articles on the theater. After the establishment of the Tatar ASSR in 1920, Burnash was chosen a member of the Tatar Central Executive Committee. Burnash wrote the plays *Khusain Mirza* (staged in 1920) and *Old Man Kamali* (Kamali kart, staged 1925). In the second play, he recreated the life of the post Civil War village; the comedy is especially noteworthy for its lively conflict, witty plot, and striking characters. Burnash is also the author of the dramas *An Errant Girl* (Adashkan kyz, 1928), *Falcons* (Lachynnar, 1934), and many anthologies of poems. He produced the first Tatar translations of Pushkin's novel in verse *Eugene Onegin,* Nikolai Ostrovskii's novel *How the Steel Was Tempered,* Gor'kii's *Mother,* Turgenev's *Fathers and Sons,* and Lev Tolstoi's *Hadji Murad.* Burnash died in January 1946.

Works: Sailanma ĕsĕrlĕr, 2 vols. (Kazan, 1959); *Molodye serdtsa: p'esy, stikhi, poėmy* (Kazan, 1969) [text in Tatar]. In Russian translation: *Sokoly,* in the almanac *Teatr narodov SSSR* (M., 1934); *Poėty sovetskoi Tatarii* (M., 1936).

References: B. Gyizzăt, "Fătkhi Burnash," *Sovet ădăbiiaty,* No. 1 (Kazan, 1958); A. Ăkhmădullin, *Fătkhi Burnash* (Kazan, 1969).

BURNÁSHEV, VLADIMIR PETROVICH (1812-1888). Russian writer. The son of a Lieutenant Governor of Orĕl Province, Burnashev was born there in 1812. Beginning his literary career in 1828, he contributed to a wide range of journals and newspapers. From 1832 to 1834 Burnash published biographical sketches of Russian manufacturers and artisans under the title "Industry of the Fatherland" in the *Severnaia pchela.* During the next three years he published children's books under the pseudonym "Viktor Bur'ianov." Belinskii praised Burnashev's first book for children, *Russian Scythe* (Russkaia kosa), but sharply criticized his later compositions intended for young readers. Some of them, written in the form of "conversations" or "strolls," contained a hodgepodge of unsystematized facts taken from the natural sciences, ethnography, economics, home life, and other areas: *A Trip through Russia with Children* (Progulka s det'mi po Rossii, 4 vols. 1837). Other books were sheerly didactic. In the early 1870s Burnashev published his memoirs covering the period from the 1820s through the 1840s, which are of some interest. In the last two years before his death, he wrote several novels with mass appeal "for the people," chiefly on historical themes. One such work appeared under the whimsical title *The Girl Cavalryman Aleksandrov-Durova* (Kavalerist devitsa Aleksandrov-Durova, 1887). He died in Petersburg on 31 January (12 February) 1888.

Works: "Moe znakomstvo s Voeikovym . . .," *Russkii vestnik,* Nos. 9-11 (1871); "Chetvergi u N.I. Grecha," *Zaria,* No. 4 (1871); *Vospominaniia ob epizodakh iz moei chastnoi i sluzhebnoi deiatel'nosti (1834-1850)* (M., 1873).

References: [Burnashev's autobiography and remarks by N.S. Leskov], *Istoricheskii vestnik,* No. 6 (1888); S.A. Vengerov, *Russkie knigi,* vols. II-III (Pb., 1898-99); *Russkii biograficheskii slovar',* vol. III (Pb., 1908); T.A. Grigor'eva, "Burnashev, V.P. (Viktor Bur'ianov)," in *Materialy po istorii russkoi detskoi literatury, 1750-1855,* fasc. 1 (M., 1927).

BURNÁSHEVA, ZAGIDA (b. 1895). Soviet Tatar poetess, CP member since 1918. Burnasheva was born on 5 (17) October 1895 in the village of Azeevo (now Riazan Oblast) in the family of a merchant and broker. Burnasheva's parents did not allow her to receive an education and she subsequently left the family. First publishing in 1914, Burnasheva devoted her work to the liberation of Tatar Women from their traditional inferior position. Her first anthology, *The Poems of Giffat Tutash* (Gyiffät tutash shigyr'lär), appeared in Moscow in 1915. Her poems "On a Moonlit Night" (Aily kichtä), "The Wanderer" (Iulchy), "In Search of an Ideal" (Ezlim), "Over the Volga" (Idel ostenda), and "From a Passionate Heart" (Ialkynly ioräktän) are imbued with lyricism and reflect Burnasheva's belief in the possibility of achieving one's goals through unflinching dedication. After the October Revolution, Burnasheva directed the women's division of the Central Asian Bureau of the CP Central Committee. From 1933 to 1955 she performed important Party work in Kirgizia.

References: M. Gainullin, "Gyiffät tutash (Zaḧidä Burnasheva),"*Azat khatyn,* No. 8 (1958).

BÚRTSEV-PROTOPÓPOV, VASILII FĒDOROVICH (Dates unknown). First Russian publisher. By profession a minor official, Burtsev-Protopopov worked at the Moscow Printing Shop in the 1630s and the early 1640s. He was the first in Russia to issue secular books in mass editions: the first Russian printed textbooks, primers, church and secular calendars. In his *Primer* (Bukvar', 1634) Burtsev-Protopopov published the poem "This visible little book" (Siia zrimaia malaia knizhitsa), of which he himself was possibly the author. He initiated the publication of small-format books, using the most advanced methods of setting and printing of his time.

References: Sbornik pamiatnikov, otnosiashchikhsia do knigopechataniia v Rossii [text by V.E. Rumiantsev], fasc. 1 (M., 1872); F.I. Bulgakov, *Illiustrirovannaia istoriia knigopechataniia i tipografskogo iskusstva,* vol. I (Pb., 1889); A.A. Bakhtiarov, *Istoriia knigi na Rusi* (Pb., 1890); I.N. Bozherianov, *Istoricheskii ocherk russkogo knigopechatnogo dela* (Pb., 1895); S.F. Librovich, *Istoriia knigi v Rossii,* 2 parts (Pb.-M., 1913-14); *Kniga v Rossii,* 2 vols. (M., 1924-25); A.A. Sidorov, *Istoriia oformleniia russkoi knigi* (M.-L., 1946); N.P. Kiselev, "O moskovskom knigopechatanii 17 v.," in *Kniga. Issledovaniia i materialy,* II (M., 1960).

BURÚNOV, KARADZHA (1898-1965). Soviet Turkmen poet, playwright, translator, Honored Artist of the Turkmen SSR (1943), one of the founders of Soviet Turkmen literature. Burunov was born on 2 August 1898 in the village of Amansha-Kapan (now the Tedzhen Raion). He first studied in a madrasah (mosque school) later at a school in the city of Tedzhen, and in 1930 graduated from Leningrad University with a degree in Eastern studies. Burunov is the author of the plays *Dakylma* (1927), about the cheerless lot of Turkmeni women in the past, *Cotton, Screws,* and the historical drama *Keimer-Ker* (jointly with B. Amanova, 1940). In addition he wrote the long poems "Tir'iakkesh" (1927) and "Eighteen Who Were Drowned" (1929), based on events of the Civil War in Turkmenia. The poem was later rewritten as a stage production in 1929. In the 1930s Burunov wrote lyric poetry and long poems for children: "Tempo," "The Pioneers Pick Cotton," "Maisa." Burunov has translated more than 40 dramatic works from the classics of Russian, Soviet, and world literature, including plays by Trenĕv, A. Ostrovskii, Gogol, Shakespeare, Lope de Vega, Schiller, and Molière. During the Second World War Burunov wrote librettos for the operas and ballets *Giul' and Bil'-Bil'* (1943), *Shasenem and Garib* (1943), *Kemine and Kazi* (1944), and *Leili and Medzhnun* (1945), as well as translating the libretto for the opera *Eugene Onegin* and the film scripts *Lenin in 1918, Lenin in October,* and *A Great Citizen.* Burunov died on 23 March 1965 in Ashkhabad.

Works: Sailanang ăserler (Ashkhabad, 1959).

References: Pisateli sovetskogo Turkmenistana. Biograficheskii spravochnik (Ashkhabad, 1955); B. Shamyradov, *Shakhyr-dramaturg G. Burunovyng òmri ve dòredijiligi* (Ashkhabad, 1961).

BUSH, VLADIMIR VLADIMIROVICH (1888-1934). Soviet Russian literary scholar, CP member since 1932. Bush was born in Petersburg on 4 (16) January 1888. A graduate of Petersburg University, Bush taught at the universities of Tashkent and Saratov after 1925, and assumed the office of secretary of the Pushkin House of the Soviet Academy of Sciences in 1931. Bush's first writings are devoted to ancient Russian literature, chiefly the works of the seventeenth century. In the early 1920s Bush studied the works of the Russian populist writers *(narodniki).* He investigated little-known archival materials for the first time in research on Gleb Uspenskii, N.E. Karonin-Petropavlovskii, A.I. Ertel, and others. The concluding book of this series was Bush's *Sketches of Literary Populism in the 70s and 80s* (Ocherki literaturnogo narodnichestva 70-80-kh gg., 1931). Bush also studied self-educated writers of peasant or working class origin. He died in Leningrad on 14 May 1934.

Works: Pamiatniki starinnogo russkogo vospitaniia (K istorii drevne-russkoi pis'mennosti i kul'tury) (Pg., 1918); *G. Uspenskii. Ètiudy* (Saratov, 1925); "O sovremennom sostoianii ustnopoeticheskogo tvorchestva v derevniakh Vol'skogo uezda," *Uchĕnye zapiski Saratovskogo gosudarstvennogo universiteta,* vol. V, fasc. 2 (1926); *Literaturnaia deiatel'nost' Gl. Uspenskogo. Ocherki* (Balakovo, 1927); "Iz knigi Raboche-krest'ianskoe dvizhenie v literaturu vo vtoroi polovine 19v.," ch. 4: "70-90-e gody," *Zvezda,* No. 8 (1934).

References: "V.V. Bush" [Obituary], *Sovetskaia ètnografiia,* No. 4 (1934); "V.V. Bush" [Obituary], *Literaturnyi Leningrad,* No. 23 (20 May 1934).

BUSLÁEV, FĔDOR IVANOVICH (1818-1897). Russian philologist and art historian. Buslaev was born on 13 (25) April 1818 in Kerensk (now Vadinsk, Penza Oblast). A graduate of Moscow University (1838), he became a professor there in 1847 and a member of the Academy of Sciences in 1881. Buslaev's works in the field of Slavic linguistics, old Russian literature, oral folk literature, and the history of the ancient Russian visual arts were for their time a landmark in the development of science, and to a large extent retain their significance today. Buslaev's views were widely respected in his time; they were based in considerable measure upon the works of the German philologists Jakob and Wilhelm Grimm and their school.

In his investigations of the Russian language, Buslaev made use of the comparative historical method. He compared modern Russian with other related

Indo-European languages and with Old Slavic, and drew upon data from old Russian documents and from folk dialects. Buslaev attempted to establish a connection between the history of a language and the life of a people, their mores, habits, legends and belief systems in such studies as *On Teaching Our Native Language* (O prepodavanii otechestvennogo iazyka, 1844), *On the Influence of Christianity on the Slavic Language. Toward a History of the Language According to the Ostromir Gospel* (O vliianii khristianstva na slavianskii iazyk. Opyt istorii iazyka po Ostromirovu evangeliu, 1848), *A Historical Grammar of the Russian Language* (Istoricheskaia grammatika russkogo iazyka, 1863). However, Buslaev's understanding of the historical development of the language was not entirely accurate. He also carefully studied and published a number of ancient manuscripts: *Paleographic and Philological Materials for a History of Slavonic Characters, Collected from 15 Manuscripts of the Moscow Synod Library* (Paleograficheskie i filologicheskie materialy dlia istorii pis'men slavianskikh . . ., 1855) and *A Historical Chrestomathy of the Church Slavonic and Ancient Russian Languages* (Istoricheskaia khrestomatiia tserkovno-slavianskogo i drevnerusskogo iazykov, 1861).

Buslaev's principal work, *Historical Sketches of Russian Folk Literature and Art* (Istoricheskie ocherki russkoi narodnoi slovesnosti i iskusstva, 1861), indicates that Buslaev at that time supported the view of the origin of folk literature in mythology. Buslaev tied together language, poetry, and mythology, and viewed folklore as the impersonal creative work of an entire people, as "fragments of ancient myths." Later he moved away from the mythological theory and subscribed to the theory of "borrowings." In his monograph *Migratory Stories* (Perekhozhie povesti, 1874), published in the collection *My Diversions* (Moi dosugi, 1886) Buslaev developed the ideas of the German philologist Theodor Benfey, who traced the path of several plots from the *Panchatantra* from ancient India to modern Europe. He came to the conclusion that the East is the source of European folklore. Buslaev's comparisons of oral poetry with written poetry, and of literature with the visual arts, particularly iconography, are valuable contributions. His book *The Russian Illustrated Apocalypse* (Russkii litsevoi apokalipsis, 1884), based on Russian manuscripts from the sixteenth to the nineteenth centuries, earned him worldwide recognition. Buslaev died on 31 July (12 August) 1897.

Works: O narodnoi poėzii v drevne-russkoi literature (M., 1859); *Moi vospominaniia* (M., 1897); *Istoricheskie ocherki po russkomu ornamentu v rukopisiakh* (Pg., 1917); *Sochineniia*, 3 vols. (Pb.-L., 1908-30); *Istoricheskaia grammatika russkogo iazyka* (M., 1959).

References: A.N. Pypin, *Istoriia russkoi ėtnografii*, vol. II (Pb., 1891); S.V. Savchenko, *Russkaia narodnaia skazka* (Kiev, 1914); M. Speranskii, *Russkaia ustnaia slovesnost'* (M., 1917); Iu.M. Sokolov, *Russkii fol'klor* (M., 1941); M.K. Azadovskii, *Istoriia russkoi fol'kloristiki* (M., 1958).

BŪTĖNAS, JULIUS (b. 1908). Soviet Lithuanian writer, CP member since 1960. The son of a peasant, Būtėnas was born on 17 (30) November 1908 in the village of Galintėnas (now the Alytus Raion). He studied at Kaunas University and taught at Vilnius University, in addition to working as a journalist and an editor.

Beginning his career in 1925, Būtėnas saw his first collection of tales in print in 1932. He has written a number of popular biographies—*Povilas Višinskis* (1936), *Vincas Kudirka* (1937), *Žemaitė* (1938) and a textbook on Lithuanian literature for use in high schools. With A. Kerganis, Būtėnas produced a play about the Lithuanian revolutionary Julius Janonis entitled *I've Fallen in Love with the Blue of the Sky* (Pamilau dangaus žydrumą, 1958).

Works: Stiklinės gonkos (Kaunas, 1932); *Prikąstas liežuvis* (Kaunas, 1933); *Mėlynieji kareiviai* (Kaunas, 1936); *Lietuvių teatras Vilniuje 1908-1918 mėtais* (Kaunas, 1940); *Žemaitės gyvenimas* (Kaunas, 1947); *Lietuvių literatūros vadovėlis*, 2 vols. (Kaunas, 1957-60); *Maironis* (Vilnius, 1957); *Istoriografo užrašai* (Vilnius, 1974); *Literato duona* (Vilnius, 1975).

BUTKÓV, YAKOV PETROVICH (1822?-1856). Russian prose writer who lived in St. Petersburg in the 1840s. His humorous sketches and novelettes belong to the formative stage of Russian realism. His short career spans the heyday of the "Natural School," and his well-received collection of sketches, *Petersburg Heights* (Peterburgskie vershiny, 1845-6) provided the occasion for a major confrontation between conservative and progressive critics over the technical and aesthetic implications of Russian naturalism. Butkov subsequently wrote nine novelettes which appeared in literary journals between 1847 and 1849, and a novel, *Steppe Idyll*. In the 1850s, Chernyshevskii called Butkov "probably the most gifted of Gogol's first followers," and a century later, Aleksei Remizov was to consider him "the most gifted of all the Russian naturalists."

Butkov was born around 1822, a free townsman *(meshchanin)*, in the remote eastern province of Saratov. He arrived in St. Petersburg in 1840, and the same year fifty-one lines of rhymed verse entitled "The Headman" (Gaidamak) appeared over his name in *Syn otechestva*. This "excerpt from a tale" with its stock Romantic epithets and Cossack setting aroused little interest, but in the summer of 1845, two stories were published serially in the popular conservative newspaper, *Severnaia pchela,* "A Proper Gentleman" (Poriadochnyi chelovek), and "A Ribbon" (Lentochka). The editor, Faddei Bulgarin, called the first story an excerpt from a novel, but Butkov never did consolidate his early pieces into a larger work. Instead he added three more sketches, "An Honorable Gentleman" (Pochtennyi chelovek), "The Go-Getter" (Bitka), "One Hundred Roubles" (Sto rublei), as well as an introduction, "An Edifying Word" (Nazidatel'noe slovo), to make up the first volume of *Petersburg Heights* (Peterburgskie vershiny), which came out in the fall of 1845.

At this time, before the appearance of the landmark *Petersburg Collection* (Peterburgskii sbornik, 1846), there was not yet a clear notion among Russian critics of a progressive "Natural School." The reviewers of *Petersburg Heights, I,* therefore, found the models for Butkov's comic technique among established traditions: Gogol's popular stories and their "laughter through tears," the glib style of the contemporary feuilleton, and the character types and slice-of-life urban settings of the physiological sketch. The originality of Butkov's pieces seemed to his readers to lie in his ability to combine features from these three sources. The reviews failed to appreciate that *Petersburg Heights* was not an *imitation* but rather a kind of implicit parody or stylization of Russian prose fiction in the first half of the 1840s. Butkov's humorous pieces invite a reader to infer that, far from being a "mirror of reality," incipient Russian realism was pervaded with sentimentalized literary cliches, largely French. Butkov achieved this effect by crowding the types and settings he wanted to expose into absurd situations, and by choosing as narrative screen the most frivolous, pun-ridden banter. In this way he not only called into question the objectivity of the physiological sketch, but also revealed its kinship with the popular literary subculture, which is to say the journal miscellany, stage farce, and even street theater. Such an ambivalent, not to say skeptical, attitude toward Russia's literary westernization had been evident in Gogol's work in the late thirties, and it was soon to be adopted by the young Dostoevskii. But for these major writers, stylization was just one aspect of a complex statement about life as well as literature. For Butkov, the metaliterary emphasis was paramount.

His stories presented scriveners, card sharps reminiscent of Gogol's "Gamblers," and such playful motifs as the absurd christening ceremony Gogol had taken from Sterne. From the feuilleton, Butkov appropriated a rambling "personalized" narrative, frequent digressions on such subjects as foreign loan words in Russian ("The Go-Getter"), and a pseudosophisticated tone which purported to inform while it merely prattled. Among the types and settings borrowed from the physiological sketch were a vociferous waiter ("A Proper Gentleman"), a hack writer ("An Honorable Gentleman"), a merchant's office ("One Hundred Roubles"), and a sleazy tavern ("The Go-Getter"). "A Ribbon" was built on a caricature of Gogol's clerk-who-can-copy-but-cannot-compose (Akakii Akakievich, Poprishchin) and a pun on the word *lentochka* ('service decoration,' 'article of feminine attire') while the scene is set in the drawing room of an immigrant German baker. In "One Hundred Roubles," the clutter of "bared" devices and motifs—to use the Russian Formalists' term—were deployed along a currently widespread sentimental plot line: a poor but well-born country boy, with dependent mother and sister, fails to make his way in the cruel city and loses his mind.

The first volume of *Petersburg Heights* got good reviews. Butkov was "talented," "original," "funny," "promising." But thanks, in part, to this successful debut, he fell victim to polemical infighting between rival publishers and critics. The conservative camp, which had brought Butkov to public attention, was watching with concern a group of young writers, including Nikolai Nekrasov, Dmitrii Grigorovich, and Evgenii Grebenka (Hrebinka), which was forming under the purported aegis of Gogol and the progressive critic, Vissarion Belinskii. In a crude attempt to discredit them and taunt Belinskii, the foremost conservative spokesman, Faddei Bulgarin, compared Butkov's "bright, genuine" humor favorably to Gogol's "filthy caricatures." In his indignant reply, Belinskii, who had maintained that only a full-blown genius like Gogol could create humor, was obliged to belittle the "caricatures" of Butkov, a mere "talent." And some months later Butkov again ran afoul of Belinskii's polemical strategy as the enthusiastic, but circumspect, critic was preparing the way for the appearance of Dostoevskii's novel, *Poor Folk*. Belinskii was trying to expand his definition of "talent" upward to include the "near-genius" of Dostoevskii, and at the same time, downward to make room for edifying non-fiction. To this end he formulated a new hierarchy of literary modes: "art," "belletristics," "reportage," and "science." Dostoevskii, as yet unpublished, fell between "art" and "belletristics," and was a "creative poet." Butkov, who served as a convenient and defenseless contrast, was relegated to the "reportage" category, and dubbed a "descriptive satirist." This label, which conditioned Butkov criticism for a century, is unfortunate in two respects. First, it ignores the baroque—and thereby truly "Gogolian"—texture of unremitting word play and grotesquerie which is the most prominent feature of Butkov's narrative style. Second, it obscures an aspect of Butkov's work which emerged more clearly in the second volume of *Petersburg Heights* and which makes Butkov a mediator between Gogol and Dostoevskii. This is Butkov's grasp, albeit tentative, of the metaphorical implications of the motifs he was stylizing.

The second volume of *Petersburg Heights,* published in 1846, contained only three stories, "Payday" (Pervoe chislo), "A Good Position" (Khoroshee mesto), and "A Dress Suit" (Partikuliarnaia para). Longer than their predecessors, these stories were close in form to the novelettes Butkov wrote later. While they still provided colorful "types" and settings (a connoisseur of liqueurs, and a courtesan's lodgings in "Payday"), they had sounder, more sustained plots. In "A Dress Suit," Butkov relates the misadventures of a young government clerk who earns his pocket money by selling to private firms envelopes he has made out of office supply paper. As the result of a chance encounter, he finds himself paying court to the daughter of one of his clients, a rich merchant. He gives up his profitable sideline for the sake of appearances, but, as a consequence, cannot afford the "dress suit" he needs to attend his young lady's birthday ball. Besides a longer, more "literary" format, Butkov was trying to articulate his own thematic emphases within the framework of Gogolian farce. He had moved away from the picaresque motifs of card sharping and the confidence game to develop a more contemporary and more cynical metaphor for artifice and illusion, the triangle, so important to Dostoevskii, which consists of the Boss, his mistress and his clerk ("A Good Position"). Similarly, in the story "Payday," Butkov produced a trope on the scrivener motif by transforming it into an expanded pun, or syllepsis, where one composite personality was split into his literal and figurative selves. The result was a "double," not of the Hoffmanesque variety, but more like Dostoevskii's Goliadkin (*The Double*).

The *Petersburg Heights, II* reviews concerned themselves with "naturalism," an issue which was by this time polarizing the world of Russian letters. Butkov's former supporters at *Severnaia pchela* renounced him, declaring that the sketches were, in fact, detailed descriptions of "filthy" urban poverty (L. Brant). Progressive critics like Valerian Maikov, Apollon Grigor'ev, and Petr Galakhov, now promoting a serious "Natural School," maintained that it was the task of literature to portray the vulgar side of life. *Petersburg Heights, II* provided them the chance to spell out their new set of criteria for art. They found Butkov's stories compassionate and, taking their cue from Belinskii, agreed that they should be read as informative reportage, even statistical surveys. Thus, by June 1846 Butkov was firmly established on the St. Petersburg literary scene, associated somewhat incongruously with a new current of objective, humanitarian writing.

Late in 1846 Butkov was called up for a twenty-five year term of military service. A prominent publisher, Andrei Kraevskii, bought him a release with the result that the promising young writer was virtually indentured to his benefactor. Over the next three years, seven of Butkov's stories appeared in Kraevskii's journal, *Otechestvennye zapiski*. They are: 1847, "The *Goriun*" (from *gore,* 'grief'), "Creditors, Love, and Other Departments" (Kreditory, liubov' i zaglaviia); 1848, "New Year" (Novyi god), "The Dark Man" (Temnyi chelovek), "Nevsky Prospect, or the Travels of Nestor Zaletaev" (Nevskii prospekt, ili puteshestviia Nestora Zaletaeva); 1849, "A Strange Story" (Strannaia istoriia), "The Miser" (Skupoi). Besides these works, two stories which appeared in *Panteon* in 1848, "Mr. Trevogin" (from *trevoga,* 'alarm'), and "Mutual Sympathizers" (Vzaimnye sochuvstvovateli), may be included in Butkov's *Otechestvennye zapiski* period.

Around this same time Butkov and Dostoevskii, who also worked for Kraevskii, became friends. Under Dostoevskii's sympathetic eye Butkov served a kind of apprenticeship, along with other young literati such as Valerian Maikov and Aleksei Pleshcheev, to whom Butkov dedicated his "Mr. Trevogin." In the stories he wrote during this period, Butkov experimented with various Gogolian narrative techniques, like alogical systems, self-deflating rhetorical figures, and verbal slapstick. He introduced dialogue, letters, and digressions—often "inserted tales"— into his stories. This tended to break up his obtrusive narrative tone, which by now tended either to *skaz,* or to a *style indirect libre* where his characters preempted the main narrator. On the thematic level, Butkov marshalled these structural devices, as well as the motifs of grotesquerie, madness, and double identities, in the service of the commanding symbol of the Dostoevskian double.

The reviews of the *Otechestvennye zapiski* stories were the first to look carefully at Butkov's texts as verbal constructs instead of "mirrors of reality . . . ." The earlier reviews of *Petersburg Heights* had confused the writer with the teller of his tales; since Butkov did actually inhabit the slums about which naturalists wrote, his readers assumed that he was describing his own surroundings. But the more sophisticated discussions of the *Otechestvennye zapiski* stories objected to his use of stereotypes instead of fresh observations drawn from life. Pavel Annenkov, in an article which introduced the term "realism" into Russian criticism, complained about Butkov's "pseudorealism," and observed that the young writer created grotesque caricatures which vied with the events in the plot "to see which would be more absurd." Thus, only at the end of his active career did Butkov's readers begin to appreciate that he was at best a *reluctant* naturalist, and another century passed before literary history found a niche for his original talent. In retrospect, it is apparent that Butkov's stories refract Gogol's narrative technique and the bizarre thematics of the young Dostoevskii. Like a prism, they reveal new functional relationships between these two seminal Russian realists, and suggest that the farces of the subculture had a major role in the development of legitimate prose fiction in the 1840s.

In 1849, the year Dostoevskii was exiled for sedition, Butkov's stories disappeared from the pages of the St. Petersburg journals, and he did not publish again for seven years. This time it was a novel, *Steppe Idyll* (Stepnaia idilliia, 1856), part farce, like the early *Petersburg Heights* sketches, and part lecture, reminiscent of the second book of Gogol's *Dead Souls* (1855). Butkov appears to have spent the intervening years in the capital, writing stories he could not sell. In 1856, at the age of 33, he died, quite forgotten, in a charity hospital.

Works: Peterburgskie vershiny, I, II (Pb., 1845-46); "Goriun," *Otechestvennye zapiski,* LI (1847); "Kreditory, liubov' i zaglaviia," *Ot. zap.,* LVI (1847); "Novyi god," *Ot. zap.,* LVI (1848); "Temnyi chelovek," *Ot. zap.,* LVII (1848); "Nevski prospekt," *Ot. zap.,* LX (1848); "Trevogin," *Panteon,* No. 2 (1848); "Vzaimnye sochuvstvovateli," *Panteon,* No. 2 (1848); "Strannaia istoriia," *Ot. zap.,* LXII (1849); "Skupoi," *Ot. zap.,* LXV (1849); *Stepnaia idilliia* (Pb., 1856).

Reprints in *Russkie povesti XIX veka, 40-50-x godov,* 2 vols. (M., 1952), I [contains "Sto rublei," "Khoroshee mesto," "Goriun," "Nevskii prospekt"] ; in *Z Petrohradskeho podkrovi* (Prague, 1956); in *Russkaia literatura XIX v. Khrestomatiia kriticheskikh materialov,* 2nd ed. (M., 1964) [contains "Nazidatel'noe slovo o *Peterburgskikh vershinakh"*] ; in Iakov Butkov, *Povesti i rasskazy* (M., 1967) [contains *Peterburgskie vershiny, I, II,* "Goriun," "Temnyi chelovek," "Nevskii prospekt"] .

Review articles: Faddei Bulgarin, *Severnaia pchela,* No. 243 (27 October 1845), 971; V.G. Belinskii, *Polnoe sobranie sochinenii* (M., 1956), X, 38-39, 354-362; L. Brant, *Severnaia pchela,* No. 186 (21 August 1846), 742-3; Pavel Annenkov, *see Vospominaniia i kriticheskie ocherki* (Pb., 1877-1881), II, 23-45.

References: Aleksandr Miliukov, "Iakov Petrovich Butkov," *Istoricheskii vestnik,* No. 2 (1881), 391-410; S.D. Ianovskii, "Vospominaniia o Dostoevskom," *Russkii vestnik,* CLXXVI (1885), 796-819; E.G. Bagirov, *"Peterburgskie vershiny* Ia. Butkova," *Uchenye zapiski Moskovskogo gosudarstvennogo pedagogicheskogo instituta,* vol. 115, No. 7 (1956), 73-109; I.S. Chistova, "Butkov i Dostoevskii," *Russkaia literatura,* No. 4 (1971), 98-110; Peter Hodgson, *From Gogol to Dostoevsky: Yakov Butkov, a Reluctant Naturalist in the 1840s* (Munich, 1976).

Peter Hodgson

BUTURLÍN, PETR DMITRIEVICH (1859-1895). Russian poet. A member of the aristocracy, Buturlin was born in Florence, Italy, on 17 (29) March 1859. He was educated in England and later became a diplomat. Buturlin's early verses were published in English in *First Trials* (1878). During the 1880s and 1890s poetry appeared in the journals *Nabliudatel', Sever, Vsemirnaia illiustratsiia,* and *Russkii vestnik,* among others. Nature, love motifs, and themes taken from classical antiquity, ancient Russian mythology and romantic Western legends predominate in Buturlin's lyrics. His contemporaries considered him a master of the sonnet. The poet's aesthetic principles are close to the poets of "pure art," and his work as a whole is imitative. The anthologies *Sibyl* (Sibilla, 1890), *Twenty Sonnets* (Dvadtsat' sonnetov, 1891), and *Sonnets* (Sonety, 1895) contain a portion of his work. Buturlin died in Tagancha on 24 July (5 August) 1895.

Works: Stikhotvoreniia (Kiev, 1897) [includes a biographical sketch and a bibliography] ; *Sonety; posmertnoe izdanie* (Kiev, 1895).

BYCHKÓ, VALENTYN VASYL'OVYCH (b. 1912). Soviet Ukrainian poet, CP member since 1943. The son of a metalworker, Bychko was born on 17 June

1912 in Kharkov. He graduated from the Kharkov Institute of popular Education in 1932 with training in language and literature and later worked on the staffs of various youth journals. First publishing in 1925, Bychko writes mainly for children and young people. The chief themes and motifs of Bychko's poetry are love of labor and the development of a feeling of collectivism, friendship, and internationalism. His verses, which are close to the folk song tradition, are both melodious and simple to understand. Bychko has translated into Ukrainian the Russian poetry of Mikhalkov, Marshak, Maiakovskii, Aliger as well as Lithuanian poets. Some of his songs have become popular.

Works: Sontse nad holovami (Kharkov-Odessa, 1935); *Perekop. Poema* (Kharkov-Odessa, 1937); *Veselka* (Kiev, 1946); *Vohnishche* (Kiev, 1949); *Lita pioners'-ki* (Kiev, 1954); *Siisia, rodisia, zerno* (Kiev, 1959); *Bilia vechirn'oho vohniu* (Kiev, 1966); *Blagoslovlialosia na svit: avtobiohrafichna povist'* (Kiev, 1969); *Sribnolittia; vybrani poezii* (Kiev, 1973); *Kolir chasu* (Kiev, 1974). In Russian translation: *Iasnyi svet: stikhi* (L., 1966); *K nam Lenin prishël: stikhi* (M., 1966); *Rassvet: avtobiograficheskaia povest'* (M., 1975); *V labirintakh svobody* (M., 1976).

BÝKAŬ, VASIL (b. 1924). Belorussian novelist. Bykaŭ was born on 19 June 1924 in Cherenovshchina, Usachi Raion, Vitebsk Oblast. He is the most important living Belorussian novelist, and indeed an outstanding figure in the field of Soviet prose as a whole. Unfortunately, he is often mistaken for a Russian owing to the deplorable practice of publishing translations without mentioning the language of origin. In many ways he is a typical product of the "Thaw," approaching with boldness and originality themes which had hitherto been treated only according to the depressingly conformist patterns of Stalinist writing. Bykaŭ's constant thematic field is the Second World War and particularly the effects of wartime Stalinism on the attitudes and fates of ordinary soldiers and partisans. Uncompromising and outspoken in the relatively relaxed atmosphere of Belorussia in the mid-1960s, he has become more circumspect in recent years while continuing to confine himself to the war theme. In the context of Belorussian prose, which is still rather thematically narrow, it is perhaps a pity that Bykaŭ practices such self-limitation, for the contemporary episodes in some of his novels (many take the form of reminiscences of the War) often afford an absorbing and convincing glimpse of present-day problems and attitudes. Plainly, however, he believes himself duty bound to continue describing the immense catastrophe of which he has been a witness. There appears to be little danger of his exhausting this theme for, unlike many war novelists who pour out their experiences in one or two books, Bykaŭ pays little attention to background and events (though setting most of his novels in places where he served), seeming able to draw on an inexhaustible well of human experience and psychological observation.

When war broke out he joined the artillery and served in an anti-tank regiment on many different fronts inside the Soviet Union and in Romania and Hungary, ending the War in Austria. Soon after the cessation of hostilities he was recalled to the army as a reservist and spent ten years in the Kuril Islands off Siberia. His first stories date from 1951 but were published only in 1956. Since that time he has lived in Grodno, working on the editorial staff of a local newspaper and several journals, most important of which is *Maladosts'*.

Bykaŭ's early work comprises some satirical sketches, several not very impressive short stories with a contemporary setting and, most notably, numerous stories about war in its various aspects. In 1959 the short novel *The Cry of the Crane* (Zhuraŭliny kryk) attracted considerable critical attention, seeming as it did to draw together the best elements of the early war stories.

In many ways this novel is typical of all Bykaŭ's subsequent work. The story describes a few hours in the life of an isolated group of soldiers who have been set the impossible task of defending a railway crossing to cover the retreat of a large section of Soviet forces. By the end five of the six have died, but in the course of the book Bykaŭ characterizes each in depth, showing the general effect on them of the War and in particular their mental and physical reactions to the hopelessness of their situation. Description of physical action and drama is minimal, the author's concern being rather directed towards individual psychology and especially the motivational springs of heroism, cowardice and treachery in the face of extreme hardship and danger. Also typical of Bykaŭ's novels as a whole is the vigorous, entirely realistic language, harsh, precise imagery with rare flashes of lyricism, a laconic, lapidary style where every detail is significant, and narrow spatial and temporal bounds extended by use of flashback, reminiscence and dream.

The Cry of the Crane has a third-person narrator, but near the center of the novel's point of view is a Belorussian youth who is experiencing military action for the first time, and it is through his consciousness that many of the events, situations and characters are seen, by means of interior monologue and other devices. He is a semi-autobiographical character (Bykaŭ was seventeen when war broke out) and he occurs in various forms in several novels, sometimes as a first-person narrator, more often not so, but always functioning as a moral point of reference against which the other characters' behavior is judged. In this, as in several other of Bykaŭ's novels, the moral judgment takes a concrete and violent form, underlining the author's own uncompromising moral stand and his conviction that evil and weakness must be resisted actively wherever they are found.

Bykaŭ's first novel, though technically still somewhat immature, in many ways sets the tone of his later works. Not merely are there none of the facile heroics commonly associated with the Soviet war novel, but the entire atmosphere is harshly unromantic, grimly and unspectacularly realistic. Amongst his contemporaries Bykaŭ somewhat resembles Yurii Bondarev and Grigorii Baklanov, although several commentators have made general comparisons with Solzhenitsyn, and it is indeed notable that in 1967 these were the three writers Bykaŭ singled out for their "honesty and talent." War serves as a catalyst of emotions, a searching test of loyalty, courage and responsibility, and the dramatic tension of his novels lies not in spectacular action or even slightly exceptional characters but in the dramatization of emotions firmly rooted in credible human beings. In the apt words of the Czech critic Václav Židlický, Bykaŭ "represents war through the dialectics of the human soul."

In the following year appeared *Treachery* (Zdrada, 1960), curiously translated into Russian as *A Page from the Front*. The main character, the villain, is a bemedalled secretary of the company Komsomol organization and a candidate for the Party, illustrating Bykaŭ's hate for political careerism and the mouthing of slogans by conservative officials who found the atmosphere of lies under Stalin a natural element and used their powers for ruthless bullying. The arbitrariness, suspicion, fear, cynicism, incompetence and treachery which so greatly increased the difficulties of the ordinary Soviet people trying to defend their homeland are also prominent in the next novel *The Third Flare* (Tretsiaia raketa, 1962), one of Bykau's most popular and successful works.

An Alpine Ballad (Alpiiskaia balada) of a year later is unexpectedly romantic in its depiction of two prisoners' attempt to escape over the Alps. The heroine, an Italian Communist, Giulia, is the most extended female portrait in Bykaŭ's writing to date, but the novel suffers from uncharacteristically stilted dialogue, particularly in Giulia's incongruous linguistic mixture of Russian, Italian and German.

Bykaŭ's longest work so far, and undoubtedly the most ambitious and interesting, is *The Dead Feel No Pain* (Miortvym ne balits', 1965) which, significantly, has not been reprinted since it first appeared in the literary journal *Maladosts'*. Unusual in its rather wide panorama of military action, the novel raises to a new and very specific level the links between past and present, already hinted at in works like *Treachery*, through interlocking chapters depicting alternately wartime and the realities of present-day Belorussia. The first-person narrator, a young sub-lieutenant in 1944, is seen also as a crippled veteran in town for the Victory Day celebrations twenty-one years later, who suddenly imagines he has recognized one of his wartime senior officers, a ruthless careerist whose reckless behavior has cost many Soviet lives. Determined to find out whether it is in fact the same man—and if so to expose and denounce him—the narrator attaches himself to an aggressive, self-satisfied middle-aged bureaucrat. Though the latter turns out to be someone else, he is no less a representative of Stalinism: a wartime public prosecutor who even after the Twentieth Party Congress has no remorse at having sent thousands of innocent people to the camps.

Friends and foes alike could not fail to perceive the novel's message: many of those who flourished under Stalin were continuing to flourish unrestricted in present-day Soviet society. *The Dead Feel No Pain* was something of a test case in Soviet Belorussian literature, being celebrated by the normally conservative Institute of Literature of the Belorussian Academy of Sciences and almost immediately attacked with the greatest vehemence by Party critics, first in *Pravda*, then in the Belorussian press. Bykaŭ made a spirited reply to these attacks in a celebrated speech at the Fifth Congress of Belorussian Writers in 1966, and it is significant that the novel which followed, *The Accursed Hill* (Prakliataia vyshynia, 1968), showed no sign of retreating from the harsh, sometimes cruel realism which had characterized his earlier work.

In 1969 Bykaŭ attempted his first novel about partisans with *The Kruhlianski Bridge* (Kruhlianski most), another highly controversial work, attacking the view that the end justifies the means, even in wartime operations. This was followed in 1970 by *The Ordeal* (Sotnikaŭ), the first of his works to be translated and published in the West. Apparently keeping to the by now expected pattern of a few men (here two partisans, Rybak and Sotnikaŭ) faced by extreme danger, leading ultimately to heroism on the one hand and betrayal on the other, it is nonetheless a work of considerable subtlety, displaying Bykaŭ's mastery of gradual characterization. The two partisans on a mission to collect provisions pass in a short space of time through a series of changing and increasingly difficult circumstances which affect their relationship and their attitudes to the people they meet. While Sotnikaŭ's uncompromising moral rigidity is not always attractive, it is ultimately his companion's conviction that the end justifies the means and that to survive at any price is more important than to die honorably that leads him to succumb to the temptations of the German police interrogator and become a member of the Polizei: Sotnikaŭ is hanged, but it is Rybak who dies spiritually.

The Dead Feel No Pain and The Ordeal are probably Bykaŭ's best works hitherto. He has continued to write prolifically in the seventies, exposing the wartime manifestations of Stalinism: the incompetence and viciousness of army commanders who aroused more fear in their soldiers than the Germans themselves; the prevailing atmosphere of suspicion, eavesdropping and threat of denunciation; the cynical preoccupation with appearances and wholesale disregard for truth all come across with striking force, rich in contemporary implication, although, in Bykaŭ's words, "such people are better camouflaged and more difficult to discern now."

Bykaŭ has an uncompromising belief in moral absolutes, to be perceived not only in the novels as a whole but also in the characteristic parable-like insertions with which various moral points are made and underlined. He is a subtle writer both in technique and psychological understanding, and his forthright moral absolutism should be seen as an indication of courage rather than any limitation of talent. His latest works, however, have shown a certain tendency to abandon these earlier unambiguous positions, turning more to plot and action to hold the reader's attention. Heinrich Böll's dictum that "a man ceases to be an artist not when he creates a weak work but when he begins to fear risks" was quoted by Bykaŭ in a short autobiographical essay of 1965, and now seems particularly relevant to his own writing in a way that could not have been foreseen in the previous decade. Even if he fails to regain his former stature, however, Vasil Bykaŭ will have played an important part in the post-Stalin renaissance of Belorussian and, indeed, Soviet prose.

Works: Vybranyia tvory ŭ dvukh tamakh (Minsk, 1974); Miortvym ne balits', Maladosts', Nos. 7-8 (1965); Prakliataia vyshynia, Maladosts', No. 5 (1968); Kruhlianski most, Polymia, No. 2 (1969); Voŭchaia zhraia (Minsk, 1975); Iaho batal'ion, Maladosts', Nos. 11-12 (1975).

References: A. Viartsinski, "Haloŭnae—praŭda . . .," Literatura i mastatstva, No. 81 (1964), 3; V. Židlický and Z. Genyk-Berezovská, Současná sovětská literatura, vol. 3 (Prague, 1966), 205-9; E. Asokina, "Vasil' Bykaŭ," Nadniomanskie byli (Minsk, 1968), 196-234; S. Andraiuk, "Aryhinalnasts' mastaka," Polymia, No. 3 (1972), 195-204; A. Adamovich, "Apovestsi Vasilya Bykava," Polymia, No. 2 (1973), 183-220; S. Hoppe, "Zu den neueren Erzählungen Vasil' Bykaus," Zeitschrift für Slawistik, No. 5 (1974), 667-80; M. Smolkin, "Z paemy chalavechykh liosaŭ," Polymia, No. 10 (1974), 220-38; V. Buran, Vasil' Bykaŭ:

narys tvorchastsi (Minsk, 1976); Arnold B. McMillin, "Vasil Bykaŭ and the Soviet Byelorussian Novel," *The Languages and Literatures of the Non-Russian Peoples of the Soviet Union* (McMaster University, Ont., 1977), 268-94.

A.B. McMillin

BÝKOV, PETR VASIL'EVICH (1843-1930). Russian writer and bibliographer. Bykov was born on 20 October (1 November) 1843 in Sevastopol. He graduated from Kharkov University with a degree in physics and mathematics. First publishing in 1861, Bykov is the author of many poems, tales, and articles. He assisted with the editing of the journals *Russkoe bogatstvo* from 1881 to 1900 and *Sovremennik* from 1911 to 1915, as well as the newspapers *Step'* in 1885-86 and *Slovo* in 1904-05. Bykov wrote numerous biographical sketches on major literary figures, which have appeared in illustrated journals and in the collected works of such writers as A.S. Afanas'ev-Chuzhbinskii, A.N. Pleshcheev, M.L. Mikhailov, I.V. Omulevskii (Fĕdorov), Leskov, Lermontov and Tiutchev. Bykov published his memoirs of literary life of the second half of the nineteenth century entitled *Silhouettes of the Distant Past* (Siluety dalĕkogo proshlogo, 1930). He died in Leningrad in October 1930.

Works: Bibliografiia sochinenii Aleksandra Stepanovicha Afanas'eva-Chuzhbinskogo (1838-1875) (Pb., 1890).

BYKOV, VASILII VLADIMIROVICH, *see* BYKAŬ, VASIL

BYKÓVA, FEKLA IVANOVNA (b. 1879). Russian folk tale narrator (*skazitel'-nitsa*), singer, and professional mourner (*voplenitsa*). Bykova was born on 19 June 1879. She worked at the Sorok Lumber Mill and lives in the Maiachnyi settlement of Belomorsk in the Karelian ASSR. Bykova has recorded more than 100 ancient laments (*plachi*) and songs for the Soviet folklorist K.V. Chistov. She has also composed works on contemporary themes, including a tale (*skaz*) about Lenin and laments about the pilots V.P. Chkalov, M.S. Babushkin, and others. Bykova is a member of the Writers' Union of the USSR.

References: Russkie plachi Karelii (Petrozavodsk, 1940), 21-50.

BYLICHKA, *see* BYVAL'SHCHINA

BYLÍNA. Russian oral epic song. A rich tradition of oral epic song survived well into the twentieth century in three areas of the Slavic world: throughout the Balkans, especially parts of Serbia, Macedonia and Bulgaria; in the Ukraine, primarily between the Desna and Dnepr Rivers; and in Russia, particularly in European Russia close to the Finnish border and the White Sea and to a lesser degree in relatively isolated areas of Siberia as well as among the Don Cossacks.

Internal evidence—for example, the names of cities and people—strongly suggests the possibility that Russian oral epic song, the *bylina* (pl. *byliny*) was flourishing at least as far back as the eleventh and twelfth centuries in Kievan Russia. The question of why the *byliny* vanished from this southern area but survived almost to the present day in the northwestern region in particular is far from clear. We do know, however, that in 1649 Tsar Aleksei Mikhailovich prohibited the "sinful" performances of a group of traveling entertainers, the *skomorokhi,* whose existence dates at least as far back as Kievan Russia and who apparently included the recitation of epic poetry as part of their repertory. The Tsar exiled them to the White Sea region, so it is possible that this act answers the question in part. The *skomorokhi* as such, however, did not survive, but perhaps the latter day performers of *byliny* inherited from them the art of oral epic song.

Even though not as well known in the West as the Russian fairy tale, the *bylina* is the folklore form which Russians are probably most proud of. This form has played a vital and viable role in the cultural life of both the uneducated masses as well as the educated Russian who for many centuries has reworked its content and form in his literary works.

There are a number of reasons which might help explain why oral epic song flourished for such a long time in Russia. Largely responsible was a predominantly rural population and its inability to read and write prior to the Soviet era. In addition, among the cultured Orthodox Russians early written literature until the seventeenth and eighteenth centuries was primarily spiritual literature. The literature of the masses, on the other hand, was oral literature, which was principally secular in nature. The survival of oral epic poetry also can be attributed to the failure of the Orthodox church to stamp out "pagan" folk beliefs and rituals. Contact with the rich oral traditions of the Finnish people and nomadic Turkic tribes likewise played a role in the long life of the *bylina*. But perhaps most important was the influence of Western Romanticism which, toward the end of the eighteenth century, was responsible for the rise of national self-awareness, resulting in an intense interest in Russia's past and its folklore. Due largely to the inspiration of the brothers Grimm, recordings and publications of Russian folklore began to appear for the first time, some of it reworked, some of it in its genuine form. One of the earliest collections of Russian *byliny* was that of Kirsha Danilov, made during the latter part of the eighteenth century and published for the first time in Moscow in 1804.

But the most significant event in the collecting and publishing of *byliny* took place in the second half of the nineteenth century. At this point interest in Russian oral epic song increased significantly, primarily because of the discovery of a treasury of folklore in the northwestern part of Russia in the 1860s, including a living oral epic tradition, by P.N. Rybnikov, an official of the civil service who had been exiled to serve in this remote area. Up to that time it was believed that the *byliny* were almost extinct as a living form in Russia. Rybnikov's discovery was so surprising that at first it was met with disbelief. After Rybnikov's discovery, however, Russian collectors began seriously to record folklore texts, and scholars likewise began to turn their attention to this living oral epic tradition, paying especial attention to the individual transmitters, particularly their repertory and style. These studies, among other things, called attention to the fact that the content of oral traditional texts was unstable from performance to performance. Even Rybnikov in his "Collectors Remarks" of the 1860s observed that epic bards do not always sing *byliny* in exactly the same way. In the 1870s A.F. Gil'ferding made an even more significant collection and study of oral epic poetry, collecting in the same region as Rybnikov and farther north than his predecessor. Gil'ferding placed even more emphasis on the repertory and stylistic characteristics of individual performers, pointing out that a singer changes a *bylina* each time he sings it, primarily by adding, substituting or leaving out certain particles, words, groupings of words, or even entire lines.

By the end of the nineteenth and beginning of the twentieth centuries a significant number of important *byliny* collections had been published and many special studies had been undertaken. Prior to the October Revolution of 1917 as well as shortly thereafter, a major trend in folklore scholarship in Russia attempted to link Russian folk poetry with Russian history, to link *byliny* heroes and events with historical personages and happenings. Another short-lived trend toward the beginning of the 1920s was formal in nature, with an emphasis on structural problems. This approach soon came under sharp official Soviet attack. As a result, studies in the thirties tended to shift toward concentration on social problems and ideological matters. By the forties the Soviet government had even begun an intensive campaign against comparative studies, against the recognition of foreign influences, against the international nature of folklore. These restrictive elements on folklore scholarship lasted well beyond the death of Stalin in the 1950s. At the present time, however, there has been a considerable amount of relaxation and more and more studies dealing with the poetics of the *bylina* are appearing.

Soviet scholars, nevertheless, continued certain traditions of the past, especially extensive collecting in the field. The first major expedition of the Soviet era, which was organized under the direction of the Sokolov brothers toward the end of the twenties, collected materials from the same area as Rybnikov and Gil'-ferding. Since that time there have been many other expeditions. Certain geographical areas have been covered again and again and the repertory of a single singer has frequently been written down several times, sometimes with a time interval of ten or more years. This has resulted in an enormous number of variants, close to 5,000, many from regions separated from each other by thousands of miles. Such extensive collecting has enabled scholars to go deeper into the nature of the changes which folklore undergoes over a period of many years.

Soviet scholars also have continued to show interest in the singer, just like Rybnikov and Gil'ferding, who were the first to gather and publish biographical data on and characterizations of those singers from whom they collected oral epic song. In a small volume published in 1924, B.M. Sokolov occupied himself with the problem of the "special talent" that a singer of *byliny* must have, observing that this talent involved more than just an exceptional memory. What was also needed, according to Sokolov, was the ability to learn a new *bylina* quickly. Sokolov pointed out that a singer of oral epic song could remember an unusually large number of verses because he had at his disposal a stock of compositional elements, such as descriptive pictures and verbal formulas, which he transferred from one *bylina* to another or repeated several times in the same *bylina*. Sokolov concluded that a *bylina* was not memorized, that only its basic content was remembered. This study led to an interesting type of folklore publication, namely one limited to the repertory of a single master practitioner of a particular folklore genre.

Also worthy of special mention is the research carried out over a period of many years by the Soviet scholars A.M. Astakhova and P.D. Ukhov, who have analyzed in detail the *bylina* tradition of the last 150 years, in particular the creative process. Both scholars have continued to draw attention to the fact that each performance of a particular *bylina* is different from all other performances of that same *bylina*.

Thus, a distinctive characteristic of the *bylina* is fluidity of the text, that is, there is no "standard version" of any one song. In this genre the very length of the song (in the Russian tradition occasionally reaching over one thousand lines) makes word-for-word exact memorization and repetition impossible. Nevertheless, if a skilled singer had the occasion to sing over and over again the same song, such as the story about how Dobrynia slew a dragon, the chances that a text would become more stable for that particular singer would increase. This type of stability is the direct result of frequent repetition; it does not arise from the idea that there is a single, unalterable text to be repeated with exactness, either on the level of word groups which are used to form a line, or on the level of themes, or on the level of the larger story patterns, that is, the *byliny* themselves. This is true, even though ideas essential to the story must be repeated for a song to be acceptable to an oral bard's audience.

Textual fluidity or instability is a direct result of a special improvisational technique of oral composition. It is a flexible technique which allows phrases considered by the individual poet to be meaningful to the story to be fitted into a specific metrical pattern.

Although there are many repeated actions, scenes, and descriptions in Russian oral epic song, they are, nevertheless, flexible. They can be expanded or contracted: the saddling of a horse may be accomplished in a half line, or may be expanded to fifty or more lines and still be considered the same "theme," because what is significant is the basic idea expressed and not the number of lines used to express it. The external form of the theme in other words is in constant flux, whereas its meaning within the context of a specific song is not. And like the themes that comprise it, the song may be long or short, according to the ability or mood of the singer, or the mood of the audience. So the shape of the song itself varies from performance to performance. What is involved is recomposition, and each recomposition is unique. Thus, each performance of a song about how Dobrynia slew a dragon is just as valid as any other performance of this song.

Although oral epic songs were usually sung by men, we know that certain women in Russia sang *byliny* with extraordinary skill at a time when the epic tradition was already on the decline, namely from around the turn of the century until shortly after the Revolution of 1917, the time when the *bylina* genre ceased being passed on orally. Since then the *bylina* has gradually ceased to exist as the creation of a living oral tradition.

The art of oral epic song was passed on for centuries by generation after generation of unlettered peasants, each of whom was the "author" of his or her performance of a *bylina*. Exactly when a particular configuration of *bylina* themes was first sung, however, is beyond our knowledge, since genuine *byliny* texts date back only to the nineteenth century. We must reconcile ourselves to the fact that we have at our disposal for reading or study the surface structure of an ancient *bylina* tradition, about whose deep structure we can only speculate. The date of the "generic" song is lost in prehistory.

The Russian *bylina* is a prime example of poetry composed in performance by people unable to read or write. It is a form of poetry that was sung, or at least chanted, to a rather monotonous melody. In modern times no musical instrument was used to accompany it. Nineteenth-and twentieth-century singers sang their *byliny* to no more than a few short melodies. The same melody was usually repeated over and over again until the end of the *bylina* was reached. T.G. Riabinin, an outstanding epic bard of the nineteenth century, sang a *bylina* of some one thousand lines about Dobrynia and Vasilii Kazimirov to the tune transcribed below:

Russian epic poetry is narrative poetry: it has a story to tell. There are no stanzas or refrains to retard the narrative. Rhymes, if they occur at all, are grammatical. For example, several successive lines might end in infinitives with similar suffixes: *poskakivat'/pomakhivat'*. Another feature of the *bylina* is repetition on a variety of structural levels, including repetition of metrical patterns, sounds, verbal expressions, large and small syntactic units, and even entire story patterns.

The language of Russian oral epic song consists of a limited vocabulary, some of it archaic, some of it reflecting the dialect features of the region in which the *bylina* was recited. Words are combined in such a way that they fit into a particular metrical and melodic pattern.

The prosodic arrangement of the *bylina* is rather free. There is considerable syllabic oscillation. The verse line, which ranges as a rule from ten to sixteen syllables, is organized by three primary accents, of which the first and third are the strongest. The external syllables, those before the first and after the third primary accent, do not carry strong stress. The number of unaccented syllables between accented ones varies in general from one to three. This rhythmical pattern can be summarized as follows: a fluctuating number of syllables, three primary accents, and a moveable caesura.

There is close interplay between the melody and the meter. The melodic line can be adjusted to the line of verse by increasing or decreasing the length of time a syllable is held. On the other hand, a verse line can be lengthened or shortened syllabically to fit the melodic line. Verbal phrases submit readily to expansion or contraction, especially through the use or omission of meaningless particles, pronoun fillers and repeated syllabic prepositions, in addition to the use of expanded or contracted morphological endings.

A large number of *byliny* hark back to ancient times, to Kievan Russia of the tenth or eleventh century. The action centers around the court of Prince Vladimir, who feasts and holds court at his palace in Kiev in the south of Russia. Prince Vladimir functions in much the same way as King Arthur, appearing only as a secondary figure. The action of a second group of *byliny* occurs in the "open plain," where Russian heroes fight the Tatars who invaded Russian territory in the thirteenth century. And a third group takes place in or near the medieval trading city of Novgorod in the north of Russia. Since the *byliny* for the most part are associated with either Kiev in the south or Novgorod in the north, it is usual to refer to them as belonging to the Kiev or Novgorod cycles.

Although diverse in content, most *byliny* are short, averaging 200-300 lines, and have a relatively simple narrative structure. A hero goes on a journey for a definite purpose, achieves his goal, and then returns home. Longer *byliny,* which rarely exceed a thousand lines, exhibit a structure that usually involves the chaining together of two or more discrete story patterns.

The basic content of most *byliny* is that of conflict between a hero and a villain. They contain migratory plots and display vestiges of an ancient, perhaps mythological substratum.

The *bylina* idealizes. The Russian heroes, aided by disguises, trickery, magic weapons, and other heroes, do not suffer defeat in combat. But while they exhibit such qualities as handsomeness and wealth which have no parallel, they tend to lack supernatural or superhuman attributes.

Byliny heroes are often endowed with names found in medieval Russian chronicles and other historical writings. This, however, says nothing about the historical veracity of the *bylina*. There is a tendency wherever oral epic poetry is recited for historical places and names to attach themselves to the story patterns and heroes.

One of the prominent themes of Russian *byliny* is the defense of the homeland by heroes, old and young, who ride heroic steeds across the open plain in order to defeat foreign invaders. The most common enemy is the Tatars, who are disposed of forthwith, even though history informs us that this was not always the case. One can generalize even more and state that one of the most common activities and chief claims to fame of *byliny* heroes is that of fighting, of success in combat, in which the hero participates alone or in which never more than a handful of Russian heroes opposes almost overwhelming numbers of the enemy.

By far the largest number of *byliny* belong to the Kiev cycle. These *byliny* are primarily stories of adventure, although incidents and scenes from domestic life are not uncommon. The range of thematic subjects consists for the most part of feasts, journeys, single combats, trials of skill in arms, sports or horsemanship, acts of insubordination followed by punishment or reconciliation, expeditions against hostile neighboring peoples, courtships, marriages and infidelities. Conflicts generally arise over tribute or women, and less frequently over an attempt to increase one's personal power or wealth. And although elements of the marvelous and superhuman are not altogether absent, exaggeration plays the greatest role.

One of the most popular heroes of *byliny* of the Kiev cycle is Dobrynia Nikitich, who frequently is sent by Prince Vladimir on diplomatic missions or who slays dragons. Or, like Odysseus, Dobrynia returns home after many years of absence only to find that his wife is about to be wed to his sworn brother, Alësha Popovich. Although Alësha Popovich plays a role in many *byliny,* he is not the main subject of independent songs.

Other well known *byliny* of the Kiev cycle concern Il'ia Muromets, who spends most of his life in warfare against the enemies of Kievan Russia. One of the most popular involves Il'ia's encounter with Solovei Razboinik (Nightingale the Robber).

Other popular *byliny* of the Kiev cycle concern Diuk Stepanovich of Galicia who goes to Kiev and finds that stories about the splendors of the court of Kiev have been exaggerated; Ivan Godinovich, who steals a bride and kills her; Khoten Bludovich, who wins a bride in spite of her mother's protests; and the last great battle of the heroes of Kiev against their Tatar foes, led by the Tatar Tsar Kalin.

Byliny of the Novgorod cycle are fewer in number than those that concern Kievan Russia. They do not deal with the defense of Russia. The two main heroes of these byliny are the rich merchant Sadko and the unruly youth Vasilii Buslaev.

Among other popular *byliny* associated neither with Kiev nor Novgorod are those about Sviatogor, a hero of gigantic stature, and Mikula Selianinovich, a superb field laborer and plowman.

In the Russian *byliny* almost as important as the hero is the hero's horse. The *byliny* heroes, especially those of Kievan Russia, are mounted, and a very close relationship exists between the horse and its master. Frequently more attention is paid to saddling the horse than to dressing the hero for a journey. This is not to suggest that dress is ignored in the *byliny*. One often encounters elaborate descriptions: sable caps, marten cloaks, elaborately patterned robes, fantastic ornamented buttons "like apples of Siberia" or buttons shaped like youths and maidens, and boots of morocco leather with high heels and pointed toes.

In addition to horse and clothing, the hero has his weapons; however, they are few. The hero is lightly armed, usually with "a taut bow with a bowstring of silk and a tempered arrow."

Women are constantly referred to in the *byliny*. They play an important role in the narrative as well, functioning both as hero and villain. Sometimes women are equivalent to male heroes; sometimes they are stronger, especially the amazon-type warriors who engage in military pursuits. Frequently women are wise, and on occasion naively frivolous. In the infrequent role of mothers, women are wise, prudent, farsighted and practical. Fathers are rarely mentioned.

The *bylina* is no longer the creation of a living oral tradition. This tradition has gradually died out in Soviet Russia, just as it has in so many parts of the world. During the early years of the Soviet period, the government attempted to breathe renewed life into the old *bylina* form. Many "new" *byliny* were created and sung about important events of the new Soviet era and its heroes—Lenin and Stalin, for example. But the revival of the *bylina* tradition was short-lived because the creation of oral epic song in Soviet Russia was on the verge of becoming a lost art. See also BOGATYRI, FOLKLORE, and EPIC.

Collections: I.F. Hapgood, *The Epic Songs of Russia* (N.Y., 1866; reprint, Westport, Conn., 1970); *Pesni, sobrannye P.N. Rybnikovym,* 3 vols. (M., 1909-10); A.M. Astakhova, *Byliny Severa,* 2 vols. (M.-L., 1938-51); *Onezhskie byliny,* eds. Ia.M. Sokolov and V.I. Chicherov (M., 1948); *Onezhskie byliny, zapisannye A.F. Gil'ferdingom letom 1871 goda,* 3 vols. (M.-L., 1949-51); *Byliny,* eds. V.Ia. Propp and B.N. Putilov, 2 vols. (M., 1958); *Drevnie rossiiskie stikhotvoreniia, sobrannye Kirsheiu Danilovym* (M.-L., 1958); N.K. Chadwick, *Russian Heroic Poetry* (N.Y., 1964).

Studies and Bibliographies: A.P. Skaftymov, *Poètika i genezis bylin* (Saratov, 1924); B.M. Sokolov, *Skaziteli* (M., 1924); A.M. Astakhova, *Russkii bylinnyi èpos na Severe* (Petrozavodsk, 1948); M.P. Shtokmar, *Issledovaniia v oblasti russkogo narodnogo stikhoslozheniia* (M., 1952); V.Ia. Propp, *Russkii geroicheskii epos* (L., 1958); A.P. Evgen'eva, *Ocherki po iazyku russkoi poèzii v zapisiakh XVII-XX vv.* (M.-L., 1963); E.M. Meletinskii, *Proiskhozhdenie geroicheskogo èposa* (M., 1963); M.Ia. Mel'ts, *Russkii fol'klor: Bibliograficheskii ukazatel',* I: *1917-1944* (L.,1966); II: *1945-1959* (L., 1961); III: *1960-1965* (L., 1967); A.M. Astakhova, *Byliny: Itogi i problemy izucheniia* (M., 1966); P.D. Ukhov, *Atributsii russkikh bylin* (M., 1970). In Western European languages: Alfred Rambaud, *La Russie épique: Étude sur les chansons héroiques de la Russie* (Paris, 1876); R. Trautman, *Die Volksdichtung der Grossrussen: Das Heldenlied,* vol. I (Heidelberg, 1935); H.M. and N.K. Chadwick, "Russian Oral Literature," *The Growth of Literature,* vol. II (Cambridge, England, 1936); A.B. Lord, *The Singer of Tales* (Cambridge, Mass., 1960); C.M. Bowra, *Heroic Poetry* (London, 1961); F.J. Oinas, "Folklore Activities in Russia," *Journal of American Folklore,* vol. 74 (1961), 362-70; Yu.M. Sokolov, *Russian Folklore* (Hatboro, Pa., 1966).

Patricia Arant

BYLINA VERSE LINE. The most ancient verse form of the Russian epic song, the *bylina* (pl.: *byliny*). There is evidence that the original metrical structure of the *bylina* line consisted of a five-syllable foot, with the stress on the third syllable, but that it permitted deviations from this model and was not strictly schematic. The *byliny* recorded by the ethnographers and folklorists of the nineteenth and twentieth centuries come from a later period, when the predominant metrical unit of the *bylina* line was reduced to four syllables. The *bylina* line most often consists of three four-syllable feet with an anapestic beginning and a dactylic ending, but in the course of an actual performance deviations may be noted both in these metrical patterns and in the number of feet. However, the majority of investigators treat the *bylina* line as a variant of tonic verse, without breaking it down into feet. Metrical variety characterizes the *byliny,* and the structure of the *bylina* line is closely tied to the improvisational character of folk singing. The *bylina* was performed in a chant, the rhythm of which is established and varied according to the text, while the end of the line was pronounced in a particularly long, drawn-out fashion. Every epic singer (*skazitel'*) made use of one, and rarely two or three, melodies for all the *byliny* which he or she performed. (See the preceding entry for an example of such a melody.) T.G. and I.T. Riabinin and M.D. Krivopolenova acquired a wide reputation as extraordinary performers of Russian epic songs.

References: A. Vostokov, *Opyt o russkom stikhoslozhenii,* 2nd ed. (Pb., 1817); F. Korsh, "O russkom narodnom stikhoslozhenii," *Otdelenie russkogo iazyka i slovesnosti AN,* vol. 67, No. 8 (1901); M.P. Shtokmar, "Osnovy ritmiki russkogo narodnogo stikha," *Izvestiia AN SSR, Otdelenie Literatury i iazyka,* No. 1 (1941); – – –, *Issledovaniia v oblasti russkogo narodnogo stikhoslozheniia* (M., 1952).

M.P. Shtokmar

BYRONISM IN RUSSIAN LITERATURE, *see* SUPPLEMENTARY VOLUME.

BYTOVÓI, SEMËN [pseudonym for KAGAN, SEMËN MIKHAILOVICH] (b. 1909). Soviet Russian writer, CP member since 1928. Bytovoi was born on 17 February (2 March) 1909 in Zhlobin, Mogilëv Province. He moved to Leningrad in 1925, where he worked and attended a literary studio associated with the journal *Rezets* (The Cutter). Beginning his literary career in 1929, Bytovoi saw his first anthology of poems, *Street of Strikes* (Ulitsa stachek), appear in 1931. In 1933 he left as a newspaper correspondent for the Far East, and it is the life of the peoples there which dominates most of his subsequent poetry: *Far East* (Dal'nii vostok, 1937), *The Wind Is from Khingan* (Veter s Khingana, 1940), and *Pacific Ocean Book* (Tikhookeanskaia kniga, 1951), and his sketches, such as *The Amur in Battle: Travel Notes* (Amur v boiu. Putevye zapisi, 1940). Bytovoi is especially interested in the history and the present life of the peoples of the North, evident in the sketches "A Train Came to Tumnin" (Poezd prishël na Tumnin, 1951), on the life of the Orochi, and "February Sun" (Fevral'skoe solntse, 1959), on the construction of an Udeg village. In his sketches Bytovoi makes use of folkloric, ethnographic, and historical materials. Although Bytovoi's poetry is noteworthy for its ethnographic accuracy, the lines often come across as cold, declarative, and lacking in true poetic feeling. Bytovoi is also well known as a translator of contemporary Chinese poetry.

Works: Dorogi: po evreiskim kolkhozam Kryma (L., 1931); *Kamchatskie vstrechi. Putevye ocherki* (L., 1948); *Tikhookeanskaia vesna* (L., 1949); *Desiat' tysiach let: Rasskazy* (L., 1953); *Stikhotvoreniia* (L., 1955); *Sady u okeana* (L., 1957); *Schast'e na sem' chasov ran'she* (L., 1964); *Svetlye vody Tymi i Romanticheskie povesti* (L., 1969); *Ot snega do snega* (L., 1972); *Obratnye adresa* (L., 1976).

BYVÁLOV, EVGENII SERGEEVICH [pseudonym: ZIUID-VEST] (1875-1943). Soviet Russian writer. Byvalov was born on 24 December 1875 in Mariupol (now Zhdanov). Educated in naval school, Byvalov served from the age of 16 as a sailor, quartermaster, boatswain, and skipper aboard merchant vessels in the Pacific Ocean. During the Civil War he commanded a gunboat. First publishing in 1921, Byvalov is the author of the tales "Children of the Deck" (Deti paluby, 1926) and "Sea Spray" (Morskie bryzgi, 1927), as well as the stories "On the 'Potëmkin' " (Na "Potëmkine," 1927), "At All Latitudes" (Pod vsemi shirotami, 1927), and "Look Out Below!" (Polundra, 1928). A screen version was made of the last story. Byvalov's tales and stories communicate the fascination of ocean fishing and the romance of the sea. They are distinguished by a stern manliness and a warm humor. Byvalov died in Moscow on 3 October 1943.

Works: Chelovek s paluby. Rasskazy (M.-L., 1927); *Dvadtsat' chetyre i odin* (M., 1928); *Dobytchiki moria. Rasskazy* (M.-L., 1931); *My povedëm korabli. P'esa* (M., 1939).

BYVÁL'SHCHINA [also BYLINOCHKA, BYL', BYLICHKA]. A short, fantastic tale in the folk tradition about encounters with evil, usually termed the "unclean force" *(nechistaia sila),* about the discovery of hidden treasures and incredible events. A *byval'shchina* tale is distinguished from a fairy tale by its pseudo-realistic character, that is, it purports to be a tale about certain incidents which actually occurred. Its opposing counterpart, the so-called *nebyval'shchina* or *nebylitsa,* is a tale of patent and premeditated nonsense. Soviet sources state that, as a result of the elimination of superstitions and the general spread of culture in the rural areas of the land, the *byval'shchina* is disappearing.

References: Iu.M. Sokolov, *Russkii fol'klor* (M., 1941), 342-43.

BZHEDUKH, see CIRCASSIAN LANGUAGE (WEST)

BZYB DIALECT, see ABKHAZIAN LANGUAGE

C

ČADARAINIS, ALEKSANDRS, see ČAKS, ALEKSANDRS

ČÁKLAIS, MĀRIS (b. 1940). Soviet Latvian poet. The son of a laborer, Čaklais was born on 16 June 1940 in the city of Saldus, Kuldīga Uezd, now the Saldus Raion. He graduated from the University of Latvia in 1964 with a degree in history and philology. Čaklais' most notable works are his anthologies *Monday* (Pirmdiena, 1965), *A Pedestrian and Eternity* (Kājāmgājējs un mūžība, 1967), *The Voice of a Leaf* (Lapas balss, 1969), and *An Outing* (Zāļu diena, 1971). He has also published a collection of poems for children entitled *Bimm-Bamm* (1973). Čaklais' poetry is concerned with moral and ethical problems, pointed up by drawing parallels between historical and contemporary events in Latvian life. As a craftsman, Čaklais uses classical meters as well as blank verse and free verse. The poet is also known as a translator of Estonian, and Czech, having rendered the works of Johan Barbarus (Vares), Nazim Hikmet, and Lazo Novomeský into Latvian.

Works: In Russian translation: *Peshekhod i vechnost'* (M., 1969); *Den' travy* (M., 1973).

ČAKS [pseudonym of ČADARAINIS], ALEKSANDRS (1902-1950). Soviet Latvian poet. Čaks was born in Riga on 27 October 1901. He left his medical studies at Moscow University in 1919 to join the Red Army, and returned to Latvia in 1921. Caks is noted among Latvian poets for his emphasis on themes of urban life, exemplified in collections such as *Heart on the Sidewalk* (Sirds uz trotuāra, 1928), *My Paradise* (Mana paradīze, 1932), and *Mirror of Fantasy* (Iedomu spoguļi, 1938). Although Čaks makes use of hyperbolic imagery, he also employs concrete detail. His most notable collections before the Second World were *Overshadowed by Eternity* (Mūžības skartie, 1937-39), *An Angel Behind the Counter* (Eņģeļis ais letes, 1935), and *Locked Doors* (Aizslēgtās durvis, 1938). His post-war production consists of the anthologies *The Patriots* (Patrioti, 1948), *Under a High Star* (Zem cēlās zvaigznes, 1948), and *To Struggle and Labor* (Cīņai un darbam, published posthumously in 1951). Čaks died on 8 February 1950 in Riga.

Works: Izlase, 2 vols. (Riga, 1960-61); *Raksti,* 5 vols. (Riga, 1971-73). In Russian translation: *Lestnitsy* (Riga, 1964); *Serdtse na trotuare* (M., 1966).

References: Ocherki latyshskoi sovetskoi literatury (Riga, 1957); *Latviešu literatūras vēsture,* vol. VI (Riga, 1962); *Istoriia latyshskoi literatury,* vol. II (Riga, 1971).

CAUCASIAN LANGUAGES. The Caucasian languages, also termed Palaeo-Caucasian or Ibero-Caucasian languages (Russian: "iberiisko-kavkazskie iazyki"), include all the languages which are spoken (or were still spoken in the nineteenth century) in the Caucasus and in the plains lying contiguously north and south, and which do not belong genetically to the Indo-Germanic, Semitic, or Turkic languages. The Indo-European languages of the Caucasus are Armenian, the Iranian languages (Ossetian, Kurdish, Tat, Talysh), Russian and Ukrainian: the Semitic languages are represented by Neo-East Aramaic (Aisor). The Turkic languages of the Caucasus include Azeri-Turkish, Kumyk, Karatai-Balkar and Nogai.

Both genetically, and according to their geographical location, the Caucasian languages are divided into three groups: the South Caucasian, or Kartvelian, the North-West Caucasian, and the North-East Caucasian languages. The Southern group consists of Georgian, Svan Mingrelian, Laz (in the Soviet Union Mingrelian and Laz are now combined into one language called Zan) and extends over the river basins of the Rioni and Middle Kura up to approximately the summit of Batumi, and in the southwest on the Black Sea coast farther to the south. The North-West Caucasian languages—Abkhaz, Abaza, Adyge, Kabardian, Ubykh—were spoken around the middle of the nineteenth century in the western Caucasus between the Kuban and the Black Sea, in the valleys of the upper Kuma and the left bank tributaries of the Middle Terek. The 28 North-East Caucasian languages, which fall into four sub-groups (Central Caucasian, Awar-Andi-Dido, Lak-Dargin, and Samur languages), are concentrated in the highlands of Dagestan. They are also called the Nakh-Dagestan group, among which a special position is accorded the Central Caucasian languages, spoken outside Dagestan (Chechen and Ingush east of the Upper Terek and south of the Middle Terek up to the central chain, Bats in the region of Akhmeti of the Georgian Soviet Republic). A still more extensive classification sets the Central Caucasian languages apart as an independent fourth group among the North-East Caucasian languages in the genuine sense. Largest of all the North Caucasian languages is Chechen with 420,000 speakers, while Awar is the most important, since alongside Kumyk and Russian it is also used outside its own language region (with 240,000 speakers) as a commercial language.

The speakers of the Caucasian languages today number approximately 5 million people within the national boundaries of the Soviet Union. Some groups formerly found in the Caucasus now reside elsewhere: the Ubykhs, after the Russian conquest of the Caucasus in 1864, left the east coast of the Black Sea (north of Khosta) and emigrated to Turkey. Ubykh speakers have now dwindled to only a few individuals; Laz is spoken in the Turkish province of Lazistan on the southeast coast of the Black Sea, and the Georgian dialects Imerkhev and Fereidanian are spoken in Turkey and southwest of Teheran, respectively. Of the three languages of the area which constitute the ancient Christian cultural languages of the Caucasus—Georgian, the extinct Caucasian Albanian, and Indo-European Armenian—Georgian is the only one of the Caucasian language family to possess an ancient tradition from the fifth century B.C., an extensive literature and its own writing system. Nevertheless, the fragmentary inscriptions of Caucasian Albanian from the sixth to the eight centuries in its own alphabet are considered a preliminary stage of the East Caucasian Udi. Besides Georgian, which is the official and school language of the Georgian S.S.R. with 3.2 million speakers (1970), eleven other Caucasian languages today have the rank of literary and school languages: Abkhaz, Abaza, Adyge, Kabardian, Chechen, Ingush, Awar, Lak, Dargin, as well as Lezgin and Tabasaran among the Samur languages. In addition to folk poetry, transmitted orally for centuries, literary masterpieces of the better-known authors, and translated literature, school texts and newspapers are published in these languages. Close literary relations exist within the North Caucasian languages and with neighboring non-Caucasian languages. Themes from the Nart epic and the Prometheus myth are widely diffused. Before the Russian conquest in the nineteenth century (the annexation of Georgia in 1801, of Armenia in 1828, the defeat of Dagestan in 1859, of the Circassians in 1864), Oriental models were predominant in the Islamized northern Caucasus. As a rule, the writing system came to be based upon the Russian alphabet, which had displaced the previous use of the Arabic, Georgian, and Latin scripts. The lexicon of the Caucasian languages has been strongly influenced through numerous loan words both from each other and from other languages, especially Persian, Ossetian, Armenian, Turkish, Arabic, and Russian.

That the North-West and North-East Caucasian languages are related seems probable on the basis of word correspondences. There are several arguable etymologies, even for the less certain genetic link with the South Caucasian languages. On the other hand, the theories which attempt to establish a link between the Caucasian languages and the ancient languages of Asia Minor (the so-called Asianic languages), such as Basque and Burushaski, among others, have remained undemonstrated.

There are typical features common to all of the Caucasian languages: the phonological differentiation of the consonant system according to a group of three-member correlations—voiceless, voiced, voiceless with laryngeal stop (or glotto-occlusive); moreover, one finds in the North-East Caucasian languages a series of geminate, or lengthened, consonants. Characteristic of the present-day Caucasian languages also is a rich consonant system, conditioned among other things by the frequency of affricates and spirants, as well as by the series of sounds (uvular, pharyngeal, laryngeal) articulated at the rear of the oral cavity. With upwards of 82 phonemes (in Ubykh), the North-West Caucasian languages are the richest in consonants of any languages on earth.

Corresponding syntactically to the Caucasian model is (1) the differentiation between the transitive ergative construction, in which the object of the transitive verb coincides with the subject of an intransitive verb in a largely unmarked nominative, while the agent stands in an oblique or special case called ergative; (2) the intransitive nominative construction; (3) the affective construction (with verbs of emotion and perception, in which the person affected stands in an oblique case or the locative). We have, for example, in Georgian: (a) *monadirem* (ergative) *moḳla* (aorist) *iremi* (nominative), "the hunter slew the deer "; (b) *monadire* (nominative) *iqo* (imperfect) *kalakši,*"the hunter was in the city"; (c) *mi-q̇uar-s kalçuli* (Old Georgian), "I love the girl" = "to me the girl is pleasing." Yet tendencies are appearing toward the substitution of the ergative by nominative constructions, and in the present tense system of the South Caucasian languages transitive verbs are already being construed nominatively.

Morphologically, an agglutinative system of inflection predominates, alongside which, however, even older features of an inflectional type (particularly in the South Caucasian and North-East Caucasian languages) are recognizable.

Typologically, contrasts exist between the type of the North-East Caucasian languages (with noun classes, impersonal verb and the use of case and post-positions) and that of the North-West Caucasian languages (with polypersonal verbs and preverbs for the expression of syntactic relations). The South Caucasian languages occupy an intermediate position: on the one hand they are moderately polypersonal, while on the other hand they also use, along with preverbs, cases and postpositions for the syntactic ordering of the elements of the sentence.

Among those who have made especially noteworthy contributions to the study of the Caucasian languages are A. Schiefner, R. von Erckert, P. Uslar, A. Dirr, N. Marr, A. Shanidze, N. Trubetskoi, G. Deeters, G. Dumézil, A. Chikobava, and H. Vogt.

Periodicals: The principal journals dealing with Caucasian linguistics are: *Sbornik materialov dlia opisaniia mestnostei i plemen Kavkaza* (Tbilisi, 1881-1926); *Iberiul-kavkaziuri enatmecniereba* (Tbilisi, 1946-); *Caucasica,* Nos. 1-11 (Leipzig, 1924-34); *Revue de Kartvelologie Bedi K'artlisa* (Paris, 1948-); *Studia Caucasica* (The Hague, 1963-); *Kartvelur enata strukturis sakitxebi* (Tbilisi, 1959-); *Ezhegodnik iberiisko-kavkazskogo iazykoznaniia* (Tbilisi, 1974-).

References: G. Deeters, "Die Stellung der Kharthwelsprachen unter den Kaukasischen Sprachen," *Bedi K'artlisa,* vol. 23 (Paris, 1957), 12-16; B. Geiger, T. Halasi-Kun, A.H. Kuipers, K.H. Menges, *Peoples and languages of the Caucasus* (The Hague, 1959); K. Bouda, *Introducción a la lingüística caucásica* (Salamanca, 1960); G. Deeters, "Die Kaukasischen Sprachen," in B. Spuler, ed., *Handbuch der Orientalistik,* I. Abt., vol. VII (Leiden/Köln, 1963), 1-79; G.A. Klimov, *Kavkazskie iazyki* (M., 1965, German translation, Hamburg, 1969); A. Chikobava, *Istoriia izucheniia iberiisko-kavkazskikh iazykov* (Tbilisi, 1965) [in Georgian]; E.A. Bokarev, K.V. Lomtatidze, eds. "Iberiisko-kavkazskie iazyki," in V.V. Vinogradov, ed., *Iazyki narodov SSSR,* vol. IV (M., 1967); K.H. Schmidt, "Problemy geneticheskoi i tipologicheskoi rekonstruktsii kavkazskikh iazykov," *Voprosy iazykoznaniia,* No. 4 (M., 1972), 14-25; I.M. Oranskii, *Die neuiranischen Sprachen der Sowjetunion,* 2 vols. (The Hague, 1975); G.A. Klimov, ed., *Strukturnye obshchnosti kavkazskikh iazykov* (M., 1978).

Karl Horst Schmidt

CAUCASIAN LANGUAGES, KARTVELIAN. The Kartvelian (Georgian *k'art'-veluri,* from *k'art'veli,* 'a Georgian') language family, also called South Caucasian or Iberian, consists of three or four languages: Georgian, the only written Kartvelian language, Svan, and Mingrelian (or Megrelian) and Laz (or Chan), these last two being regarded by most Georgian linguists as two closely related dialects of one language, called by them Zan. The Kartvelian languages are spoken in the Georgian SSR in the USSR and along the Black Sea coast of Eastern Anatolia in Turkey, in the region called Lazistan. Although there have been numerous attempts to link the Kartvelian languages genetically with other linguistic groups (most notably with the languages of the North Caucasus), no such connections can be regarded as clearly demonstrated and Kartvelian stands at the present as an independent family. Most scholars regard the Transcaucasus as the original homeland of these languages.

Georgian and Zan stand closer to each other than to Svan, which in many respects is the most conservative of the Kartvelian languages. In the generally accepted scheme of Deeters the relationship between these languages can be summarized in the following manner:

PROTO-KARTVELIAN

Svan   Zan   Georgian

Laz   Mingrelian

(For further information on Georgian, see the separate article.)

Svan (self-designation: *lušnu nin* [from mu-švan, 'a Svan' with prefix *lu-*] ; Georgian: *svanuri ena;* Russian *svanskii iazyk*). There are an estimated 35 thousand speakers of this language, living in the high mountains of the Georgian former province of Svanetia, consisting today of the Mestia (Upper Svanetia) and Lentexi *rayons.* The area is bordered on the north by the main crest of the Caucasus range (the border between the Georgian SSR and the RSFSR), on the northwest by the border with the Abkhaz ASSR, and on the south and southeast by the former provinces of Mingrelia and Rača-Leč'k'umi. Svan is an unwritten language; its speakers use Georgian as their literary language.

Zan (Georgian: *zanuri ena;* Russian: *zanskii iazyk*). Although the Mingrelian and Laz linguistic areas are now separated by Georgian-speaking territory, it is believed that in the past the two dialects of Zan formed a continuum (*ca.* 1800 years ago). *Laz* (self-designation: *lazuri nena;* Georgian: *čanuri ena* or *lazuri ena;* Russian: *chanskii (lazskii) iazyk*) is spoken primarily in Turkish Lazistan, along the Black Sea coast from the Soviet border west approximately to Trebizond (Trabzon). Turkish census figures list 50 thousand speakers, although the number is probably larger. Laz speakers in Turkey are bilingual, speaking also Turkish. Only one village in Georgia, Sarpi, on the Black Sea coast at the Turkish border, is part of the Laz speech continuum, although emigrants from the Laz speech area have settled along the Georgian Black Sea coast in and near such towns as Bat'umi, Oč'amč'ire, Soxumi (Sukhumi), and Gudaut'a. *Mingrelian* (self-designation: *margali nina;* Georgian: *megruli ena;* Russian: *mingrel'skii iazyk*) is spoken in the Georgian SSR in a region bounded approximately by the boundary of the Abkhaz ASSR on the northwest, the Egrisi crest to the north, the C'xeniscqali (Tskhenistskali) river to the east, the Rioni to the south, and the Black Sea to the west. In the north Mingrelian borders with the Svan linguistic area, to the northwest with Abkhaz, and to the southeast with Georgian. The approximately 300 thousand speakers of Mingrelian use Georgian as their literary language.

Phonology. The Kartvelian languages share with most other languages of the Caucasus a three-way opposition in the stop series: voiced, voiceless aspirate and voiceless glottalized. The consonantal systems are:

	Georgian								Svan	Zan
Labial	b	p^h	p'	m					w/v	f (Laz)
Dental	d	t^h	t'							
	ż	c^h	c'	n	z	s	r	l		
Palatal	j	$č^h$	č'	ž	š				y	y
Velar	g	k^h	k'							
Postvelar			q'	ġ	x	h	q^h	ʔ		

(Superscript ^{h} indicates aspiration and an apostrophe ' indicates glottalization, ż represents a sound similar to Russian *dz*, c a sound similar to Russian *ts*, j similar to *dzh*, and ġ a sound similar to the South Great Russian pronunciation of standard Russian *g* (that is, a *gh*). Kartvelian languages are characterized by so-called "harmonic clusters," which consist of labial, dental or palatal stops or affricates followed by the corresponding velar or post-velar stops or fricatives, e.g., *bg*, $p^h k^h$, *p'k'*, *bġ*, $p^h x$, *p'q'*, etc. Such harmonic clusters tend to function as single consonants in the phonological system.

Georgian has a five vowel system: *a, e, i, o, u*. Zan has the same system, although some Mingrelian dialects also have *ə*, a high central vowel. In addition to the five vowels above Svan also has the fronted vowels *ü, ö, ä*, (the results of *umlauting*, that is, fronting under the influence of a following front vowel) and *ə*. All nine vowels in Svan can occur distinctively long and short. Oppositions of length are not distinctive in Georgian or Zan. Stress is not distinctive in Georgian or Zan but is contrastive in Svan.

In general, the Kartvelian languages have more limited consonantal systems and larger vocalic systems than the Northwest Caucasian languages (Abkhaz-Adyghei). With respect to the Northeast Caucasian languages (Dagestan-Nakh), Kartvelian has fewer consonants and vowels.

Morphology. Noun. The Kartvelian languages are all characterized by well-developed systems of nominal declension. Georgian and Svan have six cases: nominative, ergative, dative, genitive, instrumental, and adverbial. Laz lacks the adverbial but has a directional case and an ablative, while Mingrelian has in addition to the cases of Georgian and Svan a terminative case. In general, nominal declension is more developed in Kartvelian than in Northwest Caucasian, while the Kartvelian declension is extremely limited in comparison to that of the Northeast Caucasian languages. In all the Kartvelian languages the plural tends to be formed agglutinatively, that is, a pluralizing morpheme is followed by the same case markers as used in the singular declension. Adjectives are not well-differentiated from substantives (nouns). When used independently (that is, not directly modifying a substantive) adjectives follow the same declension as substantives; when used attributively (that is, directly modifying a noun) they are either not declined at all or have a restricted declension. Neither the category of grammatical gender nor that of grammatical class is found in these languages.

Verb. The extreme complexity of the Kartvelian verbal system contrasts with the relative simplicity of the nominal system. Verbs can be classified (on a combination of formal and semantic grounds) into various classes: "transitive" or "active," "passive," "middle," "indirect" (that is, basically verbs of sensation or emotion, *verba sentiendi*), etc. The individual Kartvelian languages have various "series" of tense and mood forms, each of which behaves similarly formally and/or semantically. Georgian and Svan have three such series: present (and future), aorist, and perfect. In Zan there is in addition a fourth, "resultative," series. Preverbs, that is, verbal prefixes, serve in all Kartvelian languages to perfectivize simple verbs (as well as often changing lexical meaning). This process of aspectual derivation is similar to that found in Russian and other Slavic languages. Unlike Russian and the Slavic languages, however, the Kartvelian languages do not derive imperfective forms from prefixed perfective verbs.

Kartvelian verbal forms are polypersonal, that is, the verbal form by itself can indicate not only the subject but also the direct and indirect objects. The notion of indirect object is broader in Kartvelian than in many Western languages and can indicate possession, benefit, location, etc. Such indirect objects generally are regarded as belonging to a special grammatical category called "version." A special version, the "subjective version," functions similarly when the beneficiary, possessor, and so forth, of the action is the subject. Kartvelian verbs can undergo transformations which delete one of the persons marked by the verb (generally the patient or direct object of a transitive verb; this process is generally called passivization), or which add a person (generally the agent of an underlyingly intransitive action or the person caused or forced to perform an action when the underlying verb is transitive). Such derived forms are called causatives. Of all the Kartvelian languages, only Svan distinguishes inclusive (including the person spoken to) and exclusive (excluding the person spoken to) forms of the first person plural. Although case in Kartvelian is marked only by suffixes, person and tense/mood are marked by a system of both prefixes and suffixes.

Syntax. The Kartvelian languages can be characterized as "left-branching," that is, modifiers such as adjectives and genitives precede the word they modify. Postpositions rather than prepositions are found. The normal (unmarked) word-order tends to be subject-object (s) -verb.

The system of case-marking of subjects and objects varies from language to language and within the various languages is dependent upon the formal-semantic class to which the verb belongs (for example, active or "passive") and the series of tense-mood forms to which a given verbal form belongs (for example, present series, aorist series, or perfect series). In Georgian and Svan for "passive" verbs the grammatical subject is always in the nominative and any indirect objects are in the dative. For active verbs (which can be transitive or intransitive) in the present series (and in Georgian in the future) the subject is in the nominative case and direct and indirect objects are in the dative. In the aorist series of these verbs the grammatical subject is in the ergative, the direct object is in the nominative and the indirect object is in the dative. In the perfect series of active verbs the phenomenon of "inversion" occurs: the subject is in the dative case and the direct object is in the nominative; morphemes marking the grammatical subject in other series mark the direct object (= patient of the action) in the perfect series while those morphemes marking an indirect object ("objective version") in the other series mark the subject (= agent) in the perfect series. In Zan two differing systems are found: in Mingrelian the subject in the present series of all verbs is in the nominative and direct and indirect objects are in the dative. As in Georgian and Svan the perfect series has inversion. But in the aorist series the grammatical subject of all verbs (independent of voice-class) is in the ergative and the direct object is in the nominative, indirect objects being in the dative. In spite of the existence of a case called "ergative," the systems of Georgian, Svan, and Mingrelian are basically nominative in structure. In Laz a closer approximation to a true ergative structure is found: here the subject of all active (= transitive) verbs is in the ergative case independently of tense-mood forms, the nominative marks direct objects, and the dative indirect objects.

In all the Kartvelian languages there is a class of verbs denoting emotions, sensations (*verba sentiendi*), which are characterized by inversion: that is, the person affected is in the dative case and the source of the sensation is in the nominative.

History. The proto-Kartvelian phonological system has been reconstructed by T'. Gamgreliże (Gamkrelidze) and G. Mačavariani. Typologically it bears strong resemblance to proto-Indoeuropean, both systems being characterized by *ablaut* and alternations between syllabic and non-syllabic sonants (that is, i/y, u/w, r, l, m, n). Roots generally have the shape CVC (consonant-vowel-consonant, where the consonant can be represented by a harmonic cluster) while suffixes have as their basic shape -VC. A given stem can have only one vowel. The inventory of consonantal phonemes was basically as for Svan, with the absence of $\check{z}$ and with the addition of a mid series of affricates and fricatives: * $\dot{z}_1$, c'_1, $c^h{}_1$, z_1, s_1. These give dentals (alveolars) in Georgian and palatals in Zan and Svan: for example, Proto-Kartvelian * $c^h{}_1en$- 'grow' (of plants), Georgian *c'en*, Zan *č'an-*, Svan *šen-*. The farther back series of palatals (* j, $\check{c}$', $\check{c}^h$, $\check{s}$) give palatals in Georgian and sequences of palatal + stop in the remaining languages; for example, Proto-Kartvelian *$\check{c}^h em$- 'my', Georgian *č'em-*, Zan *č'k'im-*, Svan *mi-šgwi-*. In Gamgreliże and Mačavariani's reconstruction, Proto-Kartvelian shows strong typological similarities in phonology and morphophonology not only to Proto-Indoeurepean, but also, at an earlier state of the proto-language, to Northwest Caucasian.

G. Klimov has reconstructed the Proto-Kartvelian nominal system, which in number of cases and in form strongly resembles the system of contemporary Svan. It seems likely that the case marking of subjects and objects found in Georgian and Svan goes back to the proto-language and that the situations found in the two major dialects of Zan represent innovations.

There are varying views on the sentence structure of proto-Kartvelian. Many scholars view the proto-language as having been of a "pure" ergative structure, that is, the agent in all transitive sentences being marked in a special "ergative" case, while the patient in these sentences was in the same case, the "absolutive" (or nominative) as the subject of intransitive verbs. Others view the proto-language as belonging to the "active" structure, wherein the verb is classified not as transitive/intransitive (as in the contemporary Kartvelian languages), but rather as active/stative. According to a third view, the "ergative" construction in the proto-language was restricted to the second series of tense-mood forms, as in contemporary Georgian.

Bibliography: (Only works in Russian and Western languages are cited. For a bibliography of works in Georgian, see: "Bibliografiia iazykovedcheskikh rabot, vypolnennykh v nauchnykh uchrezhdeniiakh Gruzinskoi SSR," *Iberiul-kavkasiuri enat'mec'niereba (Iberiisko-kavkazskoi iazykoznanie),* vol. 9-10 (Tbilisi, 1958), 377-495; "Bibliografiia izdanii Instituta iazykoznaniia Akademii nauk Gruzinskoi SSR (1936-1972)," *Iberiul-kavkasiuri enat'mec'niereba (Iberiisko-kavkazskoe iazykoznanie),* vol. 19 (Tbilisi, 1974), 195-318. (For works on Georgian, see under that language.)

Kartvelian, general: G. Deeters, *Das kharthwelische Verbum* (Leipzig, 1930); A. Chikobava, "O lingvisticheskikh chertakh kartvel'skikh iazykov," *Izvestiia AN SSSR, OLYa,* vol. 7, vyp. 1 (1948); – – –, "Kartvel'skie iazyki, vvedenie," *Iazyki narodov SSSR,* vol. 4 (M., 1967), 15-21.

Kartvelian, historical: A. Chikobava, "Kartvel'skie iazyki, ikh istoricheskii sostav i drevnii lingvisticheskii oblik," *Iberiul-kavkasiuri enat'mec'niereba (Iberiisko-kavkazskoe iazykoznanie),* vol. 2 (Tbilisi, 1948), 225-275; G. Klimov, *Sklonenie v kartvel'skikh iazykakh v sravnitel'no istoricheskom aspekte* (M., 1962); K. Schmidt, *Studien zur Rekonstruktion des Lautstandes der südkaukasischen Grundsprache* (Wiesbaden, 1962); G. Klimov, *Etimologicheskii slovar' kartvel'skikh iazykov* (M., 1964); T. Gamgreliże (Gamkrelidze) and G. Mačavariani, "Sistema sonantov i ablaut v kartvel'skikh iazykakh," *Sonantt'a sistema da ablauti k'art'velur enebsi* (Tbilisi, 1965), 381-474; Thomas Gamkrelidze, "A Typology of Common Kartvelian," *Language,* vol. 42 (1966), 69-83; A. Chikobava, "K voprosu ob otnoshenii kartvel'skikh iazykov k indoevropeiskim i severokavkazskim iazykam," *Voprosy iazykoznaniia,* No. 2 (1970), 50-62.

Svan: V. Topuria, "Svanskii iazyk," *Iazyki narodov SSSR,* vol. 4 (M., 1967), 77-94.

Zan: N. Marr, *Grammatika ch'anskogo (lazskogo) iazyka* (Pb., 1910); I. Kipshidze, *Grammatika mingrel'skogo (iverskogo) iazyka* (Pb., 1914); R. Bleichsteiner, *Kaukasische Forschungen; I. Georgische und mingrelische Texte* (Wien, 1919); G. Dumézil, *Contes lazes* (Paris, 1937); – – –, *Documents anatoliens* (Paris, 1967); A. Kiziria, "Zanskii iazyk," *Iazyki narodov SSSR,* vol. 4 (M., 1967), 62-76.

Howard I. Aronson

CAUCASIAN LANGUAGES, NORTH-EASTERN (Russian: "nakhsko-dagestanskie" languages). One of the three branches of the Caucasian (Ibero-Caucasian or Palaeo-Caucasian) languages, spoken in the Dagestan and Chechen-Ingush Autonomous Soviet Republics, that is, in the mountain uplands of Dagestan and west-ward in the contiguous area lying east of the Upper and south of the Middle Terek up to the principal range of mountains. Its speakers are also known under the collective term "Lezgins." The North-East Caucasian languages are separated from the Caspian Sea on the north by Kumyk, and in the south by Azerbaijani. The group comprises 28 languages and is more sharply divided than the other two branches of the Caucasian languages. The following sub-groups are distinguished:

(I) The Central Caucasian, Nakh or Veinakh languages (Ingush *wai nakh*, 'our people'), which are called North-East Caucasian languages in a narrower sense by many investigators as an independent, Central Caucasian language family along-side the Dagestan languages. They encompass the "kist" group, consisting of Chechen, which, with its 613,000 speakers, is the largest among the North Cau-casian languages, and Ingush (158,000 speakers), as well as Bats (2,500 speakers, 1959). Chechen-Ingush are spoken in the Chechen-Ingush Autonomous Soviet Republic (capital, Groznyi), Bats is spoken in the Akhmeti region within the Georgian Soviet Republic. Among the Chechen dialect may be noted the Akki dialect (transitional to Ingush), and the language of the Pankisi-Kists, who, in the first half of the nineteenth century, emigrated to three villages on the Alazan River in Georgia. Chechen and Ingush have the status of literary languages. From 1944 to 1957 the Chechens and Ingush were resettled in Central Asia.

(II) The Awar-Andi-Dido languages are spoken in west Dagestan, where they established themselves between groups I and III, which share with each other many common features. They fall into three sub-groups: (1) Awar, which, next to Russian and the Turkic Kumyk, represents the most important among the com-mercial languages of Dagestan, is spoken by about 396,000 people, and on the basis of the dialect of Khunza and the reformed military language (bol ma.c) of Imam Shamil is also used by the speakers of sub-groups two and three (below) as a literary language and language of communication; (2) eight Andi languages (Andi, Botlikh, Godoberi, Karata, Bagulal, Chamalal, Tindi, Akhwakh), spoken by about 35,000 people in the valley of the Middle Andi Koisu; (3) four Dido or Tets languages (Dido, Hinukh, Khwarshi, Kapuchi), spoken by a few thousand people on the Upper Andi Koisu.

(III) Lak and Dargin are two independent languages with the status of literary languages; their speakers dwell between groups II and IV; Lak, known previously also as Kazikumukh, is a language of 86,000 speakers, broken into five dialects; the 231,000 speakers of Dargin are divided into three dialectal groups with nu-merous local idioms: (1) the Urakh group, with Khiurkili (or Khiurkani, the old denomination for the common language); (2) the Akusha group, the basis of the present-day literary language; (3) the Tsudakhar group, to which Kubachi, con-sidered a unique dialect, also belongs.

(IV) The ten Samur or Lezgin languages are spoken by about 350,000 people in South Dagestan and the north Azerbaidzhan Soviet Socialist Republic (in the river basins of the Samur and the Giulgerychai). They include the literary lan-guages Lezgin (more than 324,000 speakers) and Tabasaran (55,000 speakers), the non-literary languages Agul, Rutul, Tsakhur, Kryz, Budukh, and with qualifi-cations Archi, Khinalugh, Udi. The basis of the Lezgin literary language is Kiuri, one of the three Lezgin dialects on which P. Uslar as early as the nineteenth century based a developed school language.

Age of the Tradition. The 28 North-East Caucasian languages enjoy no long-standing literary tradition, if one disregards the scattered documents which derive from the nineteenth century, and some few in Awar, dating from the fifteenth century. Writing was based previously on the Arabic, Latin, and at times also on the Georgian alphabets. Today, as a rule, the Cyrillic symbols serve to render the school and literary languages for Chechen, Ingush, Awar, Lak, Dargin, Lezgin and Tabasaran. The language of the Albanians [Caucasian] enjoyed the use of its own alphabet, which the Georgian philologist E. Abuladze discovered in 1937 in an Armenian manuscript of the fifteenth century; beside this the language is transmitted through fragmentary inscriptions of the sixth to eighth centuries from the Azerbaijani village of Mingechaur. Albanian is assumed to live on in present-day Udi. Until their conversion to Islam in the course of the eighth to the thirteenth centuries, the speakers of Albanian were one of the Christian peoples of the Caucasus, alongside the Iberians (Georgians) and the Armenians.

Genetic Relationships. It is certain that the four sub-groups of the North-East Caucasian languages are related, springing originally from a common North-East Caucasian base language. Moreover, N. Trubetzkoy, in his North-Caucasian word correspondences (*Wiener Zeitschrift für die Kunde des Morgenlandes,* No. 37 [1925], 76-92), has made probable the genetic relationship between the North-East and the North-West Caucasian languages. The precise reconstruction process, however, has not yet been produced; it presupposes the production of reconstructed models for the individual sub-groups and their comparison for the derivation of the North-East Caucasian base language. The reconstructed model thus produced must ultimately be compared with the model for the North-West Caucasian base language. Less certain appears to be the relationship of both the North-Caucasian groups to the South Caucasian group, although here, too, there are arguable correspondences in evidence, such as Klimov's reconstruction (1969, p. 68):

West Caucasian	East Caucasian	South Caucasian	Meaning
*g^wa	*da-ḳw	*gul-	heart
*psə	*sswan-	*sul-	soul
*cca	*cer	*ca(l)-	number
*ttə⟩a	*ba-r⟩ (?)	*d⟩e- 'Day'	sun

All attempts to compare genetically the North-East Caucasian languages further with other language families (the Asianic languages of ancient Asia Minor, or Basque and Burushaski, among others), and to establish common bonds have, on the contrary, up to this time not led to convincing results.

Loan Relationships. Still little studied are the layers of loan words in the North-East Caucasian languages originating particularly in Arabic, Turkic and Russian, and made possible by the Arab invasion of the seventh century, leading to Islamization by the contiguity of the Kumyks in the north and Azerbaijani-Turks in the south, and by the Russian occupation in the nineteenth century. Other sources are Iranian (particularly Persian and Ossetian) and Georgian.

Typology. Phonologically, the North-East Caucasian languages display strongly developed consonant systems (particularly in groups IV and II). Besides the three series of voiced, voiceless, and voiceless consonants with glottal closure (glotto-occlusive), which are found in all the Caucasian languages, the North-East Caucasian languages have long geminate consonants (the so-called correlation of intensity), which, however, are not distributed equally in the individual languages. Numerical differences in the total number of consonants in various North-East Caucasian languages are explained also by the presence or absence of lateral, labio-velarized pharyngealized and palatalized phoneme series. The points of articulation in the rear of the oral cavity include uvulars, pharyngeals, and laryngeals. Affricates and spirants are well-represented. The poverty of vowel inventories typical of Caucasian languages is not true for group I and some languages of group II. Pharyngealized, nasalized, affected and lengthened vowels contribute in individual cases, besides diphthongs, to an increase in the total number of vowels. Tone is absent in North-East Caucasian languages; stress is based on intensity and is weak and, in general, subordinate to sentence stress; one exception is Lezgin, with the stress on the second syllable of the word. Examples of the phonological relevance of stress are rare, as in Awar *hó·co,* 'threshing floor,' vs. *ho·có,* 'condensed grapejuice.'

Morphologically, agglutination predominates. Functional vowel alternation is an archaism (as Awar *betér,* 'head'; genitive, *boṭról;* nominative plural, *buṭrúl*) and indicates flectional vestiges.

The North-East Caucasian languages lack the category of gender (as do all Caucasian languages), but have class inflections instead. This means that substantives are differentiated selectively by class. Grammatical agreement of the elements of the sentence referring to substantives (attributes, predicates) is established through class signs: for example, Tabasaran *ermi ṭi-r-khnuw,* "the man flew" (in which *r* is the sign for the class "human"), vs. *dzhaka ṭi-w-khnuw,* "the bird flew" (in which *w* is the sign for the class "not-human"). While one can establish four semantically distinct classes for the reconstruction of the North-East Caucasian base language—(1) masculine rational, (2) feminine rational, (3) other beings, (4) names of objects, collectives—the number of classes in the attested individual languages ranges from zero (Udi, Lezgin, Aqul), to eight (Bats). Most languages, however, have three- or four-class systems.

Also characteristic of the North-East Caucasian languages is the lack of the category of person in finite verbs. Impersonality is, however, sometimes counteracted in individual languages by the tendency toward the development of inflection in the verb by person (mostly by the addition of the personal pronoun), for example, in the Udi present tense of the verb 'to make,' *besun:*

Singular	Plural
1. besa-z(u)	besa-jan
2. besa-n(u)	besa-nan
3. besa-ne	besa-ḋun

The case system is strongly developed and has as a rule four grammatical cases (nominative, ergative, genitive, dative) which are opposed to a large number of local cases. The base is the unmarked nominative, which coincides as an undefined form with the stem of the word; from this is derived an oblique stem, formed by suffixes or vowel alternation, which usually serves simultaneously as the ergative, and as the basis for further declension. With local cases, the declension consists in so-called series formation: the oblique stem provides the base form for the essive cases (in some languages up to 8 cases, answering the question *where*?). From the essives, in turn, are derived the allatives (answering the question *to where*?), the ablatives (answering the question *from where*?), and sometimes even the translatives (answering the question *through where*?). An example is the Tabasaran indefinite (that is, nominative) *ɣwan*, 'stone,' the oblique stem (or ergative) *ɣwan-dzhi*, the locative (with the meaning of static location underneath) *ɣwan-dzhi-kk*, 'under the stone,' from which comes the allative *ɣwan-dzhi-kk-na*, indicating motion, or placement 'under the stone.' As a corollary to this system of indicating local relations by case affixes and postpositions on the noun, the pre-verbs in the North-East Caucasian languages (with the exception of group IV) play only a subordinate role.

The North-East Caucasian languages differentiate syntactically (according to the model valid for all Caucasian languages) between three constructions: (1) the transitive ergative construction, in which the object of a transitive coincides in the nominative with the subject of an intransitive verb, while the agent stands in an oblique or special case, the so-called ergative; (2) the intransitive nominative construction; (3) the affective construction (with verbs of emotion and perception), with the affected person in an oblique case or the locative. The "basic order" points to the unmarked order subject-object-verb, modifier before modified (with features of group inflection), subordinate clause before principal clause. In the subordinate clauses, the finite verb is replaced by converbs (that is, participles, gerunds, verbal substantives). The connection between the subordinate and the main clause is made by the finite verb at the end of the main clause.

Literature. The North-East Caucasian literatures consist of works of folk poetry transmitted in an ancient oral tradition as well as of relatively recent products of the better-known authors. Intimate structural relationships exist between the North-West Caucasian literatures and also the literatures in the Indo-European and Turkic languages of the Caucasus. In particular, Chechen, Ingush, Awar, Lezgin, Tabasaran, Lak, and Dargin possess rich anonymous folk epics. Among the Dargins and Laks lyric poetry is also well developed. Drama and theater are especially evident among the Lezgins and the Laks. Before the Russian conquest of the Caucasus, Oriental-Islamic influences in literature were predominant, and thereafter Russian, and later Soviet models became widespread. Particularly well known poets are, among others, Jetim Emin (d. 1878), the "Father of Lezgin poetry," the Lak Pan-Islamist Jusup-Kadi Murkelinskii (d. 1918) and the Awar Makhmud from Kokhab-Roso (d. 1919). Writers who underwent Soviet influence later in their lives were the Lezgin S. Stal'skii (1869-1937), G. Tsadasa (1877-1951), who founded socialist Awar poetry, and the Lak writer E. Kapiev (1909-1944). Newspapers also appear in the North-East Caucasian written languages. The basis has been laid for an extensive literature of translated works.

References: N. Trubetzkoy, "Nordkaukasische Wortgleichungen," *Wiener Zeitschrift für die Kunde des Morgenlandes,* vol. 37 (1930), 76-92; – – –, "Die Konsonantensysteme der ostkaukasischen Sprachen," *Caucasica,* 8 (1931), 1-52; – – –, "Zur Vorgeschichte der ostkaukasischen Sprachen," *Melanges J. Van Ginneken* (Paris, 1937), 171-178; G.B. Murkelinskii, red., *Iazyki dagestana,* vyp. II (Makhachkala, 1954); G. Deeters, "Bemerkungen zu K. Bouda's 'Südkaukasisch-nordkaukasischen Etymologien,' " *Die Welt des Orients,* II, No. 4 (1957), 282-391; A. Chikobava, red., *Bibliografiia iazykovedcheskoi literatury ob iberiisko-kavkazskikh iazykakh,* vol. I: *Gorskie iberiisko-kavkazskie iazyki* (Tbilisi, 1958); Y.D. Desheriev, *Nakhskie iazyki* (M., 1958); A. Shanidze, "Iazyk i pis'mo kavkazskikh albantsev," *XXV mezhdunarodnyi kongress vostokovedov* (M., 1960); E.A. Bokarev, *Vvedenie v sravnitel'no-istoricheskoe izuchenie dagestanskikh iazykov* (Makhachkala, 1961); G. Deeters, "Die kaukasischen Sprachen," in B. Spuler, ed., *Handbuch der Orientalistik,* I. Abt., Vol. VII (Leiden/Köln, 1963), 1-79; Y.D. Desheriev, *Sravnitel'no-istoricheskaia grammatika nakhskikh iazykov i problemy proiskhozhdeniia i istoricheskogo razvitiia gorskikh kavkazskikh narodov* (Groznyi, 1963); K.H. Schmidt, "Die west- und ostkaukasischen Literaturen," in W.v. Einsiedel, ed., *Die Literaturen der Welt in ihrer mündlichen und schriftlichen Überlieferung* (Zurich, 1964), 1065-1077; N. Trubetzkoy, "Der Bau der ostkaukasischen Sprachen," *Wiener Slavistisches Jahrbuch,* 11 (1964), 23-30; G.A. Klimov, *Kavkazskie iazyki* (M., 1965; German translation, *Die kaukasischen Sprachen* [Hamburg, 1969]); A.F. Nazarevich, R.F. Jusufov, redd., *Istoriia dagestanskoi sovetskoi literatury,* 2 vols. (Makhachkala, 1967); V.V. Vinogradov, red., *Iazyki narodov SSSR,* vol. IV: *Iberiisko-kavkazskie iazyki* (M., 1967); G.B. Murkelinskii, red., *Sravnitel'no-istoricheskaia leksika dagestanskikh iazykov* (M., 1971); N.G. Volkova, *Etnonimy i plemennye nazvaniia Severnogo Kavkaza* (M., 1973); S.M. Khaidakov, *Sravnitel'no-sopostavitel'nyi slovar' dagestanskikh iazykov* (M., 1973); – – –, *Sistema glagola v dagestanskikh iazykakh* (M., 1975); G.B. Murkelinskii, red., *Iazyki dagestana, vyp.* III (Makhachkala, 1976).

Karl Horst Schmidt

CAUCASIAN LANGUAGES, NORTH-WESTERN. *The People and Their Languages.* In the north-west region of the Caucasus are found scattered the remnants of a once numerous people whose languages form a distinct linguistic family, the North-Western Caucasian languages. This family has three main sub-divisions: Circassian, Ubykh and Abkhaz-Abaza. The Circassian branch, the most northerly one, can further be divided into an Eastern (or Upper) and a Western (or Lower) branch. The Eastern branch is sometimes referred to as Kabardian, as the literary language (Russian *kabardino-cherkesskii iazyk*) is based upon the dialect Greater Kabardian. This branch is spoken in and around the Kabardino-Balkarian ASSR and the Karachai-Cherkess Autonomous Oblast. Furthermore, two villages in the Adygei Autonomous Oblast also speak Eastern Circassian dialects, (Geiger *et al.,* 1956, pp. 431-432). In this sub-division there are nine dialects, seven of which are closely related forms of Kabardian, but two others, Besleney or Besney and Kubano-Zelenchuk, are divergent enough from Kabardian to qualify as separate languages in their own right. The Western branch of Circassian is sometimes called Kyakh, (Paris 1974, pp. 14-23), meaning 'lower country,' perhaps as it was bordered on the north by the lower course of the Kuban River. These dialects center in and around the Adygei Autonomous Oblast. The literary form of West Circassian (Russian: *adygeiski iazyk*) is based upon the Chemgwi or Temirgoy dialect. This sub-division, more varied than the Eastern one, contains at least eight dialects, many of them quite divergent from one another: Chemgwi or Temirgoy, Bzhedukh, Yegerukay, Khatukay, Abdzakh or Abadzakh, Haku-chi, Shapsugh, and Natukhay. These dialects followed old West Circassian tribal lines. Historically attested tribes such as the Mamkhetoy and Makhoshey may have had distinct dialects. These last two are no longer found in the Soviet Union, but may persist in the Middle East. We should further note that many of these dialects have diverse sub-dialects: for example, Bzhedukh can be further divided into Khamych and Chercheney; there seem to be several forms of Abdzakh.

After the tsarist conquest of the Caucasus in 1864 the majority of the Circas-sians, both West and East, all the Ubykhs and most of the Abaza fled to the Ot-toman Empire, and persist to the present in isolated groups throughout the Mid-dle East. There are about 100,000 speakers of West Circassian dialects still in the Caucasus and perhaps twice that number of speakers of East Circassian.

The Ubykh branch in many ways occupied a linguistically intermediate posi-tion between the Circassian and the Abkhaz-Abaza branches, sharing many fea-tures of its more numerous linguistic cousins. Never very numerous, the Ubykhs all migrated to Turkey. Consequently Ubykh is no longer spoken in the Soviet Union and, regrettably, is virtually extinct in Turkey, its speakers numbering no more than 24 (Vogt 1963). There is evidence that at one time Ubykh consisted of two divergent dialects (Dumézil 1965, pp. 266-269), but only one persists.

The Abkhaz-Abaza branch falls into two distinct languages: Abkhaz and Abaza. Abaza consists of five closely related dialects: Tapanta, Dudaruko-Bibard, Lo-Kuban or Karapago or Kubina, Kum-Lo or Koydan (Russian *krasnovostoch-nyi*) and Yegiboko. The literary language (Russian *abazinski iazyk*) is based upon the Tapanta dialect. All Abaza speakers are bilingual in Abaza and Kabardian and live in scattered villages in and around the Karachai-Cherkess Autonomous Oblast. They number approximately 15,000. The Abkhaz languages consist of four dia-lects: Bzyb, Abzhwi, Samurzakan and Ashkharwa or Shqarawa or Zelenchuk Abaza. This last Ashkharwa dialect is linguistically transitional between the other Abkhaz dialects and Abaza. The literary language (Russian *abkhazski iazyk*) is based upon a mixture of the closely related Abzhwi and Samurzakan dialects, sometime collectively termed Southern Abkhaz. From 1860 to 1874 (Deeters 1963, pp. 8-11), the Bzyb dialect was used as a literary standard. The vast ma-jority of the Abkhazians remained in their homeland after the tsarist conquest and today enjoy their own republic, the Abkhazian ASSR, an administrative unit of the Georgian SSR. Despite this there are only about 93,000 people who speak Abkhaz.

We should note that the Abkhaz have a sort of secondary language or jargon called the Woodsman's or Hunter's language (Klimov 1969, p. 31). Used on the hunt in times past in order to confuse the animals, it consists in substituting alternative forms for a wide range of nouns. A similar hunting jargon seems to have existed among the Circassian nobility

The North-Western Caucasian languages have long been assumed to be related to one another and in fact there is little reason to doubt this. The languages are quite divergent from anything in Eurasia, near or far, and indeed show many traits that set them apart from the other Caucasian languages. Despite the many shared traits exhibited within this language family, actual efforts at reconstruction have met with tremendous difficulties and the only success to date has been reconstructing some of the forms of Proto-Circassian (Kuipers 1963; 1975). Often it is assumed that the North-Western languages are remotely related to the North-Eastern Caucasian Nakh and Dagestan languages, but there is nothing yet to substantiate this belief. It is not surprising, therefore, that all efforts to relate the North-Western languages to languages outside of the Caucasus, such as Basque or some of the ancient languages of the Middle East, have yielded no fruit. Linguistically the North-Western languages are so unusual that they must have had a long and idiosyncratic history. It is reasonable to expect, therefore, that it would be difficult to unravel their past and relate them explicitly to one another, much less relate the group as a whole to languages outside the family.

Phonology. The number of sounds used distinctly to convey information in a language, that is, the number of phonemes or phonological inventory usually numbers between 25 and 35, of which anywhere from 3 to 12 or so are vowels and the rest glides, such as 'y' and 'w', and consonants. The North-Western languages are extraordinary, therefore, in that the smallest consonantal inventory is 48 (for Kabardian, Kuipers 1960), and the largest (for some interpretations of Abaza, Genko 1955) may be as high as 87 or 88. Inventories of 68 (for Bzhedukh West Circassian, Kuipers 1963) and 69 (for Bzyb Abkhaz, Bgazhba 1964) are about average for the consonant and glide systems. This remarkable welter of consonants is contrasted with a type of vocalic system that is exceedingly rare among the world's languages. All these languages have a so-called vertical vowel system consisting of only two vowels:

(1)   mid   ə

        low   a

The mid vowel, called schwa, is the neutral vowel found in English words such as "but." The second is a vowel similar to the 'a' in English "bat" or "father." This low vowel has a long form in Circassian, Ubykh and Abkhaz, but for each there is strong evidence that such long vowels are derived from various underlying forms, as in (2).

(2)   Circassian   /ā/ ← /aa/ or /ah/

        Ubykh   /ā/ ← /aa/

        Abkhaz   /ā/   (written "aa")   ← /aʕ/ or /aḥ/

One has to go all the way to New Guinea to find in the Ndu language family a language, Manambu, which clearly has such a vocalic system (Allen and Hurd 1972; Pike 1964). In fact the enormous size of the consonantal systems go hand-in-hand with the smallness of the vocalic systems. The vowels assimilate to their surrounding consonants in all qualities except the lowness which contrasts the two vowels and by this means provide helpful cues to the speakers for distinguishing among the numerous and subtle contrasts shown among the consonants.

The consonantal systems in these languages are remarkable not merely for their size, but also for the thoroughness with which they make use of all the articulatory points of the vocal tract (Kuipers 1956), and the remarkable extent to which they modify the basic articulations with secondary ones. Thus, consonants are made at the lips (labial), the tooth ridge (alveolar), behind this ridge where the 'ch' of German "ich" is made (alveo-palatal), in the area of English 'ch' (palato-alevolar), in the area of the 'k' in English "keep" (palatal), at the soft palate as in the 'c' in English "coop" (velar), at the back margin of the soft palate (uvular), in the throat (pharyngeal), and at the larynx (laryngeal). This is every possible articulatory point but one, and if we take into account the sound produced by blowing air through clenched teeth, which is a variant of a palatal phoneme found in West Circassian, then we have all points. Furthermore, in many of these languages consonants may be rounded, labialized, velarized, pharyngealized, made with advanced tongue root (the 'ee' in "beet" has advanced tongue root as opposed to the 'i' in "bit"), or various combinations of these secondary articulations. Some sounds are made with the tongue blade (laminal), and contrast with others made with the tip (apical). Short and long consonants also occur. Consonants can occur voiced, voiceless and ejective (with simultaneous closure of the vocal cords), and in West Circassian there is frequently a contrast of aspiration imposed upon the voiceless series. Most unusual are the advanced tongue root and pharyngealized uvulars (the latter both plain and rounded), found in Ubykh and Abkhaz-Abaza, and the ejective spirants found in Circassian. Rarer yet are the aspirated spirants in some forms of West Circassian. Tables 1-3 give the phonological inventories for some representative languages.

As though these enormous inventories were not enough, these languages combine consonants into formidable clusters. This reaches an extreme in Abaza, as may be seen in (3).

(3)   Abaza

a. /q̄č̌ˠq̄qʼˠa/   'pillow case'   b. /q̄ḥʷḥʷàra/   'to harrow'

c. /skʷš̌ə/   'year'   d. /ʕʷč̌ʼʷʕʷəs/   'man, mortal,

e. /č̌ʷš̌ʷš̌ʷara/   'to paint'   f. /č̌ʷḥʷḥʷə/   'nude'

g. /č̌ʷḥʷč̌ʷə/   'splinter'   h. /gʷtpssʕara/   'to have a
                                                                terrible
                                                                fright'

In Circassian various phonological processes can give rise to clusters in which some consonants are fully articulated while others are run together or co-articulated. In (4) we denote such co-articulated segments by running a ligature between them (for further examples, *see* CIRCASSIAN, WEST). This is an exceedingly subtle contrast.

(4)   Bzhedukh West Circassian

a. /zatʰayś́ʷəɬha/ → /zatʰayś́ʷɫ̰h/ 'shut up (you plural)!'

b. /wəpqχʰar/ → /p̰pqχʰar/   'your limbs, your frame'

Table 1

Bzhedukh West Circassian Phonological Inventory

labial	pʰ	p	b	p'	—	f	—	—	w
alveolar	tʰ	t	d	t'	—	s	z	—	
(affricates)	cʰ	c	ʒ	c'	—	ṣ	ẓ	ś'	
alveo-palatal	—	—	—	—	—	—	—	—	
(round)	č̣ʰʷ	čʷ	ǯ̌ʷ	—	—	ṣʷ	ẓʷ	ś'ʷ	
(lateral, l-like)	—	—	—	—	—	ł	λ	ł'	
palato-alveolar (laminal)	č̣ʰʸ	čʸ	ǯ̌ʸ	č'ʸ	ṣ̌ʰʸ	ṣ̌ʸ	ẓ̌ʸ	—	y
(apical)	čʰ	č	ǯ̌	č'	šʰ	ṣ̌	ẓ̌	—	
palatal	—	—	—	—	χʰ	χ	g	—	
velar	—	k	—	k'		—	—		
(round)	kʰʷ	kʷ	gʷ	k'ʷ		—	y		
uvular	qʰ	q	—	—		x	ɣ̣		
(round)	qʰʷ	qʷ	—	—		x̣ʷ	ɣ̣ʷ		
pharyngeal						ḥ̣	ʕ̣		
laryngeal				ʔ		ḥ			
(round)				ʔʷ					

vowels: ə a

m n r

Where Cʰ = a voiceless aspirated consonant and C' = an ejective consonant
/cʰ, c, ʒ, c'/ = [tʰsʰ, ts, dz, t's'], and similarly for /č̣ʰʷ, č̣ʰʷ, etc./.

Table 2

Ubykh Phonological Inventory

labial	p	b	p'	f	–	w	m
(pharyngealized)	p̄	b̲	p̄'	–	v̲	w̲	m̲
alveolar	t	d	t'			n	r
(round)	tʷ	dʷ	t'ʷ				
(affricates)	c	ʒ	c'	s	z		
(round)	cʷ	ʒʷ	c'ʷ	sʷ	zʷ		
(apical)	ċ	ʒ̇	ċ'	ṡ	ż		
(lateral)	–	–	ƛ'	ɬ	l		
alveo-palatal (round)	–	–	–	śʷ	ź'ʷ		
palato-alveolar (laminal)	čʸ	ǯʸ	č'ʸ	šʸ	žʸ		
(apical)	č	ǯ	č'	š	ž		
palatal	kʸ	gʸ	k'ʸ	χ	ǧ	y	
velar (round)	kʷ	gʷ	k'ʷ	χʷ	–		
uvular (advanced tongue root)	qʸ	–	q'ʸ	xʸ	ɣʸ		
(plain)	q	–	q'	x	ɣ		
(round)	qʷ	–	q'ʷ	xʷ	ɣʷ		
(pharyngealized)	q̄	–	q̄'	x̄	ɣ̄		
(pharyngealized, round)	q̄ʷ	–	q̄'ʷ	x̄ʷ	ɣ̄ʷ		
laryngeal				h			

vowels: ə
         a

Where /tʷ, dʷ, t'ʷ/ are phonetically [pt̚ bd̚ p't̚'] and
/cʷ, ʒʷ, c'ʷ, sʷ, zʷ/ are [tsᶲ, dzᵝ, t's'ᶲ', sᶲ, zᵝ].

Table 3

Bzyb Abkhaz Phonological Inventory

labial	p	b	p'	f	v	f'	w	m
alveolar	t	d	t'				n	r	l
(round)	tʷ	dʷ	t'ʷ						
(affricates)	c	ʒ	c'	s	z				
(apical)	ċ	ʒ̇	ċ'	ṡ	ż				
(apical, round)	ċʷ	ʒ̇ʷ	ċ'ʷ	ṡʷ	żʷ				
alveo-palatal (round)	–	–	–	śʷ	źʷ				
palato-alveolar	čʸ	ǯʸ	č'ʸ	šʸ	žʸ				
(velarized)	č	ǯ	č'	š	ž				
palatal	kʸ	gʸ	k'ʸ	–	–	y			
velar	k	g	k'	–	–				
(round)	kʷ	gʷ	k'ʷ	–	–				
uvular (advanced tongue root)	–	–	q'ʸ	xʸ	ɣʸ				
(plain)	–	–	q'	x	ɣ				
(round)	–	–	q'ʷ	xʷ	ɣʷ				
(pharyngealized)	–	–	–	x̄	–				
(pharyngealized, round)	–	–	–	x̄ʷ	–				
pharyngeal				ḥ	ʕ				
(round)				ḥʷ	ʕʷ				

vowels: ə

　　　　　　 a

Where / tʷ, dʷ, t'ʷ / are phonetically [p̪t, b̪d, p̪'t'],
/ ċʷ, ʒ̇ʷ, ċ'ʷ, ṡʷ, żʷ / are [t̪s̪ᶠ, d̪ẕᵛ, t̪'s̪'ᶠ', s̪ᶠ, ẕᵛ],
/ ʕ / plus either vowel yields phonetically [ā], and / ʕʷ / is [yʷ],
(French [ɥ]).

Apart from widespread processes that involve the appearance or disappearance of vowels, particularly the mid one, schwa, there is not a great deal of sound change in these languages. In that they have enormous phonological inventories and outlandish clusters they seem complex enough. Adding complex phonological rules to such systems would seem to be too much. Besides one can hardly imagine what changes such rules could effect in complex languages such as these without creating intolerable confusion.

Even without extensive rules for sound change, it is easy to see why these languages, usually spoken rapidly, can make a striking acoustic impression even upon the somewhat worldly and jaded sensibilities of the professional phonetician.

Morphology. In addition to complex phonological inventories the North-Western languages have very complex morphologies as well. Grammatical gender is not expressed in the languages except to a limited extent in the Abkhaz-Abaza verb. There are usually two cases in Ubykh and Circassian, none in Abkhaz-Abaza. Nouns can also show suffixed postpositions and adjectives, so that one can have nouns as complex as noun-adjective-case-postposition in Circassian and Ubykh. Most morphology takes place with the verb.

The North-Western verb is a sentence in microcosm, inflecting not merely for the subject of a sentence, but for almost every other noun as well. Such verbal elements are usually referred to as indices and are prefixed to the verb. They serve the function met by pronouns in most other languages, though the North-Western languages have pronouns as well. These prefixed indices can co-occur with a wide range of other prefixes, expressing location, direction, purpose, tense, adverbial nuances, causation, benefit, intrusion into a kingroup by a stranger, and nuances conveyed by generic or referential nouns. A smaller, but yet significant, set of suffixes can also be appended to express tense, number of subject or object and occasionally other nouns, negation, reference to a previous identical action or return to a previous state, directional nuances, potentiality, participial function, and reference to a specific instance of an activity. It is not at all unusual to find in a discourse that after the main nouns have been stated the balance of the sentences consist largely of verb forms (Allen 1956). Forms such as (5) are usual and those such as (6), while rare, are quite possible.

(5)　　Bzyb Abkhaz:

　　　/y–w–ź̀ə–s–ʕʷ–ayt'/　it-you(masculine)-to-I-write-present
　　　'I am writing (it) to you (masculine)'

(6)　　Bzhedukh West Circassian:

　　　/zə–qə–a–z–fa–ʔa–ś̆ʷə–s–ya–tʰə–ž̆ɣ̆ə–ya–χʰa–gʷara–ra–r/
　　　self-horizon-to-what-for-upright-you(plural)-I-make-stand-again
　　　past-plural-referential-participle-absolutive case
　　　'the reason why I made you all get yourselves up again (remote action)'

The form in (6) would be used as a noun and would refer to some specific instance of awakening some people.

Returning to the morphology of the noun we may note that one of the most striking aspects is the extensive use of compounding to form words that in other languages would be expressed by simple roots. An example of this may be seen in (7).

(7)   Bzhedukh West Circassian:

      a. /pq/   'bone, limb, frame'

      b. /śḥa-pq/   head-frame = 'skull'

      c. /wəna-pq/   house-frame = 'house frame'

      d. /ƛə-pq/   blood-frame = 'tribe, clan, sort'

      e. /warəd-ə-pq/ song-connective vowel-frame = 'melody'

      f. /ʔa-pq-ƛa-pq/ hand-frame-foot-frame = 'body'

We may note also that the Circassian languages show a contrast between inalienable possession (possession of items, body parts or blood kinsmen, that are an integral part of the possessor), and alienable possession (incidental ownership or association). In (8), from Bzhedukh again, we may see such a contrast at work.

(8)   a. /s-qʷa/ my-son = 'my son' (inalienable, said only to true son)

        b. /s-yə-qʷa/ my-possession-son = 'my boy' (alienable, a friendly gesture said to any boy)

Such contrasts as (8), together with the compounding in (7), indicate that semantic processes that are probably at work in most languages but remain obscured by word forms are transparent in the North-Western languages.

Syntax. The North-Western languages are all ergative. This means that the subject of an intransitive sentence and the object of a transitive accord with their verb for plurality and where cases are found share the same case ending. This is a general Caucasian feature. To an English speaker such sentences look passive or in some other way backwards. In fact this is not the case since these languages have a type of construction, called the anti-passive, which produces sentences that, although they look more normal to us, are actually comparable in many ways to our passives. In all the languages some verbs, oddly, are always anti-passive, though reasons for this are poorly understood. The pervasive ergativity of these languages is one of the most difficult aspects to deal with in trying to learn one of them.

The normal word order in a sentence is verb final. When an object or indirect object occur, one has the order: subject - indirect object - object - verb. Often the indirect object may be moved before the verb. Though adjectives usually follow the noun they modify, whole sentences when used as relative clauses precede the noun they modify, the head noun. Special indices on the verb of such a relative clause link it to its head noun. Sentential complements to verbs also precede the verb that they modify. Such complements along with relative clauses can produce complex syntactic patterns that have yet to be fully understood by the linguist. It may tentatively be stated, however, that to simplify some of these constructions, as well as for other reasons, many of these languages have available a wide range of rules that involve movement of sentence constituents to the right to the end of the sentence, often with the concomitant appearance of the verb 'to be' at the end. In Abkhaz and Abaza, and seemingly in Circassian as well, one of the constituents that is so moved is the interrogative pronoun in a question. This behavior is unusual in that it violates a putative linguistic universal regarding question formation. Ubykh lacks this question formation rule and, in fact, has the least number of rightward movement rules of any of the languages in the family.

The syntax of the North-Western languages is complex and as yet is poorly understood. (More details can be found in this encyclopedia in the entry CIRCASSIAN, WEST, already referred to.) The syntax, however, is only the least examined part of a rich and elaborate linguistic realm. Certainly more interesting insights, many of theoretical significance to the linguist, await the worker in this language family. We may close by extending a comment made by Yakovlev, an early and brilliant worker, about Kabardian (Kuipers, 1960, p. 12), to the entire family, that indeed the North-Western Caucasian languages are among "the most remarkable languages that have ever been the object of linguistic investigation."

Bibliography: J.C. Catford, "The Kabardian Language," *Le Maître phonétique,* vol. 78 (1942); 15-18; A.N. Genko, *Abazinskii iazyk* (M., 1955); A. Kuipers, "The North-West Caucasian Languages," *Analecta Slavica* (Amsterdam, 1956), 195-205; B. Geiger *et al., The Caucasus,* Human Relations Area File-35, Columbia-1 (New Haven, Conn., 1956); S.S. Allen, "Structure and System in the Abaza Verbal Complex," *Transactions of the Philological Society* (1956), 127-76; M.L. Abitov *et al., Grammatika kabardinocherkesskogo literaturnogo iazyka* (M., 1957); A. Kuipers, *Phoneme and Morpheme in Kabardian* (The Hague, 1960); H. Vogt, *Dictionnaire de la langue oubykh* (Oslo, 1963); A. Kuipers, "Proto-Circassian Phonology: an Essay in Reconstruction," *Studia Caucasica,* vol. 1 (The Hague, 1963), 56-92; G. Deeters, "Die kaukasischen Sprachen," in B. Spuler, ed., *Handbuch der Orientalistik,* 1 Abt., Bd. 7: *Armenisch und kaukasischen Sprachen* (Leiden and Köln, 1963), 1-79; E.V. Pike, "The Phonology of the New Guinea Highlands," in *New Guinea, the Central Highlands,* special publication of *American Anthropologist,* vol. 66, No. 4, part 2 (1964), 121-32; Kh.S. Bgazhba, *Bzybskii dialekt abkhazskogo iazyka* (Tbilisi, 1964); G. Dumézil, *Documents anatoliens sur les langues et les traditions du Caucase,* vol. III: *Nouvelles études oubykh* (Paris, 1965); G.V. Roagava and Z.I. Kerasheva, *Grammatika adygeiskogo iazyka* (Krasnodar and Maikop, 1966); G. Dumézil, *Documents anatoliens sur les langues et les traditions du Caucase,* vol. V: *Études abkhaz* (Paris, 1967); G.V. Klimov, *Die kaukasischen Sprachen* (Hamburg, 1969); J.D. Allen and P.W. Hurd, "Manambu Phonemes," *Te Reo,* vol. 15 (1972), 36-44; C. Paris, *La Princesse Kahraman, contes d'Anatolie en dialecte chapsough (tcherkesse occidental)* (Paris, 1974); A. Kuipers, *A Dictionary of Proto-Circassian Roots* (Lisse, Holland, 1975); J. Colarusso, "The Languages of the North-West Caucasus," G. Thomas, ed., *The Languages and Literatures of the Non-Russian Peoples of the Soviet Union* (Hamilton, Ontario, Canada, 1977), 62-153.

John Colarusso

CHAADÁEV, PETR YAKOVLEVICH (1794-1856). Russian philosopher. Though not a professional writer, Chaadaev has often been considered the first Russian philosopher to articulate the problem of Russia's national destiny in an incisive and resonant way, in terms of its relationship with other civilizations and societies.

Chaadaev was born in 1794 in Moscow, according to some sources, or in Nizhnii Novgorod, according to others. A member of the Russian gentry, Chaadaev was brought up in a cosmopolitan French atmosphere. At the age of fifteen he entered Moscow University where he embarked upon a study of history and philosophy under the supervision of the most distinguished contemporary professors, the representatives of the Russian School of Historical Scepticism. In 1812 Chaadaev joined the army and served in the Napoleonic campaigns. After the war he became associated with the circles of the future Decembrists, Ivan Yakushkin, Nikolai Turgenev, the Muraviev-Apostol brothers, and with such distinguished men of letters as Petr Viazemskii, Nikolai Karamzin, Aleksandr Griboedov and, especially, young Aleksandr Pushkin.

In 1817 Chaadaev was considered one of the most brilliant men in the upper circles of Russian society, with the prospect of a promising career as a future aide-de-camp to tsar Alexander the First. However, a revolt of the Semënovskii regiment in 1820, and Chaadaev's particular role as a messenger carrying the unfortunate news to the tsar, influenced Chaadaev's decision to retire from the service in 1821. He suffered an intense spiritual crisis at that time, which affected his health, and in 1823 he went abroad to recuperate. Chaadaev's travels through Western Europe lasted for three years. He visited most of the European capitals, continued his studies in Western thought, and met several famous figures including Schelling, whose ideas significantly influenced Chaadaev's own philosophical views.

Upon his return to Russia in 1826, Chaadaev led a melancholy, secluded life. It was during the years 1829-1831 that he composed the most important work of his life, the eight *Philosophical Letters,* in which he expressed his pessimistic views on Russia's history and culture.

In 1831 Chaadaev joined several intellectual circles of Moscow society. His *Letters,* circulated in large numbers, became well known to some of his friends. But it was the publication of one of them which resulted in a nation-wide scandal and a personal disaster. In 1836 his "First Philosophical Letter" was published in *Teleskop* (Telescope) by Nikolai Nadezhdin, the editor of the journal and an established university professor. The "Letter" contained a passionate rejection of Russia and drew a strong reaction from the authorities. Chaadaev was proclaimed officially insane, and put under police surveillance and medical supervision. The publication of *Teleskop* was discontinued forever and Nadezhdin was exiled to a remote village in northern Russia.

Because of this unfortunate event Chaadaev was unable to take the active role in Russia's cultural life he may have wished. Still he was not forbidden guests, and at his regular Monday reception became a Moscow celebrity, a respected and often admired philosopher-oracle of the Moscow drawing rooms. His numerous letters, aphorisms, and articles, including his "Apology of a Madman" (1837), were never published during his lifetime. By the end of his life, Chaadaev was convinced that Russia had a positive historical mission to perform in the future. He died in his native Moscow in 1856.

Chaadaev's views on Russia can be regarded as a search on a grand scale for the general pattern of Russian civilization. In fact, Chaadaev's views consist of a number of negative conclusions derived from his philosophy of history. The most fundamental supposition in Chaadaev's philosophical views was the idea of the universal nature of the historical process, viewed as a realization of the Kingdom of God on Earth—a utopian social and religious system which would unite all European nations spiritually and morally in one Christian Church. Chaadaev saw the idea of Christianity, the only movement consistently to foster moral progress and enlightenment, as the truly universal idea in Western European history. He was particularly attracted to the Roman Catholic Church, which represented for him the ideological unity of medieval Western Europe, a unity of human thought. Chaadaev's basic criticism of Russia was closely connected with his disappointment over Russia's non-participation in this historical unity.

Russia, with her Orthodox Christianity and her non-Western culture, stood outside the historical process. In the "First Philosophical Letter," Chaadaev articulated in a powerful way the question of Russia's historical and cultural position between East and West. Although Russia belonged to the East geographically, Chaadaev maintained that his country did not belong to the culture of the East. All the values of the Eastern world were absorbed by the Western tradition, uniting all Christian nations of Europe into a single historical process, and leaving Russia outside the cultural heritage of either world.

As a "Northern" country, Russia had merely a geographical meaning, and as such she could only be described in terms of her physical expanse. In fact, the political power of the Russian Empire represented only material, uncivilized, physical forces. In all Russian history there was no single spiritual idea, which for Chaadaev was the *conditio sine qua non* of an independent national character. By the simple geographical fact of their birth, Russians were destined to live outside history, and this was the main reason for their meaningless, useless lives. Chaadaev consciously identified himself with the "illegitimate" Russian children.

According to Chaadaev, the miserable status of Russian life was rooted in two significant facts from the past: first, Russia's acceptance of a corrupted form of Christianity from Byzantium as the basis for the Russian Orthodox Church; and second, the Tatar and Mongol invasion, which introduced the spirit of servility into Russian life. However, in his opinion, foreign bondage merely strengthened the servile features deeply rooted in the nature of the Russian nation. Paradoxically enough, Russians "naturally" became enslaved at the time they liberated themselves from the Tatar yoke. According to Chaadaev, slavery in Russia had a completely different character from the system of bondage found in ancient Rome or the United States. Servility became, in fact, an integral part of the Russian national character, with its source in Russian religion and the Russian way of life. This servility symbolized the dark barbarian kingdom of ignorance, while Western Europe, because of Christianity, abolished serfdom and in so doing cleared the way for the enlightenment. For this reason slavery in Russia—the

ideological and historical consequence of her geographical and religious isolation—became one of the main obstacles to cultural rapprochement with Western
Europe.

Chaadaev's pessimistic views of Russia gradually changed after 1830, the year
of the July Revolution in France. The turbulence in Paris destroyed his long-
cultivated image of traditional Western European cultural values and political
stability. At the same time, he was strongly influenced by the views of his ideological opponents, the Slavophiles. As early as 1833, Chaadaev emphasized the
advantages of Russia's special position in the "European family" because of her
youthfulness. The philosopher began to believe that Russia could, through a synthesis of theoretical knowledge of Western European historical experience with
her own spontaneous national character, freely project her own future. Moreover, Russia was in a position to make independent judgements and thereby find
correct solutions not only in the West, but also in the course of development of
all mankind. Thus Chaadaev's newly awakened nationalistic pride in Russia can
be understood with reference to his belief in Russia's future spiritual leadership
of Western civilization.

Chaadaev belonged neither to the Slavophiles nor to the Westerners. Nevertheless, he significantly influenced both groups, and, stimulated by his controversial
ideas, they entered into the now-famous Westerner-Slavophile polemic of the
1840s. Chaadaev did not share the Westerners' belief in social and political progress based on capitalistic transformation in Western Europe, nor could he follow
the Westerners' revolutionary ideas. Chaadaev's conservatism and the religious
overtones of his philosophy of history bear more resemblance to the Slavophiles'
ideology. However, it cannot be sufficiently emphasized that he disagreed with
their high estimate of Russian Orthodoxy. From 1830 onward Chaadaev passionately blamed the Slavophiles for their superficial patriotism which obscured
the image of Peter the Great and the values of Western European civilization. In
several of his writings Chaadaev criticized the Slavophiles' denunciation of Peter
the Great for his sudden break with Russia's past. For Chaadaev Peter imposed
no foreign customs on Russian life, but merely expressed in a forceful way the
desire to break away from Russia's isolation and backwardness. As Chaadaev saw
it, the Slavophiles' patriotism led them into a paradoxical position diametrically
opposed to his own: as a result of their search for Russia's national character,
they began to glorify the East as the proper goal of Russia's destiny. This, he felt,
actually might have condemned Russia to a new period of backwardness.

Chaadaev's commanding personality, his notoriety, the mysterious and often
scandalous circumstances of his life, and his controversial views attracted and
stimulated many Russian writers. During his lifetime, Chaadaev became the victim of vicious lampoons, poems, and even dramas. Denis Davydov's "Contemporary Song" (Sovremennaia pesnia, 1836, pub. 1840) and Nikolai Yazykov's "To
the Aliens" (K nenashim, 1844) may serve as examples. In particular, the play by
Mikhail Zagoskin, The Dissatisfied (Nedovol'nye, 1835), portrayed Chaadaev in a
most pejorative way, in order to satirize the westernized gentry. On the other
hand, a number of contemporary men and women of letters like Fedor Glinka,
Evdokiia Rostopchina and Aleksandr Pushkin, took note of the rumor that

Chaadaev was the prototype of Chatskii, the main character of Aleksandr Griboedov's *Woe from Wit* (Gore ot uma, 1824).

Griboedov and Chaadaev had been friends since their student days at Moscow University (1808-11) and their involvement in Freemasonry and the Decembrist circles. Griboedov's famous comedy portrays the conflict between an educated young Russian liberal, Chatskii, and contemporary Russian society. The young hero suffers from alienation, a lack of understanding, and, finally, from slander and condemnation by his countrymen. One is tempted to see a parallel between this and the atmosphere of slander and gossip which marked Chaadaev's difficult position at the time of the revolt of the Semenovskii regiment in 1820, which encouraged him to retire from the army in the following year. Griboedov began work on his *Woe from Wit* in December 1821. Moreover, Chaadaev's name bear some resemblance to the name of Chatskii, which, in the early versions of the play, is spelled "Chadskii," thus suggesting that Chaadaev may have served as a prototype for this figure.

But Chaadaev's most important literary influence can best be seen perhaps in a number of Pushkin's works. The friendship between Chaadaev and Pushkin was often treated by contemporaries, and later by commentators, in ways that tended toward the legendary and the symbolic.

Pushkin dedicated several verses to Chaadaev: "To the Portrait of Chaadaev" (K portretu Chaadaeva, 1817); "To Chaadaev," "The love, hope and silent fame . . ." (K Chaadaevu; Liubvi, nadezhdy, tikhoi slavy . . ., 1818); "To Chaadaev," "Why the cold suspicions . . ." (Chaadaevu; K chemu kholodnye somneniia . . ., 1820). In these poems he expressed the liberal ideas of their youth, as well as his warm appreciation for Chaadaev's intellectual guidance and moral support at the time of Pushkin's political idfficulties. Especially in Pushkin's third poem dedicated to Chaadaev, "In the country where . . ." (V strane, gde . . ., 1821), one can find a complete literary portrait of the young philosopher, his eccentricities, idealism, and contempt for mediocrity. To some extent these qualities are also developed in the literary image of Evgenii Onegin, the hero of Pushkin's novel in verse.

Several of Pushkin's poems, letters, and diary notations, indicate that the poet's interest in Chaadaev became more intense at the time of his initial work on the first chapter of *Eugene Onegin* in 1823. The complex and often contradictory character of the title hero bears recognizable similarities to the young Chaadaev. In the first chapter of the novel, Pushkin refers directly to Onegin as a "second Chaadaev" for his foppish appearance. Chaadaev's initials appeared in the first draft of another part of the same chapter. Moreover, Onegin's general way of life, his feelings of alienation and superiority, his depressed state of mind—his Russian *khandra*—all bear a certain similarity to the young Chaadaev in the early 1820s. Thus, Chaadaev is frequently pointed to in literary studies, particularly Soviet, as a prototype for Chatskii and Onegin, especially in the context of the "superfluous man" figure who appeared in the literary works of the first half of the nineteenth century.

During his mature years, Chaadaev was anxious to share his philosophical views with Pushkin. The poet was one of the first readers of the *Philosophical*

Letters. Pushkin's correspondence, articles, and literary works make it clear that he had been profoundly moved by Chaadaev's basic ideas about the superiority of Western European civilization and Russia's cultural and historical backwardness, but it is equally clear that Pushkin did not share all of these views. Pushkin responded to Chaadaev's pessimism with his own search for Russian national identity. Although he agreed with much of Chaadaev's criticism of contemporary life, Pushkin emphasized the need to employ a different historical scale in evaluating Russia's culture.

Although the evidence is inconclusive, Eikhenbaum believed that the poet Mikhail Lermontov responded to the publication of the "First Philosophical Letter" with his poem of 1836 "Oh great man! There is no reward . . ." (Velikii muzh! Zdes' net nagrady . . ., published only in 1875).

But it is Lermontov's poem "Meditation" (Duma) of 1838 which is considered to be perhaps the clearest poetic expression of Chaadaev's thought, or at least repeats many of the principal themes of the *Letters*—the emptiness of Russian life and the premature old age of Russian youth—although these ideas were also part of the "spirit of the times."

Chaadaev also appealed to Dostoevskii's novelistic imagination. While bitterly opposed to all of Chaadaev's views, Dostoevskii considered for some time making Chaadaev a character in his unrealized novel *The Life of a Great Sinner.* Moreover, many of Chaadaev's views are placed in the mouth of Versilov in *A Raw Youth* (1875), one of which was Dostoevskii's favorite idea that Russians possess a unique ability to adapt to other national cultures.

A detailed study of Chaadaev's influence on Russian literature remains to be written. There can be no question, however, that his impact on all aspects of Russia's intellectual and literary development was profound.

Works: P.Ya. Chaadaev, *Sochineniia i pis'ma* (M., 1913); R. McNally, ed., "Chaadaev's Philosophical Letters Written to a Lady," *Forschungen zur osteuropäischen Geschichte,* vol. XI (Berlin, 1966); P.Ya. Chaadaev, *Lettres philosophiques adressées à une dame* (Paris, 1970). In English translation: Peter Yakovlevich Chaadaev, *Philosophical Letters* and *Apology of a Madman* (Knoxville, Tennessee, 1969); *The Major Works of Peter Chaadaev* (Notre Dame, 1969).

References: Ch. Quenet, *Tchaadaev et les lettres philosophiques* (Paris, 1931); D. Shakhovskoi, "P.Ya. Chaadaev: Neopublikovannaia stat'ia," *Zven'ia,* Nos. 3-4 (1934), 354-90; – – –, "Neizdannyi proekt proklamatsii P.Ya. Chaadaeva 1848 g.," *Literaturnoe nasledstvo,* vols. 22-24 (1935), 679-82; N.V. Riazanovskii, *Russia and the West in the Teaching of the Slavophiles* (Cambridge, Mass., 1952); A.A. Lebedev, *Chaadaev* (M., 1965); W. Lednicki, *Russia, Poland and the West* (Port Washington, N.Y., 1966); R. McNally, *Chaadaev and His Friends* (Tallahassee, Florida, 1971); G. Cook, "Chaadaev's First Philosophical Letter: Some of the Origins of Its Critique of Russian Culture," *Jahrbücher für Geschichte Osteuropas,* vol. XX, No. 2 (1972), 194-209; J. Brun-Zejmis, "The Cost of Petrine Progress: Some Notes on Pushkin's and Chaadaev's Evaluation of Peter the Great," *Journal of Thought,* vol. 13, No. 1 (January, 1978), 32-39.

Chaadaev and Russian Literature: M.V. Nechkina, *A.S. Griboedov i Dekabristy* (M., 1951); F.F. Seeley, "The Heyday of the 'Superfluous Man' in Russia,"

The Slavonic and East European Review, vol. XXXI, No. 16 (December 1952), 92-112; Yu.N. Tynianov, "Siuzhet *Goria ot uma," Pushkin i ego sovremenniki* (M., 1969), 347-414; M.O. Gershenzon, "Chaadaev and Pushkin," *Stat'i o Pushkine* (M., 1926), 31-42; F.I. Berelevich, "P.Ya. Chaadaev i A.S. Pushkin," *Uchenye Zapiski Tumenskogo gosudarstvennogo pedagogicheskogo instituta,* vol. XVIII (1962), 121-47; J. Brun-Zejmis, "Malen'kie tragedii and Povesti Belkina: Western Idolatry and Pushkinian Parodies," *Russian Language Journal,* XXXII, No. 111 (1978), 65-75; M.Yu. Lermontov, *Polnoe sobranie sochinenii,* vol. II (M.-L., 1936), 166-69, 194-98.

Julia Brun-Zejmis

CHACHÓT, YAN (1796-1847). Belorussian-Polish poet and folklorist. Chachot was born to the minor nobility on 17 July 1796 in the village of Maliushchi (now Grodno Oblast). Completing preparatory school with the Dominicans in 1815, he entered Vilnius University and studied until financial straits forced him to abandon his education two years later. Still he joined the nationalist secret student society, the "Philomats," later called the "Philorets." Chachot wrote songs and dramatic scenes in Belorussian for their secret meetings.

Arrested with fellow student and fellow "Philoret," Adam Mickiewicz, Chachot was exiled in 1823 first to Ufa, then to Tver. He returned to Belorussia only in 1833, where he was employed as an office clerk, a tutor and a librarian in vicinity of Lepel.

Pursuing his ethnographic interests, Chachot collected Belorussian folksongs, eventually publishing about 1000 of them in six collections between 1837 and 1846. Typical of these works is the collection *Peasant Songs from Around the Neman and the Dvina* (Piosnki wieśniacze z nad Niemna i Dźwiny, 1839).

Chachot was one of those liberal Belorussian writers of the first half of the nineteenth century whose cultural orientation was Polish, but who were caught up in the surge of regional nationalism which followed the Napoleonic wars. Chachot's original works reflect that nationalism, as well as the Romantic concern for local color, in his literary ballads based on Belorussian legends. Chachot's lyrics show his study of folk songs and his sympathy for peasant life. Soviet sources criticize the poet for having identified the interests of the peasants with those of the landowners.

Chachot died in great poverty on 23 August 1847 in Druskininkai, Lithuania.

Works: Jezowe, Jaroszowe, and *Adamowe i Tomaszowe* (1819), recorded in *Archiwum filomatów,* Vol. III: *Poezja filomatów,* Jan Czubek, ed. (Cracow, 1922); Piosnki wieśniacze z nad Niemna i Dźwiny, z dołączeniem pierwotwornych w mowie sławiano-krewickiéj (Wilno [Vilnius] , 1844); Piosnki wieśniacze z nad Niemna i Dźwiny, niektóre przysłowia i idiotyzmy, w mowie sławianokrewickiej . . . (Wilno [Vilnius] , 1846); Piesni ziemianina . . . (Wilno [Vilnius] , 1846).

References: A. Loika, *Adam Mitskevich i belaruskaia literatura* (Minsk, 1959); A. Mal'dzis, *Padarozhzha u XIX stagoddze* (Minsk, 1969), 12-25; *Historyia belaruskai dakastrychnitskai litaratury,* vol. II (Minsk, 1969), 31-34; Arnold B. McMillin, "Jan Čačot in Byelorussian and Polish Literature," *The Journal of Byelorussian Studies,* vol. II, No. 1 (1969), 57-69; S. Swirko, *Z kregu preromantyzmu filomackiego* (Warsaw, 1972).

CHÁEV, NIKOLAI ALEKSANDROVICH (1824-1914). Russian playwright, novelist. Chaev was born on 26 April (8 May) 1824 in Nerekhta Uezd, Kostroma Province. He graduated in law from Moscow University in 1850 and entered civil service in the Royal office. Until the mid-1880s Chaev occupied the post of director of the Moscow Armory. Besides acting as chairman of the Society of Lovers of Russian Literature (1872-74 and again 1878-84), Chaev had an important voice in theatrical affairs. Upon the death of playwright Aleksandr Ostrovskii, Chaev assumed the position of director of reportory of Moscow theaters, and that of president of the Society of Russian Dramatic writers. His works include a range of dramatic efforts: the comedies *Know Our Own* (Znai nashikh, 1875) and *The Sour Puss* (Biriuk, 1876); the tragedy *The Mother-in-Law* (Svekrov', 1870); the chronicle plays *Prince Aleksandr Mikhailovich Tverskoi* (1864), and *The False Dimitrii* (Dimitrii Samozvanets, 1865). He died on 16 (29) November 1914 in Moscow.

Works: Bogatyri (M., 1873); *Poema* (M., 1878); *Tsar' i velikii kniaz' vseia Rusi Vasilii Ivanovich Shuiskii. Letopis' v litsakh* (M., 1886); *Stikhotvoreniia* (M., 1896); *1612 god i izbranie na tsarstvo Mikhaila Fedorovicha Romanova. Letopis' v litsakh* (M., 1912).

References: P.V. Annenkov, *Vospominaniia i kriticheskie ocherki* (Pb., 1879), 323-32; A.M. Skabichevskii, *Sochineniia,* 3rd ed., vol. I (Pb., 1903), 783-88; L.M. Lotman, *A.N. Ostrovskii i russkaia dramaturgiia ego vremeni* (M.-L., 1961).

CHAGHATAI GURUNGI, *see* SUPPLEMENTARY VOLUME.

CHAGHATAI LANGUAGE. A classical literary Turkic language of the Central Asian group which played a role among Turkic tribes somewhat analogous to that of Latin in Western Europe. Although the exact period of its predominance is given variously by different Turkologists, it was in use from the beginning of the fifteenth to the beginning of the twentieth century.

Derived from "Chaghatai Khan," the second son of Chingis Khan, who died in 1242, "Chaghatai" designates that Turkic language which became dominant under the Timurids in the Chagatai Khanate, particularly in the fifteenth century.

Although used principally by Uzbeks, the existence of literary masterpieces in Chaghatai by Navai and Babur, among others, lent the language immense prestige for the next four hundred years. Consequently, it was used by Turkic peoples whose linguistic norms diverged from those of Chaghatai. The brief renaissance of Chaghatai literature in the nineteenth century was not sufficient to sustain it and Chaghatai gave way to modern Uzbek. The Chaghatai language occupies an intermediate position between its predecessors the Khakanian and Khorzmian Turkic, and the modern Turkic languages Uzbek and New Uigur. Recent scholarship (since the 1930s) refers to the Chaghatai language also as "Old Uzbek." See also UZBEK LANGUAGE.

References: A.N. Samoilovich, "K istorii literaturnogo sredneaziatsko-turetskogo iazyka," in *Mir-Ali-Shir* (L., 1928); S.E. Malov, "Mir Alisher Navoi v istorii tiurkskikh literatur i iazykov Srednei i Tsentral'noi Azii," *Izvestiia ANSSR, Otdelenie literatury i iazyka,* vol. 6, vyp. 6 (1947); A.M. Shcherbak, *Grammatika starouzbekskogo iazyka* (M.-L., 1962); E.I. Fazylov, *Starouzbekskii iazyk,* 2 vols.

(Tashkent, 1966-71); E.N. Nadzhip, "O srednevekovykh literaturnykh traditsiiakh i smeshannykh pis'mennykh tiurkskikh iazykakh," *Sovetskaia tiurkologiia,* No. 1 (1970); C. Brockelmann, *Osttürkische Grammatik der islamischen Literatursprachen Mittelasiens* (Leiden, 1954); Janos Eckmann, *Chagatay Manual* (Bloomington, Ind., 1966).

CHAGHATAI LITERATURE, *see* UZBEK LITERATURE.

CHÁGOVETS, VSEVOLOD ANDRIIOVYCH (1877-1950). Soviet Ukrainian theatrical scholar. Chagovets was born on 18 February 1877 in the village of Starokostiantinov. In 1900 he completed Kiev University with a degree in history and philology, and from 1901 to 1918 wrote as a theater reviewer. He took an active part in the development of the repertoire and the direction of the Mikola Sadovs'kyi Theater (Gogol's *Inspector General* and Lesia Ukrainka's *Stone Guest*). Since 1917 he has written the scenarios for Gogol's *Taras Bulba,* Gor'kii's *Mother* and *Childhood,* and Kuprin's *Duel.* His original works include the play *Doina,* libretto for Dan'kevich's ballet *Lileia,* and Svechnikov's *Marusia Boguslavka,* memoirs *(Z temriavy mynuloho),* and sketches of the works of Lysenko, M. Zan'kovets'kaia, P. Saksahans'kyi, I. Mar'ianenko, I. Patorzhins'kyi, and others. He died on 20 December 1950.

Works: Prepodobnyi Feodosii Pecherskii, ego zhizn' i sochineniia (Kiev, 1901); *P.K. Saksahans'kyi: zhyttia i tvorchist'* (Kiev, 1951); *Zhyttia i stsena* (Kiev, 1956).

CHAIÁNOV, ALEKSANDR VASIL'EVICH [pseudonyms: KREMNEV, IVAN, and BOTANIN, KH.] (1888-1939). Soviet Russian writer, economist. Chaianov was born on 17 (29) January 1888 in Moscow. Although Chaianov's publications are primarily in economics, he also wrote a small number of belletristic works which include a collection of verses entitled *Lelia's Book* (Lelina knizhka, 1912), and five realistic-fantastic tales, stylized in imitation of the Russian prose of the early 19th century: "The Story of a Barber's Doll, or The Last Love of the Moscow Architect M." (Istoriia parikmakherskoi kukly, ili Posledniaia liubov' moskovskogo arkhitektora M., 1918), "Venediktov, or Memorable Events in My Life" (Venediktov, ili Dostopamiatnye sobytiia zhizni moei, 1922), "The Venetian Mirror, or The Remarkable Adventures of a Glass Man" (Venetsianskoie zerkalo, ili Udivitel'nye pokhozhdeniia stekliannogo cheloveka, 1923), "The Extraordinary, but True Adventures of Count Fedor Mikhailovich Buturlin" (Neobychainye, no istinnye prikliucheniia grafa Fedora Mikhailovicha Buturlina, 1924), and "Julia, or Rendezvous near Novodevich'i Monastery" (Iuliia, ili Vstrechi pod Novodevichem, 1928). Finally, he is known for one short "sketch" of a peasant utopia, "My Brother Aleksei's Journey into the Land of Peasant Utopia" (Puteshestvie moego brata Alekseia v stranu krest'ianskoi utopii, 1920). Attacked as a defender of kulak interests, Chaianov was arrested in the early thirties, and died in prison in 1939. He has been posthumously rehabilitated.

Works: Petrovsko-Razumovskoe v ego proshlom i nastoiashchem (M., 1925); *Staraia zapadnaia graviura* (M., 1926).

References: B. Smirenskii, "Podrazhatel'nye povesti," in his *Pero i maska* (M. 1967); O. Lasunskii, "Chaianovskie izdaniia," *Pod'em,* No. 3 (1968).

CHAIKÓVS'KYI, ANDRII YAKOVYCH (1857-1935). Ukrainian writer. The son of a clerk, Chaikovskii was born on 15 May 1857 in the city of Sambor (now the Lvov Oblast) in the Ukraine. He graduated from Lvov University (1883) and became a lawyer. In a number of works of the last decade of the nineteenth century, he wrote novelettes reflecting realistic scenes of Galician life of that period: "Oliun'ka" (1895), "In a Strange Nest" (V chuzhim hnizdi, 1896), short stories "An Offence of Honor" (Obraz honoru, 1895), "Who's to Blame?" (Khto vynen?), and "More Beautiful than Death, Lower than Slavery" (Krashche smert', nizh nevoliu). According to Soviet sources, conservatism and the nationalistic narrowmindedness of his world view were the cause of his inimical attitude toward the October Revolution. Several of his works are cited as reflecting such views: the tales "He Showed His Gratitude" (Viddiachyvsia), "Oleksii Kornienko," and "Colonel Krychevs'kyi." Chaikovs'kyi died on June 1935 in the city of Kolomyia, now Ivan Franko Oblast, Ukrainian SSR.

Works: Oliun'ka. Povisti ta opovidannia (Lvov, 1966).

References: Iu. Mel'nychuk, *Slovo pro pys'mennykiv* (Lvov, 1958); V. Beliaev, "Ob'ektyvnist' chy ob'ektyvizm?," *Radians'ke literaturoznavstvo,* No. 1 (1960).

CHAIKÓVSKII, MODEST IL'ICH (1850-1916). Russian playwright, librettist, translator, music critic. The brother and biographer of Peter Il'ich Chaikovskii, Modest was born on 1 (13) May 1850 in Alapaevsk, now Sverdlovsk Oblast. Graduating from the Petersburg School of Jurisprudence in 1870, he served in the legal department in Simbirsk (now Ulianovsk). First publishing in 1874 as a music and theater critic, Chaikovskii is the author of *The Benefactor* (Blagodetel', staged 1881; revised edition entitled *Fighters* [Bortsy, 1897]). His most popular plays were *Lizaveta Nikolaevna* (1884), *The Symphony* (Simfoniia, 1890), *The Hangover* (Pokhmel'e, 1890), *A Day in Petersburg* (Den' v Peterburge, 1892), *Prejudices* (Predrassudki, 1893), and *A Fear of Life* (Boiazn' zhizni, 1895), staged in the Malyi and Aleksandriinskii theaters. His musical training and his experience as a dramatist assured his skill as a librettist. From his pen came the opera librettos for *The Queen of Spades* (1890), *Iolanta* (1891), E.F. Napravnik's *Dubrovskii* (1895), A.N. Koreshchenko's *The Ice House* (Ledianoi dom, 1900), A.S. Arenskii's *Nal and Damayanti* (1904), and S.V. Rakhmaninov's *Francesca da Rimini* (1904). He wrote the major biography, *The Life of Petr Il'ich Chaikovskii* (Zhizn' Petra Il'icha Chaikovskogo, 3 vols., 1900-01), and was one of the founders of P.I. Chaikovskii Museum in Klin. Chaikovskii died 2 (15) January 1916 in Moscow.

Works: Dramaticheskie sochineniia, vol. I (M., 1900).

References: V.V. Iakovlev, "M.I. Chaikovskii—avtor opernykh tekstov," in his *Izbrannye trudy o muzyke,* vol. I (M., 1964), 417-81.

CHÁINIKOV, KUZ'MA PAVLOVICH [pseudonym: GERD, KUZEBAI] (1898-1937). Soviet Udmurt writer, folklorist. Chainikov was born in 1898 in the family of a peasant in the village of Bol'shaia Dok'ia (now the Mozhginsk Raion of the Udmurt ASSR). After completing the Kukarsk Teachers' Seminary, he taught school in the village of Bol'shaia Ucha. He was extremely active in the early years of the Soviet period organizing education work among the Udmurt population of Viatka Province.

From 1922 to 1926 Chainikov studied in the Briusov Moscow Literary Institute and afterwards was a graduate student in the Institute of the Peoples of the East of the USSR. He was thereafter assigned the directorship of a regional museum in Izhevsk. For two years he taught Udmurt language and literature in a regional Soviet Party school. In 1932 he was arrested under the false charge of "bourgeois nationalism," and on 14 October 1937 he died in prison. In 1958 he was rehabilitated after a review of his case.

Soviet sources fault Chainikov's poetic works for viewing the Revolution as a means of solving limited national problems such as allowing schools, theaters, businesses and the courts the use of the Udmurt language, but not as a solution to class questions.

His poetry stresses particularly the awakening of the Udmurt people to political life and cultural building. But he is criticized also for having expressed regret at the passing of the Udmurt past, the customs and mores of the older generations. He wrote for example, about the pagan worship of Keremet in the beautiful birch grove behind the village, while at the same time he praised the Revolution, which aimed to destroy the religious past.

As an ethnographer and folklorist, Chainikov participated in several folklore expeditions in the twenties, publishing his records of the sayings and saws, riddles, and songs of the Udmurt people, as well as articles on various kinds of oral creativity of the Udmurts.

Chainikov was also known as the author of textbooks. His reading books for elementary schools *Warm Rain* (Shunyt zor) and *New Path* (Vil' siures) have been repeatedly reprinted.

Works: Malmyzh udmurt kyrzan"es (n.p., 1920); *Iugyt siures vyle* [drama] (n.p., 1919). The following titles were published under the name K. Gerd: *Krez'chi. Kylbur"es* (Izhevsk, 1922); *Shunyt zor* (Izhevsk, 1924); *Sias'kaiak'kis' muz":em. Kylbur"es* (Izhevsk, 1928); *Vil' siures* (Izhevsk, 1929); *Leget"es. Kylbur"es* (Izhevsk, 1931); *Kylbur"es no poemaos* (Izhevsk, 1963); *Pichiosly salam* (Izhevsk, 1965). In Russian translation: *Lirika* (Izhevsk, 1965).

References: Pisateli Udmurtii. Biobibliograficheskii spravochnik (Izhevsk, 1963); A. Tok, *Nezabyvaemye gody. Vospominaniia* (Ioshkar-Ola, 1970); A. Arsharuni, *Vstrechi s proshlym* (M., 1971).

CONTENTS